US Foreign Policy and Global Standing in the 21st Century

This book examines US foreign policy and global standing in the twenty-first century.

The United States is the most powerful actor in world politics today. Against this backdrop, the present volume examines how the foreign policies pursued by Presidents George W. Bush and Barack Obama have affected elite and public perceptions of the United States. By examining the United States' standing from the perspective of different actors from across various regions, including China, Russia, Latin America, and the Middle East, while also assessing how these perceptions interact with the United States' own policies, this books presents a fresh interpretation of the United States' global standing. In doing so, the volume evaluates how these perceptions affect the realities of US power, and what impact this has on molding US foreign policy and the policies of other global powers. A number of books address the question of which grand strategy the United States should adopt and the issue of whether or not the United States is in relative decline as a world power. However, the debate on these issues has largely been set against the policies of the Bush administration. By contrast, this volume argues that while Obama has raised the popularity of the United States since the low reached by Bush, the United States' credibility and overall standing have actually been damaged further under President Obama.

This book will be of much interest to students of US foreign policy, US national security, strategic studies, Middle Eastern politics, international relations, and security studies generally.

Efraim Inbar is Professor in Political Studies at Bar-Ilan University and the Director of the Begin-Sadat (BESA) Center for Strategic Studies, Israel. He is author/editor of numerous titles, including most recently *The Arab Spring, Democracy and Security: Domestic and Regional Ramifications* (Routledge, 2013).

Jonathan Rynhold is Senior Lecturer of Political Studies at Bar-Ilan University, Israel, Director of the Argov Center for the Study of Israel and the Jewish People, and a Senior Researcher at the Begin-Sadat (BESA) Center for Strategic Studies. He is author of *The Arab–Israeli Conflict in American Political Culture* (Cambridge University Press, 2015).

BESA Studies in International Security
Series Editor: Efraim Inbar

Middle Eastern Security
Prospects for an arms control regime
Edited by Efraim Inbar and Shmuel Sandler

Religious Radicalism in the Greater Middle East
Edited by Bruce Maddy-Weitzman and Efraim Inbar

The National Security of Small States in a Changing World
Edited by Efraim Inbar and Gabriel Sheffer

Israeli Strategy after Desert Storm
Lessons of the Second Gulf War
Aharon Levran

The Politics and Economics of Defense Industries
Edited by Efraim Inbar and Benzion Zilberfarb

Democratic Societies and Their Armed Forces
Israel in comparative context
Edited by Stuart A. Cohen

US Allies in a Changing World
Edited by Barry Rubin and Thomas A. Keaney

Armed Forces in the Middle East
Politics and strategy
Edited by Barry Rubin and Thomas A. Keaney

The Gulf War of 1991 Reconsidered
Edited by Andrew J. Bacevich and Efraim Inbar

Democracies and Small Wars
Edited by Efraim Inbar

Religion in World Conflict
Edited by Jonathan Fox and Shmuel Sandler

Radical Islam and International Security
Challenges and responses
Edited by Hillel Frisch and Efraim Inbar

US–Israeli Relations in a New Era
Issues and challenges after 9/11
Edited by Eytan Gilboa and Efraim Inbar

The New Citizen Armies
Israel's armed forces in comparative perspective
Edited by Stuart A. Cohen

Israeli Statecraft
National security challenges and responses
Yehezkel Dror

The Arab Spring, Democracy and Security
Domestic and international ramifications
Edited by Efraim Inbar

US Foreign Policy and Global Standing in the 21st Century
Realities and perceptions
Edited by Efraim Inbar and Jonathan Rynhold

US Foreign Policy and Global Standing in the 21st Century
Realities and perceptions

Edited by Efraim Inbar and Jonathan Rynhold

LONDON AND NEW YORK

First published 2016
by Routledge
2 Park Square, Milton Park, Abingdon, Oxon OX14 4RN

and by Routledge
711 Third Avenue, New York, NY 10017

Routledge is an imprint of the Taylor & Francis Group, an informa business

© 2016 selection and editorial matter, Efraim Inbar and Jonathan Rynhold; individual chapters, the contributors

The right of the editors to be identified as the authors of the editorial matter, and of the authors for their individual chapters, has been asserted in accordance with sections 77 and 78 of the Copyright, Designs and Patents Act 1988.

All rights reserved. No part of this book may be reprinted or reproduced or utilized in any form or by any electronic, mechanical, or other means, now known or hereafter invented, including photocopying and recording, or in any information storage or retrieval system, without permission in writing from the publishers.

Trademark notice: Product or corporate names may be trademarks or registered trademarks, and are used only for identification and explanation without intent to infringe.

British Library Cataloguing-in-Publication Data
A catalogue record for this book is available from the British Library

Library of Congress Cataloging-in-Publication Data
Names: Inbar, Efraim, 1947– editor of compilation. | Rynhold, Jonathan editor of compilation.
Title: US foreign policy and global standing in the 21st century : realities and perceptions / edited by Efraim Inbar and Jonathan Rynhold.
Other titles: U.S. foreign policy and global standing in the 21st century | United States foreign policy and global standing in the 21st century
Description: New York, NY : Routledge, 2016. | Series: BESA studies in international security | Includes bibliographical references and index.
Identifiers: LCCN 2015031157| ISBN 9781138938489 (hardback) | ISBN 9781315675619 (ebook)
Subjects: LCSH: United States–Foreign relations–21st century.
Classification: LCC JZ1480 .U158 2016 | DDC 327.73–dc23
LC record available at http://lccn.loc.gov/2015031157

ISBN: 978-1-138-93848-9 (hbk)
ISBN: 978-1-315-67561-9 (ebk)

Typeset in Baskerville
by Wearset Ltd, Boldon, Tyne and Wear

Contents

List of figures	ix
List of tables	x
Notes on contributors	xi
Introduction EFRAIM INBAR AND JONATHAN RYNHOLD	1

PART I
The United States today — 13

1 **Lessons from 15 years of war** — 15
ELIOT COHEN

2 **The US foreign policy debate: déjà vu?** — 27
HENRY R. NAU

3 **Obama: the reluctant realist** — 41
STEVEN DAVID

4 **Public opinion and Obama's foreign policy** — 63
EYTAN GILBOA

PART II
Regional perceptions — 89

5 **The United States' standing in China: Chinese attitudes toward the United States** — 91
JIAN WANG

6 **Seoul–Washington alliance: the beginning of independence?** — 109
ALON LEVKOWITZ

7 Change and continuity in Russian perceptions of the United States 123
DMITRI (DIMA) ADAMSKY

8 India's perspective of US political leadership and foreign policy 139
C. UDAY BHASKAR

9 US–Latin American relations and the role of the United States in the world: the view from Latin America 159
ARIE M. KACOWICZ

PART III
The Middle East 179

10 Obama and the Middle East: illusions and delusions 181
EFRAIM KARSH

11 US counter-proliferation policy: the case of Iran 198
EMILY B. LANDAU

12 Erdoğan's Turkey and Obama's United States 213
EFRAT AVIV

13 Vultures over the Nile: US–Egypt relations between Hosni Mubarak to Abdel-Fatteh al-Sisi 230
YEHUDA U. BALANGA

14 Israeli attitudes to the Obama administration 248
YAELI BLOCH-ELKON AND JONATHAN RYNHOLD

15 The impact of a transformed US global stance on Israel's national security strategy 267
SHMUEL SANDLER

Index 284

Figures

2.1	Graph of security and democracy	29
4.1	Isolationism versus internationalism	65
4.2	US commitment to NATO	67
4.3	Obama job approval	68
4.4	Obama's foreign policy approval	69
4.5	Obama's leadership approval	69
4.6	Afghanistan war: a mistake?	71
4.7	Iraq war: a mistake?	72
4.8	Handling terrorism	73
4.9	US role as world leader	78
4.10	Party preferences: coping with international terrorism and military threats	80
14.1	The importance of close relations with the United States to Israeli security	252
14.2	The United States: a loyal ally of Israel	253
14.3	US willingness to aid Israel in the event it is faced with an existential crisis	254
14.4	The importance of various factors to Israeli security	255
14.5	President Obama's approach toward Israel	256
14.6	Threats to Israel's existential interests	257
14.7	President Obama's policies toward the Middle East	257
14.8	Obama's policies and US standing in the Middle East	259
14.9	The United States' standing in the Middle East	260
14.10	Israeli security and the United States' standing in the Middle East	261
14.11	US and Israeli interests in the Middle East	261
14.12	Support for Israeli military action if diplomacy fails to halt Iran's drive for nuclear weapons	262
14.13	Support for Israeli military action in the event that diplomacy fails to halt Iran's drive for nuclear weapons and the United States opposes an Israeli air strike	263
15.1	US–Israel parallelogram of forces	269

Tables

4.1	Desirability of US leadership in world affairs	66
4.2	Toughness in foreign policy and national security	70
4.3	Obama's job rating on foreign policy crises and issues (2013)	74
4.4	Obama's approval rating on foreign policy issues (2014–2015)	75
4.5	Respect for the United States in the world	79
4.6	Party preferences: views of global threats	81
4.7	Party preferences: US importance and power	81
4.8	Party preferences: respect by other countries	82
6.1	Support of South Koreans for becoming a nuclear state (in %)	113
6.2	Public appraisal of influence of China vs United States (in %)	118
9.1	Proportion of population with favorable perception of the United States (in %)	166

Contributors

Efraim Inbar is a Professor of Political Studies at Bar-Ilan University and the Director of its Begin-Sadat (BESA) Center for Strategic Studies. His area of specialization is Middle Eastern strategic issues, with a particular interest in the politics and strategy of Israeli national security.

Jonathan Rynhold is the Director of the Argov Center for the Study of Israel and the Jewish People in the Political Studies department at Bar-Ilan University, where he also serves as deputy head of the department and as a Senior Researcher at the Begin-Sadat (BESA) Center for Strategic Studies. Dr Rynhold's research focuses on Israeli foreign policy, the Middle East peace process, and US–Israeli relations. His latest book, entitled *The Arab–Israeli Conflict in American Political Culture*, was recently published by Cambridge University Press.

Dmitry (Dima) Adamsky is Associate Professor at the Lauder School of Government, Diplomacy and Strategy at the Interdisciplinary Center (IDC) Herzliya, and is a Head of the BA Honors track in strategy and decision making. His research interests include international security, strategic studies, cultural approaches to international relations, modern military thought, nuclear strategy, and US, Russian, and Israeli national security policy. His books *Operation Kavkaz (Maarachot)* and *The Culture of Military Innovation* (Stanford University Press) earned the annual prizes, in 2006 and 2012 respectively, for the best academic works on Israeli security.

Efrat Aviv is a Lecturer in the Department of Middle Eastern Studies at Bar-Ilan University, Israel. She conducted her postdoctorate research at the Begin-Sadat Center for Strategic Studies (BESA). She is a Fellow at the Vidal Sassoon International Center for the Study of Anti-Semitism and at BESA.

Yehuda U. Balanga is a Lecturer in the Department of Middle Eastern Studies at Bar-Ilan University, and a visiting scholar at the Moshe Dayan Center, Tel-Aviv University. Dr Balanga's academic research focuses on the Great Powers' involvement in the Middle East, particularly in Egypt and Syria, and the results of these interventions.

C. Uday Bhaskar is the Director of the Society for Policy Studies in New Delhi. He retired from the Indian Navy in early 2007 after 37 years of service. He was Director of the National Maritime Foundation from 2009 to 2011, and was previously with the Institute for Defence Studies and Analyses (IDSA), New Delhi, from 1989 onwards, where he served as a Senior Fellow, Deputy Director (1996–2004), and Director, until late 2005. He has edited books on nuclear, naval/maritime, and international security issues, and has contributed over 60 research articles to journals in India and abroad.

Yaeli Bloch-Elkon is a Senior Lecturer and Vice-Chair of the School of Communication at Bar-Ilan University. She is also an Associate Research Scholar at the BESA Center for Strategic Studies, and at Columbia University's Institute for Social and Economic Research and Policy (ISERP), New York. Bloch-Elkon's research interests include media, public opinion and foreign policy, terrorism and counterterrorism, and partisan polarization, using statistical methods. She co-authored *Selling Fear: Counterterrorism, the Media and Public Opinion* (University of Chicago Press, 2011), which received several significant international awards.

Eliot Cohen is the Robert E. Osgood Professor of Strategic Studies at Johns Hopkins University's School of Advanced International Studies. He directs the Strategic Studies Program at SAIS and the Philip Merrill Center for Strategic Studies, which he founded. From April 2007 through January 2009 he served as Counselor of the Department of State. His books include *Supreme Command: Soldiers, Statesmen, and Leadership in Wartime* (Anchor, 2002) and, most recently, *Conquered into Liberty: Two Centuries of Battles Along the Great Warpath that made the American Way of War* (Free Press, 2011).

Steven David is a Professor of International Relations at the Johns Hopkins University. His main areas of focus are international security, the politics of the developing world, and US foreign policy. David is the author of three books and articles that have appeared in such journals as *Foreign Affairs*, *International Security*, *World Politics*, *Israel Affairs* and *The American Interest*.

Eytan Gilboa is a Senior Researcher at the BESA Center, a Professor of International Communication, and Director of the School of Communication and the Center for International Communication at Bar-Ilan University. He specializes in US–Israeli relations, US policy in the Middle East, US and Israeli politics, public opinion, international communication, and public diplomacy.

Arie M. Kacowicz is the Chaim Weizmann Chair in International Relations and a Professor in the Department of International Relations at Bar-Ilan University. His areas of interest include theories of international relations, international relations of Latin America, globalization, and global governance. His most recent book, *Globalization and the Distribution of Wealth: The Latin American Experience, 1982–2008* was published by Cambridge University Press in 2013.

Efraim Karsh is Professor Emeritus of Middle East and Mediterranean Studies at King's College London, and a Professor of Political Studies at Bar-Ilan University, where he is also a Senior Research Associate at the BESA Center for Strategic Studies. He is editor of the *Middle East Quarterly* and *Israel Affairs*, and the author of 15 books, including: *Palestine Betrayed* (Yale, 2010); *Islamic Imperialism: A History* (Yale, 2006); *Arafat's War: The Man and his Battle for Israeli Conquest* (Grove, 2003); *Empires of the Sand: The Struggle for Mastery in the Middle East 1798–1923* (Harvard, 1999); and *Fabricating Israeli History: The "New Historians"* (Routledge, 1997).

Emily B. Landau is a Senior Research Fellow and Head of the arms control and regional security program at the Institute for National Security Studies (INSS), Tel Aviv University. She has published and lectured extensively on: nuclear proliferation, regional security, and arms control efforts in the Middle East; efforts to confront the proliferation challenges posed by Iran and North Korea; Israel's nuclear image and policy; and developments in US and global arms control thinking regarding weapons of mass destruction in the post-Cold War world.

Alon Levkowitz is a Researcher at the Begin Sadat Center for Strategic Studies at Bar-Ilan University. He teaches Korean politics and Asian security and international relations at Bar-Ilan University and the Hebrew University of Jerusalem. His research interests include Korean politics and security, Asian civil society, and Asian regional international organizations.

Henry R. Nau is a Professor of Political Science and International Affairs at the Elliott School of International Affairs, The George Washington University. From January 1981 to July 1983, Dr Nau served on President Reagan's National Security Council staff as White House sherpa responsible for G-7 summits and international economic affairs. From 1975–1977 he served as Special Assistant to the Undersecretary of Economic Affairs in the Department of State. And from 1963–1965, he served as a Lieutenant in the US Army with the 82nd Airborne Division. His published books include, among others, *Conservative Internationalism: Armed Diplomacy Under Jefferson, Polk, Truman, and Reagan* (Princeton University Press, 2013).

Shmuel Sandler is a Senior Research Associate at the BESA Center, and a Professor of Political Science at Bar-Ilan University and at several regional colleges associated with Bar-Ilan. He holds the Yehuda Avner

Chair in Religion and Politics at Bar-Ilan University, and has served as Dean of the University's Faculty of Social Sciences. His fields of study include theories of international relations, Israeli politics and foreign policy, US foreign policy, and religion and international relations.

Jian Wang is Director of the USC Center on Public Diplomacy and an Associate Professor at the University of Southern California Annenberg School for Communication and Journalism. His books include *Shaping China's Global Imagination: Branding Nations at the World Expo*, *Soft Power in China: Public Diplomacy through Communication* (editor, Palgrave Macmillan, 2013), and *Foreign Advertising in China: Becoming Global, Becoming Local* (Wiley-Blackwell, 2000).

Introduction

Efraim Inbar and Jonathan Rynhold

This book is about the United States' standing in the world. That is, it is about how other states and their citizens, as well US citizens themselves, perceive the United States in the international arena. Is it perceived as strong or weak, resolute or vacillating, reliable or perfidious, revolutionary or conservative, moral or immoral? The answers to these questions will greatly affect the United States' ability to conduct its foreign policy successfully. The higher a state's standing – its reputation, prestige and credibility – the easier it will be for it to pursue its objectives at a lower cost in terms of blood and treasure. For as Morgenthau (1954, 27) recognized, while military and economic power is grounded on certain objective material factors, "political power is a psychological relationship between those who exercise it and those over whom it is exercised."

That much is relatively uncontroversial. However, there is a big debate about what constitutes the most important basis for a state's standing. Is it more important for a state to be liked or feared? One the one hand, it can be argued that it is more important to be feared. For if enemies do not fear you, this will encourage adventurism on their part. Equally, if allies do not trust your resolution and reliability they will defect to the other side (Kagan 1995). On the other hand, it can be argued that being liked reduces the possible reasons for conflict in the first place, and that generating a very fearful reputation may drive otherwise disparate states to unite in a counterbalancing formation (Pape 2005; Walt 2006).

A second issue concerns the relative importance of a state's standing vis-à-vis political elites and public opinion. Of course it is desirable to be both feared and liked by both elites and publics. But it is often impossible to pursue one objective without cost to the other. Thus, the assertive grand strategy pursued by George W. Bush during his first administration enhanced fear of the United States among Middle Eastern leaders such that Colonel Qadaffi surrendered Libya's nuclear program, while at the same time drastically reducingthe United States' popularity with public opinion throughout most of the world. In contrast, Obama's restrained grand strategy increased the United States' popularity with public opinion abroad (Pew 2006, 2012, 2013a, 2013b), while, as argued in this volume by several authors, simultaneously reducing the fear of the United States among political elites in states hostile to it, such as Iran and North Korea.

The United States' standing and grand strategy

The United States remains extremely powerful militarily, far more powerful than any other state. Even after major cuts in the defense budget under Obama, US military spending constitutes about 40 percent of global military expenditure, more than four times as much spending as the next state, China. Moreover, the United States has a huge lead in power projection capabilities, with ten aircraft carriers; China and Russia have only one aircraft carrier each. Aside from this, US technology means that it also retains a significant qualitative edge (Macias *et al.* 2014; SIPRI 2015).

In economic terms, the United States remains the state with the largest economy, but the world economy is essentially multilateral, with the European Union's combined economy exceeding that of the United States, while China is catching up with it fast (World Bank 2013; Knoema 2015). Indeed, despite the United States' continued dominance, it is clear that US material power is in relative decline, though there is a major debate about the extent of that decline, its speed, and its strategic significance. Some have argued that the US can retain its dominant position for the foreseeable future if it demonstrates the will and skill to do so (Lieber 2012; Beckley 2011; Kagan 2012; Joffe 2009; Drezner 2011a; Nye 2011); while others argue that the process of decline is upon it and that this is best managed by a cautious strategy of retrenchment (Kupchan 2002, 2012; Zakaria 2009; Layne 2009; Pape 2009; Posen 2014; Rachman 2011). In any case, much of public opinion across the world (with the notable exception of opinion among the United States' East Asian allies) believes that Chinese power will eventually eclipse that of the United States (Pew 2013b).

In terms of soft power appeal, US culture and values remain far more popular than China's, though in the wake of 9/11 there has been much debate about the growth of anti-Americanism (Katzenstein and Keohane 2007; Rubin and Rubin 2005; O'Connor and Griffiths 2006). Some have argued that anti-Americanism is essentially a prejudice grounded on a hatred of the United States' liberal democratic values (Ajami 2003; Berman, 2004; Hollander 1995; Markovits 2007; Revel 2003), and/or the political interests of dictatorial regimes (Rubin 2002). These authors focus on the ideological foundations – radical Islamist or leftist – of the most vehement forms of anti-Americanism. Others argue that anti-Americanism is primarily a result of an assertive, interventionist US foreign policy, especially that of George W. Bush (Telhami 2002; Pape 2005; Chiozza 2009), and they point to the decline in positive attitudes toward the United States under Bush and their partial recovery under Obama (Datta 2012). Some consider these trends in public opinion to be strategically significant (Datta 2012), others are not convinced (Katzenstein and Keohane 2007).

Indeed, George W. Bush and Barack Obama pursued very different grand strategies, which were informed by very different answers to the issues discussed above. Following the end of the Cold War, a unipolar world emerged, with the United States as the dominant power (Huntington 1999; Mastanduno 1997). Against this background, from 9/11 until midway through his second administration, Bush pursued an interventionist grand strategy of "primacy," which rested on the assumption that the United States could maintain its dominance, and that the best way to preserve its standing was through an assertive, and relatively unilateral, approach (Halper and Clarke 2004; Daalder and Lindsay 2003). On the one hand, such an approach was designed to induce in the United States' enemies and competitors a healthy fear and respect. In the wake of 9/11, the United States would demonstrate that it was neither weak nor decadent. On the other hand, the Bush administration tended to the view that the core of anti-Americanism was ideological. On this basis, its democratization agenda was supposed to increase the popularity of the United States in the long run, the model being the transformation of German and Japanese attitudes toward the United States after 1945.

Meanwhile, the first Obama administration emerged at the time of a renewed wave of international relations literature, once more heralding the US decline in world affairs (Posen 2007; Zakaria 2009; Layne 2009; Rachman 2011; Kupchan 2012). In contrast to Bush, Obama pursued a cautious grand strategy of retrenchment, underwritten by the belief that this is the best way to manage the decline of US power (Drezner 2011b; Dueck 2015). The administration, whose rhetoric was marked both by cautious realism and idealistic dovish liberalism, operated on the assumption that the Bush strategy had severely damaged US standing, and that the way to restore that standing was to adopt the opposite strategy, namely a cautious, multilateral, and non-interventionist approach. In this vein, Obama sought to improve the United States' standing by reaching out to the Arab public and to the regime in Iran, in an effort to make the United States appear less threatening and more likable.

Outline of the book

This book originated in the many discussions about the standing of the United States in world affairs that were held at the Begin-Sadat (BESA) Center for Strategic Studies at Bar-Ilan University. We were concerned about the contours of US foreign policy in the new millennium, particularly in our region, the Middle East. We were not surprised by the unsuccessful attempts to create an Iraq or an Afghanistan in a US image. We were not convinced that the noble US goal of turning such countries into democracies, in order to prevent them from becoming incubators for terrorist organizations, was realistic. Therefore, gradually terminating overseas commitments to attain impossible political objectives made sense.

Investing in such projects was costly and came at the expense of domestic priorities. Indeed, recommendations for greater restraint in US foreign policy were written at BESA (Posen 2007, 2014).

Yet most of us were disturbed by the direction of US diplomacy under President Barack Obama. His presidency has clearly seen US clout eroded in several regions, notably in Eastern Europe, the Far East, and the Middle East. The attempts to engage with foes, such as Iran or Syria, raised eyebrows. US "leadership from behind" in the case of Libya, and the rosy expectations of the Arab Spring, were met with skepticism. Our meetings with scholars from other countries showed that the unease with US foreign policy was widespread. Indeed, much of Obama's foreign policy actions appeared to confirm the declinist theory, even though the United States is probably still able to reassert itself and snap back as the leading global power.

The first section of the book focuses on the picture within the United States itself. It begins with Eliot Cohen's review of US involvement in recent wars, in Iraq and Afghanistan and against al-Qaeda. The chapter charts US military successes and failures in these conflicts, before turning to their likely consequences. On the tactical level, he points to the successful use of UAVs, signals intelligence, and video-teleconferencing between the president and post-conflict leaders in Afghanistan and Iraq as positive lessons to draw for the future. On the negative side of the ledger, he argues that the United States' failure sufficiently to understand the societies it was dealing with led to serious mistakes in post-war reconstruction. For example, regarding Afghanistan he argues that the United States should not have attempted to reshape the Afghan polity against its societal grain. He also suggests that in future US counterinsurgency strategy should be focused primarily on military and governance issues, and not on development. More generally, Cohen argues that the United States will be less willing than in the past to engage in large-scale, expeditionary warfare. The United States has not become isolationist or pacifist, but it will likely use force more selectively. While these wars were not as economically draining as is commonly assumed, they generated more partisan division and discord than the Vietnam War, a fact which will likely affect the lessons each of the two parties will learn from them. Cohen concludes by noting that however maladroit much of the US conduct of these wars was, that is to some extent the nature of all war; and cautions that we will not know for some time what the consequences of these campaigns are and what would have happened if they had not been waged (Iraq), or had been waged differently.

Moving from the military sphere to grand strategy, Henry Nau analyzes the US foreign policy debate. He identifies three approaches – nationalist, realist, and internationalist – that have tended to dominate this debate, with their prominence rotating in a cyclical fashion. Thus, after a surge of internationalism under George W. Bush, Barack Obama now beckons the

United States to come home. Neo-nationalists in both parties agree with him and pledge, short of another attack, never to put boots on the ground again in foreign wars. Realists also counsel restraint, but worry about lagging defense spending and warn that great powers cannot retire from global affairs; while internationalists, on the defensive, insist that transformation, not stabilization, of world affairs remains the essential goal. However, this is not the whole picture, for Nau has uncovered a fourth tradition, *conservative internationalism*, as exemplified by Presidents Polk and Reagan. This tradition affirms the objectives of *liberal internationalism*, namely the goal to spread freedom (unlike realism); but it uses the means or instruments of *realism* to back up this effort, namely military power (unlike the soft-power emphasis of liberal internationalism). It also pursues an end goal that is less ambitious than liberal internationalism and closer to *nationalism* and *realism*: namely, a world of decentralized nation-states in which sister democratic republics retain their national sovereignty, rather than a centralized world of international institutions.

While Nau's chapter focuses on the debate over different approaches to US foreign policy in general, Steven David's chapter provides an overarching analysis of President Obama's approach to foreign policy in particular. David argues that the widespread criticism that Obama's policy has lacked a coherent strategy is misplaced. Instead, he contends that Obama's strategy has adhered very closely to the traditional realist theory of international relations. As such, Obama's foreign policy has been marked by restraint and retrenchment, reflecting what Obama believes to be the limits of US power, and avoiding the squandering of resources on what he has concluded are futile causes and marginal threats. Indeed, he has been cautious in the use of force, restrained in efforts to promote democracy and human rights, opposed to the direct involvement of US troops, and insistent on others sharing the burden for world order. For David, this strategy rests on the realist belief that force should only be used to protect vital interests, coupled with the convincing case made by the administration that these vital interests are not under serious threat anywhere. However, in conclusion, David warns that the cumulative effect of noninvolvement can erode US credibility. The growing recognition that the United States cannot be depended upon to enforce international order may create so great a threat to US interests that by the time the United States wakes up to the danger, it can only be met at a terrible cost.

In contrast to David, some have argued that Obama's foreign policy has been driven by the US public's increased unwillingness to engage internationally following the perceived failures of the wars in Iraq and Afghanistan. In his chapter on US public opinion toward Obama's foreign policy, Eytan Gilboa vehemently rejects this thesis. While Gilboa accepts that there was public support for ending the US interventions in Iraq and Afghanistan, and that public opinion on some foreign policy issues has been polarized along party lines, he nonetheless argues that Obama's foreign policy actually ignored important consensual aspects of public opinion toward foreign policy. As such he concludes that there was no isolationist constraint on US foreign policy. Indeed, despite Afghanistan and Iraq, the public continued to support an active role for the United States in world affairs, wanted the United States to lead the world, and strongly supported the long-standing US commitment to NATO. In addition, the public did not think Obama was tough enough on national security. Moreover, they disapproved of his handling of the crises in the Middle East and his handling of relations with key states such as Russia, China, Mexico, and Israel. While US citizens supported the negotiations on the Iranian nuclear program, they were very skeptical about Iranian intentions to implement any deal, and they strongly rejected his preference for bypassing Congress with regard to any permanent agreement with Iran.

The second section of the book focuses on perceptions of the United States' standing across different regions of the world. Here we begin with the United States' most important international relationship, the one with China. This is the subject of Jian Wang's chapter, which analyzes how the Chinese public perceives the United States. Although China is not a democracy, public opinion increasingly matters as a result of the modernization process that has been underway since reforms were first introduced in 1978. According to Wang, there is a contrast between Chinese perceptions of US foreign policy on the one hand, and attitudes toward US society and culture on the other. The Chinese tend to view the United States' global role negatively, along with aspects of US policy toward China, which they perceive as aiming to curtail China's rise. However, US values, business practices, technology, and culture are held in high regard, as reflected in patterns of Chinese investment, travel, study, and entertainment. Somewhat surprisingly, the chapter concludes that Chinese perceptions of the United States have been rather stable in the twenty-first century, and that any changes have been the result of shifts in domestic Chinese realities, rather than shifts in US policies.

The rise of China has become an important intervening variable in the relations between the United States and some of its Far East allies. The next chapter, by Alon Levkowitz, focuses on the bilateral relations with an important US ally in the Far East, the Republic of Korea. He analyzes South Korea's perceptions of the United States and China, and the ways in which the regional and global arenas influence Seoul's policies. This chapter shows that although the South Korean public attaches great importance to the alliance with the United States, the South Korean political and military milieus have doubts regarding the credibility of the alliance and of US commitments. While some security aspects demonstrate Seoul's security dependence on Washington, others reflect a gradual shift in South Korea's security policy, toward greater independence. This shift reflects South Korea's changed self-perception to that of a middle-power state, and its growing skepticism regarding Washington's commitment to Korea's security.

The change and continuity in Russian perceptions of the United States are analyzed by Dima Adamsky. His chapter traces the evolution of Moscow's self-image in the context of US foreign policy in general and toward Russia specifically. It covers the transition from euphoria and disillusionment in the 1990s, to the emergence of strategic competition in the 2000s, culminating in the current state of geopolitical confrontation. This is the background for understanding the main components of the current Russian threat perception with regards to the United States, in the foreign and security spheres, in terms of energy, and in the domestic sphere. All of these combine to explain Moscow's current approach to the West. The chapter compares and contrasts contemporary "bottom-up" Russian anti-Americanism with its Soviet "top-down" equivalent. Adamsky concludes with the main strategic issues on the Russian agenda vis-à-vis the United States, and outlines the main principles guiding Moscow's view of the way ahead.

India is a rising power in the international arena, and its perspective on US political leadership and foreign policy is central to world politics. C. Uday Bhaskar's chapter reviews this subject. The new partnership between India and the United States in the post-Cold War era, and its radical manifestation, is reflected in the most recent development in the bilateral relationship – namely the invitation extended to US President Barak Obama to be the chief guest at the Indian Republic Day Parade on January 26, 2015. In many ways, the trajectory from Jawaharlal Nehru through Indira Gandhi to Narendra Modi is reflective of the dramatic change that has taken place in India's perceptions of the US role in global affairs – although wariness about US foreign policy still persists. While India does not wish to become an alliance partner with the United States, it is nonetheless drawn to the United States because it is wary of the rise of China and of growing Chinese assertiveness. Bhaskar concludes that in the long run, ensuring that India maintains the appropriate degree of strategic equipoise, and enabling it to realize its latent economic and military potential, has an existential underpinning that will benefit both the eagle and the elephant.

Another region examined in the book is Latin America, and perceptions of the United States' standing among Latin American states is the subject of Arie Kacowicz's chapter. Latin America is a highly significant region for the United States. It is the largest foreign supplier of oil to the United States, and an important partner in the development of alternative fuels, as well as being one of its fastest-growing trading partners. Although there is a perception in Latin America that there has been a significant decline of US hegemony in the region, very few Latin American leaders have shown more than a superficial interest in copying the late Hugo Chávez's model of anti-Americanism. Most are well aware of the overwhelming strength of the United States, and they are pragmatic enough to work hard on maintaining good relations with the United States. As for public opinion, Kacowicz argues forcefully that it is time to move beyond the caricature that depicts Latin America as a self-perceived helpless victim of an oppressive US imperialism, which uses and abuses the tools of globalization in order to continue its neo-colonial exploitation. Even though there are genuine sentiments of anti-Americanism, overall, globalization, trade, and economic opportunities attract more than they repel. On average, the region's citizens are favorable toward the United States, and they are more likely to view it through the lens of economic opportunity than as a threat.

The Middle East has been the focus of much of the US diplomacy in the twenty-first century, and is treated extensively in this volume. Efraim Karsh claims in his chapter that Barack Obama has done more than any of his predecessors to foster sterile stereotypes of Arabs and Muslims that have little to do with reality. Worse, Obama's attempt to translate these misconceptions into actual policies has resulted in a string of disasters: the failure to contain Tehran's quest for nuclear weapons; the disruption of Washington's relations with key regional allies; the surge of Islamist terrorism; the fragmentation of the Iraqi state; and the collapse of the Palestinian–Israeli peace talks. All of this has plunged the United States' regional standing to its lowest ebb in decades.

Emily Landau focuses on the US counter-proliferation policy toward Iran. Her chapter focuses on the major constraints that have hobbled Western efforts to halt Iran's nuclear development for more than a decade. Landau argues that whether international negotiators have focused on attempting to alter proliferators' behavior through inducements ("carrots") or through application of pressure ("sticks"), they have found that it is the proliferator that tends to gain the upper hand in negotiations, due to its determination at the strategic level and its ability to play a superior tactical game at the negotiating table. Indeed, the P5+1 group under the leadership of the United States has been structurally hampered in this way in its negotiations with Iran. The political context within which their efforts are carried out has a crippling effect on their ability to garner the kind of unified and determined stance necessary to compel a nuclear proliferator effectively to back away from its military aspirations and uphold its commitment to remaining non-nuclear.

Another important regional actor in the Middle East is Turkey, which is covered by Efrat Aviv. The ruling AKP government (since 2002) has signaled that it will not automatically follow the US lead. Turkey, a non-permanent member of the UN Security Council, has held the position of secretary general of the Organization of Islamic Conference (OIC), and is also a member of the G-20 group of nations. Turkey has the world's eighth-strongest military, is a NATO member, and has multilateral relations with various political actors. It also sees itself as an emerging power in the Balkans, the Middle East, and Central Asia. This article examines Turkish–US relations over the last decade, and presents the attitudes of

Turkish public opinion toward the United States. The article begins by analyzing the impact of the 2003 US invasion of Iraq on bilateral relations; it then goes on to assess the impact of several other foreign policy issues on the relationship. Subsequently, the Turkish domestic scene is reviewed; here the focus is on assessing the attitudes of the Turkish public toward the United States.

Since the 1970s, Egypt has been one of the main pillars of US strategy in the Middle East. But when Egypt experienced a period of unrest during the Arab Spring, and was in greater need of US support than ever, it seemed that US support wavered. The chapter written by Yehuda Blanga documents the role of US hesitancy in the demise of the Hosni Mubarak regime, US support for the Muslim Brotherhood regime, and the cold shoulder given to the regime of General Abdel al-Fattah al-Sisi, symbolized by the suspension of US military assistance to Egypt. Egypt and other US allies in the Middle East view such inconsistencies very critically.

Israel is one of the United States' closest allies, and closely follows the direction of US foreign policy, yet it has had a problematic relationship with the Obama administration. The chapter by Yaeli Bloch-Elkon and Jonathan Rynhold focuses on the attitudes of the Israeli public toward the United States during the Obama era, from 2009 through 2014. While surveys and analysis of US public opinion toward Israel are numerous, surveys of the other side of the equation are rare, and this chapter serves to fill that gap. Overall, the polls show that Israelis strongly support the United States and that they overwhelmingly view the relationship with the United States as vital to Israeli security. Indeed, they rank the "special relationship" as more important for Israeli security than any other factor, with the exception of Israel's own military capabilities. They also clearly view the United States in general as a reliable ally of Israel. However, Israelis were evenly divided as to whether Obama's approach to Israel is a positive one, and even more significantly, a clear majority of Israelis viewed Obama's policies in the Middle East in a negative light. This was found to be true for the administration's policies toward the Islamic State in Syria and Iraq (ISIS), the Iranian nuclear issue, and the Israeli–Palestinian peace process.

Meanwhile, in another chapter about Israel, Shmuel Sandler argues that a change in the role of the United States in the Middle East would have severe implications for Israel's security. A reduced US presence in the region would lead to regional instability and upset the balance of power between Israel and its neighbors. A return to pre-1967 Israeli strategy would be likely, featuring preventive and preemptive strikes, and disproportionate punishment in order to build deterrence. A partial US exit would also increase Israel's threat perception and hence its need for strategic depth, leading to unilateral annexation of strategic territory, such as in the area along the Jordan River and on the Golan Heights. Finally, Sandler contends that a United States unable to prevent a nuclear Iran could compel Israel to strike at the Iranian nuclear infrastructure.

The BESA Center for Strategic Studies has been a wonderful intellectual home for producing this book, and for hosting the conference on which it is based. Its administrative staff deserves our thanks for the logistical support given throughout the project. Liana Rubin was especially helpful, while Daniel Barnett, the linguistic editor, improved the product. Finally, the contributors to this collection have worked hard to accommodate our comments and to meet the deadline. We are grateful to all.

Bibliography

Ajami, Fouad. 2003. "The Falseness of Anti-Americanism." *Foreign Policy* 183: 52–61.
Berman, Russell A. 2004. *Anti-Americanism in Europe*. Stanford, CA: Hoover Institution Press.
Beckley, Michael. 2011. "China's Century? Why America's Edge Will Endure." *International Security* 36 (3): 41–78.
Chiozza, Giacomo. 2009. *Anti-Americanism and the American World Order*. Baltimore, MD: Johns Hopkins University Press.
Daalder, Ivo, and James Lindsay. 2003. *America Unbound: The Bush Revolution in Foreign Policy*. Washington, DC: Brookings.
Datta, Monti Narayan. 2012. *Anti-Americanism and the Rise of World Opinion*. Cambridge: Cambridge University Press.
Drezner, Daniel. 2011a. "China Isn't Beating the U.S." *Foreign Policy* 184: 67.
Drezner, Daniel. 2011b. "Does Obama Have a Grand Strategy?" *Foreign Affairs*, July/August.
Dueck, Colin. 2015. *The Obama Doctrine: American Grand Strategy Today*. Oxford: Oxford University Press.
Global Firepower. 2015. "The United States of America Military Strength," January 4. www.globalfirepower.com/country-military-strength-detail.asp?country_id=United-States-of-America.
Halper, Stefan, and Jonathan Clarke. 2004. *America Alone: The Neo-Conservatives and the Global Order*. Cambridge: Cambridge University Press.
Hollander, Paul. 1995. *Anti-Americanism: Irrational and Rational*. New Brunswick, NJ: Transaction Publishers.
Huntington, Samuel P. 1999. "The Lonely Superpower." *Foreign Affairs*, March/April: 35–49.
Joffe, Josef. 2009. "The Default Power: The False Prophecy of America's Decline." *Foreign Affairs* 88 (5): 21–35.
Kagan, Donald. 1995. *On the Origins of War and the Preservation of Peace*. New York: Doubleday.
Kagan, Robert. 2012. *The World America Made*. New York: Knopf.
Katzenstein, Peter J., and Robert O. Keohane, eds. 2007. *Anti-Americanisms in World Politics*. Ithaca, NY: Cornell University Press.
Knoema. 2015. "World GDP Ranking 2015: Data and Charts." http://knoema.com/nwnfkne/world-gdp-ranking-2015-data-and-charts.
Kupchan, Charles. 2002. *The End of the American Era*. New York: Random House.
Kupchan, Charles. 2012. *No One's World: The West, The Rising Rest, and the Coming Global Turn*. New York: Oxford University Press.

Layne, Christopher. 2009. "The Waning of U.S. Hegemony – Myth or Reality? A Review Essay." *International Security* 34 (1): 147–172.
Lieber, Robert J. 2012. *Power and Willpower in the American Future*. Cambridge: Cambridge University Press.
Macias, Amanda, Jeremy Bender, and Skye Gould. 2014. "The 35 Most Powerful Militaries in the World." *Business Insider*, July 10. www.businessinsider.com/35-most-powerful-militaries-in-the-world-2014-7.
Markovits, Andrei S. 2007. *Uncouth Nation: Why Europe Dislikes America*. Princeton, NJ: Princeton University Press.
Mastanduno, Michael. 1997. "Preserving the Unipolar Moment: Realist Theories and U.S. Grand Strategy after the Cold War." *International Security* 21 (4): 49–88.
Morgenthau, Hans. 1954. *Politics Among Nations*, 6th edition. New York: Knopf.
Nye, Joseph S. Jr. 2011. *The Future of Power*. New York: Perseus.
O'Connor, Brendon, and Martin Griffiths. 2006. *The Rise of Anti-Americanism*. London: Routledge.
Pape, Robert A. 2005. "Soft Balancing against the United States." *International Security* 30 (1): 7–45.
Pape, Robert A. 2009. "Empire Falls." *National Interest* 99: 21–34.
Pew Research Center. 2006. "America's Image Slips, But Allies Share U.S. Concerns Over Iran, Hamas." *Pew Global Attitudes and Trends*, June 13. www.pewglobal.org/2006/06/13/americas-image-slips-but-allies-share-us-concerns-over-iran-hamas/.
Pew Research Center. 2012. "Global Opinion of Obama Slips, International Policies Faulted." *Pew Global Attitudes and Trends*, June 13. www.pewglobal.org/2012/06/13/global-opinion-of-obama-slips-international-policies-faulted/.
Pew Research Center. 2013a. "America's Global Image Remains More Positive Than China's, But Many See China Becoming World's Leading Power." *Pew Global Attitudes and Trends*, July 18. www.pewglobal.org/files/2013/07/Pew-Research-Global-Attitudes-Project-Balance-of-Power-Report-FINAL-July-18-2013.pdf.
Pew Research Center. 2013b. "Global Image of the United States and China." *Pew Global Attitudes and Trends*, July 18. www.pewglobal.org/2013/07/18/global-image-of-the-united-states-and-china/.
Posen, Barry. 2007. "The Case for Restraint." *American Interest* 3 (2): 7–32.
Posen, Barry. 2014. *Restraint. A New Foundation for U.S. Grand Strategy*. Ithaca, NY: Cornell University Press.
Rachman, Gideon. 2011. "American Decline: This Time It's for Real." *Foreign Policy* 184: 59–65.
Revel, Jean-Francois. 2003. *Anti-Americanism*. San Francisco: Encounter Books.
Rubin, Barry. 2002. "The Real Roots of Arab Anti-Americanism." *Foreign Affairs* 81 (6): 73–85.
Rubin, Barry, and Judith Colp Rubin. 2005. *Hating America: A History*. Oxford: Oxford University Press.
SIPRI. 2015. "The 15 Countries with the Highest Military Expenditure in 2014." www.sipri.org/googlemaps/milex_top_15_2014_exp_map.html.
Telhami, Shibley. 2002. "Understanding the Challenge." *Middle East Journal* 56 (1): 9–18.
Walt, Stephen M. 2006. *Taming American Power: The Global Response to US Primacy*. New York: W. W. Norton & Co.
World Bank. 2013. "Gross Domestic Product 2013." http://databank.worldbank.org/data/download/GDP.pdf.
Zakaria, Fareed. 2009. *The Post-American World*. New York: W. W. Norton & Company.

Part I
The United States today

1 Lessons from 15 years of war

Eliot Cohen

The importance of the last 15 years

The debate over the United States' use of force in the world will be shaped for the next several decades by the experience of three wars: the war against al-Qaeda and its affiliates; the Afghan war; and, most controversially, the Iraq war. All three were, or swiftly became, wars without discernible fronts, in which progress was obscure; all three involved tremendous domestic and international controversy; all three were waged by two presidents whose outlooks were in many respects very different, yet who did many of the same things.

The partisan temper that surrounds these conflicts makes it both difficult and important to gain some distance on these events, and insofar as is possible, to consider them with a dispassionate eye. One way of doing this is to imagine ourselves looking back on these wars from a much longer period ahead than we normally do, and to ask the kinds of questions that future historians are likely to pose about them.

Where did the wars begin?

In one way the answer to this question is simple: with the events of September 11, 2001. But of course future historians will question that easy assignment of a date, noting the ways in which US support for the *mujahedeen* in the anti-Soviet *jihad* of the 1980s paved the way for the Afghan war; the roots of the conflict with Iraq stretching back at least to the invasion of Kuwait in 1990; and the contest with radical Islam as far back as Sayyid Qutb's unfortunate visit to Colorado in the late 1940s. Nonetheless, it is the shock of 9/11, and the ensuing change in the US temperament and attitude toward the use of force in South Asia and the Middle East, that deserves attention.

It is absurd to claim that there was some ending of innocence here. The territory of the United States, and certainly US citizens abroad, had been attacked before. But the 9/11 attacks were very much a bolt out of the blue, conducted on a scale and with an effectiveness that few could have imagined within the scope of a non-state actor, and directed against symbolic targets of tremendous significance. Secretary of State Rice used to say that for those who were in the White House on that day, as she was, every day thereafter passed in high government service was September 12 – accompanied by a deep fear that it was really September 10.

These three wars were distinct, yet united by that central fact. The 9/11 attacks contributed to a mood of emergency and deeply felt threat to the homeland, and in some measure to the global order that the United States had maintained since 1945.[1] They were united as well by larger developments extrinsic to the United States, chiefly a crisis in the Arab world, which, in the years since it won independence from European colonial rules had charged down a number of dead ends (pan-Arabism, revolutionary socialism, strong man leadership), and whose order had been upended by lopsided wealth produced exclusively by oil, a demographic explosion, and repeated humiliation, as it saw it, at the hands of the West, to include Israel.[2] Beyond this lay a larger crisis in the much wider Muslim world, which can be most broadly understood as a crisis of modernity. This too fed off the crisis in the Arab world, particularly through the oil-rich states (and their citizens) who funded radicalizing madrassahs and movements.

The wars were linked in other ways as well: US decision makers, not altogether implausibly, saw a connection between al-Qaeda and the Iraqi regime – a connection not nearly as deep, we now think, as they imagined. But in the atmosphere of 9/11, and on the basis of the scraps of intelligence available to decision makers, it was not an unreasonable hypothesis to investigate. The wars against al-Qaeda and the Taliban were, obviously, wars of immediate reaction to 9/11; the Iraq war was too, to some extent, but had also to do with the brewing crisis that had resulted from the incomplete ending of the 1991 war.[3] The elaborate regime of sanctions and inspections directed against Saddam that had been constructed after the rescue of Kuwait was crumbling; it had been bolstered by repeated attacks on the Iraqi regime (e.g., Operation Desert Fox in 1998), but one way or another the Iraqi conundrum would need to be faced.

The question of the origins of these wars is important because of its relevance to strategic choices. By 1940 or 1942, the question of what had allowed Hitler to gain power– the terms of the Versailles treaty, the Allies' failure to end World War I with a march on Berlin, the brilliance of a particularly dangerous demagogue, or a development in strains of German culture going back to Martin Luther – made little difference. This question was important to historians and political thinkers, but from the point of view of strategists, it was peripheral. The business at hand was the shattering of German military power and the drive on Berlin. In the United States' recent wars, however, the question of the origins of the wars has been highly relevant to the strategic choices US leaders have confronted. And in the failure to think deeply about the origins of these wars lie some of the mistakes and errors committed in all three.

What went right?

At a time of disillusionment with these wars it is particularly important to begin with the large number of things that went well from a strategic point of view. In the case of al-Qaeda, the first attack on the homeland was the only successful one; the central al-Qaeda organization was put under a great deal of pressure, and its leader was eventually killed by a US raid into Pakistan. This war in the shadows was conducted successfully (from a tactical point of view, at least) across two administrations.

The Afghan war saw the swift overthrow of the Taliban, construction of a reasonably stable, reasonably open government through the first decade of the twenty-first century, and steady support by the Afghan population for a large foreign presence. This situation should be compared with those in countries like South Korea in the early 1950s, and South Vietnam in the early 1960s, by which standards the Kabul regime does not look quite as bad as some think. In the case of Iraq, the regime was swiftly dispatched, and after a period of tremendous turbulence several insurgencies (former regime elements, al-Qaeda in Iraq, and the Sadrists, among others) were crushed. A central government was constructed, and infrastructure restored enough to permit growing oil exports. By 2008 it was the judgment of most outside observers that Iraq was on a fragile trajectory to success – depending, crucially, on US support, mentoring, and pressure.

In all three cases, the United States did *not* spend unsustainable amounts of money to achieve these ends. From 2001 to 2014, the United States spent something like $3.4 trillion on the Afghan and Iraq wars, using a very broad definition of directly war-related expenses; by some accounts, it has accrued another $1 trillion in war-related obligations to future veterans. These are huge numbers, no doubt – until one realizes that US defense spending never cracked 6 percent of GDP during these years. By contrast, it had been in the range of 10 percent and above in the 1960s, and around 8 percent in the 1980s.[4]

The United States did not need to reintroduce conscription to fight these wars, and although the quality of volunteers dipped to some extent, in most respects the quality of the armed forces remained extraordinarily high, particularly in the officer and NCO corps. Grievous though the losses were, they were an order of magnitude lower than in previous conflicts. About 4,400 Americans died in Iraq, and another 2,200 in Afghanistan, for about 6,600 overall – about a sixth as many as died in Korea and an eighth as many as died in Vietnam. Because of advances in military medicine, wounded rates were conversely much higher in these more recent wars.

The innovations

It is worth remembering the point of departure of US ground forces. The United States' last large war had been in 1991, with Iraq; it was a war fought the way the US army liked it: mainly in the desert, against a generally static enemy. The conflicts of the post-9/11 period were, with the exception of the brief opening phase of the Iraq war, nothing like that. When the wars began it was a commonplace – one with plenty of precedents in military history – that counterinsurgency operations were low-technology, and in some ways unsophisticated, operations. As US leaders soon learned, this was no longer true.

The biggest operational – and with it, tactical – innovation, of course, was, in fact, the return to counterinsurgency: a set of military operations neglected in US military thought since Vietnam. Indeed, when I conducted a survey for the Defense Policy Board in 2004 on US counterinsurgency doctrine I discovered, to my surprise, that the extant manuals were still those written for Vietnam. The newer manuals were about different forms of peacekeeping and humanitarian intervention. The new doctrinal manual issued in 2006, FM 3–24, was a step, but only a step, in recovering some of that knowledge.

The greatest *tactical innovations* were as follows:

- First and foremost, the development of the most extraordinary man-hunting operations ever seen, first in Iraq and later in Afghanistan, in which black special operations units were repeatedly able to find, capture, or kill senior enemy operatives – and to do so at a high rate. Although Israel, in particular, has had similar success in its theater of operations, as had the British in Northern Ireland, the US operations were performed on a scale and over an extent of territory unprecedented in military history.[5]
- Second, the deployment of UAVs (unmanned aerial vehicles) on a theater-wide scale for the first time in military history, and for many purposes, to include for targeted killing of enemy leaders. To be sure, Israel had used UAVs over Gaza and in southern Lebanon for tactical purposes, and indeed the United States had made extensive use of drones during the Vietnam War. Still, the Predator and Global Hawk programs now allowed the United States to conduct sustained surveillance of targets hundreds of miles from US forces, and to deliver precision fire power against them on a routine basis. As the old Soviet saying went, quantity has a quality all its own, and in the course of these wars the United States deployed several hundred large-scale UAVs, and many times that number of smaller platforms.[6]
- Third, dramatic breakthroughs in tactical signals intelligence. One area in which FM 3–24 had it wrong, in retrospect, was in its emphasis on HUMINT at the expense of SIGINT and other forms of technical intelligence gathering. While much of this subject remains classified, it is publicly known that the United States developed the ability to monitor cellphones and similar electromagnetic devices. In the connected world

of the 2000s, cellphones were widespread, and that proved a vulnerability to many terrorist groups.
- For the rest, a lot of what was done – to include, for example, walling off neighborhoods in Baghdad or deploying small units in neighborhoods – was not particularly new, but effective nonetheless.[7]

The question of *institutional adaptation* to the challenge of the new conflicts was much more problematic.

As is well known, the United States military simply did not do much to prepare itself for the foreseeable tasks of military governance that it would confront, particularly in Iraq. Until quite late in the Iraq war, and to some extent to the present day, the United States military never mastered the art of detainee operations, for both intelligence gathering and subverting the insurgents. Eventually, pretty good training and mentoring programs for the Afghan and Iraqi militaries were created – but they were rushed, and under-resourced for a very long time, particularly in terms of assigning quality US personnel to these missions. More to the point, they were not sustained over the long haul, being understood in terms of decades rather than years.

These were not new problems, and indeed, all of them could have been found in the challenges the United States faced in Korea and Vietnam, and indeed elsewhere throughout the Cold War.[8] They may be lumped together in Carl von Clausewitz's dictum that "in the absence of a true theory of war, routine methods take over, even at the highest level" (Howard *et al.* 1984, II: 4). Indeed, in that sentence lies the explanation for many US mistakes in these wars.

A more open question is the creation of the Provincial Reconstruction Teams, or PRTs, an innovation begun in Afghanistan that then was applied on a larger scale in Iraq, and curiously, reintroduced to Afghanistan. The PRTs, and what one might call militarized development more broadly, require a thorough study. It is not clear to what extent they paid off. Certainly, a lot of development money went astray. The issue is not merely waste – war is by definition wasteful – but rather how much benefit was achieved, and in some cases how much damage was done by well-intentioned but misplaced use of externally funded development. To take one example: as a government official I visited Tikrit, Saddam Hussein's home town, where a well-intentioned commander had used his Commander's Emergency Response Program (CERP) funds to buy a German water purification plant for the local community. In the absence of coordination with the Iraqi ministries for training of key personnel, maintenance, and spare parts, the plant failed after less than a year. And the local population was, if anything, more aggrieved as a result than if they had received no such gift in the first place. As the Iraqis said, "If you can put a man on the moon, why can't you do this?" To their minds, the only obvious explanation was some kind of deeper plot to humiliate them.

The deeper question, and more disturbing, is whether at the end of the day development is critical to the practice of counterinsurgency. Evidence suggests that it may not be. Although it is important to help build institutions of governance, the most external forces probably can and should do is to build security institutions and hold the ring against insurgents while something approaching effective governance is created. In any case, this is one of the deeper lessons of Iraq and Afghanistan that will require future study.

The *organizational story* of the last 15 years is also mixed. On the one hand, the United States displayed some models of civil–military cooperation at the top that were indispensable successes, among them the partnerships between Lieutenant General David Barno and Ambassador Zalmay Khalilzad in Afghanistan early on, and later between General David Petraeus and Ambassador Ryan Crocker in Iraq. In both cases, the civil and military authorities co-located their headquarters (literally a hundred feet apart or less), and worked in tandem. Unfortunately, these were matched by some dysfunctional, and indeed poisonous, relationships in the same countries.

At the level of *high command* in Washington, the two key innovations were the creation of a deputy national security adviser specifically for these conflicts, and the regular use of video-teleconferencing between the president and key foreign leaders. Although both innovations had their perils, both ended up giving direction and coherence to US war efforts. Both, however, had their costs. In the Obama administration there was increasing tension between the Department of Defense and the deputy national security adviser, whom it regarded as usurping the right of providing military advice to the president. In the latter case, one president had built personal relationships through teleconferencing that his successor did not wish to maintain. Arguably, the collapse in US–Iraqi and US–Afghan government relationships had a lot to do with the curtailment of what had been a remarkable level of direct contact between leaders in those countries and the president of the United States.[9]

What went wrong?

This is a much longer list, alas, but four particular failures stand out:

Understanding the societies the United States was dealing with. The truth is that any society is difficult to understand, and those of Iraq and Afghanistan in particular were extraordinarily so. Indeed, we often find it hard to understand movements of opinion and attitude in our own societies, which can often act in surprising ways. Minor examples of this might include the astonishingly swift adoption of gay marriage and legalization of marijuana in the United States. In countries as different as Iraq and Afghanistan, the potential for surprise was even greater.[10]

Inevitably, most of our understanding of these places was taken from rare and controlled pre-war visits or, which was much more problematic, the opinions of refugees from these countries. Here again, the distortions were more complicated than one might think. In the case of Iraq, for example, refugees did not overestimate the hostility to Saddam Hussein throughout the country. They did, however, overestimate the coherence of the society and of older, largely secular and technocratic elites. If one of the big mistakes of the US invasion was its failure to anticipate the chaos that would envelop Iraq afterward, this was due to a failure to understand just how shattered that society had been by the rise of the Ba'ath Party and the Hussein dictatorship, the Iran–Iraq war, the first Gulf war, the ensuing isolation and sanctions, and yet another US invasion. Indeed, in both Iraq and Afghanistan, Americans (and others) failed to understand how traumatized these societies had become by decades of war and savage repression. In Iraq that worked against the United States; curiously, in Afghanistan it worked the other way, as a normally somewhat xenophobic population welcomed US intervention against the Taliban.

A very different kind of mistake was the US failure to help shape an Afghan state, after the shattering of the Taliban regime, which went with the grain of Afghan society, as opposed to centralizing power in a way that could never work. In both cases, the United States failed to think through, in a serious way, the real challenges of military governance in anything like the way it had during World War II as it began planning for the occupation of Italy and Germany. Particularly in the case of Iraq, the United States would have done better to resort to local governance combined with US military supervision for some period of time, building national institutions of governance with more care (and less dubious assistance from the United Nations).

The United States also, of course, took far too long to understand its enemy, or rather enemies.[11] Some cases in point include US officials' persistent references to the enemy in Iraq as "bitter enders" or "former regime elements," and with it our failure to recognize the conflict for what it was: a civil war in which we were inevitably embroiled. Similarly, the United States found it very difficult to figure out who the Taliban members were, and to what extent they could be divided or split from one another. The US government was for years unwilling to recognize that both Pakistan and Iran were conducting lethal covert warfare against it, and to react. Similarly, the United States believed that al-Qaeda had been defeated, or nearly so, when in fact it was merely metastasizing, most recently in Syria and Iraq, but also in the Maghreb, Yemen, and some parts of Africa.

Planning for long conflicts. Both the Bush and the Obama administrations did a wretched job of preparing the public and sustaining domestic support for what were bound to be long conflicts. In fact, US popular support for these wars lasted longer than one might reasonably have expected: until July 2009, for example, US popular support for the war in Afghanistan topped 60 percent; even in the case of Iraq, support for the war lasted at least three years. But neither president during this period put much effort – hardly any at all – into explaining these wars to the US people or securing their support for them. From the point of view of a historian of previous wars, it was a remarkable lapse in wartime leadership.

In the same way, the US government staggered through these wars on a consistently short-term basis. A particularly notorious case was the failure to introduce mine-protected (MRAP) vehicles until quite late in the Iraq war – 2007 to be exact – even though the technology was in no way exotic. The argument was that the war would soon be over, and that it therefore did not make sense to introduce a new class of vehicles which were not expected to have much utility in other conflicts.[12]

Similarly, the government stinted on the expansion of force structure needed to keep a large force overseas on a decent rotational basis. The result, during the period of maximum strain in Iraq, was imposing rotations of 14 months or more on soldiers who had in many cases already served in combat once, twice, or even three times before. Moreover, although the US military created some new organizations – military training teams, or the Afghan Hands program – by and large it proved reluctant to create new kinds of units and organizations, rather than merely generate brigade combat teams which could then be re-missioned.

Coalition management. NATO, in particular, was poorly adapted for the Afghan war. In retrospect, it was a terrible mistake to put NATO into a fight for which it was not prepared, and in which the convoluted chain of command – to a German general sitting in Brunssum, Netherlands, of all places – could offer nothing but trouble. Indeed, one of the great lessons of these wars is never to use NATO for anything other than its original purpose: the defense of Western Europe against Russia, a mission that, alas, remains of importance to this day.

In other respects, I would argue that on the whole the United States did pretty well at managing several large coalitions, with one major exception: handling the problem of detainees as a result of the war on al-Qaeda and the initial attack on Afghanistan. The United States failed to build a consensus on the sensitive legal issues associated with handling detainees from these shadow wars. On the whole, US leaders dealt reasonably effectively with their Iraqi and Afghan counterparts, although on occasion they yielded to congenital US over-optimism about what their allies could accomplish.

Higher war direction. Civil-military relations at the top were a problem for both administrations. President Bush was initially hands off on too many things; Obama did not understand how to manage his generals; neither got a real grip on bringing the full force of the US government to bear on the problems confronting Washington; and neither was able effectively to solicit a range of opinions from the military, nor to groom a generation of military leaders who could handle these wars. It is striking, for example, that President Obama found himself having to rebuild the team that had won in Iraq – Crocker–Petraeus – for Afghanistan, despite the exhaustion of both men.[13]

These wars saw the relief of not one but three four-star commanders: Admiral Fox Fallon; General David McKiernan; and General Stanley McChrystal. And behind the scenes there was a great deal more hidden friction. During the Bush administration the joint chiefs of staff fumed as the administration turned to a retired army general (Jack Keane) for military advice; the Obama administration saw even worse friction between the chairman of the joint chiefs of staff, Admiral Mike Mullen, and the deputy national security adviser, retired Lieutenant General Douglas Lute.

And the higher organization of our efforts in the field was often similarly inadequate. In Afghanistan, on my first trip in 2007, I counted seven parallel chains of command waging war: US forces (Operation Enduring Freedom); the NATO-led International Security Assistance Force; Combined Security Transition Command – Afghanistan, which had charge of training Afghan forces but was, in fact, directing some operations; so-called Black SOF; White SOF (reporting back to the US); the CIA's paramilitary operations; and completely indigenous Afghan operations being conducted by the Afghan National Directorate of Security. This bizarre, divided organization of US high command made real unity of command impossible.

Legacies

These faults – and there are many others, unfortunately – which in different forms spanned two administrations, left a number of corrosive legacies.

"War weariness." This is a curious concept in a number of ways (after all, these were wars fought without conscription or increased taxation), but is with us for better or worse.[14] As of June 2014, 50 percent of the US population thought the war in Iraq a mistake, and the numbers for Afghanistan were similar. All the data showed considerable reluctance of the US population to engage in Libya, Syria, or Ukraine, although substantial minorities were willing to do so. These numbers have to be qualified in two ways: similar polling data show that the US people are unhappy with a US withdrawal from the world, and with the foreign policy of the Obama administration. Perhaps more importantly, the US population had received no argument from the administration, and above all the president, in favor of its involvement in these conflicts. Nonetheless, whether war weariness really does exist, it is believed to exist, and that counts for a great deal in presidential decision making.

Restraint and a light footprint in the Middle East. No matter what US public opinion says, its government has chosen to disengage as much as possible from this region, with consequences in Libya, Syria, Iraq, and Iran that are now visible. This strategic decision, however, was driven less by public opinion than by strategic conviction that further US intervention would be counterproductive, and that the Middle East was a giant sideshow in comparison to Asia. And, it should be noted, the US government has remained quite willing to use force against Islamic militants, even to the point of (reluctantly) reintroducing thousands of US troops to Iraq. But it does so tentatively and quite likely on a scale unlikely to be effective.

Deep partisan bitterness. This was an unnecessary but distinguishing feature of the domestic politics of these wars from roughly 2005 to 2012. Oddly enough, by contrast, the Vietnam war elicited tremendous domestic turmoil, but not this level of animosity between parties. The 2008 presidential election was partly a referendum on the Iraq war, although that was by no means the main feature of it. Arguably, however, the Obama administration's foreign policy troubles have diminished some of the partisan argument about foreign policy. Indeed, it is quite possible that a new consensus will emerge after 2016, more prudent than some of the Bush decisions and more assertive than Obama's policies.

Neo-isolationism? This is a trickier issue. In fact the US foreign policy consensus would appear *not* to be isolationist, although it is not clear what exactly it is. Sorting that out will be a major challenge for future leadership. The latest Pew polls, for example, show that 53 percent of the US public say the world's problems would be worse without US involvement, while 40 percent say US involvement makes those problems worse. What is interesting is that this division does not align with "left" and "right." Critically, there are neo-isolationist voices in both parties (Rand Paul and Bernie Sanders being two key examples). But the most likely presidential candidates in 2016 will probably be somewhere between Bush and Obama in their world views.

A distorted force structure. This distortion has been both physical (lots of counterinsurgency capacity at the expense of conventional power), and intellectual. More important, however, is the way in which other states took advantage of 15 years of US distraction: China, Russia, and Iran, in particular, used the time to build up their militaries. The Europeans became more divided from the United States, and continued down the path of unilateral disarmament. It is unlikely, and perhaps impossible, that the United States will experience a replay of the early 1980s, when US preeminence was re-established remarkably swiftly through a conventional and nuclear reconstruction of its armed forces.

That said, the United States remains the most powerful country on earth. If its armed forces were stretched by these wars, they also accumulated invaluable experience and combat hardening. Behind that, the US economy remains on balance the healthiest in the Western world, and the essential elements undergirding its power – demographics, capital markets, innovation base, and the like – remain solid. US military power, which is recuperating from these wars, rests on solid foundations.

What does all this mean for the future?

Clearly, the United States will be less willing than in the past to engage in large-scale, expeditionary warfare. But it would be a mistake to think that it has become a nation of pacifists. Rather, it is more likely, particularly in the wake of the catastrophes in Libya, Syria, Iraq, and quite possibly in other places, that it will look for, and find, more selective ways of using force. Moreover, however maladroit much of the US conduct of these wars was, that is to some extent the nature of all war – something too easily forgotten, particularly after the military campaigns of the 1990s, which made war look way too easy. And one last thought: we do not know, and will not know for some time, what the consequences of these campaigns are, or what would have happened if they had not been waged (Iraq), or had been waged differently. If there is one judgment to be made with confidence, it is that historians 30 years from now will think of them quite differently than we do today.

Notes

1 A good history remains to be written, and the University of Virginia historian Melvyn Leffler is now working on one. However, the memoirs of key participants, including President Bush (2010), then National Security Adviser Condoleezza Rice (2011), and Secretary of Defense Donald Rumsfeld (2011) convey the sense of threat and urgency.
2 This is a large subject, but Bernard Lewis (2003), Bassam Tibi (2012), and the many occasional writings of Fouad Ajami are good starting points.
3 The best journalistic work on the Iraq war is that of Michael R. Gordon and Bernard E. Trainor (2006). It will be a considerable period of time before historians do justice to this topic.
4 The best overview of war costs is that of Amy Belasco (2014).
5 The best first-hand account is by General Stanley McChrystal (2013). McChrystal was the mastermind of the manhunting operation in both Iraq and Afghanistan.
6 This can be tracked through the annual volumes of the International Institute for Strategic Studies' "The Military Balance." See IISS (2015, 49).
7 For a very good account by an American brigade commander in Iraq, see Peter R. Mansoor (2008).
8 A short, and not always completely reliable, account of the development of US counterinsurgency doctrine is that of Fred Kaplan (2013). On Vietnam and Iraq, see Bing West (2008).
9 The best first-hand account of this is that of Robert Gates (2014); an unsourced and not entirely reliable external view is Bob Woodward's (2010).
10 The memoir of the undersecretary of defense for policy at the outset of the Iraq crisis, Douglas Feith (2008), is illuminating on what policy makers knew, or thought they knew.
11 However, in the aftermath a remarkable research project helped reconstruct this. See the study by Kevin M. Woods *et al.* (2013), which was originally government sponsored.
12 A British adviser to the US commander in Iraq, opposed to the original intervention, makes a compelling case for the need to have remained much longer; see Sky (2014).

13 Gates (2014) is the best account of civil-military relations during the late Bush and early Obama administrations.
14 The best polling data on US attitudes toward foreign policy can be found at the Pew Research Center's Foreign Affairs and Policy website www.pewresearch.org/topics/foreign-affairs-and-policy/.

Bibliography

Belasco, Amy. 2014. *The Cost of Iraq, Afghanistan, and Other Global War on Terror Operations Since 9/11*. Washington, DC: Congressional Research Service.
Bush, George W. 2010. *Decision Points*. New York: Crown.
Feith, Douglas. 2008. *War and Decision: Inside the Pentagon at the Dawn of the War on Terrorism*. New York: HarperCollins.
Gates, Robert. 2014. *Duty: Memoirs of a Secretary at War*. New York: Alfred A. Knopf.
Gordon, Michael R., and Bernard E. Trainor. 2006. *Cobra II*. New York: Pantheon.
Howard, Michael, Peter Paret, and Rosalie West. 1984. *Carl Von Clausewitz: On War*. Princeton, NJ: Princeton University Press.
IISS. 2015. *The Military Balance 2015*. London: Routledge.
Kaplan, Fred. 2013. *The Insurgents: David Petraeus and the Plot to Change the American Way of War*. New York: Simon and Schuster.
Lewis, Bernard. 2003. *The Crisis of Islam: Holy War and Unholy Terror*. New York: Modern Library.
Mansoor, Peter R. 2008. *Baghdad at Sunrise*. New Haven, CT: Yale University Press.
McChrystal, Stanley. 2013. *My Share of the Task*. New York: Penguin, 2013.
Pew Research Center. www.pewresearch.org/topics/foreign-affairs-and-policy/.
Rice, Condoleezza. 2011. *No Higher Honor*. New York: Crown.
Rumsfeld, Donald. 2011. *Known and Unknown*. New York: Sentinel.
Sky, Emma. 2014. *The Unraveling: High Hopes and Missed Opportunities in Iraq*. New York: Public Affairs.
Tibi, Bassam. 2012. *Islam and Islamism*. New Haven, CT: Yale University Press.
West, Bing. 2008. *The Strongest Tribe: War, Politics, and the Endgame in Iraq*. New York: Random House.
Woods, Kevin M., Michael R. Pease, Mark E. Stout, Williamson Murray, James G. Lacey, and the Joint Center for Operational Analysis and Lessons Learned. 2013. *Iraqi Perspectives Project: A View of Operation Iraqi Freedom from Saddam's Senior Leadership*. CreateSpace.
Woodward, Bob. 2010. *Obama's Wars*. New York: Simon and Schuster.

2 The US foreign policy debate
Déjà vu?

Henry R. Nau

Long-term students of US foreign policy debate will undoubtedly have experienced, as I have, a sense of "déjà vu" in the contemporary US foreign policy debate. A very small number of foreign policy approaches are adopted, one after another, in repeating cycles.

The contours of the US foreign policy debate were set at the inception of the Republic. Thomas Jefferson held out the *internationalist* hope that the new US republic would not only change domestic politics from monarchy to republicanism, but also world politics from war to peaceable trade and diplomacy. Alexander Hamilton championed the *realist* course, pursuing alliances and coveting territory, including filibusters on the United States' western border, to defend the new nation's security. George Washington advocated the *nationalist* course, prioritizing independence and warning against both ambition and alliances in foreign affairs.

These three approaches – nationalist, realist, and internationalist – became the United States' standard foreign policy traditions. Andrew Jackson and his protégé James K. Polk lionized the nationalist *quest* for independence by the imperialist *conquest* of the North American continent (Kagan 2006; McDougall 1997). Teddy Roosevelt and Richard Nixon reified the realist game of great power politics, taking the morally ambivalent world as it is, rather than as internationalists might wish it to be (Kissinger 2014). And, after two devastating world wars thought to reflect the bankruptcy of this realist world, Woodrow Wilson and Franklin Roosevelt designed the great internationalist experiments to transform world affairs, the League of Nations and the United Nations (Smith 2012).

Cycling in foreign policy

The debate among these standard traditions has produced repeated cycles in US foreign policy. Under the influence of nationalism, the United States hunkers down to protect its borders and hemisphere, as it did before World Wars I and II, after Vietnam, and as it is doing again today after Iraq and Afghanistan. It retreats, essentially until it is attacked again (think of Pearl Harbor and 9/11), and then after repulsing the attack it reacts, in internationalist mode, to spread democracy through peaceful diplomacy and trade, using force only as a "last resort" after diplomatic and economic sanctions have failed, and then only with multilateral support.

Realism often weighs in on both sides as the pendulum swings. It helps nationalists to "pull back" from failed internationalist experiments, as the United States is doing today after Iraq and Afghanistan (Posen 2014); but it also supports internationalist efforts to "police the world" when the United States is in an expansionist mode – think of realist support for UN efforts in the first Persian Gulf War (Bush and Scowcroft 1998). The United States hides or retreats to avoid conflicts, and then after it is attacked it overreaches to transform the world, while never establishing a sustained presence in the world that might reduce the probability of attack at an acceptable cost to the US public.

The cycling continues today. After a surge of internationalism under George W. Bush (recall the Middle East Democracy Initiative), Barack Obama has brought forces and focus back to the United States from Afghanistan and Iraq. Neo-nationalists in both parties (Elizabeth Warren (Vinik 2014) and Rand Paul (2014)) agree with him and pledge, short of another attack, never to put boots on the ground again in foreign wars. Realists (Hillary Clinton (2014) and Senator Marco Rubio (2014)) also counsel restraint, but worry about lagging defense spending and warn that great powers cannot retire from global affairs. Meanwhile, internationalists (Senator John McCain (2014) and former Secretary of State Madeleine Albright (2003)) insist that transformation, not stabilization, of world affairs remains the essential goal, either through regime change (in Syria or Iran) or multilateral agreements (chemical weapons ban in Syria and nuclear agreement with Iran). Internationalists bent on regime change are on the defensive, as will be those bent on multilateral agreements if the Iran nuclear agreement fails.

None of the standing traditions offers a way for the United States to stay in the world on an ongoing basis at a sustainable cost. None combines the pursuit of freedom in the world with a willingness to back up diplomacy with the use of force. Nationalists and realists are willing to use force but only when it is necessary, which usually means after an attack, and then only to restore the status quo – as in the first Persian Gulf War. Internationalists, especially the multilateral agreement type, are reluctant to use force as long as there is any hope for negotiations, reserving force as a "last resort" only if negotiations fail, and then only with multilateral agreement.

A fourth tradition: conservative internationalism

What can be done? I propose a fourth way of thinking about the United States' role in the world that might mediate between nationalism and realism on the one hand and liberal internationalism on the other. I call this tradition *conservative internationalism* (see Nau 2013). It has always been a part of our historical experience, but it has been generally neglected in the academic literature and debate on US foreign policy – not least because there are few conservative scholars in the academy. Conservative internationalism combines critical parts of the other traditions, and fills a large gap in the traditional debate.

It affirms the objectives of *liberal internationalism*, namely the goal to spread freedom (unlike realism); but it uses the means or instruments of *realism* to back up this effort, namely military power (unlike the soft power emphasis of liberal internationalism). And it pursues an end goal that is less ambitious than liberal internationalism and closer to *nationalism* and *realism*: namely, a world of decentralized nation-states in which sister democratic republics retain their national sovereignty and live side by side, with independent military capabilities. These sister republics do not engage in militarized competition or disputes, because democracies do not threaten or go to war with one another. In short, the vision is of a decentralized world of democratic peace, rather than a centralized world of international institutions. For conservatives, internationalism does not mean international institutions or a post-nationalist world.

Figure 2.1 depicts this conservative internationalist alternative in comparison to the standing traditions of nationalism, realism and liberal internationalism. It shows the obvious gap of a tradition that promotes democracy through armed diplomacy. This, in contrast to realism (which seeks only to promote stability, but relies on the earlier use of limited force before and during negotiations), and to liberal internationalism

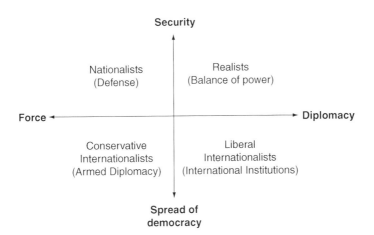

Figure 2.1 Graph of security and democracy (source: Nau, Henry R.; *Conservative Internationalism.* Copyright © 2014 Princeton University Press. Reprinted by permission of Princeton University Press).

(which reserves the use of force for later, and inevitably larger, interventions after negotiations fail).

To be sure, using force early to preempt the greater use of force later is risky in the short run, and is hard to sell to a war-weary public. It is risky in the short run because it may provoke negotiating partners to retaliate, leading to a spiral of armaments and conflicts: the so-called slippery slope. But failing to counter the early use of force by negotiating partners in the short run risks a larger conflict in the long run. George Shultz (1993) once aptly put it this way: "…last [resort] means no other, and by that time the level of force and the risk involved may have multiplied many times over." It is tough to sell because it is never possible to prove that something that does not happen was preempted or prevented; instead, because it doesn't happen, it is usually considered not to have been very likely.[1]

In recent decades neoconservatives have sensed the absence of a conservative internationalist tradition. They were refugees from the standard traditions. Senator Henry "Scoop" Jackson and Jeane Kirkpatrick were liberal internationalists who felt that negotiations with the Soviet Union had to be backed up by a more assertive military policy. Condoleezza Rice and Charles Krauthammer (2004) were realists who felt that military power had to be used for something more than just the cynical defense of the status quo; they sought to "tilt the balance of power toward freedom." But the neoconservatives found no tradition that cared about both the spread of freedom and the need, in negotiations with despots, to use force before negotiations fail. The determination of neoconservatives to arm US diplomacy paid off in forcing an unexpected end to the Cold War – but can't be proved. And their leadership role in the invasion of Iraq is considered by some to have been provocative – which is easier to prove.

Neocons themselves were and are a diverse group – some more optimistic about nation building than others, some more opposed to negotiations than others (see Fukuyama 2006). The domain I propose is one large enough to accommodate all conservative internationalists – for example, both President Reagan, who always intended to negotiate with the Soviet Union (located near the vertical axis in the lower left-hand quadrant of Figure 2.1), and Secretary of Defense Caspar Weinberger, who wished to negotiate with the Soviet Union later if ever at all (located farther away from the vertical axis in the conservative internationalism quadrant).[2] My hope is to add another important voice to the debate among nationalists, realists, and liberal internationalists, so that in the long run all traditions will be represented equally in a healthier debate about US foreign policy.

Let me quickly identify five traits of conservative internationalism, and thereby show how it differs from the standard traditions and would add an important new element to future US foreign policy debates. I'll give a few examples along the way, from the foreign policies of four US presidents I have previously written about – Jefferson, Polk, Truman, and Reagan – and from some of the current crises in the world.[3]

Conservatism in the United States

First, conservative internationalism is *conservative*, not liberal. In the United States, that means an emphasis on limited central government and on the moral and religious nature of human society. Conservatives see progress more in terms of a "moral" or political struggle with despots in which, as President Reagan once said, freedom is always only one generation away from being lost.

Liberals, by contrast, favor activist central government and are more optimistic about human society. They believe that science and modernization will do more than moral confrontation to improve the world; history is on our side, and if we are patient enough, globalization will eventually ensnare despotic regimes in the labyrinth of mutual benefits and negotiations without the need to use much force (think of US policy toward China).

These different orientations result in contrasting views of world affairs. Conservative Americans envision a more decentralized world in the future, where world institutions are limited, national sovereignty and patriotism are respected, and countries struggle individually and collectively toward greater freedom in the world. They prefer global competitive free markets to international institutions. Liberal Americans, on the other hand, look to international institutions to chart the future. They see a world in which countries come together increasingly in centralized institutions to solve collective goods problems of arms control, environment and poverty. They anticipate a reduction of national sovereignty as countries learn the habit of cooperation and become more tolerant, pluralist and democratic within the context of global institutions. They opt for global governance over capitalism.

Thomas Jefferson nicely illustrates this conservative orientation of limited government and rational skepticism. It is one reason why, in my judgment, he qualifies as a conservative, not the liberal internationalist he is often portrayed as.[4] He is the icon of today's Tea Party United States.

Jefferson put primary emphasis on individuals, not central government: "Sometimes it is said that man cannot be trusted with the government of himself. Can he then be trusted with the government of others?" Self-government came first. At the international level, he put the emphasis on states, not union, with national sovereignty as a priority. In considering new entities in the Louisiana Territory that might join the Union, Jefferson was indifferent as to whether they became states of the United States or separate nation-states: "Keep them in the union, if it be for their good," he said, "but separate them, if it be better."[5]

Jefferson also put primary emphasis on politics (namely a struggle) over expertise (or science): "If there be any among us who would wish to dissolve this Union or to change its republican form, let them stand undisturbed as monuments to the safety with which error of opinion may be tolerated where reason is left free to combat." Jefferson believed in the public square and the prevailing of educated public argument, rather than in experts or bureaucrats regulating outside or above the public arena on the basis of superior knowledge or science. He wanted to be remembered for founding the University of Virginia, rather than for being president. And he wanted elections, not the courts, to settle disputes. He never challenged the constitutionality of the Alien and Sedition Acts, one of the most blatant violations of the US Constitution, by which the Federalist government under John Adams imprisoned some 300 journalists who supported Jefferson's Republican Party (and no journalists who supported the Federalist Party). He simply said that the elections of 1800 and 1804 resolved the issue; the public square discredited the Acts.

Internationalism vs nationalism/realism

Second, conservative internationalism is *internationalist*, not nationalist. Traditionally conservatives identified as realists or nationalists; only liberals were internationalists. The nationalist–internationalist divide concerns whether foreign policy is primarily about defense and security, or about spreading freedom, human rights, and democracy. Nationalists and realists say defense; internationalists, both conservative and liberal, say spreading freedom.

Both sides have a point. The debate will persist. But I have found Reagan's approach to be highly instructive.

He started with the solid *nationalist* position that the United States, as a country that practices freedom, must be defended. He told the Republican Convention in 1964: "If we lose freedom here [in the United States], there is no place to escape to." If freedom is lost in Vietnam, the Vietnamese flee to the United States. But where do Americans go, if freedom is lost in North America? It was an interesting insight because it recognized the United States' role as the world's leading constitutional republic, expanding the white male franchise in the nineteenth century more rapidly than in any other country, including pre-existing Dutch and English republics.

But Reagan also grasped the *internationalist* position, saying already in 1952 (yes, that's 1952):

> America is less a place than an idea ... the idea of the dignity of man, the idea that deep within the heart of each of us is something so Godlike and precious that no individual or group has a right to impose his or her will upon the people.

(Nau 2013, Ch. 7)

In 1983, at the height of the Cold War struggle, he warned us not to distance ourselves from the great moral struggles of the world: "I urge you to beware the temptation of pride – the assumption of blithely declaring yourself above it all … and thereby to remove yourself from the struggle between right and wrong and good and evil" (ibid.).

So, for Reagan, freedom started at home but, as an idea, transcended the United States' borders. He sensed that freedom's plight at home was somehow inextricably linked with freedom's plight abroad. And he was right. If the United States does not care about freedom in the world, how much will it care about freedom at home? When the United States neglected freedom abroad in the 1920s and 1930s, US freedom suffered. The Ku Klux Klan peaked in the United States with five million members; and white-sheeted wizards marched down Philadelphia Avenue, 30,000 strong, in a brazen blizzard of bigotry. On the other hand, when the United States cared about freedom in the world after World War II and rescued Europe from totalitarianism, it made more progress on civil rights at home than at any time since the Civil War.

So if the United States improves the prospects of freedom abroad, it improves the prospects of US defense. Think of how much safer the United States is in 2014 compared to 1914: Europe today is "whole and free," and democracy thrives in non-Western cultures in Japan, South Korea, Taiwan, and hopefully Turkey.[6]

Armed diplomacy

But now we arrive at a problem, which brings me to my third point: the need for armed diplomacy, or backing up diplomacy by force.

If we truly care about freedom abroad, we are likely to encounter more pushback from non-democratic countries than expected by liberal internationalists, who believe that despots can be negotiated into submission. Despots use force to maintain their power at home; surely they will use it abroad as well. Reagan, who had a knack for putting matters pithily, said: "If they do that to their own people, think what they will do to us if they get the chance."

So if we intend to negotiate seriously with despots, as liberal internationals advocate, it will be necessary to back up our diplomacy with force, not only when negotiations fail, but in order to give negotiations the best chance to succeed.

By use of force, I mean three things: build-up of force (e.g., higher defense spending); deployment of force (e.g., putting US forces in Europe and Asia); and direct intervention in other countries by force (e.g., Vietnam, Afghanistan, and Iraq). Presidents Truman and Reagan, the bookends of a successful strategy to win the Cold War, offer great examples of the use of force to make negotiations succeed. They deployed force through defense build-ups – NATO and Reagan's defense build-up; they pushed back on the ground to block military options outside negotiations – Truman in Berlin and Korea, Reagan in Afghanistan, Central America and Southern Africa; and Reagan developed bargaining chips to reduce, not just limit, arms – the Intermediate-Range Nuclear Forces (INF) Treaty.

Truman recognized much sooner than Franklin Roosevelt would have (which is why Truman is a conservative, not liberal, internationalist) that if negotiations with the Soviet Union were going to make any headway, the United States would have to deny the Soviet Union military options outside the negotiations. So he established NATO to contain the Soviet Union and prepare the way for eventual negotiations – the détente of the 1970s. Reagan's arms race served the same purpose. If the Soviets believed they could achieve their objectives by an arms race outside negotiations, why would they negotiate *seriously*?

It is a serious mistake to assume that Reagan's first-term military build-up served no purpose once the Soviet Union had a leader, namely Mikhail Gorbachev, who was willing to negotiate. Gorbachev, and the military in the Soviet Union, had to be convinced that the Soviet Union could not win an arms race in competition with the United States. Gorbachev conceded the point to the Politburo in October 1985, only six months after he came to office (Brooks and Wohlforth 2000). "Gentlemen," he said, "the last thing we can afford is an arms race with the United States. We will lose." Here was the negotiating payoff of Reagan's defense build-up, and the reason why Gorbachev subsequently negotiated seriously (rather than because he was just a nice guy).

A second purpose for arming diplomacy is to deny the negotiating partner *leverage on the ground*, in arenas outside and surrounding negotiations. President Truman, for example, later regretted his failure in May 1945 to follow Winston Churchill's recommendation and leave Western forces in Czechoslovakia, to use as leverage on the ground to negotiate a better deal with Moscow on Berlin and Poland. But Truman had already moved toward a more muscular Soviet policy in 1946, much sooner than Franklin Roosevelt would have. And in June 1948 he decided to maintain a military presence in West Berlin, against the counsel of all his advisors. Reagan's Freedom Fighters served the same purpose at the end of the Cold War. Resistance to Soviet-sponsored aggression in Afghanistan, Africa and Central America put the Kremlin on notice that there were no easy or cheap alternatives to negotiations (see Kagan 2014).

Finally, military force serves as leverage for trade-offs *inside* negotiations. NATO deployed Intermediate-Range Nuclear Forces (INF) missiles in 1983 to have something to trade off against Soviet SS-20s. As Reagan told the National Security Council in February 1982: "They won't negotiate seriously until we have something to trade!" He was right. The Soviet Union negotiated seriously only after the INF deployment, and the superpowers eliminated all INF weapons in an historic arms *reduction* agreement in December 1987.

Arming diplomacy involves the use of a little force early during negotiations to avoid the use of more force later, after negotiations fail. There are risks to early intervention, to be sure. But the risks are actually less than waiting. Using a little force early on is likely to escalate the conflict only if the other side is bent on achieving its objectives outside negotiations. And if that's the case, it is better to learn that sooner rather than later. If the other side is only opportunistic and not aggressive, the early use of force denies an objective the adversary is already predisposed to forego if confronted.

Still, with all the advantages of bolstering diplomacy with the use of force, it is not possible to arm diplomacy in all cases. George W. Bush's call to end tyranny in every nation is simply Pollyannaish. How then can we maintain discipline in the use of armed diplomacy to pursue the enlargement of freedom? Conservative internationalism does so in two ways. It intervenes to spread liberty only in priority cases where the battle for freedom is most important and most likely to succeed; and it uses military leverage not to defeat an adversary in some conventional military sense, but to achieve a timely compromise and to move outcomes toward freedom, even if solutions are less than perfect and may have to be revisited in the future.

This brings me to my last two points. They are crucial, and demonstrate that conservative internationalism employs the prudence of realism, but for the purpose of expanding freedom rather than merely for preserving the status quo.

Setting priorities

Conservative internationalism sets priorities by distinguishing where the battle for freedom is most consequential and most likely to succeed. And that means pursuing this battle primarily on the major borders that separate existing free countries from despotic ones. The defense and spread of democracy in countries on the borders of existing democratic societies matter more than in countries in regions remote from existing democracies.

The two main fault lines of freedom today lay along the borders of existing freedom in Europe and Asia, generally the countries between Russia and the free states of Europe (such as Turkey, Ukraine, and the Balkans), and between China and the free countries of Asia (such as Japan, South Korea, Taiwan, and India). A third fault line lies between Israel and its authoritarian neighbors, but Israel is the sole democracy in the Middle East and the prospects for democracy in other countries of the region are considerably less than along the borders of Europe or Asia. Moreover, nothing will do more to help democracy in the Middle East than to win the battle for freedom in Turkey, Ukraine, and the Balkans. Conversely, the rollback of freedom on the border of Europe will further isolate democracy in the Middle East.

When threats arise along these main fault lines, the United States must take the lead to defeat them *and* then stay on to defend and promote democracy. Why? Two reasons: first, because the loss of freedom in these countries (say, the Balkans in the 1990s, or Ukraine, Turkey or the Korean peninsula today) would be highly detrimental to the cause of freedom generally, bringing the threat of despotism closer to the center of the democratic world; and second, because the costs of pursuing freedom in these countries are considerably less than elsewhere in the world, given the existence of powerful next-door democratic neighbors and markets that help promote freedom. Think of NATO's role during the Cold War in Germany and of the US–Japan and US–South Korea alliances in Asia today. And think of the role the European Union played in Eastern Europe during the economic and political transformation of these countries after the Cold War. In these border areas the success of democracy is both imperative and affordable because they lie right next door to existing democracies.

That's not the case for countries in regions remote from existing free countries. These countries lie outside the immediate orbit of free countries and closer to the orbit of authoritarian neighbors; think here of Georgia in the Caucasus, Iraq and Syria in the Middle East, Libya in North Africa, Afghanistan in Southwest Asia, and, say, Burma or Mongolia on the border of China.

When threats arise in these regions (e.g., the Taliban in Afghanistan, or now the Islamic State in Syria and Iraq), the United States should certainly take the lead to defeat them, but should not stick around to promote democracy. The required approach is to get in and out as quickly as possible, putting in place a local government that can counter the threat, at least in the short term (such as the early Hamid Karzai government in Afghanistan). In these cases it is necessary to pick a government to replace the one that is a threat and make the situation a little better. But it is not necessary to commit to constructing a full-blown democracy over an indefinite time span. The US public, or for that matter any democratic public, will not support sustained nation building where the stakes are too low.

This is the crux of Obama's problem in Syria. He does not support Bashar Assad, yet he cannot decide on an opposition group to replace Assad. Since it is impossible to defeat something with nothing, the United States is probably going to have to live with Assad, at least in the short term. Remember, Syria is not on the main borders of existing freedom. So the idea is to deal with the threat posed by radical Islamists without doing any extended nation building. Yes, the United States may leave behind weak and in many ways undesirable governments, but it's doing that today anyway in Afghanistan and Iraq *after ten years and more*. It would have been better to leave earlier, in 2005–2007, and to be in a position to go back in again should the threat re-emerge, than to be in the position the United States is in today in Iraq or Afghanistan (and was earlier in Vietnam). Now there is no public support to go back in again under any circumstances, short of another deadly attack on the United States or its allies.

Unfortunately, over the past decade, the United States has pursued exactly the reverse priorities. To defeat terrorism, it intervened massively in remote regions, namely Afghanistan and Iraq, and stayed on to try and promote democracy. Meanwhile it neglected, or possibly even hurt, the cause of democracy where it struggles to emerge on the borders of existing free countries. Ukraine fell under greater Russian influence and now intervention; Turkey was weakened by the US decision to invade Iraq, and drifts away from both Israel and democracy; Pakistan (next to India) was destabilized by US policy in Afghanistan; and South Korea drifted away from Japan politically and closer to China economically.

Prioritizing is difficult and therefore often left undone. Failure to prioritize leads to mission creep and to the danger that the adversary sets the agenda, while US assets are spread across a wider and wider arena of costly engagements. This process in turn contributes to overreach and, when the costs become too high, to pullback and retrenchment.

Timely compromise

Finally, for my fifth and final point, the purpose of military leverage is not in the first instance to win wars; it is, as Reagan believed, to win the negotiations and the peace.

While conservative internationalism holds that diplomacy is never used without the backup of force (i.e., armed diplomacy), it also maintains the corollary: *never use force without backing it up with diplomacy.* The purpose of armed diplomacy is not to win wars, but to cash in short-term military gains for long-term gains in freedom. Fighting wars to unconditional surrender is not only difficult, it is unaffordable, because it has to be followed by unconditional nation building. There is virtually no government or society left after unconditional surrender, as in Iraq in 2003, and the nation must be rebuilt.

Now, this kind of massive nation building was indeed carried out by the United States and its allies in Germany and in Japan after World War II, with both countries on the border of existing freedom at the time, and in the shadow of a huge Soviet threat. The project took 50 years and trillions of dollars; and it was both successful and worth it. To appreciate this, it's sufficient to consider the scenario of having to face Vladimir Putin today with Germany and Italy also ruled by Putin-like governments. However, the United States has had enough experience elsewhere in remote regions, for example in Vietnam, to know that it cannot make that kind of effort where the stakes are much lower. In those situations, the United States should be willing to take a weakened enemy today and get out, to come back another day if necessary.

President James K. Polk was a master of this aspect of conservative internationalism. He launched four major forays to acquire the southwest territories of California and New Mexico. Each time he combined a diplomatic initiative with the threat of force (as in the initial Slidell mission to purchase New Mexico and California) or the use of force with a diplomatic off-ramp (as in the Beach, Atocha, and Trist missions).[7]

President Polk ultimately compromised when his military leverage was at its peak. US military forces sat in Mexico City, the capital of Mexico, in February 1848, and many in Congress and the public (e.g., the poet Walt Whitman) urged that the United States stay in Mexico to build a better nation. But Polk accepted a less than perfect pace agreement, the Treaty of Guadalupe Hidalgo, negotiated by an envoy he had fired four months earlier, because he knew his military leverage would wane, and he sensed that the costs of a long-term occupation would be unacceptable (a "bleeding Ireland" was the concern at the time). As a result, US forces were completely out of Mexico within six months. Compare that to Vietnam, Afghanistan, and Iraq.

The real knock against George W. Bush is not that he used force too much but that he did not follow it up with diplomacy, as his father did after the first Persian Gulf War. Within six months of the end of the first Persian Gulf War, Bush the father launched the Madrid Conference, from which the Oslo Accords emerged. As broken as those Accords appear today, they represented noticeable progress at the time. By contrast, Bush the son dithered for four years after the second Persian Gulf War before launching his own Middle East peace initiative. Nothing of any consequence resulted from that endeavor.

Compromise is always a controversial matter. President Reagan risked the support of his most ardent supporters when he proceeded to sign nuclear arms accords with the Soviet Union. But compromise – not any compromise but one that moves freedom forward at the time – is the art of the game, if the costs of pursuing freedom are to be contained within a range that the US public can support and sustain over the long run.

Summary

So, in summary, the main features of conservative internationalism are:

- It is *conservative*, meaning dedicated to limited government and seeing progress as a moral struggle for freedom, not a "slam dunk" consequence of international institutions and the advance of science and modernization.
- It is *internationalist*, meaning that it seeks to shift the types of domestic regimes in the system toward democracy and to transform anarchy into democratic peace. It does not accept the realist or nationalist world view of a struggle to preserve the status quo in permanent coexistence with despots.

- It wields *armed diplomacy* before and during negotiations, not only once negotiations fail, because despots use force continuously, and no negotiations will get the attention of despots unless despots are blocked from achieving their objectives by force outside negotiations.
- But armed diplomacy is used with discipline: to serve freedom *where it matters most and has the best chance of success*, namely on the borders of existing free countries; and to serve peace by making *timely compromises*, trading military leverage for diplomatic solutions that, however imperfect, move the needle of freedom forward in the world.

An increased awareness of the conservative internationalist tradition, and its inclusion in our foreign policy debate, can help the United States to stop the cycling between overreach and withdrawal. It offers a way to be internationalist, that is, to care about spreading freedom in the world; while also being conservative, that is, combining force and diplomacy to create a world in which national sovereignty is retained, but nations are increasingly free, and live side by side in peace, with no need for global institutions or one-world government.

Notes

1 A good example is the preemptive use of force by NATO in the early 1950s. Did it prevent a hot war in Europe, such as occurred in Korea, or did it provoke the Cold War when neither a hot war nor a Cold War was necessary or likely?
2 The other quadrants likewise include diverse versions. Liberal internationalism includes one-world government advocates, neo-liberal institutionalists, and human rights advocates. Realism includes classical realism, neo-realism, offensive and defensive realism. Nationalism includes isolationists, regionalists (Monroe Doctrine), and imperialists.
3 The examples are drawn from the case studies in Nau (2013, Chs 4–7 and Conclusion).
4 For the standard interpretation of Jefferson as a liberal internationalist, see Tucker and Hendrickson (1990).
5 For quotes in this and next paragraph, see Nau (2013, Ch. 5).
6 On the other hand, Reagan did not believe that freedom had a single nationalist face. Freedom would look different in other cultures, but there would be three overriding universal characteristics: (1) rotating parties in power through free and fair elections; (2) all institutions, especially the military, accountable to elected officials; and (3) civil rights to speak, assemble, worship, vote, etc., making it possible to have free and fair elections.
7 For details, see Nau (2013, Ch. 5).

Bibliography

Albright, Madeleine. 2003. *Madame Secretary: A Memoir*. New York: Miramax.
Brooks, Stephen G., and William C. Wohlforth. 2000. "Power, Globalization, and the End of the Cold War." *International Security* 25 (3): 29.
Bush, George, and Brent Scowcroft. 1998. *A World Transformed*. New York: Knopf.
Clinton, Hillary Rodham. 2014. *Hard Choices*. New York: Simon and Schuster.

Fukuyama, Francis. 2006. *America at the Crossroads: Democracy, Power, and the Neo-Conservative Legacy.* New Haven, CT: Yale University Press.

Kagan, Robert. 2006. *Dangerous Nation.* New York: Knopf.

Kagan, Robert. 2014. "Obama Should Take Another Look at Some U.S. Foreign Policy 'Failures.'" *Washington Post,* October 31. www.washingtonpost.com/opinions/robert-kagan-obama-should-take-another-look-at-some-us-foreign-policy-failures/2014/10/31/ebecd42c-611b-11e4-91f7-5d89b5e8c251_story.html.

Kissinger, Henry. 2014. *World Order.* New York: Penguin.

Krauthammer, Charles. 2004. "Democratic Realism: An American Foreign Policy for a Unipolar World." Irving Kristol Lecture, American Enterprise Institute, Washington, DC, February 12.

McCain, John. 2014. "Peace Through Strength." Speech to Reagan National Defense Forum, Simi Valley, California, November 15. www.mccain.senate.gov/public/index.cfm/speeches?ID=158e34c3-2766-4ec4-aad5-4ba5b477330d.

McDougall, Walter. 1997. *Promised Land, Crusader State.* Boston, MA: Houghton Mifflin.

Nau, Henry. 2013. *Conservative Internationalism: Armed Diplomacy Under Jefferson, Polk, Truman and Reagan.* Princeton, NJ: Princeton University Press.

Paul, Rand. 2014. "The Case for Conservative Realism." *National Interest,* October 23. http://nationalinterest.org/feature/rand-paul-the-case-conservative-realism-11544.

Posen, Barry R. 2014. *Restraint: A New Foundation for American Grand Strategy.* Ithaca, NY: Cornell University Press.

Rubio, Marco. 2014. "American Strength: Building 21st Century Defense Capabilities." Remarks prepared for delivery at the Willard Hotel, Washington, DC, September 17. www.rubio.senate.gov/public/index.cfm/press-releases?ID=82ca57f5-c05e-4d75-b53a-bcb98b390139.

Shultz, George. 1993. *Triumph and Turmoil.* New York: Charles Scribner's Sons.

Smith, Tony. 2012. *America's Mission.* Princeton, NJ: Princeton University Press.

Tucker, Robert W., and David C. Hendrickson. 1990. *Empire of Liberty: The Statecraft of Thomas Jefferson.* New York: Oxford University Press.

Vinik, Danny. 2014. "Why Won't Elizabeth Warren Reveal Her Foreign Policy Positions?" *New Republic,* October 23. www.newrepublic.com/article/119965/elizabeth-warrens-foreign-policy-positions-are-mystery.

3 Obama

The reluctant realist

Steven David

There is no shortage of criticism for President Obama's foreign policy. The president is seen as weak, indecisive, naive, afraid to lead, and fearful of using force. Most of all, many have argued, it is impossible to figure him out. He seems to be constantly improvising without any ideological or intellectual compass to guide him. This failure to explain why he acts as he does, and the underlying worry that Obama himself may not understand the rationale for his decisions, lie at the heart of much of the unease many feel about Obama, both in Israel and, for that matter, in the United States.

I argue that, in fact, Obama's foreign policy is no mystery. It can be explained as adhering very closely to traditional realist theory. In each of his major foreign policy decisions, far from being random or inexplicable, Obama has behaved as a realist. To be sure, a realist foreign policy is not necessarily a good foreign policy, and Obama's actions demonstrate many of the shortcomings of this approach. Nevertheless, demonstrating that Obama's foreign policy follows realism challenges the view that his actions defy explanation. Those who criticize Obama's approach have not yet understood that their problem is as much with realism as it is with the president. This is all the more remarkable in light of the fact that many of Obama's fiercest critics describe themselves as realists.

My argument is made in three parts. First, I put forth my own understanding of realism. Second, in the bulk of the essay, I examine Obama's major foreign policy decisions, explaining why the great majority of them are consistent with realist precepts. I conclude by examining the implications of Obama's approach for world politics.

Realism

What is realism?

There are probably as many views of realism as there are scholars and practitioners who claim to abide by it.[1] In its simplest form, realism is an approach or theory that purports to describe the way the world behaves. Central to realism is the belief that the world we live in is just as the world has always been and will always be. We may wish to believe that human nature can be transformed, that states will not go to war, or that the international system could somehow end its anarchic nature, but these are pipe dreams.[2] If we seek to minimize the wars and conflicts that do erupt, and make the best of a very bad situation, it is critical not to fall prey to the illusion that humankind can escape its condition. Instead, in order to survive and prosper in this grim world, we must work with the world as it is.

Just what is this realist world? Realism paints a very bleak picture of world politics, in which states struggle over power with the constant threat of war lurking in the background. Cooperation among states is severely limited, and lasting peace impossible. The explanations for this state of affairs lie in three main assumptions that realists make about international politics. First, as Hans Morgenthau argues (2006, 3–4), we have to acknowledge that human nature is fixed and flawed. People are predisposed to struggle for power, which is stronger than any impulse to act for the good of all. This desire for power often leads to conflict, something for which we need to be prepared. For John Mearsheimer, international anarchy, not human nature, is the underlying assumption of the realist. Anarchy means that we live in an international system composed of states which have no government above them to settle disputes. In this anarchic international system, states possess the ability to hurt and even destroy other states. Making matters worse, it is impossible to discern the intentions of other states. An arms build-up in a neighboring state may be offensive or defensive. Since it is impossible to know for sure, in a world characterized by international anarchy, one must assume the worst. For realists, the most important challenge for leaders is to figure out how to preserve the survival of their states in this threatening environment. Finally, realists assume that leaders are rational in the sense that they are sensitive to costs. Leaders may be evil and they may miscalculate, but they will reasonably weigh the costs and benefits of a given decision before acting (see Waltz 2003, 13–14; Mearsheimer 2014a, 30, 32).

These assumptions drive state behavior. Since countries seek to survive in a threatening world where there is no world government to come to their rescue, states must rely on themselves for their protection. Relying on other states or – even worse – international institutions to help them, is foolish and potentially deadly (Mearsheimer 2014a, 33). Given that nearly one-third of countries have been wiped off the world map since 1816, this concern with survival is understandable and pressing (Fazal 2007, 3). Leaders cannot allow their personal morality to affect foreign policy if doing so imperils the existence of their state. For realists, the greatest immorality is allowing their country to be destroyed. Humanitarian interventions that drain resources from states, leaving them ill-prepared to deal with challenges to their vital interests, must not be undertaken. As Michael Mandelbaum (1996) argued, foreign policy should not be "social work."

States should avoid ideological crusades to spread their form of government to others. What matters in realism is the power and intent of potential adversaries, not the form of government a state has. Scarce resources should not be wasted on marginal concerns while vital interests are neglected. As the prominent US realist and commentator Walter Lippmann warned, governments cannot allow their commitments to exceed their capabilities.[3] For the United States, vital interests are the protection of its security, its economic wellbeing, and its core values, as well as those of its key allies in Europe, parts of Asia, and the Persian Gulf. For all other concerns, the United States is advised to adopt a strategy of "offshore balancing," meaning it should keep the bulk of its military forces away from conflicts and only intervene as a last resort when vital interests cannot be protected any other way (Walt 2005, 222–223). In order to be a successful offshore balancer, the United States needs to be a "buck passer," that is, to get others who have more at stake to do the fighting while it watches from afar.[4] Force must be used when necessary, but only as a last resort. Because we live in a world of equilibrium, where states resist threats, forceful policies will simply drive countries into the arms of their competitors.[5] By abstaining from the use of force in most circumstances, the United States is able to focus its efforts where it matters most, while encouraging other countries to do more for themselves.

Obama and realism

The case for Obama following realist principles can be found first in what he says. Despite his reputation as a starry-eyed idealist, Obama's key speeches convey a strong realist message, which perhaps draw from the influence of the realist theologian, Reinhold Niebuhr, whom Obama calls "one of my favorite philosophers" (Brooks 2007). In accepting the Nobel Peace Prize in December 2009 (largely for his rhetorical support for the transition to a world without nuclear weapons), Obama made clear his commitment to realism. After discussing the debt he owed to Martin Luther King's and Mahatma Ghandi's teachings on non-violence, Obama went on to say:

> But as head of state sworn to protect and defend my nation, I cannot by guided by their [King's and Gandhi's] examples alone. I face the world as it is and cannot stand idle in the face of threats to the American people. For make no mistake: Evil does exist in the world. A non-violent movement could not have halted Hitler's armies. Negotiations cannot convince Al-Qaeda's leaders to lay down their arms. To say that force may sometimes be necessary is not a call to cynicism – it is a recognition of history, the imperfections of man and the limits of reason.
>
> (*New York Times* 2009)

These views echo Niebuhr's opposition to pacifism and the need to confront evil forcefully when it arises. As such, they are very much in the mainstream of classical realism.

Obama's rhetoric in support of realism continued with his speech at West Point, in May 2014, billed as a major foreign policy address. In his remarks, Obama sought to place US foreign policy in a middle ground, between calls for military intervention in such places as Syria and demands that the United States stay away from foreign entanglements altogether. For vital interests, Obama's message was clear and fully consistent with realism:

> The United States will use military force, unilaterally if necessary, when our core interests demand it; when our people are threatened, when our livelihoods are at stake; when the security of our allies is in danger ... [I]nternational opinion matters, but America should never ask permission to protect our people, our homeland, our way of life.
> (*Washington Post* 2014)

However, when vital US interests are not threatened, Obama made it clear that other states should bear much of the burden.

> [W]hen issues of global concern do not pose a direct threat to the United States ... then the threshold for military action must be higher. In such circumstances, we should not go it alone. Instead we must mobilize allies and partners to take collective action. We have to broaden our tools to include diplomacy and development ... and, if just, necessary and effective, multilateral military action.
> (*Washington Post* 2014)

The view that military force should be reserved for the direst threats, while less pressing challenges be addressed with a cautious, multilateral effort that does not squander US resources, is one fully consistent with realism.

These speeches, along with other remarks by Obama, present a vision of realism in which the United States should avoid the direct intervention of forces except where vital interests are threatened, should not get dragged into conflicts of peripheral concern, should stay away from costly humanitarian interventions, should encourage other states to act on their own, and should always be careful that the costs of an action do not exceed its benefits. A policy of realism, then, is a policy of restraint. It is an approach that best defines the foreign policy of Barack Obama.

Obama's realist policies

More important than what President Obama says he will do is what he actually does. Examining Obama's record of major foreign policy decisions, it is impossible not to be struck by how well they conform with realism. Obama's "pivot" to Asia, the handling of Iran's nuclear program, the reaction to Russia's intervention in Ukraine, and the response to the "Arab Spring" all followed realist precepts. This is not to suggest that everything Obama has done fits neatly into the realist paradigm; rather that, taken overall, Obama's policies have been consistent with realism, even when he has pursued them reluctantly.

Pivot to Asia

The Obama administration's decision to "pivot" to Asia is a clear demonstration of its realist inclinations. President Obama made it clear that the United States would pay renewed attention to Asia when he told the Australian Parliament in November 2011 that "I have made a deliberate and strategic decision: as a Pacific nation, the United States will play a larger and long-term role in shaping this region and its future" (White House 2011). The message from Obama (amplified by his Secretary of State, Hillary Clinton) marked a significant shift away from traditional US policy. While Asia had always been important to the United States, Obama was now saying that the United States would no longer be diverted by secondary concerns in regions such as the Middle East, but would instead make focusing on Asia its top priority. Obama's administration was the first to elevate Asia to this status (Shambaugh 2013).

The substance of the pivot to Asia includes security, economic, and diplomatic initiatives. On the security front, Obama promised that any cuts in the future US defense budget, some of which have been mandated by Congress, would not affect the US military budget for Asia. As the US defense budget shrinks, therefore, Asia would be kept whole, accounting for an ever greater proportion of US defense expenditures (Chye 2012). The United States would also work to enhance its formal and informal alliance relationships with Asian states. The United States already maintains formal alliances with Japan, South Korea, the Philippines, Thailand, and Australia. It will enhance those relationships, while concluding "strategic partnerships" with other states to ease the security costs of maintaining order in Asia (Parameswaran 2014).

The economic dimension of the pivot included strengthening the Trans-Pacific Partnership (TPP), which expanded in 2012 and is designed to provide a free-market alternative to the Chinese model of state capitalism. Washington would also work with other multilateral institutions, such as the Association of Southeast Asian Nations (ASEAN) and the Asia-Pacific Economic Cooperation Forum (APEC), to enmesh Asia further into the US economic sphere.

Moreover, greater diplomatic attention would be paid to Asia. The President would visit more often, more US government personnel would be stationed there (the US embassy in Beijing has the largest staff in the world), and additional agreements would be signed (Shambaugh 2013, 14). Tangible consequences of the renewed attention to Asia were noticeable during Obama's November 2014 visit, when the United States concluded agreements with China on restricting greenhouse emissions, easing trade and visa restrictions, and taking steps to avoid military confrontations between US and Chinese military forces.

From a realist perspective, it is easy to see why Asia needs to be the primary focus of the United States. Militarily, six of the world's ten largest armies are in Asia: China, India, North Korea, South Korea, Pakistan, and Vietnam; two of which – China and North Korea – possess nuclear weapons (Sahu 2014, 551). Asia is responsible for more than half of the world's global economic output and nearly half of worldwide trade, supporting 850,000 US jobs (Clinton 2011, 13). The United States trades more than twice as much with Asia than Europe, and Asia is the largest source of imports and the second-largest source of exports for the United States (Shambaugh 2013, 11). Over 4.2 billion people – 60 percent of the world's population – live in Asia. By almost any measure, Asia is the most important continent to US interests and, for that matter, to the world.

The intrinsic importance of Asia has meant and continues to mean that the United States cannot allow it to be controlled by any single state. The United States went to war with Japan to prevent its domination of Asia, and presumably would resist attempts by any other state from achieving dominance over this critical continent. Today, of course, that means preventing China from achieving hegemony over Asia, which in turn requires that the United States demonstrate that it is willing and able to help Asian states counter Chinese expansion. As the country with the world's largest population, second-highest gross development budget (poised to overtake the United States in the coming years), and second-highest (and one of the fastest growing) defense budgets, China has the raw capability to dominate its Asian neighbors. Chinese behavior in recent years has heightened US concerns. Aggressive Chinese moves in the South China Sea (an area that may contain more oil than Saudi Arabia), and especially China's efforts to assert control over the Senkaku/Diaoyou islands, have produced frightening confrontations with Japan, while raising fears in Vietnam and the Philippines. The United States is especially worried that China aims to push US naval operations beyond Japan and perhaps to the second island chain of the Marianas, limiting the US ability to defend Taiwan and its other Asian allies (Kelly 2014, 484).

The realist case for the "pivot" to Asia is, if anything, overdetermined. The military and economic role played by Asia itself justifies the United States' focus on the region, while the rise of China adds urgency to US fears. Realists are quick to highlight the dangers of conflict when a rising hegemon (China) confronts an existing great power (the United States).[6] Whether one believes war between China and the United States is a realistic prospect, the mere possibility of a clash, together with fears of growing

Chinese influence in Asia, explain the Obama administration placing increased emphasis on Asian and Chinese affairs. From a realist perspective, expending scarce resources on intractable Middle East disputes while Asia receives scant attention makes no sense. Realists assert that a great power's interests must follow where the world's military and economic assets are found, which means Asia, and particularly China. Obama's decision to focus on Asia and China conforms fully to realism and is, if anything, long overdue.[7] The only remaining question is whether Obama's behavior in Asia will match his words. Thus far, the US military presence in Asia has not been appreciably increased, raising questions among Asia's leaders regarding US determination. Only by quelling those concerns through concrete actions will Obama's declared pivot realize its realist ends.

Iran

President Obama has repeatedly said that he will not rely on containment or deterrence to deal with Iran, but instead will prevent Iran from acquiring nuclear weapons in the first place.[8] In order to accomplish this, Obama has imposed harsh economic sanctions on Iran to force it to disable much of its nuclear enrichment capability, which could be used to produce an atomic bomb. The imposition of sanctions led to Iran signing an interim agreement (the Joint Plan of Action) in November 2013 that froze parts of its nuclear program in exchange for limited relief from sanctions.[9] The interim accord was designed as a precursor to a comprehensive agreement that was supposed to end the potential for Iran to develop nuclear weapons, in exchange for the removal of all sanctions. That agreement (Joint Comprehensive Plan of Action) was reached in July 2015. The agreement curtailed (but did not eliminate) Iran's nuclear capability for ten to 15 years, in exchange for an end to sanctions. The agreement holds out the promise of delaying Iran's march toward developing nuclear weapons, but at the cost of legitimizing its status as a nuclear threshold state.[10]

Although it looks like Obama is taking a tough stance toward Iran, his policy is more conciliatory than it might appear. While Obama has stressed that "all options are on the table" to stop Iran from developing a nuclear weapon, the prospect of a US military strike against Iranian nuclear facilities appears increasingly remote.[11] Especially with the successful conclusion of negotiations, virtually no one believes the United States is about to attack Iran. Uncertainty about being able to destroy Iran's nuclear facilities, the prospect of horrific Iranian retaliation in the wake of an attack, and the hope that diplomacy will eventually dissuade Iran from developing nuclear weapons have all apparently convinced US officials not to launch a strike.[12] Those who argue that a US military attack could succeed, and that maintaining a military option would at least be useful in pressuring Iran, have been sidelined.[13] Obama has not only virtually eliminated the prospect of a US attack, he has also worked to ensure that Israel would not attack Iran either. The US policy of "no Iranian nuclear weapons" is pointedly less demanding than the Israeli policy of "no Iranian nuclear weapons *capability*" (Hymans and Gratias 2013). By raising the threshold for a US attack, Obama is signaling the Israelis that they too must hold off on striking Iran until an actual weapon is produced. The message is clear. Especially as diplomacy looks as though it may bear fruit, the United States will not strike Iran, and it expects Israel to follow suit.

Obama's policy toward Iran follows a realist path in that it expends limited effort for limited ends. Obama does not want the Iranians to get nuclear weapons, but he is not willing to pay much of a price to stop them from doing so. US policy seeks to dissuade Iran from acquiring a nuclear capability because Washington recognizes that a nuclear-armed Iran would threaten Israel, other US allies, and may spur proliferation elsewhere. Countering these threats justifies the effort to apply sanctions and pursue diplomacy to prevent a nuclear-armed Iran.[14] Obama's focus on sanctions to bring about a negotiated agreement and his refusal seriously to contemplate a military attack against Iran's nuclear program, reflects not only the costs of such an attack but also the limited threat that a nuclear-armed Iran poses to the United States. Although Iran threatens US allies, such as Israel, the threat it poses to the United States is less direct, making the use of US force less attractive. Hurting Iran economically is one thing; going to war with Iran is something else. The threshold for the use of force in a realist world is high, and is not met by an Iran that does not directly threaten US vital interests and may be willing to limit its nuclear capabilities.

Obama's reluctance to use force is also explained by the forgiving attitude that realists have toward the acquisition of nuclear weapons. Many realists are sympathetic to countries that seek to acquire nuclear arms. In an anarchic and threatening world, with no one to rely on but oneself, nuclear weapons provide an indispensable life insurance policy for insecure states. Far from being a threat, some realists see nuclear weapons as a stabilizing force for peace. In this view, nuclear acquisition by Iran may not be welcomed, but in the final analysis, a nuclear-armed Iran could be contained and deterred.[15] A policy of using limited means to deal with what is seen a limited threat of Iranian nuclear acquisition is fully in accord with the benign view of nuclear weapons that lies at the heart of contemporary realism.

Ukraine

Obama's reaction to Russia's actions toward Ukraine is what one would expect from a realist president. Putin's annexation of Crimea, combined with his sending Russian arms and advisers to assist separatists in eastern

Ukraine, provoked a response from Obama that was more noteworthy for what he did not do than what he did. At no point did Obama or NATO threaten military action to counter Russian aggression. Instead, Obama and NATO have sought to punish Russia by employing escalating economic sanctions that target wealthy supporters of Putin and high-level officials of the Russian government. Insofar as a Western threat exists, it is to expand the sanctions to other parts of the Russian economy. No one seriously believes that the United States (or NATO) is prepared to use force to reverse Putin's gains, and no one expects NATO to offer membership or protection to Ukraine. The response of the United States and its European allies to the first forcible takeover of territory in Europe since World War II has been to limit themselves to mild economic punishment that is unlikely to reverse Russian actions.[16]

While some may bemoan the lack of a more forceful policy, Obama and the West are behaving consistently with realism in several respects. Realists believe in a balance of interests in which one defers to the state that has the biggest stake in a given issue (Betts 1987). Ukraine is a vital interest to Russia and is of only secondary importance to the United States and the West. Russians consider Ukraine to be part of their country and see Ukrainians as fellow Russians. Ukraine has served as a launching point for countless invasions into Russia; Russians understandably fear a pro-Western Ukraine on their border, and millions of ethnic Russians in Ukraine look to Moscow for support against a government they do not trust.[17] For the United States, the plight of Ukraine is mostly humanitarian, which, in a realist world, cannot match Moscow's stakes.

Realists emphasize that the direct use of force should be reserved for threats to one's vital interests. Ukraine meets that criteria for Russia, but not for the United States. Moreover, despite its decline, Russia is a great power with thousands of nuclear weapons and a formidable conventional military force. To start down a road that may lead to war for secondary concerns would be a blatant violation of realism, and one that Obama is apparently not prepared to exercise. Equally important, realists tell us that states are far more likely to counter threats than to yield to them (Walt 1987). Seen in this light, Russian aggression can be expected to move Ukraine (and other endangered countries) closer into the Western orbit, eventually giving Washington what it seeks without the costs and risks of using military force (von Eggert 2014, 55; Mankoff 2014, 67–68). In short, Putin's moves against Ukraine present a classic case for realist restraint.

Afghanistan

Obama's policy toward Afghanistan has been to withdraw US troops as quickly as feasible. Although Obama came into office in January 2009 having campaigned on a platform that, while Iraq was a war of choice, defeating the Taliban, who had harbored the 9/11 al-Qaeda terrorists, was a "war of necessity," he quickly came to the conclusion that Afghanistan was a lost cause (Indurthy 2011). He recognized that the United States had real interests in Afghanistan, including the opportunity to deny terrorists a base to launch further attacks against the United States, preventing the Taliban from toppling the Afghan government, and providing time for the Afghan forces to be able to defend themselves. For Obama, however, these interests did not warrant an open-ended US commitment. As such, with the exception of a "surge" of US troops in December 2009, Obama has consistently moved to cut US forces, culminating in a May 2014 timetable that would remove all US troops from Afghanistan by the end of 2016. As Secretary of Defense Robert Gates remarked, "For him [Obama] it's all about getting out" (Gates 2014, 557).

The policy pursued by Obama in Afghanistan fits the realist model of not expending resources on peripheral or hopeless causes. Afghanistan mattered, but it was hardly a vital US interest. When Obama approved the surge, he did so in the belief that the additional troops, combined with a cooperative attitude from Pakistan and better governance from the Afghans, would enable the Taliban to be defeated at an acceptable (US) cost (Gates 2014, 569–570). It soon became obvious, however, that the 30,000 extra US troops would not stem the Taliban tide, because the conditions necessary for success were not present. The Afghan government remained corrupt and ineffective, and Pakistan continued to support the Taliban.[18]

Under these circumstances, only a major new US intervention offered any hope of defeating the Taliban, since the Afghan forces themselves were not up to the task (Biddle 2013, 49). While Afghanistan might be worth a limited US effort (and Obama did accede to military requests that US forces be allowed to undertake combat missions against the Taliban in 2015), it certainly was not worth the deployment of hundreds of thousands of additional troops, especially given the US public's souring toward the whole affair (Mazzetti and Schmitt 2014). Far better, Obama concluded, to keep a token force of several thousand US advisers in Afghanistan to bolster Afghan forces, in the hope that perhaps at some point the Afghans could do the job themselves. Obama's frequent announcements of troop withdrawal deadlines ensured that the United States would not spend needless blood and treasure on what he believed to be a losing cause. In so doing, he was trying to guarantee that the United States would not again be wasting scarce resources on an unworthy prize, a realist approach if there ever was one.

The Arab Spring

One of the most demanding tests of Obama's commitment to realism stemmed from the events surrounding what became known as the "Arab Spring." Initial hopes that the Arab Spring would usher in a new era of freedom and democracy for the Middle East quickly evaporated. Instead of US interests being reinforced by the wave of protests, Washington saw some of its strongest friends threatened or removed from power, resulting in a renewed US focus on the Middle East. Obama's reaction to the Arab Spring did not always follow the realist paradigm. The nature of the challenges he confronted differed, as did the kind of threat they posed to US interests, which helps account for the lack of uniformity in the US response. Nevertheless, most of the policies Obama eventually settled upon were in conformity with realism, and in those instances where he departed from realist principles he made sure to limit his exposure. This can be seen by focusing on four of the key US policies followed in the wake of the Arab Spring: the reaction to the toppling of Mubarak in Egypt, the intervention in Libya, coping with the Syrian insurgency, and dealing with the mounting threat posed by ISIS.

Egypt

Obama's policy toward Egypt was marked by two quandaries, both of which were resolved in a manner supportive of realism. The first predicament was presented by the escalating protests against Hosni Mubarak in the winter of 2010–2011. The United States had maintained a close relationship with Mubarak ever since he assumed power, following the assassination of Anwar Sadat in 1981. Washington welcomed Mubarak's adherence to the peace treaty with Israel, his cooperation with Washington on anti-terrorist measures, and his stewardship over the strategic Suez Canal. As such, when demonstrations erupted in Egypt demanding Mubarak's ouster, Obama and his advisers were conflicted.

Obama's national security chiefs, including Secretary of Defense Robert Gates, National Security Adviser Tom Donilon, and Secretary of State Hillary Clinton wanted the United States to stand by Mubarak: to urge reforms, but not to call for his immediate ouster. They were concerned not only about what regime would follow Mubarak's (especially with the powerful Muslim Brotherhood waiting in the wings), but also about the impression made on other leaders who depended on US support (Gates 2014, 504–505; Clinton 2015, 343). Many of the more junior members on the National Security Staff, however, sided with the protestors, and with their calls for democracy and dignity. They wanted Obama to demand that Mubarak leave immediately.

Obama resolved this dispute in favor of the National Security Staff when he told Mubarak on February 2 that he had to leave office "now" (Gates 2014, 505; Clinton 2015, 343). Following an intensification of the mass protests demanding his ouster, Mubarak did indeed resign his post on February 18, and was replaced by a transitional government. Elections followed, resulting in the selection of Mohammed Morsi, a leader of the Muslim Brotherhood, who took office in June 2012.

Obama initially welcomed Morsi's election. By most accounts, Morsi was chosen in a free and fair election, and it set a good example to demonstrate that religious Muslims will prosper if they play by the rules. Moreover, Morsi agreed to continue to adhere to the peace treaty with Israel and played a pivotal role in ending the 2012 Gaza war. Obama's welcoming of Morsi, however, proved to be short lived. Morsi began to rule Egypt as a dictator, eliminating centers of power that did not adhere to the Muslim Brotherhood's line, suspending the right of the judiciary to review presidential decisions, and purging military officers he suspected of being disloyal. Morsi's actions produced a renewal of major protests in Egypt, leading to his overthrow by the military on July 3, 2013, and eventual replacement by the head of the Egyptian military, Abdel Fattah el-Sisi.

Sisi's takeover created the second dilemma for Obama. On the one hand, he did not want to endorse the toppling of a democratically elected president, especially one in the Muslim world. To do so reinforced the view that Washington only backed democracy when it supported US policy. On the other hand, Obama did not want to alienate the Egyptian military, the one force for stability in Egypt. Nor did Obama wish to upset Egyptian liberals, who had backed the effort to remove the autocratic Morsi. In the end, Obama elected to support Sisi. Obama refused to label Sisi's toppling of Morsi a "coup" (which it was, but declaring it as such would have led to the end of US aid), he largely ignored Sisi's brutal crackdown on the Muslim brotherhood and his arrest of Morsi, and continued to provide generous US assistance to Egypt.[19]

Obama's decisions to abandon Mubarak and back Sisi followed realist principles. It is true that Obama's demand for Mubarak to leave office went against the self-styled realists of his administration, and seemingly supported the promotion of democracy over hard-headed US interests. But Obama's decision was dictated as much by pragmatism – what the United States could accomplish with reasonable means – as it was by any adherence to ethical practice. At the point that Obama demanded Mubarak's departure, the Egyptian president was already on the ropes, the target of ever increasing, violent demonstrations. With the Egyptian army showing signs of ending its support of Mubarak, there was little that the United States could do to save the Egyptian leader, short of a massive intervention. Washington might not have been on the "right side of history" in backing Mubarak's demise, but it was on the right side of the balance of power in Egypt, making this a very pragmatic decision. Obama's move to support Sisi was even more in the realist tradition. By choosing to overlook the forceful overthrow of an elected leader in order to curry favor with the Egyptian military, Obama clearly placed himself in the realist camp that values the furthering of US national interest over the promotion of democracy.

Libya

Obama's decision to intervene in Libya for essentially humanitarian purposes marked a departure from realism, but the limited extent of US involvement ensured that the deviation did not undermine the overall realist direction of his foreign policy. The seeds of the intervention were planted in February 2011, when Libya's dictator, Muammar Qadaffi, violently suppressed peaceful protests against his rule. Qadaffi's actions precipitated a near-civil war, with rebels in the eastern section of the country seeking to topple his rule. With Qadaffi's forces having the upper hand, fears grew in Libya and throughout the international community that he would unleash a blood bath, particularly in Benghazi, which had become the source of much of the revolt. In response to these concerns, and under intense US prodding, the United Nations Security Council accepted a request from the Arab League to enforce a no-fly zone and authorized international action to use "all necessary measures" to protect Libyan civilians.[20] This was one of the first instances of the United Nations employing its "responsibility to protect" doctrine, by which outside states have the right (and perhaps the obligation) to intervene to safeguard the lives of civilians in other countries.[21] The next day, March 18, President Obama declared that the United States, together with its NATO and Arab allies, would enforce the UN resolution. The US-led coalition (taken over later by NATO) then launched a series of air and missile strikes blunting Qadaffi's offensive.[22] The rebels achieved superiority by the summer, killed Qadaffi in October, and set up a new transitional government. Without a single US or NATO casualty, and at a cost of only a few billion dollars, an impressive victory appeared to have been won.[23]

As successful as the Libyan operation may have seemed, it certainly did not appear to be driven by realist concerns. Although odious, Qadaffi did not threaten the United States. On the contrary, he cooperated with US efforts against al-Qaeda, ended his weapons of mass destruction programs, and generally moved his country in a pro-Western direction (Gvosdev and Takeyh 2012). Robert Gates, who opposed the intervention (along with National Security Adviser Donilon and Vice President Joe Biden) so strenuously that he considered resigning over the issue, argued that the United States had no vital interests in Libya to justify getting involved (Gates 2014, 511). For Obama, however, the opportunity to stop a massacre at an acceptable cost carried the day. Obama's ignoring of national interests to intervene in Libya, simply to protect people from a brutal government, seemingly not only contradicted realism, but (for some) marked a new "post-realist" chapter in US foreign policy in which humanitarian interventions would become much more frequent (Gvosdev and Takeyh 2012).

In fact, there is less to Obama's departure from realism than meets the eye. As Obama himself noted, the Libyan intervention brought together a set of distinct conditions – an impending humanitarian disaster; UN,

NATO, and Arab support; the ability to act in a way that did not put US troops at risk – that would only rarely be repeated elsewhere. Indeed, the refusal of Obama to intervene in the far more deadly Syrian civil war suggests that the United States will stay away when interventions would be costly to the United States. Moreover, the United States had a realist interest in preventing Libya from disintegrating and spreading instability to the Middle East and Africa. Even Gates acknowledged that although the vital interests of the United States were not engaged in Libya, its allies felt their vital interests *were* affected, "and therefore we had an obligation to protect them" (Gates 2014, 521). As for the costs incurred in protecting innocent lives, even realists will not balk at acting for humanitarian interests if the price in blood and treasure to the United States is minimal, and if key allies do the heavy lifting (see for example Lynch 2012, 46). Insofar as Libya represented a divergence from Obama's realist path, it was a reluctant and anomalous one.

Syria

Obama's reactions to the Syrian civil war both violated and conformed to realist doctrine. His clearest violation came in his response to the use of chemical weapons by Bashar al-Assad's government. Beginning with peaceful protests in the spring of 2011, disturbances in Syria escalated quickly to a full-scale civil war that threatened Assad's hold on power. Fearing that Assad would be tempted to use his vast quantities of chemical weapons to defeat the insurgents, Obama publicly tried to deter him from doing so. In August 2012, following reports that the Syrian government was transferring large amounts of chemical weapons out of storage and preparing them for immediate use, Obama announced that moving or using substantial amounts of chemical weapons would cross a "red line" that would "change my calculus" regarding US involvement in the civil war (Baker *et al.* 2013). Despite Obama's warning, Syria launched a series of chemical attacks, including a massive strike in August 2013 that killed over 1,400 civilians, among them 400 children. With Secretary of State John Kerry lambasting the Syrians for their use of chemical weapons, it appeared that a US military strike was imminent. Instead of launching an attack, however, Obama sought the approval of Congress, and when it appeared that Congress would not support a military strike, Obama seized upon a Russian offer for Syria to disarm on its own.

Syria did indeed give up its chemical weapons, but this success did little to lessen the damage done to US credibility. After all, Obama had drawn a "red line" and implied US military action should Syria cross it; yet Syria crossed it anyway, and no military action followed. As former Secretary of Defense Leon Panetta remarked,

> [Obama] sent a mixed message, not only to Assad, not only to the Syrians, but [also] to the world. And that is something you do not

want to establish in the world, an issue with regard to the credibility of the United States to stand by what we say we were gonna do.

(Miller 2014)

For realists, the minor victory of getting Syria to rid itself of chemical weapons was not worth the damage done to US credibility. In this instance, Obama could hardly be said to have acted in a realist manner.

Meanwhile, the rebellion in Syria continued, raising questions as to whether the United States would assist the Syrian insurgents in their efforts to topple Assad. In what many saw as a surprising move, Obama in 2012 rejected the advice of his Secretaries of State and Defense, and of the director of the CIA, by deciding against providing major assistance to the Syrian rebels (Clinton 2015, 463). Obama certainly wanted Assad gone, but questioned whether US support could accomplish this at an acceptable cost. Unlike Qadaffi, Assad had an effective military willing to fight for him and, in Iran and Russia, important allies who would not look kindly on seeing him deposed by a US-supported effort. Obama doubted that US arms would make much of a difference given the large amounts of weapons already flowing to Syrian rebels from countries like Saudi Arabia and the United Arab Emirates. Moreover, it was unclear to Obama whether enough "moderate" Syrian rebels existed to make a difference – whether "(an) opposition made up of former doctors, farmers (and) pharmacists" could bring down the Syrian dictator (Gass 2014). More likely, weapons supplied by the United States would fall into the hands of radical insurgents, as with US support of the Afghan *mujahedeen* (Clinton 2015, 463).

Equally important was the fact that the Syrian insurgency did not threaten US vital interests. To be sure, the revolt created an enormous humanitarian disaster, as tens of thousands of innocents were killed and millions more were driven from their homes. As the fighting spilled over borders, Turkey, Jordan, and Lebanon found themselves imperiled as refugees burdened their support services. Nevertheless, vital US interests were not at stake in Syria, a country that shared few values with the United States, had no US military bases, and was not a major oil producer.[24] Syria mattered, but not enough for the United States to do much to end its civil war.

ISIS

Obama's restrained reaction to the Syrian insurgency changed somewhat with the advent of ISIS (Islamic State in Iraq and Syria – though it goes by other names as well). The success of ISIS in conquering large swathes of territory in Iraq and Syria alarmed a large cast of characters who had nothing in common except their fear of ISIS' growing influence. They included Turkey, Jordan, Saudi Arabia, Iran, the Kurds, Iraqi Shi'ites, and even Assad himself (who belatedly woke up to the threat it posed to his rule). At the same time ISIS inflamed public opinion in the United States (and throughout much of the Western world) by filming the decapitation of some of its prisoners, including three US citizens (Landler 2011).

Obama responded to the escalating ISIS threat by calling for direct US military involvement (but no ground troops) while increasing assistance to the indigenous groups most threatened. At first, US support was limited to air strikes against ISIS targets in Iraq to protect US diplomatic personnel stationed in the Iraqi city of Erbil, and the Yazidis, a religious minority targeted by ISIS. Although the air attacks were the first direct US intervention in Iraq since the withdrawal of US troops, Obama was careful to limit the US commitment, declaring, "I will not allow the United States to be dragged into fighting another war in Iraq" (White House 2014a).

A month later, in September 2014, reacting to continued ISIS advances and a shift in US attitudes toward a more activist response, Obama announced a further escalation of US involvement. The United States would now launch air strikes against ISIS targets throughout Iraq (not simply to protect the Yazidis or US diplomats) and against a range of targets in Syria as well. The goal now went beyond humanitarian objectives, becoming to "degrade and ultimately destroy" ISIS (White House 2014b). To that end, supplementing the air strikes, additional US military advisers would be sent to Iraq, bringing their numbers to around 1,500, and military assistance to Syrian insurgents would be ramped up. Despite this increased support, Obama was careful to maintain that the overall US effort would be limited to supporting indigenous forces in the region, and he took pains once again to emphasize that "We will not get dragged into another ground war in Iraq" (ibid.). Two months later, in November 2014, Obama doubled the US presence by ordering an additional 1,500 troops to Iraq to train Iraqi and Kurdish troops, in anticipation of a spring offensive against ISIS. Once again, Obama was careful to emphasize that US forces would not engage in direct combat, but would simply advise the Iraqi and Kurdish forces (Cooper and Shear 2014).

With the exception of Obama's clumsy "red line," his policies toward Syria and ISIS closely followed realist guidelines. The Syrian civil war and the ISIS threat it spawned justifiably provoked US concerns, but never really endangered vital US interests. To be sure, Obama worried about the effects of the conflict on important US friends in the region (such as Turkey, Jordan, and Iraq), on US citizens radicalized by the civil war returning to the United States bent on committing mayhem, and on the humanitarian tragedy that grew worse with each passing day. As important as these concerns were, however, none rose to the level of endangering core interests of US security or economic wellbeing. As such, it made sense for Obama to limit the US response, especially when the Syrian civil war was largely confined to Syria.

As the threat to US interests grew with the rise of ISIS, so too did US actions to defeat it, but always with the qualification that there be no major intervention by US forces. Reinforcing the limited nature of the US response was Obama's belief that the actors most threatened should do the most to defeat the threat they faced. The Iraqis, Kurds, and Syrian rebels, therefore, needed to play the principal role in this drama. The United States would support them with weapons, training, and advisers, but in the final analysis it was up to them to save themselves. In this manner, the United States has acted very much as a "buck passer," placing the main responsibility on those who have the most at stake, which is exactly what realists would recommend.

Conclusion: assessing Obama's realism

With few exceptions, Obama's major foreign policy decisions have conformed to realist precepts. The pivot to Asia followed the realist admonition to focus one's efforts in those areas of the world that possess the greatest military threats and economic wealth. The nuclear negotiations with Iran showed the willingness to use economic sanctions to contain a dangerous adversary, but also conformed with the realist belief that nuclear proliferation is not a major threat (because adversaries can be deterred) and is certainly not worth going to war over. Also not worth a war was Russia's incursion into Ukraine, including the seizure of Crimea. Although this represented the first forcible change of borders in Europe since World War II, it did not pose a threat to US vital interests and thus did not justify a major power confrontation.

The decision to leave Afghanistan conformed well to the realist view of not sinking resources into a losing cause, especially one whose impact is peripheral to US concerns. Obama's acquiescence to the removal of Mubarak, the ascendancy of Morsi, and the latter's replacement by Sisi represented the recognition of the limits of US power to control the internal politics of another state, and the willingness to overlook objectionable leaders who are supportive of US interests. Obama's view that the principal burden of defeating Assad and ISIS must rest with indigenous forces in the Middle East who are most threatened, and not with US troops, is fully consistent with the realist practice of buck passing. To be sure, Obama's humanitarian intervention in Libya and his abandonment of the "red line" in Syria marked departures from realism, but neither action proved costly to the United States, nor did they undermine the overall realist thrust of his foreign policy.

It is easy to imagine Obama following a different, non-realist path. A US president intent on transforming the world might have chosen to delay reaching out to China until it improved its human rights policy, to launch a military strike against Iran's nuclear facilities, to remain in Afghanistan, to roll back the Russians from Crimea, to stand by Mubarak (or Morsi), to arm the Syrian rebels much earlier, and to deploy ground troops to eliminate ISIS. Alternatively, a more isolationist president might have decided to make little effort to embrace Asia, to end sanctions against Iran, to leave Afghanistan long ago, to accept Russian moves in Crimea as legitimate, and to allow the Arab Spring to unfold without any US interference. That Obama's policy sits into the middle of these extremes does not make it right, but it reinforces its realist credentials.

In sum, Obama's foreign policy has not sought to transform the world, but has accepted it "as is." He has been cautious in the use of force, restrained in efforts to promote democracy and human rights, opposed to the direct involvement of US troops, and insistent on others sharing the burden for world order. At the same time, in accordance with realist principles, Obama's foreign policy is not isolationist or pacifist. He has not shrunk from the use of force when he believes it can do good at an acceptable cost. Moreover, he has proved sensitive to the realist concern not to squander resources on what he believes to be marginal threats, which might leave the United States ill-prepared to deal with future challenges from powerful adversaries. Obama's foreign policy has been one of restraint and retrenchment, reflecting what he believes to be the limits of US power, and avoiding the squandering of US resources on what he has concluded are futile causes.

None of this is to suggest that Obama's realism has necessarily produced an admirable foreign policy. Around the world, many view Obama's foreign policy as having been a disaster, because they see in Obama's restraint an abdication of the United States' responsibility in the world. The United States, it is argued, remains the world's only "indispensable" power. It alone provides what order there is in an otherwise anarchic world. This role, however, is undermined by adhering too closely to realist principles. A policy of realism for the United States can easily shift into a policy of isolationism similar to that practiced in the 1920s and 1930s, even when this is not the intention of the policy makers.

The United States is fortunate in that its "vital interests" – defined as preserving its security, economic wellbeing, and core values – are not under serious threat anywhere. As such, a convincing case can be made against the use of force, especially the direct use of US troops, for almost any threat. Indeed, as we have seen, Obama has been skillful in limiting US involvement across a wide range of issues. Over time, however, the cumulative effect of non-involvement can erode US credibility and promote challenges to US concerns. The word gets out that the weak can get away with more, encouraging disruptive behavior as the "indispensable" nation looks the other way. Just as a frog will supposedly not leap from a pan if the heat is raised ever so slowly, the growing recognition that the United States cannot be depended upon to enforce international order may create a threat to US interests so great that by the time the United States wakes up to the danger, it can only be met at a terrible cost.[25] It is this fear that drives some to see Obama's foreign policy as an unqualified failure.

Whether Obama's realist approach deserves this harsh criticism remains to be seen. On the one hand, he has avoided costly quagmires such as the 2003 Iraqi intervention, while also ending the United States' longest war in Afghanistan. On the other hand, China is extending its influence over East Asia, Iran continues on its path toward achieving the capability to produce nuclear weapons, Russia is increasing its influence over Ukraine, the Taliban is poised to take over Afghanistan as soon as the United States departs, and the Middle East is wracked with an unprecedented level of mayhem. Obama may reassure us that the United States' vital interests are not yet threatened by any of these developments, but their overall impact is frightening nonetheless. The point, however, is not to declare that realism is good or bad for the world or for the United States. Rather, that far from being arbitrary, naive, and muddled, Obama's foreign policies are consistent with realism. If one wishes to understand what he has done and is likely to do in the future, realism, for better or worse, is the best guide.

Notes

1 Three of the most distinguished works that inform modern realism are Morgenthau (2006), Waltz (2010), and Mearsheimer (2014a). For ways in which realism should inform US foreign policy, see Walt (2005).
2 On why warfare will never end because of the nature of mankind, states, and the international system, nobody does it better than Kenneth Waltz (2001), especially chapter VIII (Conclusion).
3 The difference between capabilities and interests came to be known as the "Lippmann Gap." See Dueck (2013).
4 For a description of "buck-passing," see Mearsheimer (2014a, 159–162).
5 The notion that states will seek to balance rather than bandwagon is a major theme of Stephen Walt's (1987).
6 For an excellent analysis of why a rising China may conflict with the United States, see Freidberg (2011).
7 Two prominent realists who worry about the rise of China are Aaron Friedberg (2011) and John Mearsheimer (2014a – especially chapter 10).
8 See, for example, Obama's remarks to the 2012 United Nations General Assembly, as cited in Goldman and Rapp-Hooper (2013, 589).
9 For the text of the interim agreement, see Joint Plan of Action 2013. For a criticism of the plan, see Drotar (2014).
10 On the problems of determining Iran's breakout capability, see Kahl, Pattani, and Stokes (2013).
11 On Obama's repeated assertions that the military option is real, see Katzman (2014).
12 On why a US military strike would not work against Iran, see Kahl (2012).
13 On why a US strike against Iran might make sense, see Kroenig (2012), and also Inbar (2006).
14 Mathew Kroenig (2012) is most alarmist about the negative effects a nuclear Iran would produce.
15 The iconic statement of this view can be found in Waltz (1981). For an updated treatment of this issue that applies to Iran, see Waltz (2012).
16 On the damage done to the Russian economy because of its intervention in Crimea, see Rautava (2014).

17 On Russian ties to Ukraine, see Lukin (2014), and also Mearsheimer (2014b).
18 On the failure of US strategy, see Eikenberry (2013), especially p. 61, and also Biddle (2013).
19 For a good account of the quandary facing Obama re: Morsi and Sisi, see Aftandilian (2013).
20 On the intense US efforts to get the UN resolution passed, see Clinton (2015), especially pp. 363–375.
21 For a brief discussion of the "responsibility to protect" and how it relates to the Libyan intervention, see Chesterman (2011).
22 For an account of the US operations against Libya emphasizing command and control issues, see Quartarro *et al.* (2012).
23 For a glowing account of NATO operations in Libya, see Daalder and Stavridis (2012).
24 On the lack of US interests in Syria itself, see Pollack (2014). Despite the absence of interests in Syria, other factors cause Pollack to argue in favor of the United States training and equipping a Syrian insurgent force.
25 For a compelling indictment of Obama's policy of retrenchment, see Robert Kagan (2014).

Bibliography

Aftandilian, Gregory. 2013. "Pitfalls in Egypt." *Parameters* 43 (3): 7–17.
Baker, Peter, Mark Landler, David E. Sanger, and Anne Barnard. 2013. "Off-the-Cuff Obama Line Put U.S. in Bind on Syria." *New York Times*, May 4.
Betts, Richard K. 1987. *Nuclear Blackmail and Nuclear Balance*. Washington, DC: Brookings Institute.
Biddle, Stephen. 2013. "Ending the War In Afghanistan." *Foreign Affairs* 92 (5): 49–58.
Brooks, David. 2007. "Obama, Gospel and Verse." *New York Times*, April 26.
Chesterman, Simon. 2011. "'Leading from Behind': The Responsibility to Protect, the Obama Doctrine, and Humanitarian Intervention after Libya." *Ethics and International Affairs* 35 (3): 279–285.
Chye, Tan Seng. 2012. "Changing Global Landscape and Enhanced US Engagement with Asia-Challenges and Emerging Trends." *Asia Pacific Review* 19 (1): 119.
Clinton, Hillary. 2015. *Hard Choices*. New York: Simon and Schuster.
Clinton, Hillary. 2011. "America's Pacific Century." *Foreign Policy*, October 11. www.us-global-trade.com/Hilary%20Clinton.Asia%20(Foreign%20Policy%20Nov.%202011).pdf.
Cooper, Helene, and Michael D. Shear. 2014. "Obama to Send 1500 More Troops to Assist Iraq." *New York Times*, November 7. www.nytimes.com/2014/11/08/world/middleeast/us-to-send-1500-more-troops-to-iraq.html?emc=edit_au_20141107&nl=afternoonupdate&nlid=50993955.
Daalder, Ivo H., and James G. Stavridis. 2012. "NATO's victory in Libya: The Right Way to Run an Intervention." *Foreign Affairs* 91 (2): 2–7.
Drotar, Matej. 2014. "Nuclear Negotiations Revisited: Challenges and Prospects toward a Final Deal with Iran." *Strategic Assessment* 17 (2): 53–63.
Dueck, Colin. 2013. "Obama's Strategic Denial." *National Interest*, March 27. www.nationalinterest.org/commentary/obamas-strategic-denial-8275.
Eikenberry, Karl W. 2013. "The Limits Of Counterinsurgency Doctrine in Afghanistan." *Foreign Affairs* 92 (5): 59–74.

Fazal, Tanisha M. 2007. *State Death: The Politics and Geography of Conquest, Occupation and Annexation.* Princeton, NJ: Princeton University Press.
Freidberg, Aaron L. 2011. *A Contest for Supremacy: China, America, and the Struggle for Mastery in Asia.* New York: W.W. Norton.
Gass, Nick. 2014. "Barack Obama rebukes Syrian fantasy." *Politico,* August 10. www.politico.com/story/2014/08/barack-obama-rebukes-syrian-fantasy-109890.html.
Gates, Robert M. 2014. *Duty: Memoirs of a Secretary at War.* New York: Knopf.
Goldman, Zachary K., and Mira Rapp-Hooper. 2013. "Conceptualizing Containment: The Iranian Threat and the Future of Gulf Security." *Political Science Quarterly* 128 (4): 589.
Gvosdev, Nicholas K., and Ray Takeyh. 2012. "Decline of Western Realism." *National Interest* 117: 8–19. http://nationalinterest.org/files/digital-edition/1325174168/117DigitalEdition.pdf.
Hymans, Jacques E. C., and Matthew S. Gratias. 2013. "Iran and the Nuclear Threshold: Where is the Line?" *Nonproliferation Review* 20 (1): 13.
Inbar, Efraim. 2006. "The Need to Block a Nuclear Iran." *Middle East Review of International Affairs* 10 (2): 85–104.
Indurthy, Rathnam. 2011. "The Obama Administration's Strategy in Afghanistan." *International Journal of World Peace* 27 (3): 14.
Joint Plan of Action. 2013. Interim agreement, Geneva, November 24. http://eeas.europa.eu/statements/docs/2013/131124_03_en.pdf.
Kagan, Robert. 2014. "Superpowers Don't Get to Retire." *The New Republic,* May 26. www.newrepublic.com/article/117859/allure-normalcy-what-america-still-owes-world.
Kahl, Colin H. 2012. "Not Time to Attack Iran." *Foreign Affairs* 91 (2): 166–173.
Kahl, Colin H., Raj Pattani and Jacob Stokes. 2013. "If All Else Fails: The Challenges of Containing a Nuclear-Armed Iran." *Center for A New American Security,* May: 13–16.
Katzman, Kenneth. 2014. "Iran: U.S. Concerns and Policy Responses." *Congressional Research Service,* July 25: 53.
Kelly, Robert E. 2014. "The 'Pivot' and Its Problems: American Foreign Policy in Northeast Asia." *Pacific Review* 27 (3): 479–503.
Kroenig, Matthew. 2012. "Time to Attack Iran: Why a Strike is the Least Bad Option." *Foreign Affairs* 91 (1): 76–86.
Landler, Mark. 2011. "Obama in Speech on ISIS, Promises Sustained Effort to Rout Militants." *New York Times,* September 10. www.nytimes.com/2014/09/11/world/middleeast/obama-speech-isis.html.
Lukin, Alexander. 2014. "What the Kremlin is Thinking." *Foreign Affairs* 93 (4): 85–93.
Lynch, Marc. 2012. "Does Libya Represent a New Wilsonism?" *National Interest* 118: 45–48. http://nationalinterest.org/files/digital-edition/1329864262/118%20Digital%20Edition.pdf.
Mankoff, Jeffrey. 2014. "Russia's Latest Land Grab: How Putin Won Crimea and Lost Ukraine." *Foreign Affairs* 93 (3): 60–68.
Mandelbaum, Michael. 1996. "Foreign Policy As Social Work." *Foreign Affairs.* 75 (1): 16–32.
Mazzetti, Mark, and Eric Schmitt. 2014. "In Secret, Obama Extends U.S. Role in Afghan Combat." *New York Times,* November 22: A1.
Mearsheimer, John J. 2014a. *The Tragedy of Great Power Politics.* New York: Norton.

Mearsheimer, John. 2014b. "Why The Ukraine Crisis Is the West's Fault." *Foreign Affairs* 93 (5): 77–89.

Miller, S. A. 2014. "The Knives are out: Panetta eviscerates Obama's 'Red Line' blunder on Syria." *Washington Times*, October 7. www.washingtontimes.com/news/2014/oct/7/panetta-decries-obama-red-line-blunder-syria/.

Morgenthau, Hans. 2006. *Politics Among Nations: The Struggle for Power and Peace* (seventh edition). New York: McGraw Hill.

New York Times. 2009. "Obama's Nobel Remarks." October 10. www.nytimes.com/2009/12/11/world/europe/11prexy.text.html?pagewanted=all&_r=0.

Parameswaran, Prashanth. 2014. "Explaining US Strategic Partnerships in the Asia-Pacific Region: Origins, Developments and Prospects." *Contemporary Southeast Asia* 36 (2): 262, 266.

Pollack, Kenneth M. 2014. "An Army to Defeat Assad." *Foreign Affairs* 93 (5): 110.

Quartarro, Joe Sr, Michael Rovenolt, and Randy White. 2012. "Libya's Operation Odyssey Dawn: Command and Control." *Prism Security Studies* 3 (2): 141–156.

Rautava, Jouko. 2014. "Crimean Crisis Will Cost Russia Too." *BOFIT Policy Brief* 1/2014: 4–5.

Sahu, Arun Kumar. 2014. "Two to Tango: The US and China in the Asia-Pacific." *Strategic Analysis* 38 (4): 551.

Shambaugh, David. 2013. "Assessing the US 'Pivot' to Asia." *Strategic Studies Quarterly*, Summer: 10–14.

Von Eggert, Konstantin. 2014. "All Politics Are Local: Crimea Explained." *World Affairs*, September/October: 55.

Walt, Stephen M. 1987. *The Origins of Alliances*. Ithaca, NY: Cornell University Press.

Walt, Stephen M. 2005. *Taming American Power: The Global Response to U.S. Primacy*. New York: Norton.

Waltz, Kenneth N. 1981. "The Spread of Nuclear Weapons: More May Be Better." *Adelphi Papers 171*. London: International Institute for Strategic Studies.

Waltz, Kenneth N. 2001. *Man, the State, and War: A Theoretical Analysis*. New York: Columbia University Press.

Waltz, Kenneth N. 2003. "More May Be Better." In Kenneth N. Waltz and Scott D. Sagan, *The Spread of Nuclear Weapons: A Debate Renewed*, New York: Norton.

Waltz, Kenneth N. 2010. *Theory of International Politics*. Long Grove, IL: Waveland Press.

Waltz, Kenneth N. 2012. "Why Iran Should Get the Bomb." *Foreign Affairs* 91 (4): 2–5.

Washington Post. "Full transcript of President Obama's commencement address at West Point." May 28. www.washingtonpost.com/politics/full-text-of-president-obamas-commencement-address-at-west-point/2014/05/28/cfbcdcaa-e670-11e3-afc6-a1dd9407abcf_story.html.

White House. 2011. "Remarks By President Obama to the Australian Parliament." November 17. www.whitehouse.gov/the-press-office/2011/11/17/remarks-president-obama-australian-parliament.

White House. 2014a. "Statement by the President." August 7. www.whitehouse.gov/the-press-office/2014/08/07/statement-president.

White House. 2014b. "Statement by the President on ISIL." September 10. www.whitehouse.gov/the-press-office/2014/09/10/statement-president-isil-1.

4 Public opinion and Obama's foreign policy

Eytan Gilboa

This chapter investigates US public opinion toward Barack Obama's foreign policy choices and priorities.[1] There are several schools of thought regarding the influence of public opinion on Obama's foreign policy. One school suggests that Obama has been a "realist," whose policy has essentially reflected prevailing trends in public opinion: fatigue from the failed wars in Afghanistan and Iraq, combined with the severe 2008 financial crisis.[2] Under these circumstances, any president, this interpretation argues, would adopt similar policies. Another school suggests he is more of an "idealist," for whom public opinion is not a major factor. On this view, it was Obama's s own background, world view, and lack of experience that has driven his policy (Drezner 2011; Joffe 2015). A third approach argues that he is neither a "realist" nor an "idealist," but an outstanding practitioner of the "liberal" tradition in international relations (Goldsmith 2014; Chesterman 2011).

Despite the central role of US public opinion in the debate over Obama's foreign policy, in actual fact very few studies have been published on this subject. Out of those that have examined this issue, many have investigated the effects of political polarization in Washington on Obama's freedom to implement the fundamental changes he had planned for US foreign policy. Richard Eichenberg (2009) analyzed polling data on Obama's first year at the White House. He found much disagreement between Republicans and Democrats on critical issues, but speculated that the president's persuasive talents and the unpopularity of the opposition would provide him with substantial room for maneuver in foreign affairs.

James McCormick (2014) has argued that public opinion in the United States is largely structured by party and ideology, but that in general, the "public mood" has been in accord with the views of the Obama administration. He adds that the public may have had little influence on Obama's policy, due to the highly centralized structure of his policy-making process. Lawrence Ciulla (2014) argues the opposite: that Obama's foreign policy doctrine has been shaped by public opinion, and that he has failed to take action on crises until the political climate was advantageous to him. In two shorter commentaries, Jeremy Rosner (2014) argues that Obama is able to ignore public opinion on foreign policy, and Josh Kraushaar (2015) suggests that this is exactly what he did on the nuclear negotiations with Iran.

This study attempts to resolve this debate about public opinion and Obama's foreign policy. It presents and analyzes major trends in US public opinion toward Obama's foreign policy and national security.[3] It explores responses to various polls taken primarily in the years following Obama's victory in the 2008 presidential elections. These polls cover: the United States' role in the world; Obama's foreign policy performance and leadership; his handling of the wars in Afghanistan and Iraq; his efforts to combat terrorism; his handling of major international crises; and the effects of his policy on the United States' standing in the world. Wherever possible and relevant, the data for the Obama era is placed within long-term trends.

This analysis finds that Obama's choice of policies has not reflected public opinion. The data show public support for the ending of the US interventions in Afghanistan and Iraq, but also much criticism of Obama's leadership and his handling of international crises. He received low marks for his performance, and majorities have felt that the United States' standing in the world has deteriorated during Obama's tenure at the White House. The public did not believe that he had a clear strategy, and it was largely divided along party lines regarding the major issues.[4] Obama has certainly been concerned about opinion trends and has made efforts to garner more public support. Often, however, he has acted against the preferences of most US citizens, who expected far better from him in terms of both performance and results.

Isolationism versus internationalism

Historically, US foreign policy has oscillated between isolationism and internationalism. After World War II, the United States emerged as one of the two superpowers in the world, and with the end of the Cold War and the collapse of the Soviet empire, it remained as the sole superpower. Despite major setbacks over the years, such as the Vietnam war, the United States has remained very active in world politics. Following the long and failed wars in Afghanistan and Iraq many thought that the public would prefer for the United States to be much less involved in world affairs. However, several indicators show a more complex picture.

A Pew Research Center (2013) survey found that 52 percent of a national sample agreed that "the US should mind its own business internationally and let other countries get along the best they can on their own" (see also Pew Research Center 2014a). Immediately after 9/11, only 30 percent held this view. Other surveys, however, have revealed a much more complex picture, with much public support remaining for internationalism and involvement. Figure 4.1 displays how polls conducted over the last 40 years by the Chicago Council on Global Affairs (2014) have

Public opinion and Obama's foreign policy 65

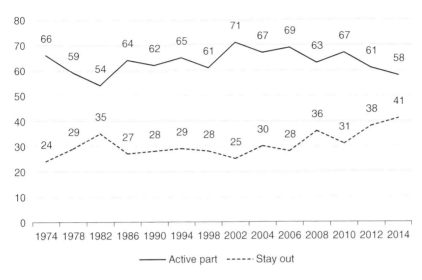

Figure 4.1 Isolationism versus internationalism (source: The Chicago Council on Global Affairs (2014, 7). Copyright © 2014 The Chicago Council on Global Affairs. The content is used with permission).

Question: "Do you think it will be best for the future of the country if we take an active part in world affairs or if we stay out of world affairs?" (%)

shown relative stability in the distribution of responses to a direct question on internationalism (see also Smeltz 2012).

The average proportion of supporters for an active US role in world affairs has remained in the region of 60 percent, and the average proportion of opponents has been around 30 percent. In 1982, this ratio narrowed to 54 percent versus 35 percent, probably due to President Jimmy Carter's poor handling of the long Iranian hostage crisis, the Soviet invasion of Afghanistan, and the world oil crisis. After 9/11, for obvious reasons, the gap grew, to 71 percent versus 25 percent. Obama began his presidency with 67 percent versus 31 percent support for an active US role in world affairs. Since then, however, support has fallen by 10 percentage points, with opposition increasing by the same amount. This decrease may have resulted from poor handling of foreign affairs and from confusion about US goals and strategies, not necessarily from a fundamental change in US attitudes. Still, a clear majority supports internationalism.

Surveys conducted by the Chicago Council between 2002 and 2014 also reveal continuing solid public support for US leadership in world affairs. Table 4.1 shows remarkable stability in the distribution of opinions over more than a decade. Overwhelming majorities of between 82 percent and 84 percent said that US leadership in world affairs is "very desirable" or "somewhat desirable." Despite the disappointments of the post 9/11 era,

Table 4.1 Desirability of US leadership in world affairs

Question: "From your point of view, how desirable is it that the United States exerts strong leadership in world affairs – very desirable, somewhat desirable, somewhat undesirable, or very undesirable?" (%)

Response	2002	2010	2012	2014
Very desirable	41	35	36	37
Somewhat desirable	42	49	46	46
Somewhat undesirable	9	12	14	13
Very undesirable	5	4	4	3

Source: The Chicago Council on Global Affairs (2014, 9). Copyright © 2014 The Chicago Council on Global Affairs. The content is used with permission.

the proportion of those holding this opinion in 2002 and 2014 was identical: 83 percent.

Another significant indicator of internationalism has been the US commitment to NATO. At the end of the Cold War, it seemed that the Western alliance had lost its *raison d'être*. But NATO survived, and has even added new members – East European countries, former members of the Soviet bloc. NATO intervened in the Kosovo war, fought in Afghanistan, and intervened in the civil war in Libya. The United States has always been the main axis of NATO. Figure 4.2 shows that public support for the US commitment to NATO has remained very high. Immediately after the Cold War, support went down to 61 percent versus 26 percent, but following 9/11 it rose to an overwhelming ratio of 76 percent to 17 percent. Two years into Obama's presidency, it remained high at 76 percent to 21 percent, and in 2014, it even reached a record high of 78 percent versus 19 percent.

Leadership

Any US president has to deal simultaneously with domestic and foreign affairs, but each sets priorities between and within each domain. Obama's goal was to concentrate mostly on domestic affairs, for three reasons: first, because he inherited a major economic and financial crisis; second, he wanted to initiate major reforms in areas such as health care; and third, he had no experience in foreign affairs. His main foreign policy goals were to end the wars in Afghanistan and Iraq and withdraw US forces from these countries; to prevent anti-American terrorism, especially on US soil; to reach reconciliation with the Muslim world; and to improve relations with Russia, China, and the developing word. His primary means included soft power, public diplomacy, multilateral diplomacy, and engaging enemies, as well as combating extreme Islamic terrorist groups such as al-Qaeda, and active participation in international organizations, even within the

Public opinion and Obama's foreign policy 67

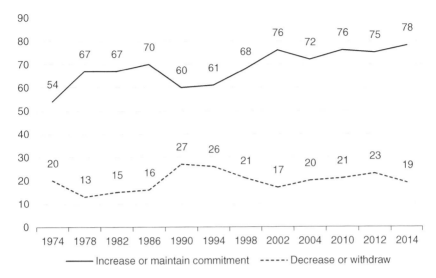

Figure 4.2 US commitment to NATO (source: Chicago Council on Global Affairs (2014, 34). Copyright © 2014 The Chicago Council on Global Affairs. The content is used with permission).

Question: "Do you feel we should increase our commitment to NATO, keep our commitment as it is now, decrease our commitment to NATO, or withdraw from NATO entirely?" (%)

discredited and infamous UN Council on Human Rights (for an early analysis of Obama's presidency, see Greenstein 2009, 2011).

However, Obama had to deal with a number of eruptions of violence and serious crises, especially in the Middle East. These included: the Arab Spring; the NATO intervention in Libya; the civil war and chemical weapons crisis in Syria; the atrocities and conquests of the Islamic State in Iraq and Syria (ISIS); the Russia–Ukraine confrontation; and negotiations to halt the Iranian nuclear weapons program, and to resolve the Palestinian–Israeli conflict. In response, his policies have been inconsistent and erratic, and have failed to achieve his declared goals (Gilboa 2009a, 2009b, 2013, 2015). One strange manifestation of Obama's style and approach was the "leadership from behind" concept (Gerges 2013; Lakoff 2013), which emerged during the NATO military intervention in Libya, initiated by France and Britain, who then pushed the United States to join them. The concept is an oxymoron. A state, especially a superpower, either leads or stays behind. This was no mere slip of the tongue by a careless senior White House official; in many ways, it represented Obama's approach to the United States' role in world affairs.

Since 2009, the polls show a substantial decrease in public approval for Obama's performance as president and his handling of foreign affairs (Gallup 2015a, 2015b). A similar sharp drop was registered in the public

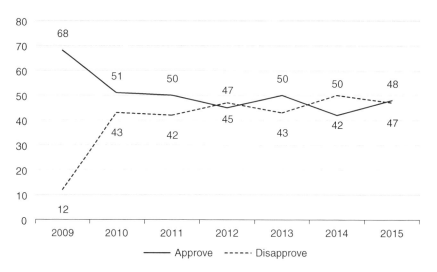

Figure 4.3 Obama job approval (source: Gallup 2015b. Copyright © 2015 Gallup, Inc. All rights reserved. The content is used with permission; however, Gallup retains all rights of republication).

Question: "Do you approve or disapprove of the way Barack Obama is handling his job as president?" (%; n=1,500; margin of error ±3)

evaluation of his leadership. Figure 4.3 shows that at the beginning of his first term, 68 percent approved of his performance as president, while 12 percent disapproved. This is usually the case when a new president assumes office, demonstrating a grace period in which to implement his campaign promises. But after only one year in office, Obama's approval rating dropped to 51 percent, and has remained low ever since. In 2015, the number of respondents who approved his presidency was equal to the number who disapproved, both below 50 percent. And in the NBC News/Wall Street Journal (NBC/WSJ) poll, his rating was negative: only 46 percent approved while 50 percent disapproved (Murray 2014; Hart Research Associates/Public Opinion Strategies 2015).

General approval for a president may be influenced by an average of his performance in both domestic and foreign affairs. A similar pattern, however, emerges in evaluations of Obama's handling of foreign affairs. Figure 4.4 shows that during his first year at the White House, majorities of 54 percent approved of his foreign policy. After only one year, the scores dropped to 47 percent, and in 2015 they went down further, to less than 40 percent. In the NBC/WSJ poll, only 36 percent approved, while 58 percent disapproved. This figure represents complete public dissatisfaction with Obama's foreign policy choices and decisions. Figure 4.4 shows the Gallup poll results, which show similar trends to those obtained by other polls.

Public opinion and Obama's foreign policy 69

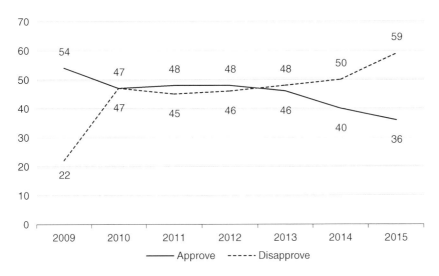

Figure 4.4 Obama's foreign policy approval (source: Gallup 2015b. Copyright © 2015 Gallup, Inc. All rights reserved. The content is used with permission; however, Gallup retains all rights of republication).

Question: "Do you approve or disapprove of the way Barack Obama is handling foreign affairs?" (%; *n* = 1,500; margin of error ±3)

The CBS News Poll has asked national samples whether Obama "has strong qualities of leadership" (PollingReport 2015a). Figure 4.5 shows a steady decline between 2009 and 2015 in positive responses, and a parallel rise in the negative responses. At the beginning of his presidency, 76 percent

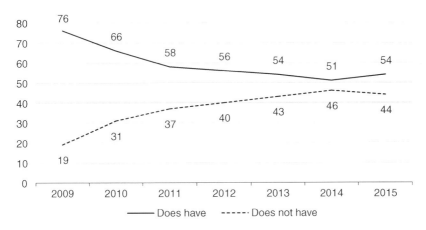

Figure 4.5 Obama's leadership approval (source: CBS News Poll (PollingReport 2015a).

Question: "Do you think Barack Obama has strong qualities of leadership, or not?" (%; *n* = 1,344; margin of error ±3)

of respondents said he had strong leadership qualities, and only 19 percent disagreed. In 2014 and 2015, the scores dropped to about 54 percent versus 44 percent. These results represent a total drop of around 20 percentage points in the positive column, and even a sharper rise of about 25 percentage points in the negative column. In 2013, Gallup found that 53 percent thought Obama was a "strong and decisive leader," while 47 percent disagreed. In 2015, this result was reversed, with 47 percent supporting this statement and 52 percent disagreeing.

The Pew Research Center has examined Obama's leadership qualities in a specific way. National samples have been asked whether Obama was sufficiently "tough" on foreign policy and national security. At the beginning, 51 percent thought his policy was "about right," while 38 percent said he wasn't tough enough (Table 4.2). In 2014, the situation was reversed. Now, only 36 percent thought his policy was about right, while a majority of 54 percent said it wasn't tough enough.

Similarly, a Pew poll in 2009 found that 74 percent of a national sample said they had "confidence in Obama to do the right thing in world affairs." This high level of confidence subsequently declined almost every year, and in 2014 stood at 58 percent. This figure still represents a clear majority, but also a drop of 16 percentage points. Despite all the other negative indicators of actual failed performance, apparently, the public still believed that Obama "may" do the right thing in world affairs.

Managing crises and global issues

For the United States, as a superpower and self-appointed "policeman of the world," almost every crisis in the world has effects and ramifications for it. US presidents have to cope with international crises and global issues, and are evaluated on their ability to manage them successfully. In July and August 2014, the CBS Poll asked a national sample the following general question: "How much confidence do you have in Barack Obama's ability to handle an international crisis?" The sample was equally divided: 52 percent said they had "a lot" or "some confidence," while 47 percent

Table 4.2 Toughness in foreign policy and national security

Question: "Is Obama, when it comes to foreign policy and national security – too tough, not tough enough, or about right?" (%)

Response	2009	2010	2012	2013	2014
Too tough	2	2	2	5	3
Not tough enough	38	47	41	51	54
About right	51	41	42	37	36

Source: Pew Research Center (2014b). Copyright © 2014 Pew Research Center. The content is used with permission.

Public opinion and Obama's foreign policy 71

had "a little" or "none at all" (PollingReport 2015a). On specific crises, however, polls have consistently revealed very negative results.

The wars in Afghanistan and Iraq

The two major US military interventions in Afghanistan and Iraq, inherited by Obama from President George W. Bush, represented a formidable challenge. During the 2008 presidential campaign, Obama promised to end both wars within a short period of time, and this commitment may have helped him to win the race to the White House. Figure 4.6 shows how the US public changed its mind on the war in Afghanistan (Gallup 2014a). When asked in 2002 if the United States had made a mistake in sending troops to fight in Afghanistan, a huge majority of 93 percent said "no," and only 3 percent said "yes." When Obama began his presidency, 68 percent still said "no," and 36 percent said "yes." By 2014, the public was equally divided on this issue, by 49 percent to 48 percent. In 2011, the NBC news poll found that 52 percent of a national sample approved NATO's decision to leave some American troops in Afghanistan until 2014, while 47 percent disapproved. In the same year, more than half (55 percent) of the American public was less confident that the war in Afghanistan will come to an end (PollingReport 2015d). In 2013, the Pew poll found that only 31 percent felt the war in Afghanistan had made the United States safer, while 21 percent said it had made the United States less safe, and 43 percent said it made no difference (Pew 2013).

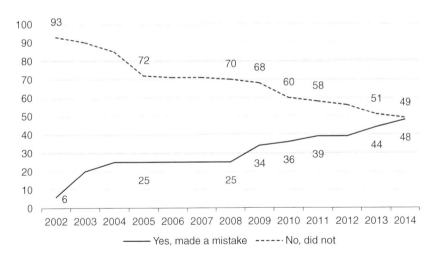

Figure 4.6 Afghanistan war: a mistake? (source: Gallup 2014a. Copyright © 2014 Gallup, Inc. All rights reserved. The content is used with permission; however, Gallup retains all rights of republication).

Question: "Looking back, do you think the United States made a mistake sending troops to fight in Afghanistan in 2001?" (%)

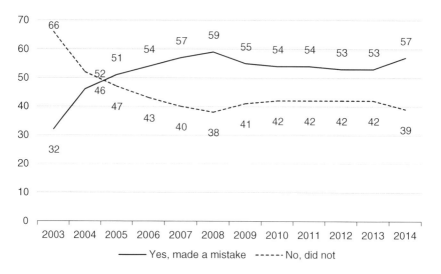

Figure 4.7 Iraq war: a mistake? (source: Gallup 2014b. Copyright © 2014 Gallup, Inc. All rights reserved. The content is used with permission; however, Gallup retains all rights of republication).

Question: "Looking back, do you think the United States made a mistake sending troops to fight in Iraq: yes, it made a mistake; or no, did not?" (%)

The results on the war in Iraq were different (Gallup 2014b). Prior to his election, Obama (2007) distinguished between the two wars, believing that the war in Afghanistan was justified while that in Iraq was not. In response to the same question asked about the war in Afghanistan, in 2004, 52 percent thought the United States had not made a mistake by sending troops to fight in Iraq, and 46 percent disagreed (Figure 4.7). Since 2007, however, the situation has been reversed. During the Obama years, slight majorities of about 54 percent said the war was a mistake, while 42 percent thought it was not. In 2010, the public was equally divided on Obama's handling of the war. In 2014, 55 percent disapproved of his policy, and only 35 percent approved. The negative score may have resulted from the handling of the Islamic State in Iraq and Syria (ISIS) advances in Iraq and Syria.

Combating terrorism

Since 9/11, another terrorist attack on US soil has been perceived by both leaders and the public as a major national security threat, and prevention has been a major goal of both Bush and Obama. Indeed, Obama continued to hunt the leaders of al-Qaeda in Afghanistan and Pakistan, and finally, in May 2011, US forces killed Osama bin Laden. Obama received

Public opinion and Obama's foreign policy 73

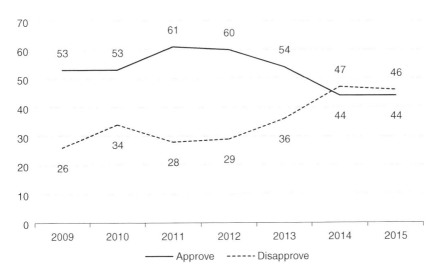

Figure 4.8 Handling terrorism (source: CBS News Poll/PollingReport 2015a (*n*=1,023; MOE ±3)).

Question: "Do you approve or disapprove of the way Barack Obama is handling terrorism?" (%)

much credit for achieving justice in this lingering search for the master terrorist. However, the public has had reservations about Obama's handling of terrorism. Figure 4.8 shows that he received reasonable marks (around 60 percent) only after the killing of bin Laden. Since then, his approval rating has been steadily declining, and in 2014 and 2015 was even below the 50 percent mark (see McCrisken 2011).

Obama's handling of the atrocities perpetrated by ISIS represents a good example of his failure to assess threats correctly and use effective means to deal with them, and of the negative public reaction to his confusing policies. After a decade of failed military intervention in Iraq, Obama wanted to end the United States' role and bring home the remaining US soldiers. The atrocities and genocide committed by ISIS, its threat to take over all of Iraq, and the beheading of two US reporters, James Foley and Steven Sotloff, forced Obama to rethink his strategy. His approach, however, was muddled. At first he said that ISIS did not represent a strategic threat to the United States. Later he revised this stance, but admitted to not having a strategy to deal with the threat. After more waves of ferocious violence, he authorized the use of airpower against ISIS, in cooperation with a limited Arab coalition, and the dispatching of thousands of military "advisers" to help the Iraqi forces.

In October 2014, the CBS Poll asked a national sample, "How would you rate the job Barack Obama has done in assessing the threat posed by ISIS militants in the past few months?" Only one-third of the respondents said his assessment was "excellent" or "good," while more than two-thirds thought his assessment was "fair" or "poor." No wonder that in March 2015, 53 percent disapproved of Obama's handling of the ISIS situation, while only 36 percent approved.

Managing crises and global issues

Responses of national samples to approval–disapproval questions on several international crises and global issues have also been mainly negative. In 2013, the Pew poll found that, on nine out of ten foreign policy issues, Obama's approval rating was negative, and below 40 percent (Table 4.3). Only on the handling of terrorism did he receive a positive rating, of 51 percent versus 44 percent. The public disapproved of his foreign policy (56 percent to 34 percent), and of his policies toward Russia (47 percent to 37 percent), Iran (53 percent to 37 percent), Afghanistan (57 percent to 34 percent), China (52 percent to 30 percent), and Syria (57 percent to 30 percent). His ratings on critical global issues were also negative. The public disapproved of his handling of global climate change (46 percent to 38 percent), of international trade (46 percent to 36 percent), and of immigration policy (60 percent to 32 percent).

Similar negative results on the same and other international issues appeared in various polls taken in 2014 and 2015. Table 4.4 shows that out of ten crises and issues, the public approved Obama's policies only toward the Ebola epidemic (47 percent to 41 percent) and Cuba (44 percent to 36 percent), but even on these issues, the approval percentage was narrow, and below 50 percent. The public disapproved of his handling of Iran (47

Table 4.3 Obama's job rating on foreign policy crises and issues (2013)

Question: "Do you approve or disapprove of the way Barack Obama is handling ____?" (%)

	Approve	Disapprove
Overall foreign policy job approval	41	53
Threat of terrorism	51	44
Global climate change	38	46
Russia	37	47
Iran	37	53
International trade	36	47
Afghanistan	34	57
Nation's foreign policy	34	56
Immigration policy	32	60
China	30	52
Syria	30	57

Source: Pew Research Center (2013, 13). Copyright © 2013 Pew Research Center. The content is used with permission.

Table 4.4 Obama's approval rating on foreign policy issues (2014–2015)

Question: "Do you approve or disapprove of the way Barack Obama is handling the current situation in/against _____ ?" (%)

	Approve	Disapprove	Poll (month.year)
Ebola	47	41	CBS (10.2014)
Cuba	44	36	CBS (12.2014)
ISIS	36	53	CBS (3.2015)
Iran	38	47	CBS (3.2015)
Iraq	37	52	CBS (6.2015)
Israel	38	50	ABC/WP (3.2015)
Israeli–Palestinian relations	30	62	Gallup (8.2014)
Ukraine	39	55	CNN (9.2014)
Russia	37	54	Gallup (8.2014)
Mexico	33	58	ABC/WP (7.2014)

Sources: PollingReport 2015a (ABC News/*Washington Post*, July 9–13, 2014, n=1,016, MOE ±3.5; ABC News/*Washington Post*, March 26–29, 2015, n=1,003, MOE ±3.5; CBS News, October 3–6, 2014, n=1,260, MOE ±3; CBS News, October 23–27, 2014, n=1,269, MOE ±3; CBS News, June 20–22, 2014, n=1,009, MOE ±3; CBS News, December 18–21, 2014, n=1,000, MOE ±3; CBS News, March 21–24, 2015, n=1,023, MOE ±3; CNN/ORC, September 5–7, 2014, n=1,014, MOE ±3; Gallup, August 7–10, 2014, n=1,032, MOE ±4).

percent to 38 percent), Iraq (52 percent to 37 percent), ISIS (53 percent to 36 percent), Israel (50 percent to 38 percent), Israeli–Palestinian relations (62 percent to 30 percent), Russia (54 percent to 37 percent), the Ukraine crisis (55 percent to 39 percent), and even Mexico (58 percent to 33 percent).

Stopping Iran's nuclear weapons program

For more than a decade, Presidents Bush and Obama have been trying to prevent Iran from becoming a nuclear power. The combination of an extreme, hostile, and aggressive Islamic theocracy and weapons of mass destruction could only be a recipe for disaster. Obama repeatedly declared that a nuclear Iran would be a major strategic threat to the United States, and promised to use any means, including military, to prevent this from happening. In order to stop the nuclear weapons program, the United States, the European Union, and the United Nations imposed severe sanctions on Iran. The ayatollahs agreed to negotiate a nuclear deal with permanent members of the UN Security Council, plus Germany (the P5+1). An intermediate agreement was reached in Geneva on November 24, 2013, and a framework for a permanent agreement in Lausanne on April 2, 2015. Both were highly controversial.

Israel, the United States' Arab allies, and many international experts vehemently criticized Obama and the framework, arguing that it would legitimize Iran as a threshold nuclear power, and would increase its capabilities to undermine regimes and expand violence. In 2015 House Speaker John Boehner invited Israeli Prime Minister Benjamin Netanyahu to present his case before a joint session of Congress. Obama criticized Netanyahu, and said he would veto any attempt by Congress to review and approve the permanent agreement, although he eventually relented, and agreed to a limited Congressional review of the final agreement.

The public viewed the Iranian nuclear program as a major security threat to the United States. Respondents preferred diplomacy and negotiations, but were ready to support the use of force, by the US or Israel, if all other means failed (Gilboa 2010). The public was not satisfied with Obama's handling of the Iranian regime and the nuclear crisis. In 2009, after the rigging of the Iranian presidential elections, and the brutal squashing of a mass protest against this fraud, the public narrowly approved Obama's timid responses by a ratio of 45 percent to 39 percent (PollingReport 2015b). Between 2013 and 2015, however, this result was reversed, and majorities came to disapprove of his policies. In January 2014, the public disapproved his handling of the situation in Iran by a ratio of 53 percent to 35 percent, and in April 2015 the disapproval rate went higher, to 58 percent versus 33 percent (Blanton 2015).

The Pew Research Center (2015; see also Poushter 2015) found that more US citizens approve of the nuclear negotiations (49 percent) than disapprove (40 percent), and the Suffolk University/USA Today Poll revealed approval of the framework for a permanent deal, by a ratio of 46 percent to 37 percent (PollingReport 2015b). Yet samples in several national polls were very skeptical about Iran's intentions to abide by the agreement. In the Pew poll, 63 percent didn't believe that Iranian leaders were "serious about addressing international concerns over their nuclear enrichment program." In an NBC News poll (Hart Research Associates 2015), 68 percent believed that Iran was either "not too likely" or "not at all likely" to abide by a nuclear agreement, compared with 25 percent who said Iran was "very likely" or "somewhat likely." A Fox News poll (Blanton 2015) revealed that 55 percent thought that the United States "can't trust anything" Iran says on its nuclear program, and only 28 percent thought otherwise. Clear majorities in several polls (76 percent in the Fox News poll, 72 percent in the Suffolk University/USA Today Poll, and 62 percent in the Pew poll) rejected Obama's position on the role of Congress, and thought that he should be required to obtain Congressional approval for any nuclear deal with Iran.

Israel

Although Israel has long been the closest and the most reliable ally of the United States in the Middle East, relations between the two countries have deteriorated during the Obama era. Although Obama has frequently acknowledged the "special relationship" with Israel and his firm commitment to its security, he has often initiated policies that have been viewed in Jerusalem as compromising Israel's vital interests. Obama and Netanyahu disagreed about critical issues such as the negotiations with the Palestinians, the US policy toward the Arab Spring, and the US-led effort to halt the Iranian nuclear weapons program (Gilboa 2008; 2009a; 2009b; 2013; 2015). At the beginning of both his first and second terms, Obama initiated aggressive attempts to achieve a comprehensive resolution of the Palestinian–Israeli conflict. Both failed. Although the Palestinians were mostly responsible for these failures, the Obama administration tended to blame Israel.

Public opinion rejected the Obama initiatives, and disapproved of his policies and his handling of the relations with Israel. In March 2013, 69 percent of the respondents in an ABC/WP poll said that the United States should leave the negotiations on a peace settlement to the Israelis and the Palestinians, and only 26 percent thought it should take the "leading role" in negotiations (PollingReport 2015c). In July and August 2014, the CBS Poll found that 59 percent thought the United States had "no responsibility to resolve the Palestinian–Israeli conflict," while 35 percent though it had. As can be seen in Table 4.4, in 2013 the public disapproved of Obama's handling of Israel by a ratio of 50 percent to 38 percent, and of his handling of Israeli–Palestinian relations by even a higher ratio of 62 percent to 30 percent. Similarly, in March 2015, over the controversy about Netanyahu's speech on Iran at the US Congress, the ABC/WP poll found that only 38 percent of a national sample approved of the "way Obama was handling US relations with Israel," while 51 percent disapproved.

The United States' standing in the world

Evaluations of the United States' standing in the world during the Obama presidency have been negative. The Pew poll found that between 2009 and 2013, the number of respondents saying that "the United States plays a less important and powerful role as a world leader than ten years ago" went up from 41 percent to 53 percent (Figure 4.9). Members of the Council on Foreign Relations also believe that US power has declined. A majority of 62 percent expressed this view, compared with 44 percent in 2009.

Gallup also found that in 2014, the public was almost equally divided on US military strength. By a ratio of 50 percent to 47 percent, respondents said that the United States was number one in the world militarily; by contrast, in 2008, 60 percent expressed this opinion while 39 percent disagreed. The public wanted the United States to be the most powerful state in the world, however. The Pew Research Center (2013) poll found that 56 percent said that the United States' policies should keep it as the only military superpower in the world, while 32 percent would accept China,

78 E. Gilboa

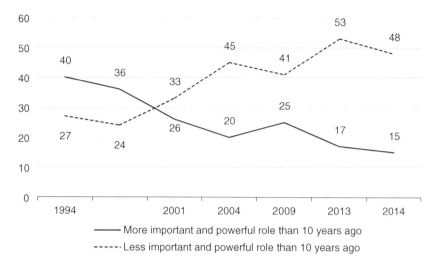

Figure 4.9 US role as world leader (source: Pew Research Center 2014b, 3. Copyright © 2014 Pew Research Center. The content is used with permission).

Question: "The US role today as world leader is: less important and powerful than ten years ago; or more important and powerful than ten years ago?" (%)

the European Union, or other countries to be as militarily powerful as the United States.

Since 2004 the public has perceived a decline in the United States' popularity in the world. At the beginning of the century, probably following 9/11, between 73 percent and 79 percent believed that the world viewed the United States "very" or "somewhat" favorably. The unpopular wars in Afghanistan and Iraq substantially reduced this rating. From 2005 to 2010, majorities believed that the United States had an unfavorable image abroad. Obama extensively employed public diplomacy to improve the United States' standing in the world, and at the beginning of his first term even won the Nobel Peace Prize. The polls show that he was able to reverse the negative trend, and that majorities now felt that the United States' standing had improved, but only slightly. The narrow positive ratio in 2014, 51 percent to 47 percent, was identical to the one registered in 2010. The Pew poll also revealed that substantial majorities thought the United States was less respected in the world (Table 4.5). The trend began in 2004, but despite his intensive public diplomacy efforts, Obama wasn't able to reverse it. Table 4.5 shows that the number of respondents saying "the United States is less respected by other countries than in the past" went up from 56 percent to 70 percent. This was the highest negative score in a decade. A Gallup poll in 2014 (PollingReport 2015a) found only 37 percent of a national sample saying they were "satisfied with the

Table 4.5 Respect for the United States in the world

Question: "Compared to the past, the United States is ____ by other countries" (%)

Response	2004	2005	2006	2008	2009	2012	2013
More respected	10	9	7	7	21	13	7
As respected	20	21	23	18	20	27	19
Less respected	67	66	65	71	56	56	70

Source: Pew Research Center (2014b). Copyright © 2014 Pew Research Center. The content is used with permission.

position of the United States in the world today." In 2002, 71 percent held this opinion.

Polarization

Bipartisanship has always been a major asset in presidential management of foreign policy and national security. Presidents make considerable efforts to cultivate bipartisanship, in order to strengthen their ability to plan and implement effective foreign policy and diplomacy. Frequently, even if the two parties differ on domestic issues, they are able to cooperate on international issues, particularly when the United States faces crises and challenges. During the Obama years, however, political polarization in the United States has grown to a level not seen in Washington at least since the Vietnam war. Obama was unable to overcome it in the domestic arena, and the party confrontations have spilled over into foreign affairs.

The Democratic Party controlled the two branches of Congress only during the first two years of the Obama presidency, losing the majority in the House in 2010, and in both the House and the Senate in 2014. The lack of bipartisanship has characterized Obama's entire presidency, but the situation deteriorated following the 2014 Republican congressional victory. It reached a nadir during the debate about the nuclear negotiations and agreements with Iran.

The public certainly preferred bipartisanship. In 2014 and 2015, a CNN/ORC poll (PollingReport 2015a) asked a national sample the following question: "In general, would you rather see Barack Obama attempt to reach a bipartisan compromise with Congress on major issues, or would you rather see Obama take unilateral action without Congress to make changes in government policy that are not supported by Republicans?" Overwhelming majorities, 67 percent versus 30 percent in 2014 and 74 percent versus 24 percent in 2015, preferred bipartisanship and compromises over unilateral action. On many issues, primarily on Iran, Obama has adopted the opposite approach.

Figure 4.10 reveals that in the last decade, except for one year, 2007, the public trusted the Republicans much more than the Democrats "to do

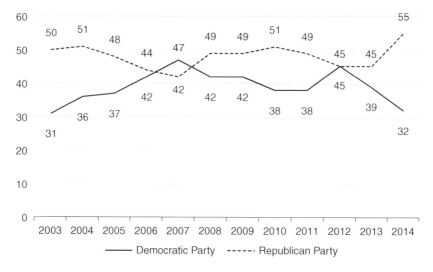

Figure 4.10 Party preferences: coping with international terrorism and military threats (source: Gallup poll (Newport 2014). Copyright © 2014 Gallup, Inc. All rights reserved. The content is used with permission; however, Gallup retains all rights of republication).

Question: "Looking ahead for the next few years, which political party do you think will do a better job of protecting the country from international terrorism and military threats?" (%)

a better job of protecting the country from international terrorism and military threats." In 2009, after Obama became president, the Republican Party held an advantage of 7 percentage points, but by 2014 this had grown to 23 percentage points, as 55 percent of Americans trusted the Republicans more, while only 32 percent preferred the Democrats.

The polls reveal substantial differences between the approaches of the two parties to threats faced by the United States and Obama's handling of foreign policy, diplomacy, and crises. Table 4.6 shows that in 2014 Republicans and Democrats had different perceptions about seven out of nine global threats to the United States. The Republicans were more worried than the Democrats about the nuclear programs of Iran and North Korea, China's emergence as a global power, the Palestinian–Israeli conflict, and Islamic extremist groups such as al-Qaeda and ISIS. The Democrats were more worried about the spread of infectious diseases and climate change. Members and supporters of both parties were equally worried about only one threat – the tension between Russia and its neighbors. Table 4.6 also shows that on these threats, except for the spread of infectious diseases and global climate change, the views of Independents were much closer to those of the Democrats.

Republicans and Democrats had very different opinions about Obama's approach to foreign policy and national security. In 2014, while 77 percent

Table 4.6 Party preferences: views of global threats

Question: "Saying each is a 'major threat' to the US" (%)

	REP	DEM	IND	R–D difference
Iran's nuclear program	74	56	45	+18
China's emergence as a world power	60	43	46	+17
The conflict between Israelis and Palestinians	60	44	45	+16
Islamic extremist groups like al-Qaeda	80	67	69	+13
The Islamic militant group in Iraq and Syria, known as ISIS	78	65	63	+13
North Korea's nuclear program	63	58	54	+5
Growing tension between Russia and its neighbors	54	54	52	0
The rapid spread of infectious diseases from country to country	49	55	50	–6
Global climate change	25	68	44	–43

Source: Pew Research Center (2014b, 8). Copyright © (2014) Pew Research Center. The content is used with permission.

Table 4.7 Party preferences: US importance and power

Question: "Saying the United States plays a less important and powerful role as leader than ten years ago" (%)

Response	2001	2004	2009	2013	2014	Changes 2001–2014
Total	26	20	41	53	48	+22
Republicans	21	8	50	74	64	+43
Independents	27	23	45	55	53	+26
Democrats	28	27	29	33	30	+2
R–D diff.	–7	–19	+23	+41	+34	

Source: Pew Research Center (2014b, 6). Copyright © 2014 Pew Research Center. The content is used with permission.

of the Republican sample thought that Obama was not "tough enough" on security issues, only 34 percent of the Democratic sample held this opinion; and while only 16 percent of Republicans thought his approach to foreign policy and national security was "about right," 56 percent of Democrats held this opinion. In the same Pew poll (Pew Research Center 2014a, 2014b), 64 percent of the Republican sample thought that "compared to ten years ago, the United States' role as a world power is less important," while 30 percent of the Democratic sample agreed with this assessment (Table 4.7).

Table 4.8 Party preferences: respect by other countries

Question: "Saying the United States is less respected by other countries than in the past" (%)

Response	2004	2008	2009	2013
Total	67	71	56	70
Republicans	47	60	68	80
Independents	74	72	59	74
Democrats	80	81	49	56
R–D diff.	–33	–21	+19	+24

Source: Pew Research Center (2013, 50). Copyright © (2013) Pew Research Center. The content is used with permission.

Similarly, in 2013, almost 80 percent of the Republican sample compared to 56 percent of the Democratic sample agreed that "the United States is less respected by other countries than in the past." It should be noted that, although the gap between the two parties on this issue was still high, 24 percentage points, a majority of the Democrats agreed that under Obama, the United States had become less respected in the world (Table 4.8).

Conclusions

Stephen Walt (2014) criticized the findings of the comprehensive survey conducted by the Chicago Council on Global Affairs, which found public support for active US leadership in world affairs. He blamed the Council for asking the wrong questions about attitudes toward Afghanistan, Syria, and Ukraine, because "real" interests and costs were omitted. He hinted that Obama's foreign policy has been well formulated and implemented, and in line with the "true" wishes of the US public. The results of this study show how wrong Walt was in his criticism and interpretation. Analysis of major trends in US public opinion toward foreign policy and national security shows that there were no isolationist constraints on Obama's foreign policy. Despite the failing wars in Afghanistan and Iraq, the US public supported an active role for the United States in world affairs, wanted the United States to lead the world, and strongly supported the long-standing US commitment to NATO.

The main problems with US foreign policy have been Obama's failing leadership and inconsistent policies. After only one year in office, the public began to express questions and reservations about his overall performance and foreign policy. The public disapproved of his performance as president and of his handling of foreign affairs, and did not think he was tough enough on foreign policy and national security. Over time, the public became unsure as to whether Obama has strong leadership qualities.

One principal requirement of leadership is to present a clear vision and clear goals. In many cases, the public has been confused about Obama's goals and policies (see the CBS News poll, PollingReport 2015a). This is primarily because his policies have not been consistent and because he has failed to explain them (Gelb 2012; Ignatius 2014). The polling data confirm this failure. In September 2013, 79 percent of a national sample said that the Obama administration had not clearly explained US goals in Syria, while only 24 percent thought he had. In June 2014, 67 percent of a national sample said Obama had not clearly explained what US goals were in Iraq; only 23 percent thought he had. In October 2014, 61 percent of a national sample said that Obama did not have a clear plan for dealing with ISIS, while only 36 percent thought otherwise.

The public disapproved of Obama's handling of most of the crises and the global issues with which he was faced. US citizens were not sure if the war in Afghanistan was a mistake or not, but they did not think it made the United States safer, and they disapproved of Obama's policy there. There has been much stronger support for the withdrawal from Iraq, but the violent success of ISIS disrupted Obama's plan. Even the ratings of his efforts to combat terrorism dropped from high positive in 2011 to negative in 2014–2015.

Various polls yielded a negative assessment of Obama's handling of crises and global issues. The public disapproved of how he handled the crises in the Middle East, US relations with Israel, and the relations between Israel and the Palestinians. US citizens supported the negotiations on the Iranian nuclear program, but were very skeptical about the Iranian intention to implement it. The public disapproved of Obama's handling of the situation in Iran and strongly rejected his plan to bypass Congress on the permanent agreement. The public also disapproved of Obama's handling of relations with Russia and the Ukraine crisis, and of US relations with China and Mexico. Obama has even received negative marks on his handling of global issues such as climate change and international trade. The only slightly positive evaluation recorded was for his handling of the Ebola crisis, and of relations with Cuba. Given this grim record, it is little wonder that the public was concerned about the deterioration in US standing and prestige in the world. Many thought that the United States had become less powerful and less important in world affairs, and less respected. They were even less sure as to whether the United States remained the strongest military power in the world.

Obama has not been led by public opinion. On the contrary, he has ignored public opinion, and refused to be constrained by it. Instead, his foreign policy has been based on his own worldview and on his beliefs in the world order and in international cooperation. His lack of experience has resulted in severe mistakes in judgment, while his inconsistent policies and frequent zigzags represent desperate attempts to preserve his approach, even when it became clear that it was not achieving its intended goals. It is quite possible that if another president had been elected in 2008, US foreign policy would have been different.

It is likely that Obama's successor, regardless of party affiliation, will adopt a different and more assertive leadership style in foreign policy formulation and implementation. In the meantime, Obama will attempt to create a heritage of two major foreign policy achievements: an agreement to stop the Iranian race to acquire nuclear weapons; and a historical rapprochement with Cuba. His chance to achieve the second is greater than the first, but even so, it would not be sufficient to erase his abysmal foreign policy record.

Notes

1 Research for this study was supported by the Center for International Communication at Bar-Ilan University. The author thanks Ori Malkin, a doctoral student at the Bar-Ilan School of Communication, for his research assistance.
2 See Chapter 3 in this volume. See also: Parmar *et al.* 2014; Lynch 2012; and Quinn 2011.
3 The study is based on the presentation and analysis of polling data sponsored and produced by various organizations. Several, such as the Pew Research Center and the Chicago Council on Global Affairs, periodically conduct comprehensive surveys of US attitudes toward foreign policy and national security. Organizations such as Gallup and groups of media outlets, including the ABC News and *Washington Post* Poll (ABC/WP), the CNN and ORC Poll, the NBC News and *Wall Street Journal* Poll (NBC/WSJ), and the CBS News Poll, frequently conduct surveys on foreign policy issues. Many results of these polls are available on the polling report website (www.pollingreport.com/). An attempt has been made to construct meaningful long-term trends, which can demonstrate stability versus fluctuations in the distribution of opinions. The more valid trends are based on the same questions and answers being asked over time by the same organization, employing identical or similar samples and techniques.
4 Former secretaries of the Obama team on foreign policy and national security severely criticized both his management and policies. See: Clinton 2014; Gates 2014; and Panetta 2014.

Bibliography

Blanton, Dana. 2015. "Fox News Poll: US Can't Trust Iran, Obama Should Get Hill Approval of Deal." *Fox News*, April 1. www.foxnews.com/politics/2015/04/01/fox-news-poll-us-cant-trust-iran-obama-should-get-hill-approval-deal/.

Chesterman, Simon. 2011. "Leading From Behind: the Reasonability to Protect the Obama Doctrine and Humanitarian Intervention after Libya." *Ethics and International Affairs* 25 (3): 279–285. http://papers.ssrn.com/sol3/papers.cfm?abstract_id=1855843.

Chicago Council on Global Affairs. 2014. *Foreign Policy in the Age of Retrenchment*. Chicago: Chicago Council on Global Affairs. www.thechicagocouncil.org/publication/foreign-policy-age-retrenchment-0.

Ciulla, Lawrence. 2014. "Obama Foreign Policy Doctrine Shaped Primarily by Public Opinion." *Pipe Dream*, October 7. www.bupipedream.com/opinion/39722/obama-foreign-policy-doctrine-shaped-primarily-by-public-opinion/.

Clinton, Hillary R. 2014. *Hard Choices*. New York: Simon & Schuster.
Drezner, Daniel W. 2011. "Does Obama Have a Grand Strategy? Why We Need Doctrines in Uncertain Times." *Foreign Affairs* 90 (4). www.foreignaffairs.com/articles/67919/daniel-w-drezner/does-obama-have-a-grand-strategy.
Eichenberg, Richard. 2009. "Public Opinion and Foreign Policy in the Obama Era." *Politique Américaine* 14. http://ase.tufts.edu/polsci/faculty/eichenberg/politiqueAmericaine.pdf.
Gallup. 2011. "New Low of 26% Approve of Obama on the Economy." http://globalpublicsquare.blogs.cnn.com/2011/08/17/new-low-of-26-approve-of-obama-on-the-economy/.
Gallup. 2014a. "Afghanistan." Gallup Historical Trends. www.gallup.com/poll/116233/afghanistan.aspx.
Gallup. 2014b. "Iraq." Gallup Historical Trends. www.gallup.com/poll/1633/iraq.aspx.
Gallup. 2015a. "Presidential Ratings Issues Approval." Gallup website. www.gallup.com/poll/1726/presidential-ratings-issues-approval.aspx.
Gallup. 2015b. "Obama Job Approval." Gallup website. www.gallup.com/poll/113980/gallup-daily-obama-job-approval.aspx.
Gates, Robert. 2014. *Duty: Memoirs of a Secretary at War*. New York: Knopf.
Gelb, Leslie. H. 2012. "The Elusive Obama Doctrine." *National Interest*, Special Issue on Politics and Geopolitics, 121: 18–28. http://nationalinterest.org/article/the-elusive-obama-doctrine-7340.
Gerges, Fawaz A. 2013. "The Obama Approach to the Middle East: The End of the American Moment." *International Affairs* 89 (2): 299–323.
Gilboa, Eytan. 2008. "The Public Dimension of American–Israeli Relations: A Comparative Analysis." In Eytan Gilboa and Efraim Inbar, eds., *US–Israel Relations in a New Era: Issues and Challenges after 9/11*. London: Routledge, 53–75.
Gilboa, Eytan. 2009a. "The US and the Arab Spring." In Efraim Inbar, ed., *The Arab Spring, Democracy and Security: Domestic and International Ramifications* London: Routledge, 51–74.
Gilboa, Eytan. 2009b. "Obama and Israel: A Preliminary Assessment." *Israel Journal of Foreign Affairs* 3: 51–58.
Gilboa, Eytan. 2010. "American Public Opinion Toward Iran's Nuclear Program: Moving Towards Confrontation." *BESA Perspectives* 117. www.biu.ac.il/Besa/perspectives117.html.
Gilboa, Eytan. 2013. "Obama in Israel: Fixing American–Israeli Relations." *Israel Journal of Foreign Affairs* 7: 19–28.
Gilboa, Eytan. 2015. "On the Brink: US Israeli Relations." *Jerusalem Report*, March: 6–7.
Goldsmith, Benjamin E. 2014. "A Liberal Defense of Barack Obama's Foreign Policy." *E-International Relations*, October 6. www.e-ir.info/2014/10/06/a-liberal-defense-of-barack-obamas-foreign-policy/.
Greenstein, Fred I. 2009. "The Leadership Style of Barack Obama: An Early Assessment." *The Forum* 7 (1): article 6.
Greenstein, Fred I. 2011. "Barack Obama: The Man and His Presidency at the Midterm." *PS: Political Science & Politics* 44: 7–11.
Hart Research Associates/Public Opinion Strategies. 2015. "NBC News/Wall Street Journal Survey (Study #15110)," March. http://online.wsj.com/public/resources/documents/NBC_WSJ_MARCH_POLL.pdf.

Ignatius, David. 2014. "Obama's Foreign Policy Needs Clarity Impact." *Leaf Chronicle*, July 15. www.theleafchronicle.com/story/opinion/2014/07/16/ignatius-obamas-foreign-policy-needs-clarity-impact/12696537/.

Joffe, Josef. 2015. "The Unreality of Obama's Realpolitik: With the President Unwilling to Project US Might, Iran and Other Bad Actors Rush to Exploit the Power Vacuum." *Wall Street Journal*, 2 February. www.wsj.com/articles/josef-joffe-the-unreality-of-obamas-realpolitik-1422923777.

Kraushaar, Josh. 2015. "On Iran Obama is Ignoring Public Opinion at His Own Peril." *National Journal*, March 19. www.nationaljournal.com/against-the-grain/on-iran-obama-is-ignoring-public-opinion-at-his-own-peril-20150319.

Lakoff, Sanford. 2013. "Leading from Behind: The Obama Doctrine and US Policy in the Middle East." *Strategic Assessment* 16 (1): 7–19. www.inss.org.il/index.aspx?id=4538&articleid=2663.

Lynch, Timothy J. 2012. "Obama and the Third Bush Term: Towards a Typology of Obama Studies." *International Affairs* 88 (5): 1101–1111.

McCormick, James M. 2014. "American Foreign Policy During the Obama Administration: Insight from the Public." In I. Parmar, L.B. Miller, and M. Ledwidge, eds., *Obama and the World – New Directions in US Foreign Policy*, second edition. London and New York: Routledge, 133–148.

McCrisken, Trevor. 2011. "Ten Years On: Obama's War on Terrorism in Rhetoric and Practice." *International Affairs* 87 (4): 781–801.

Murray, Mark. 2014. "NBC/WSJ Poll: Obama's Foreign Policy Rating Plummets Even without Iraq." NBC News, June 17. www.nbcnews.com/politics/first-read/nbc-wsj-poll-obamas-foreign-policy-rating-plummets-even-without-n133461.

Newport, Frank. 2014. "Republicans Expand Edge as Better Party Against Terrorism." Gallup website, September 11. www.gallup.com/poll/175727/republicans-expand-edge-better-party-against-terrorism.aspx?utm_source=democrats%20international%20terrorism&utm_medium=search&utm_campaign=tiles.

Obama, Barack. 2007. "Renewing American Leadership." *Foreign Affairs* 86 (4): 2–16. www.foreignaffairs.com/articles/62636/barack-obama/renewing-american-leadership.

Panetta, Leon. 2014. *Worthy Fights: A Memoir of Leadership in War and Peace.* New York: Penguin.

Parmar, Inderjeet, Linda B. Miller, and Mark Ledwidge eds. 2014. *Obama and the World: New Directions in US Foreign Policy*, second edition. London and New York: Routledge.

Pew Research Center. 2013. *America's Place in the World 2013.* Washington, DC: Pew Research Center. www.people-press.org/2013/12/03/public-sees-u-s-power-declining-as-support-for-global-engagement-slips/.

Pew Research Center. 2014a. "Confidence in the US President." Pew Global Indicators Database. www.pewglobal.org/database/indicator/6/.

Pew Research Center. 2014b. "As New Dangers Loom, More Think the U.S. Does Too Little to Solve World Problems," August 28. Pew Research Center website. www.people-press.org/2014/08/28/as-new-dangers-loom-more-think-the-u-s-does-too-little-to-solve-world-problems/2/.

Pew Research Center. 2015. *More Approve than Disapprove of Iran Talks, But Most Think Iranians are "Not Serious."* Washington, DC: Pew Research Center. www.people-press.org/2015/03/30/more-approve-than-disapprove-of-iran-talks-but-most-think-iranians-are-not-serious/.

PollingReport. 2015a. "President Obama and the Obama Administration." www.pollingreport.com/obama_ad.htm.
PollingReport. 2015b. "Iran." www.pollingreport.com/iran.htm.
PollingReport. 2015c. "Israel." www.pollingreport.com/israel.htm.
PollingReport. 2015d. "Afghanistan." www.pollingreport.com/afghan.htm.
Poushter, Jacob. 2015. "Americans (Especially Republicans) Distrustful of Iran as Nuclear Deal Looms." Pew Research Center website, March 18. www.pewresearch.org/fact-tank/2015/03/18/americans-republicans-distrustful-of-iran-nuclear-deal/.
Quinn, Adam. 2011. "The Art of Declining Politely: Obama's Prudent Presidency and the Waning of American Power." *International Affairs* 87 (4): 803–824.
Rosner, Jeremy D. 2014. "Obama Can Ignore Public Opinion on Foreign Policy." *Time Magazine*, August 8. http://time.com/3093659/obama-iraq-foreign-policy-polling/.
Smeltz, Dina. 2012. *Foreign Policy in the New Millennium: Results of the 2012 Chicago Council Survey of American Public Opinion and US Foreign Policy*. Chicago: Chicago Council on Global Affairs. www.amicc.org/docs/2012_CCS_Report.pdf.
Walt, Stephen M. 2014. "Survey Says: The Chicago Council's New Report Might Have Answers as to What Americans Want When it comes to Syria, Afghanistan, and Ukraine." *Foreign Policy*, September. http://foreignpolicy.com/2014/09/26/survey-says/.

Part II
Regional perceptions

5 The United States' standing in China
Chinese attitudes toward the United States

Jian Wang

Introduction

The relationship between the United States and China is arguably the most consequential bilateral relationship of our times for both countries and beyond. Despite growing and strengthening ties, US–China relations seem more volatile and fragile than ever. Indeed, competing and conflicting interests abound between the two countries, and there are genuine differences in the policies they pursue and the values they embody. This complex bind is likely to be further complicated and tested by current and future international and domestic events. Nevertheless, the bottom line is clear: the US–China relationship is simply too consequential to be allowed to falter and fail. The cost of mishandling it would be enormous, if not disastrous, for the two populations and for the rest of the world. The crucial question then becomes how to manage the tensions and conflicts amid growing contacts between the two countries, and especially in light of China's expanding global footprint, including such new initiatives as the Silk Road Economic Belt and the 21st Century Maritime Silk Road programs.

While the two governments have publicly committed to pursuing a "positive, cooperative and comprehensive" relationship, there is nevertheless a "trust deficit" between Beijing and Washington (Lieberthal and Jisi 2012). Trust is invariably a function of risk, and the level of perceived risk is heightened in times of great uncertainty. US–China relations have always been complex and, at times, tumultuous. Amid the ups and downs of this relationship, the countries' popular perceptions of each other matter, as they form the climate of opinion in which policies and actions are considered, chosen, and pursued.

This chapter focuses on Chinese public perception of the United States in recent years. It addresses three main questions: (1) What is the importance of Chinese public perceptions for US–China relations?; (2) What are the attitudes toward the United States among the Chinese public?; and (3) How do we explain the drivers of Chinese perceptions and their potential consequences?

In this context, the public perception of a country is defined as a generalized, expressed view of the country by its foreign publics. And how we perceive other countries is by and large a function of our self-perception. Despite China's remarkable economic and social transformations over the last several decades, the country faces a host of international relations challenges, as well as internal challenges, to its continued development. A major complication in managing the US–China relationship, and indeed China's rise, is the country's uncertain domestic situation, which encompasses growing inequality, environmental degradation, mass urbanization, and ethnic strife. The forms that Chinese power will take will also in large part depend on how the Chinese public comes to see the world, and particularly how it views China's relationship with the dominant power, the United States. Given the rise of the Chinese middle class, the expanding, dynamic media and communications landscape, and an increasingly decentralized society, public opinion has assumed growing importance for a wide range of political, economic, and cultural matters in contemporary China. So the first part of this chapter examines the significance of the bilateral relationship, and the role within it of Chinese public perception of the United States.

The next part of the chapter provides a review and analysis of existing public opinion polling data on Chinese perceptions of the United States, including image salience, valence, and attributes. This part then presents a quasi-reality check, through various examples of the United States becoming a prime destination for Chinese private investment, tourism, study abroad, and entertainment.

The third and final section of the chapter is devoted to discussing the main contours of Chinese perception of the United States, in terms of its heterogeneity and stability. I infer that, despite Chinese antipathy toward certain aspects of the United States, the country's overall standing among the Chinese public has been largely positive and stable. I explain these characteristics in terms of China's mixed contemporary identities and China's evolving vision of its place in a changing world order.

Before I proceed, it is important to note the role of a country's public image in international relations. A nation's image is comprised of perceptions held by foreign publics, as well as those based on self-image. For this discussion, I focus only on the former, and consider only perceptions that are expressed as views and opinions, and are thus detectable through various representations and indicators. A country's image is also a multidimensional concept, for people may view favorably certain aspects of a country while disliking others (Katzenstein and Keohane 2007). Furthermore, the ownership of a country's image is external, rather than internal. In other words, it is about others' perceptions rather than self-perception. As Walter Lippmann put it, such opinions "are not in continual and pungent contact with the facts they profess to treat. But the feelings attached to those opinions can be even more intense than the original ideas that provoke them" (Lippman 1922, 154).

The significance of country image lies its implications for possible future actions by stakeholders, based on the salience and valence of certain country perceptions. Generally speaking, ordinary citizens do not have informed views or coherent opinions on matters related to foreign policy issues (Holsti 1991). They tend to use shortcuts, such as abstract principles and country image, to form a view on foreign policy (Johns 2009). Nor is it certain that, even in circumstances where public perception of a country is salient, there are direct and effective linkages between public opinion and policies (see, for example, Kull and Ramsay 2000; Powlick and Katz 1998; Baum and Potter 2008; Todorov and Mandisodza 2004).

While country perception does not necessarily have a direct impact on policy making, a positive perception does have "strategic value," for it creates an enabling environment in which countries may pursue their political and economic goals and policies in the global arena; while a negative image nurtures a disabling opinion environment, which threatens effective policy pursuits (Leonard 2002). This is particularly the case given the contemporary information and communication ecology, which is instantaneous and interactive. In short, a nation's image is an indicator of the strength of a country's symbolic power, which reflects and affects the nation's standing in the global arena. As Robert Jervis (1970, 6) wrote some time ago, in international relations a desired image and reputation can often be "of greater use than a significant increment of military or economic power." Joseph Nye extended E. H. Carr's notion of "power over opinion" and advanced the concept of "soft power," which he defines as a country's ability to get what it wants through appeal and attraction (Nye 2004). Overall then, foreign perceptions of a country form a crucial element in the symbolic domain of its power.

Why does Chinese public perception matter?

In both academic literature and think tank analysis, there is general consensus on the centrality of US–China relations, in spite of constant headline-grabbing events and conflicts from other parts of the world. And the consensus spans a broad spectrum of political ideologies and orientations. As Henry Kissinger asserts, "The relationship between China and the United States has become a central element in the quest for world peace and global wellbeing" (Kissinger 2011, xvi). Making a similar point, Andrew Nathan and Andrew Scobell observe that

> China has become one of a small number of countries that have significant national interests in every part of the world.... And perhaps most important, China is the only country widely seen as a possible threat to US predominance.
>
> (Nathan and Scobell 2012, 32)

As they also note, managing the fraught bilateral relationship is Beijing's foremost foreign policy challenge (ibid., 33). Likewise, managing the rise of China, as Ashley J. Tellis argues, "remains the central geopolitical challenge facing the United States" (Tellis 2012, 75). Kishore Mahbubani has sounded a similar note, as he writes, "[i]n geopolitics, the most important relationship is always between the world's greatest power (today America) and the world's greatest emerging power (today China)" (Mahbubani 2013, 147). John Ikenberry states that "it is not exaggeration to say that US–China relations, more than any other bilateral relationship, will shape the overall character of twenty-first-century world politics" (Ikenberry 2012). Meanwhile, most acknowledge that the relationship is also a complex one. As David Shambaugh writes, "[t]hese two titans are tangled together in innumerable ways – strategically, diplomatically, economically, socially, culturally, environmentally, regionally, internationally, educationally, and in many other domains" (Shambaugh 2012, 3).

Taken together, the United States and China represent one-fourth of the world's population, one-third of the economic output, one-fourth of global trade, over 40 percent of CO_2 emission, and nearly half of the world's defense spending (see US–China Bi-National Commission on Trust-Building and Enhancing Relations 2014). The two countries have a disproportionate impact globally. It is not difficult to understand why the relationship between the two countries matters a great deal to others.

Competition and rivalry between the United States and China appear inevitable. Their relationship is generally framed as that of a rising power challenging an incumbent power, with variant analytical thrusts and interpretations. There are basically three scenarios in the relationship outcome: a zero-sum game; a win-win situation; and a negative-sum scenario.

Most of the attention has been focused on the zero-sum outcome. The conceptual expectation when a rising power (China) challenges a sitting power (the United States) is one of security competition and military conflict, because the dominant power will naturally resist the rising power's drive to overtake its incumbent position. Many have pointed to historical precedents to demonstrate that military conflict is inevitable in such power transition, with the exception of the United States' replacement of Britain in the first part of the twentieth century. After all, the United States and China have different histories, political systems, and cultural norms. Indeed, such a belief is shared in both countries. To the Chinese, the United States is a revisionist power that "seeks to curtail China's political influence and harm China's interests" (Nathan and Scobell 2012, 33).

On the other hand, the liberal-internationalist school of thought contends that the dynamics of international order have changed fundamentally, in light of the unprecedented globalization facilitated by widespread, instantaneous communication technologies and the emergence and diversification of global actors. There are more incentives and opportunities for countries to cooperate than to compete and destroy. In the US–China case, James Steinberg and Michael O'Hanlon have argued, "The lack of intense ideological competition, as well as the absence of bilateral territorial disputers or imperial ambitions by either side, suggest grounds for hope" (Steinberg and O'Hanlon 2014, 13). The two countries are far more interconnected and interdependent than most tend to realize, through commerce and culture, a trend which is only growing. This provides the basis for John Ikenberry's argument that

> China will find itself increasingly rising up *within* the existing international order – rather than rising up and challenging this order from the outside. The United States and China will compete for power and influence, but they will do so within a structural setting shaped by liberal and Westphalian systems.
>
> (Ikenberry 2012, 57)

As Lee Kuan Yew observed, "Sino-US relations are both cooperative and competitive. Competition between them is inevitable, but conflict is not" (Allison *et al.* 2013, 38). This view is mirrored in Chinese discourse and visions of the US–China relationship. According to Andrew Nathan and Andrew Scobell's (2012) analysis, the mainstream opinion in China is not to challenge the United States in the foreseeable future, for the United States will remain the dominant superpower despite its relative decline.

Whether one holds a deterministic view or a more optimistic view, the key challenge remains how to manage tensions and conflicts effectively between the two countries. The United States has pursued a mixed strategy of containment and engagement toward China since the end of the Cold War. The two-pronged policy of "congagement" – military containment and economic engagement – has enjoyed bipartisan support; but is also seen as a paradoxical tangle and, in Justin Logan's (2013) words, a "hopeless contradiction." The United States cannot have it both ways, making China more powerful through economic engagement while at the same time seeking to contain its power and influence. Lee Kuan Yew also pointed out, "You cannot say you will engage China on some issues and isolate her over others. You cannot mix your signals" (Allison *et al.* 2013, 46).

The Obama administration has continued with this general policy orientation. It reflects an increasingly common view that the US–China relationship will be characterized by "a blend of cooperation, competition, and discord" (Harding 2012). Most importantly, as Harry Harding argues, the outcomes of these scenarios will depend on

> the two countries' definition and prioritization of their national interests, their ability to identify common goals and to work together to advance them, and their skill at managing the differences in interests and values that could foster competition or conflict.
>
> (Harding 2012, 389)

At the same time, the Obama administration's China policy does have a sharpening focus on the Asia-Pacific region through its "strategic pivot to Asia" initiative, later rephrased as "rebalancing toward Asia" to avoid misinterpretation in terms of implied US military intentions. China has not been invited to join the Trans-Pacific Partnership, a pan-Asia-Pacific free trade pact, in which the United States is playing a leading role. As Mark Landler wrote in the *New York Times*, "America's eastward shift has left the Chinese deeply suspicious of American motives, with some analysts in China arguing that the United States is trying to encircle the country" (Landler 2012). While Obama's China policy embodies consistent themes in the United States' China policy over the past couple of decades, it is certainly not viewed in China, among elites and the general public, as being more cooperative or pro-Chinese than before. In the Chinese view, containment has been a constant in the United States' relations with China as the latter's relative power grows, but containment is not necessarily always the most salient element. For example, the most contentious issue in the bilateral relationship was previously Taiwan, but this issue has receded in prominence and significance for the Chinese. In other words, the bilateral relationship in spheres beyond security matters is also critical in shaping Chinese perceptions of the United States.

Needless to say, there are many complications in managing this complex relationship. Chief among them are the geopolitical uncertainties in regions where the two countries' interests and values diverge and may collide. The disputes in the South and East China Seas in recent years are illustrative of such challenges.

Within the United States, the "crisis of becoming number two" will become more acute. US leaders and populations alike are not prepared for the impending reality that the US economy will be superseded by China's in the near future, given the likely continuation of China's growth trajectory. Kishore Mahbubani writes, "When Americans finally wake up to the realization that their economy is number two in the world, it is more than likely that an acrimonious debate will begin with the famous question 'Who lost America's number one spot?'" (Mahbubani 2013, 158). Such a scenario will put enormous pressure on domestic policy debates, and will surely be less conducive to effectively managing the relationship. However, it should be noted that China's continued rise is not preordained. As Ashley J. Tellis observes, "Although US–China relations will continue to embody the inherent contradiction where Beijing's rise is sustained by an international order subsidized by Washington, it must be remembered that China's definitive success as an emerging power is not yet certain" (Tellis 2012, 81). The most important uncertainty remains within China. China's modernization strategy is anchored around loosening top-down, central command over all aspects of the society. Although the government retains control over ideology and politics, its relative loss of control means that it is in greater need of public legitimacy; hence the growing importance of public opinion.[1] The country faces grave challenges internally to maintain domestic stability and regime legitimacy. For example, the following four issues heighten domestic tensions and threaten internal stability.

First is the growing social and economic inequality in light of rampant, systemic corruption. Despite the remarkable overall increase in wealth among Chinese people, China's Gini coefficient – a widely used indicator of economic inequality – has grown from 0.45, 20 years ago, to 0.73 in 2012 (Kaiman 2014). According to a 2013 Pew Research Center survey (Poushter 2013), inflation, corruption, and inequality are the top three concerns of the Chinese public, followed by air pollution, water pollution, and food safety. More than half of the survey respondents (53 percent) viewed corrupt officials as a major problem. About the same proportion (52 percent) was concerned about the rich–poor gap. The current Xi Jinping administration has launched a major anti-corruption drive, purging some of the highly placed officials. The crackdown has helped Xi to consolidate his power base, but it is also evident that the government is acting on an issue that has broad public resonance within China.

The second potential threat to regime stability is environmental degradation. China's economic growth over the last several decades has exacted a huge cost in the quality of air, water, and soil. As noted in the Council on Foreign Relations' report, 'China's Environmental Crisis',

> As the world's largest source of carbon emissions, China is responsible for a third of the planet's greenhouse gas output and has sixteen of the world's twenty most polluted cities. Life expectancy in the north has decreased by 5.5 years due to air pollution, and severe water contamination and scarcity have compounded land deterioration problems. Environmental degradation ... has also bruised China's international standing as the country expands its global influence, and endangered its stability as the ruling party faces increasing media scrutiny and public discontent.
>
> (Xu 2014; see also *The Economist* 2013)

The third problem facing China domestically is mass urbanization and the associated demographic challenge, in part as a consequence of the "one-child" policy implemented in the 1980s. In 2011, for the first time in Chinese history, more people lived in cities than in countryside. According to a report by the Chinese Academy of Social Sciences, by 2030 China will become the world's most aged society, with a high proportion of people over 65 (People's Daily Online 2010). Such a demographic composition will slow down per-capita economic growth. How to create job opportunities for the massive urban population while at the same time maintaining high productivity will present a severe challenge to government policy and domestic stability.

A fourth source of domestic instability lies in ethnic strife in the western regions of China, especially Tibet and Xinjiang. The most salient ethnic tensions and violence are those between the dominant Han group, Tibetans, and Uighurs, and are rooted in economic, cultural, and political causes. The manifestations of such ethnic discord are no longer restricted to the western part of China where most Tibetans and Uighurs reside; it has periodically spread to major urban centers elsewhere.

All four of these issues exist within a fast-changing, more decentralized China, with the world's largest emerging middle class – projected to reach 700 million in 2020 (Euromonitor 2007), double the size of the US population – and the world's largest digital social media space. In short, the domestic situation is in flux and is volatile. The regime's internal legitimacy and, by extension, China's overall prospects are indeterminate.

Meanwhile, China's international identity is also in flux. An understanding of the shifts in China's world view over time is essential here. For most of its history, China did not have a national identity per se, let alone an international one. It saw the world as an extension of itself, and prided itself on its cultural superiority to all other states, reflected in its tributary system. But this conception of the world was shattered with the incursions of foreign powers into China in the mid-nineteenth century and the resultant political turmoil. China entered the phase generally called the "Century of Humiliation," which lasted from the First Opium War of 1840–1842 to the establishment of the People's Republic of China in 1949. The country barely "limped along in the international system"; it was neither a Western colony like India, nor a modernized state like Japan (Scott 2008, 2). China's remarkable socioeconomic achievements in recent decades have ushered in a new phase, signaling a re-emergent, more confident China. Yet the country is still characterized by an interplay of pride and humiliation (Callahan 2010). Such complex and conflicting feelings are also present in the Chinese public's view of the country's international relations. In the case of the US–China relations, unlike China's relations with Japan, there is a lack of "legacies of episodes of contention" or traumatic historical experiences that become a "more or less permanent ideational feature" of the bilateral relations (McAdam 2007).

China now needs to address a host of international relations challenges to create a favorable, secure environment for the country's development. The Xi administration has outlined its foreign policy strategy, comprising: neighborhood diplomacy (secure, friendly neighbors); a sound, stable framework for major-country relations; strengthening relations with developing countries; and advancing multilateral diplomacy (Xinhuanet 2014).

In short, the twin sources of Chinese regime legitimacy are rising living standards and nationalism. Continuing to improve the living standards of ordinary Chinese requires the country to sustain and expand economic engagement with others, chief among them the United States. Meanwhile, the US military containment policy toward China activates intense nationalistic sentiments among the Chinese public. These considerations put contradictory pressures on the bilateral relations.[2] Given a fragile domestic situation and an equally challenging international environment, Chinese public perceptions and attitudes concerning the dominant power – the United States – become ever more relevant. In other words, a positive perception of the United States by the Chinese public creates an enabling environment in which both countries can pursue political and economic goals and policies; whereas a hostile Chinese public perception puts pressure on both governments' diplomatic stance, leaving less wiggle room for policy maneuver and implementation.

What are Chinese public perceptions of the United States?

How, then, is the United States viewed by the Chinese public? Country image, a generalized public perception of a country, can be assessed and analyzed in a variety of ways, including: public opinion polling; public discourse, such as mediated representations in news, literature, pop culture, and cultural artifacts; and country-of-origin associations with businesses and products. For this discussion, we examine public opinion polls at the aggregate level, which provide a good indication of how the United States and its relationship with China have been viewed by the Chinese public. Granted, public opinion polling is not a tidy business. Results and their interpretation depend on a variety of factors, such as sampling type and quality, how questions are constructed, and the broader social and historical context in which the polls are undertaken. Polls in China are typically taken in major cities, thus only representing Chinese citizens from urban centers. Nevertheless, when conducted well and over a long period of time, polls are useful for helping us understand the basic contours and patterns of mass attitudes and sentiments.

The overview presented here provides a snapshot of the tacit knowledge people have of another country. Specifically, we highlight three areas of public perception: favorability rating; views of the United States' global role; and views of US soft power. We mainly rely on several prominent surveys, and on surveys that have been analyzed by academic scholars. The questions were phrased in different ways across these surveys, thus providing multiple angles for examining the Chinese public's perceptions of the United States.[3]

Before discussing the polling results, it is important to situate this review in its historical context. The Chinese popular perception of the United States has gone through many different phases, against the backdrop of changing international relations dynamics and changes to China's own foreign policy. During World War II and before the founding of the People's Republic, the United States was China's ally and friend. During the first two decades of the People's Republic, the United States was viewed as an imperialist power and a superpower in competition with the other superpower, the Soviet Union. The end of the Cold War marked the United States' hegemonic power status. Over the last decade, the United States has remained the dominant power in an increasingly distributed international system, with China's ascent at the forefront. Wang Jisi (2005) aptly captures the vicissitudes of the Chinese public perception of the United States since 1949: a paper tiger to be defeated by the worldwide anti-imperialist alliance; a superpower locked in ideological and security struggle with the Soviet Union; an inspiration for China's modernization project; and an opponent to China's rise. In contemporary times, the Chinese public generally believes the United States is the most important country for China, both currently and in the foreseeable future, well ahead of Russia, the European Union, and Japan.

Favorability ratings

The Pew Global Attitudes surveys show that over the last decade favorable Chinese views of the United States have fluctuated within the 30 percent to 50 percent range. In the last two years, for instance, the ratings were 40 percent in 2013 and 50 percent in 2014 (slightly below the median positive rating of about 60 percent among the 44 countries surveyed).[4] The 2012 Committee of 100[5] survey found that there was substantial distrust among the Chinese public of the United States, with 56 percent of the Chinese respondents indicating that China should trust the United States only a little or not at all. In reviewing the Beijing-based Horizon Group's surveys between 2001 and 2009, Chuanjie Zhang (2011) found that the Chinese general perception of the United States was rather consistent, with a practical view of the US–China relationship standing somewhere between friendship and enmity. The one difference noted in the review is that general Chinese impressions of the United States have diversified over the years, from an impression of wealth and power to also include more politically related feelings (Zhang 2011, 19). A series of surveys of Beijing residents between 1998 and 2004 found that the overall amity toward the United States declined from more than 60 (based on a 0–100 scale) in 1998 to less than 40 in 2004, and that attitudes toward US foreign policy were substantially negative; while those with higher socioeconomic status and better education tended to view the United States more favorably (Johnston and Stockmann 2007).

Views of the United States' global role

Since 2005, the BBC has conducted an annual survey to gauge the global public's view of various countries' influence in the world. Over the last ten years, Chinese respondents have consistently viewed the United States' influence as mainly negative. In 2005, 62 percent of the Chinese respondents said that US influence was negative (and only 22 percent said positive). The most recent poll shows the negative response at 59 percent (as against 18 percent positive). In between these years, the negative numbers have fluctuated in the range of 40 percent to 50 percent.[6] According to the 2014 Pew Global Attitudes survey, when asked "How much does the Unites States take into account China's interests?," Chinese respondents were quite divided: half of them said "a great deal" or "a fair amount", while 44 percent reported "not too much" or "not at all." The same survey also shows that the majority of Chinese (55 percent) still view the United States as the world's leading economic power, as compared to the global median of 45 percent. On the other hand, 59 percent of Chinese respondents believed that China will eventually replace or has replaced the United States as superpower.[7]

Views of US soft power

The Chinese public is receptive to many aspects of US soft power and holds favorable views toward US technology and business, and toward its democratic values. For instance, a comparison of the Pew polling results in 2007 and 2012 shows that the Chinese admired the United States' technological and scientific advances (80 percent in 2007; 73 percent in 2012). The Chinese also liked US ways of doing business (49 percent in 2007; 43 percent in 2012). With regard to US popular culture (music, movies, and television), the views were quite split. In 2007, 42 percent said they liked US popular culture, while 46 percent disliked it. In 2012, an equal number of respondents (43 percent each) said they liked or disliked US popular culture. It is interesting to note that US ideas about democracy were well received. In 2007, 48 percent of Chinese respondents indicated their liking for US-style democracy (as opposed to 36 percent indicating dislike). The positive view of US-style democracy increased to 52 percent in 2012. Likewise, in 2007, 38 percent of the Chinese respondents thought it was a good idea (in contrast to 39 percent saying a bad idea) for US ideas and customs to spread in China. In 2012, the positive view grew to 43 percent while concerns decreased to 34 percent.[8]

In comparing two surveys conducted by the Chinese Academy of Social Sciences, which polled elite segments of the Chinese public in 2001 and 2004 respectively, Mei Zhao found the respondents' views of the United States were mixed and varied: "the most prominent characteristic of Chinese views of America is love-hate ambivalence" (Zhao 2005, 62). Such a pattern is confirmed by other surveys over the years. As noted in an analysis of Chinese youth perception of the United States based on Horizon Group data from 2000 to 2009, "[m]any have gradually established a positive opinion of the United States in the general sense, and have great confidence in the Sino-US bilateral relationship, while at the same time having huge concerns that the United States will pose a worrisome threat in the future" (Jiang *et al.* 2011, 61).

The United States as a destination for investment, tourism, and study

The Chinese public's largely ambivalent views aside, the United States has become a go-to destination for Chinese private investment, tourism, and study abroad. There has been an influx of Chinese investment in the United States, growing from $58 million in 2000 to $14 billion in 2013, with investment ranging from acquisitions of companies to residential real estate (Gusovsky 2014). The motivations for Chinese investment in the United States are varied, and include: Chinese companies want to be closer to their US customers; wages in China have been rising; changes in the Chinese model of growth; and a sense that investment in the United States is protected (see, for example, Wallace 2015). The fact that Chinese private investors have excess savings in their home country is an important driver. In 2013, Chinese émigrés accounted for 80 percent of the US government's EB-5 investor visa program, which grants US residency status to individuals investing $1 million in the United States (Cole 2014). It is noteworthy that the number of investment visas issued to wealthy Chinese individuals has more than doubled over the past few years.

The United States is also now a major destination for Chinese tourists. In 2013, the United States received 1.8 million Chinese tourists. Although China ranked seventh in the overall arrivals market, it posted the strongest annual growth (23 percent). In terms of visitor spending, Chinese tourists spent nearly $9.8 billion, making China the sixth-biggest spender country in the United States. The year set a record in Chinese visitor spending, on the heels of four consecutive years of double-digital growth (US Department of Commerce 2013).

In international education, China is the largest supplier of foreign students to the United States, with 274,000 Chinese students studying in the United States during the 2013–2014 academic year, while India came in a distant second (103,000). Chinese student enrollment grew by 16 percent over the prior year (Institute of International Education 2014). And unlike two decades ago, the vast majority of Chinese students are self-financed, and benefit from the increasing levels of acceptance of international students at state universities. Most are degree-seeking students and tend to have a broader cultural experience in the United States than short-term language students. There is also a substantial number of students coming to the United States at the pre-collegiate level.

US popular culture in China

The US brand of popular culture continues to be attractive to Chinese audiences. As China is poised to become the largest film market in the world by 2020, US films and television shows are drawing in bigger Chinese audiences. In 2014, the number-one box office hit in China was *Transformers: Age of Extinction*. Among the top ten highest-grossing films, five were Hollywood productions: *Transformers: Age of Extinction*; *Interstellar*; *X-Men: Days of Future Past*; *Captain America: The Winter Soldier*; and *Dawn of the Planet of the Apes* (Box Office Mojo 2014).

Despite Chinese censorship and restrictions, US TV series have found many fans in China. The Netflix series 'House of Cards' was released in February 2014 on China's leading video site Sohu and received 103 million views by the year's end, more than double Netflix' global subscriber base (Jiang 2015). Other shows make their way into China through pirate channels. Even "The Daily Show" with Jon Stewart, a political satire show from the US Comedy Central channel, has been widely popular in China (Liu 2014).

In addition, the US NBA is one of the most popular brands in China, with 70 million followers on Sina Weibo and Tencent's microblog platforms. It recently signed a five-year deal to carry the league's content with China's digital powerhouse Tencent, worth $500 million (Sin 2014). Another Chinese online platform LeTV has reached an agreement to stream PAC-12 men's basketball games in China (Frater 2015). In sum, there is ample evidence to suggest that the Chinese public is attracted to the United States in a wide range of areas, from popular culture to tourism and private investment.

Summary and conclusion

Based on the above discussion, we can identify three features of how the United States is viewed by the Chinese public. First, Chinese perceptions of the United States are diverse and multidimensional. The Chinese public form views on wide-ranging aspects of the United States, from security and political ideology to economy and culture. There is no one single theme that dominates contemporary Chinese perceptions of the United States. Such heterogeneity is similar to the multidimensional perceptions of the United States in some other regions (see examples in Katzenstein and Keohane 2007).

Second, there is a divergence in the perception of US foreign policy and international behavior vis-à-vis the United States as a society and culture. This pattern is also found in other countries (ibid.). The Chinese tend to view negatively the United States' global role, along with aspects of US policy toward China that are perceived as aiming to curtail China's growth. On the other hand, US values, business, technology, and culture are held in high regard. The Chinese encounter with US values and soft power assets does not seem to provoke broad public anxiety or fear. On the contrary, there is behavioral preference for US offerings when it comes to investment, travel, study, and entertainment. In short, despite such ambivalence, these contrasting views and feelings do not seem to create problems for the Chinese; in fact, the seemingly incoherent generalized views toward the United States are compartmentalized and coexist.

Third, Chinese perceptions of the United States have been generally consistent and stable over the last decade. There have been fluctuations in popular sentiments toward the United States, most probably influenced by news events at the times of the surveys. Such relative stability reflects the basic assumptions and collective beliefs the Chinese public have about the United States as a country and China's relationship with it. As Wang Jisi has pointed out,

> China's image of the United States is to a great extent its mirror image, and reflects its own national aspirations, identity, traits, and culture. In fact, China's changing image of the United States is more the result of changing Chinese realities than changing US realities.
>
> (Wang 2005, 19)

In this regard, mixed and shifting Chinese identities shape Chinese perceptions of the United States. Contemporary China defies simple categorization. It exhibits multiple identities: China is both a developed and developing economy; socialist/communist and capitalist; modern and traditional; urban and rural. These contrasting and competing identities are often fraught with tension. For the Chinese public, the United States serves as an inspiration for China's own modernization aspirations, as the country strives for prosperity and strength to regain global prominence and respectability. Hence the Chinese public react negatively if they perceive that other countries, and the United States in this case, are pursuing policies and practices that aim to stem China's growth.

Public opinion in China plays a growing role in Chinese foreign policy making. As Yufan Hao observes, these days there are a host of actors and forces that seek to influence foreign policy outcomes, including

> netizens on the internet, the mass media, opinion makers both in the media and in the academic community, technocrats within the bureaucratic apparatus, random public opinion, think tanks and research institutions, the business community, and other sub-national entities within Chinese society.
>
> (Hao 2012, 129)

Furthermore, public opinion in China can play two roles: one is that the government gauges public opinion as part of the policymaking process; the other is for policymakers to mobilize public opinion in support of policy positions (ibid., 138). Since the US–China relationship is one of the most prominent foreign policy matters, we expect the Chinese government (as well as the US government) to pay close attention to how the United States is viewed by ordinary Chinese citizens, and to manage policy positions in the context of the opinion environment. At times the differences between the

United States and China may be overstated. Despite differing political ideologies, both countries have demonstrated pragmatism in addressing differences and conflicts.

This review also raises several theoretical concerns. The public opinion polls we typically rely on for assessing country perceptions are conventional polls, while there are now analytical tools that enable us to assess online opinions toward issues and countries. We often find more strident anti-US sentiments in the Chinese online space. But the issue of how we should make sense of the relationship between standard opinion polls and online sentiment analysis is both a conceptual question and an empirical challenge. Moreover, as noted earlier, country perceptions by the general public are often diffuse and ephemeral, and are affected by news of the day. Among the often multidimensional perceptions, which are more crucial in affecting the policy environment? Is it when these country perceptions are emotionalized and moralized, for instance? The underlying analytical challenge remains: to understand how country perception constrains or facilitates policy making and implementation. A comparative analysis of the role of country perception in bilateral relations between Japan–China and US–China may be illuminating. Anecdotal evidence suggests that in the Sino-Japanese relations Chinese public perceptions of Japan do put a limit on the Chinese government's policy maneuver. Finally, as bilateral relations more often than not take place in a multilateral context, and as countries such as China increasingly engage in multilateral diplomacy, this kind of bilateral analysis needs to be cast in the broader multilateral framework.

Notes

1 The author thanks the article reviewer for suggestions.
2 The author is grateful for the suggestions made by the article reviewer.
3 Most of these surveys focus on the content and structure of perceptions and attitudes, rather than on intensity.
4 See polling results from various years at the Pew Global Attitudes website, www.pewglobal.org/.
5 The Committee of 100 is an advocacy group made up of prominent Chinese American citizens, with the goal of advancing Chinese–US causes and furthering US–China relations. From time to time it commissions opinion surveys on US–China relations. See www.committee100.org/.
6 See various polls by the BBC and GlobalScan, www.globescan.com/.
7 See Pew Global Attitudes and Trends website, www.pewglobal.org/.
8 See Pew Global Attitudes and Trends website, www.pewglobal.org/.

Bibliography

Allison, Graham, Robert D. Blackwill, Ali Wyne, and Henry A. Kissinger. 2013. *Lee Kuan Yew: The Grand Master's Insights on China, the United States, and the World.* Cambridge, MA: MIT Press.

Baum, Matthew A., and Philip B.K. Potter. 2008. "The Relationships Between Mass Media, Public Opinion, and Foreign Policy: Toward a Theoretical Synthesis." *Annual Review of Political Science* 11: 39–65.

Box Office Mojo. 2014. "China Yearly Box Office 2014." www.boxofficemojo.com/intl/china/yearly/?yr=2014&p=.htm.

Callahan, William A. 2010. *China: The Pessoptimist Nation*. Oxford: Oxford University Press.

Cole, Michael. 2014. "Wealthy Chinese Accounted for 80 percent of US Investor Visas in 2013." Forbes, May 13. www.forbes.com/sites/michaelcole/2014/05/13/wealthy-chinese-accounted-for-80-of-u-s-investor-visas-in-2013/.

Economist. 2013. "China and the Environment: The East Is Grey," August 10. www.economist.com/node/21583245/print.

Euromonitor International. 2007. "China's Middle Class Reaches 80 Million," July 25. http://blog.euromonitor.com/2007/07/chinas-middle-class-reaches-80-million.html.

Frater, Patrick. 2015. "China's LeTV to Stream US Basketball Season." *Variety*, February 11. http://variety.com/2015/digital/news/chinas-letv-to-stream-u-s-basketball-season-1201430910/.

Gusovsky, Dina. 2014. "Why Chinese money is flooding American markets." CNBC, September 17. www.cnbc.com/id/102001876#.

Hao, Yufan. 2012. "Domestic Chinese Influence on US–China Relations." In David Shambaugh, ed., *Tangled Titans: The United States and China*. Lanham, MD: Rowman & Littlefield, 129.

Harding, Harry. 2012. "American Visions of the Future of US–China Relations: Competition, Cooperation, and Conflict." In David Shambaugh, ed., *Tangled Titans: The United States and China*. Lanham, MD: Rowman & Littlefield, 389.

Holsti, Kalevi J. 1991. *Change in the International System: Essays on the Theory and Practice of International Relations*. Brookfield, VT: Edward Elgar.

Ikenberry, G. John. 2012. "The Rise of China, the United States, and the Future of the Liberal International Order." In David Shambaugh, ed., *Tangled Titans: The United States and China*. Lanham, MD: Rowman & Littlefield, 53–74.

Institute of International Education. 2014. "Open Doors 2014 Data." www.iie.org/Research-and-Publications/Open-Doors.

Jervis, Robert. 1970. *The Logic of Images in International Relations*. Princeton, NJ: Princeton University Press.

Jiang, Changjian, Shen Min, and Ju Hong. 2011. "The United States in Chinese Students' Eyes." In Douglas G. Spelman, ed., *The United States and China: Mutual Public Perceptions*. Washington, DC: Wilson Center, 61.

Jiang, Steven. 2015. "The End or To Be Continued? Top US TV Shows Face Uncertain Fate in China." CNN, January 2. www.cnn.com/2014/12/28/world/asia/china-tv-shows/.

Xinhuanet. 2014. "Xi Eyes More Enabling International Environment for China's Peaceful Development," November 30. http://news.xinhuanet.com/english/china/2014-11/30/c_133822694.htm.

Johns, Robert. 2009. "Tracing Foreign Policy Decisions: A Study of Citizens' Use of Heuristics." *British Journal of Politics and International Relations* 11: 574–592.

Johnston, Alastair Iain, and Daniela Stockmann. 2007. "Chinese Attitudes Toward the United States and Americans." In Peter J. Katzenstein and Robert O. Keohane, eds., *Anti-Americanisms in World Politics*. Ithaca, NY: Cornell University Press, 157–195.

Kaiman, Jonathan. 2014. "China Gets Richer But More Unequal." *Guardian*, July 28. www.theguardian.com/world/2014/jul/28/china-more-unequal-richer.

Katzenstein, Peter J., and Robert O. Keohane. 2007. "Varieties of Anti-Americanism: A Framework for Analysis." In Peter J. Katzenstein and Robert O. Keohane, eds., *Anti-Americanisms in World Politics*. Ithaca, NY: Cornell University Press.

Katzenstein, Peter J., and Robert O. Keohane, eds. 2007. *Anti-Americanisms in World Politics*. Ithaca, NY: Cornell University Press.

Kissinger, Henry. 2011. *On China*. New York: Penguin.

Kull, Steven, and Clay Ramsay. 2000. "Challenging US Policymakers' Image of an Isolationist Public." *International Studies Perspectives* 1 (1): 105–117.

Landler, Mark. 2012. "Obama's Journey to Tougher Tack on a Rising China." *New York Times*, September 20.

Leonard, Mark. 2002. *Public Diplomacy*. London: Foreign Policy Center.

Lieberthal, Kenneth, and Wang Jisi. 2012. "Addressing US–China Strategic Distrust". John L. Thornton China Center Monograph Series, number 4.

Lippmann, Walter. 1922. *Public Opinion*. New York: Harcourt, Brace and Company, Inc.

Liu, Chaoran. 2014. "Not Lost in Translation: Why Is Jon Stewart Popular in China?" *CPD Monitor* 5 (3). http://uscpublicdiplomacy.org/pdin_monitor_article/not-lost-translation-why-jon-stewart-popular-china.

Logan, Justin. 2013. "China, America, and the Pivot to Asia." *Cato Institute Policy Analysis* 717.

Mahbubani, Kishore. 2013. *The Great Convergence: Asia, the West, and the Logic of One World*. New York: PublicAffairs.

McAdam, Doug. 2007. "Legacies of Anti-Americanism: A Sociological Perspective." In Peter J. Katzenstein, and Robert O. Keohane, eds., *Anti-Americanisms in World Politics*. Ithaca, NY: Cornell University Press, 251–269.

Nathan, Andrew, and Andrew Scobell. 2012. "How China Sees America." *Foreign Affairs* 91 (5): 32–47.

Nye, Joseph S. Jr. 2004. *Soft Power: The Means to Success in World Politics*. New York: PublicAffairs.

People's Daily Online. 2010. "China's Percentage of Elderly Highest in 2030," September 12. http://en.people.cn/90001/90776/90882/7137446.html.

Poushter, Jacob. 2013. "Inflation, Corruption, Inequality Top List of Chinese Public's Concerns." Pew Research Center, November 8. www.pewresearch.org/fact-tank/2013/11/08/inflation-corruption-inequality-top-list-of-chinese-publics-concerns/.

Powlick, Philip J., and Andrew Z. Katz. 1998. "Defining the American Public Opinion/Foreign Policy Nexus." *Mershon International Studies Review* 42 (1): 29–61.

Scott, David. 2008. *China and the International System, 1840–1949: Power, Presence, and Perceptions in a Century of Humiliation*. Albany, NY: State University of New York Press.

Shambaugh, David. 2012. "Tangled Titans: Conceptualizing the US–China Relationship." In David Shambaugh, ed., *Tangled Titans: The United States and China*. Lanham, MD: Rowman & Littlefield, 3.

Sin, Ben. 2014. "NBA Looks to Asia for Next Growth Spurt." *New York Times*, March 14. www.nytimes.com/2014/03/15/business/international/nba-looks-to-asia-for-next-growth-spurt.html?_r=0.

Steinberg, James, and Michael O'Hanlon. 2014. *Strategic Reassurance and Resolve: US–China Relations in the Twenty-First Century*. Princeton, NJ: Princeton University Press.

Tellis, Ashley J. 2012. "US–China Relations in a Realist World." In David Shambaugh, ed., *Tangled Titans: The United States and China*. Lanham, MD: Rowman & Littlefield, 75–102.

Todorov, Alexander, and Anesu N. Mandisodza. 2004. "Public Opinion on Foreign Policy: The Multilateral Public that Perceives Itself as Unilateral." *Public Opinion Quarterly* 68 (3): 323–348.

US Department of Commerce. 2013. "Top 10 International Markets: 2013 Visitation and Spending." http://travel.trade.gov/pdf/2013-Top-10-Markets.pdf.

US–China Bi-National Commission on Trust-Building and Enhancing Relations. 2014. "Building U.S.-China Trust through Next Generation People, Platforms & Programs." USC Annenberg School for Communication and Journalism, and Peking University School of International Studies. http://uschinaexchange.usc.edu/sites/default/files/us-china-trust-2014.pdf.

Wallace, Lewis. 2015. "A Look Inside the Fuyao Glass Factory – And Why Chinese Companies Are Coming To The US," WYSO, February 12. http://wyso.org/post/look-inside-fuyao-glass-factory-and-why-chinese-companies-are-coming-us.

Wang, Jisi. 2005. "From Paper Tiger to Real Leviathan: China's Images of the United States since 1949." In Carola McGiffert, ed., *Chinese Images of the United States*. Washington, DC: CSIS Press, 9–22.

Xu, Beina. 2014. "China's Environmental Crisis." Council on Foreign Relations, April 25. www.cfr.org/china/chinas-environmental-crisis/p12608.

Zhang, Chuanjie. 2011. "Chinese Citizens' Attitudes toward the United States 2001–2009." In Douglas G. Spelman, ed., *The United States and China: Mutual Public Perceptions*. Washington, DC: Wilson Center, 17–25.

Zhao, Mei. 2005. "Chinese Views of America: A Survey." In Carola McGiffert, ed., *Chinese Images of the United States*. Washington, DC: CSIS Press, 62.

6 Seoul–Washington alliance
The beginning of independence?

Alon Levkowitz

President Barack Obama has repeatedly reiterated that the United States is committed to South Korea's security. In his meeting with South Korean President Park Geun-hye at the White House on May 7, 2013, he declared: "The commitment of the United States to the Republic of Korea will never waver" (Crabtree 2013). His statement demonstrated Washington's commitment to the defense of the Republic of Korea and the important interests that Washington shares with Seoul. Washington has stated many times that it sees South Korea as an important ally, and as a strategic and economic partner in Asia (Manyin *et al.* 2014).

During the same visit to Washington, President Park Geun-hye said: "Building on the extraordinary accomplishments of the last 60 years, we are determined to embark on another shared journey toward peace in the Korean Peninsula, toward cooperation in Northeast Asia, and finally, toward prosperity around the world" (Lee 2013). When Park hosted Barack Obama on April 25, 2014, he said: "Of all the US presidents, the number of his visits to Korea has outnumbered that of his predecessors. This reflects President Obama's special interest in Korea, and his full commitment to further strengthening the US–ROK alliance" (President's News Conference, April 25, 2014).

In his words, President Park stresses the importance of the US alliance not only for Korea, but for Northeast Asia as a whole. The statements by both presidents emphasize the importance of the relations between Seoul and Washington, and the central role played by the alliance between them, not only in military terms, but also in terms of economic growth and regional prosperity.

South Korean public opinion polls also show that support for US–South Korean relations is relatively high, and even that the support for President Obama is 10 percent higher than it was for President George W. Bush (Fisher 2013). These polls demonstrate how important these relations are for South Koreans.

Relations between South Korea and the United States have gradually changed throughout the years since the Korean war and the formal alliance that was signed in 1953. Relations between the two states were influenced by regional and global factors such as the Cold War, security tensions in the Korean Peninsula, international relations between the Asian states, and the economy. Domestic politics, both in South Korea and the United States, was another factor that influenced relations, including the perceived status of South Korea by the South Korean government, and the political agenda of the South Korean presidents at the Blue House (Cheong Wa Dae) and the US presidents at the White House (Kim 2007).

While the official statements by President Obama and President Park stress the importance of the alliance and the special relations between their countries, they do not reflect these changes, nor the tensions that exist between the two states. The relations between South Korea and the United States display characteristics of a multi-sphere interaction. These spheres are parallel, integrated, and sometimes conflicting. For example, in the security sphere, South Korea's dependence on the United States increases, while South Korea concurrently attempts to increase its security independence. At the same time, the economic sphere might cause tension between Seoul and Washington, due to the two countries' changing economic interests in the context of China's rising economic importance in East Asia and globally.

Although South Korean public opinion polls reveal stability in the favorable way that US–South Korean relations have been perceived in recent years, and despite President Barack Obama's initiation of the "pivot to East Asia," ensuring the growth of US commitment to Asia (Asan Institute for Policy Studies 2012), the political and security echelons in South Korea express increasing concerns about Washington's commitment to South Korea. These concerns are reflected in political statements and in unofficial discussions within the South Korean administrations. Such concerns have influenced South Korea's foreign and security policies toward China, North Korea, and Japan, as well as toward the United States, throughout the years.

This paper will primarily analyze: the relations between South Korea and the United States; the relations between South Korea and China; South Korea's perceptions of the United States and China; and the ways in which the regional and global arenas influence Seoul's policies. The paper will show that although the South Korean public attaches great importance to the alliance with the United States, the South Korean political and military milieus have doubts regarding the credibility of the alliance and of US commitment, yet also acknowledge South Korea's dependence on the military alliance with the United States. It will show that Washington plays a dominant role in some elements of Seoul's foreign and security policies, while ceding dominance to other players in the region in other spheres, such as economic and political issues. The paper will also show that, while some security aspects demonstrate Seoul's security dependence on Washington, others reflect a gradual shift in South Korea's security policy, towards greater independence. This shift is an expression of South

Korea's changed self-perception to that of a middle-power state (Lee 2012), and of skepticism regarding Washington's commitment to Korea's security.

The first section of the paper will briefly review the main factors that influence South Korean public opinion of foreign and security issues. The second section, divided into two sub-sections, will discuss the security sphere of South Korea–United States relations. The first sub-section will discuss the change in South Korea's nuclear policy, how this is linked to changes within the alliance between the two states, and how it serves to indicate a change in Seoul's independence policy. The second sub-section will discuss the issue of command structure, the external and internal debates about the transfer of command from US control to South Korean control, and how this change affects the relations between the two states.

The third section will analyze the economic sphere, the impact of the rising Chinese economy on South Korea, and South Korea's perceptions of China as a regional balance versus Japan.

Factors influencing South Korean public opinion

Relations between South Korea and the United States, and the alliance between them, are perceived in South Korean public opinion polls in an increasingly favorable manner. But this has not always been the case, and in the past, attitudes toward the United States have on occasion been highly negative and critical. Several factors influence South Korean public opinion of the country's main ally: the North Korean threat; anti-Americanism in Korea; Korea's self-perception as a middle power; the political arenas in Seoul and Washington; and demographic changes in South Korea.

The North Korean military threat plays an important factor in South Korean public opinion. The increase or decrease of this threat can influence the polls, although in some cases, the public will be less concerned about North Korea and more concerned about the reactions of other regional states. The South Korean leadership, on the other hand, will be more concerned about North Korea.

Anti-US opinion has been present across different social strata within Korean society over the years, and has influenced polls accordingly (Oh and Arrington 2007). In particular, anti-US opinion increases in South Korean society in the wake of unexpected and unpleasant events involving the United States. Such was the case following the IMF crisis in 1997, the killing of two South Korean girls by US soldiers in 2002, and the 2008 US beef protests in Korea (Pew Research Center 2014), all of which resulted in very low public opinion ratings regarding the United States.

South Korea's self-perception affects public attitudes toward China, North Korea, and Japan, and Seoul's relations with the United States. Initially, Seoul did not perceive itself as an active force in the global arena, but since the 1990s Seoul has come to see itself as a middle-power state, which includes growing involvement in the regional and global arena (Kim 2014). This change is also reflected in public opinion polls.

Political relations between Seoul and Washington also influence Korean public opinion polls, and periods of discord between the South Korean and US administrations have been reflected in poll results. For example, during the administrations of Kim Dae-jung and Roh Moo-hyun the polls were more favorable (excepting the beef incident), compared to Lee Myung-bak's administration (Moon 2011).

An in-depth analysis of South Korean attitudes toward the United States shows that there is a generation gap, with the attitudes of the younger generation diverging from those of the older generation on various issues. For example, while the older generation will be more pro-United States, more anti-North Korea, and more conservative, the younger generation does not follow this pattern, and in some cases might lean to the other side in the polls (Kim 2014; Pollack 2006, 88).

The security sphere

The nuclear issue – a nuclear South Korea – sounds of independence?

The United States-Republic of Korea alliance is a vital element in South Korea's national security. The alliance includes a nuclear umbrella, military cooperation between the two armies, and the presence of US forces in Korea and in the region that are on alert in case Korea is attacked, all of which constitute important elements of South Korea's defense against a possible North Korean attack. Throughout the years, the tensions between Seoul and Washington have increased whenever the United States considered partially withdrawing its military forces from Korea (Levkowitz 2008). Tensions peaked during the era of President Jimmy Carter and President Park Chung-hee, and again in 2002 during the Yangju highway incident, in which two South Korean girls were killed by a US army vehicle (Cha 2000; Oberdorfer 1999, 194). According to public opinion polls conducted by the Asan Institute for Policy Studies between 2011 and 2014, South Korean public support for South Korea–United States relations, and for the alliance with the United States, has been very high throughout this period, rising above 80 percent in 2013 and above 90 percent in 2014. Despite this high level of public support, doubts are being raised about the credibility of the alliance, especially as regards US nuclear deterrence of North Korea.

The possibility of South Korea becoming a nuclear state has not been viewed positively by Washington, mainly because of the concern that this would lead to nuclear proliferation in the region. In the 1970s, Washington pressured Seoul to abandon its plans to develop a nuclear program (Hong 2011). Even when North Korea began to develop its nuclear capabilities, no public discussion of the nuclear option was held in South Korea, although some scholars claimed that stabilization of the Korean Peninsula would be dependent on South Korea obtaining nuclear capabilities (Waltz 1981). Extended US nuclear deterrence, and until 1991 the tactical nuclear weapons stationed in South Korea (Dalton and Jin 2013), allowed Seoul to avoid developing its military nuclear capabilities on the one hand, while allowing Washington to abstain from pressuring Seoul not to develop or obtain nuclear weapons on the other hand. For a long time, the debates on developing nuclear capabilities, or becoming a nuclear threshold state, were held behind closed doors, or within limited security and academic milieus.

Over the last decade, however, this debate has become more public. Politicians, policy makers, journalists, and scholars have begun to discuss this issue openly, in South Korea and also in the United States.

For example, Chung Mong-joon from the Saenuri (New Frontier) Party, and a former presidential conservative candidate, has said:

> We, the Korean people, have been duped by North Korea for the last 20 to 30 years, and it is now time for South Koreans to face the reality and do something that we need to do. Nuclear deterrence can be the only answer. We have to have nuclear capability.
>
> (Kwon 2013)

South Korean commentators have begun to debate this issue, with some of them publicly supporting the option of becoming a nuclear state (Demick 2013), while South Korean public opinion polls have begun indicating public support for the idea. Table 6.1 shows that, since 2010, public support for the South Korean nuclear option has risen, while opposition to it has declined. These data indicate that, despite the very high level of public support for the US alliance, there are serious doubts regarding the commitment of the United States, and the credibility of the deterrence it provides.

In the United States, Colby (2014), Santoro (2014), and Bandow (2014) have all proposed that leaving Seoul free to develop nuclear weapons might be the best way to respond to the DPRK's persistent threat. According to their analysis, South Korea should consider developing nuclear weapons in order to deter North Korea, and the United States should consider this option as well.

Table 6.1 Support of South Koreans for becoming a nuclear state (in %)

Year	2010	2011	2012	2013
Support	56	63	66	66
Oppose	44	37	34	31

Source: Asan Institute for Policy Studies.

But as Hayes and Moon have illustrated (2014), this option is more complicated than it seems, and may carry implications for regional politics and security, bringing about less security rather than more. Bruce Klinger, former deputy chief for Korea in the CIA's Directorate of Intelligence under President Bill Clinton, said that this issue is a "non-starter" (Dorell 2013), which is one indicator of Washington's policy on this issue.

One might have expected that Washington's "pivot to Asia" policy would be understood as strengthening US commitment to its allies in Asia. But it seems that the pivot gives rise to concerns in Korea that it will allow Japan to play a bigger security role, as discussed later in this paper. Professor Han Yong-sup of the Korea National Defense University pinpoints the problem, saying that the calls for the South Korean nuclear option are indicators for the lack of credible US extended deterrence (Kwon 2013).

Indeed, the public debate on South Korea's military nuclear option indicates a gradual crack in the alliance with the United States, underscoring two issues: First, it raises doubts in South Korea about the dependability of the alliance, especially in terms of deterrence of North Korea, and it questions Washington's willingness to use force. South Korean concerns about this latter issue may have future implications for the stationing of US forces in South Korea. But at present, these concerns have not yet reached a point where they might destabilize the security relations between the two states.

The second issue is the incremental process of security independence that Seoul has begun to pursue over the last decade.

The discussion of the nuclear option within the political milieu in South Korea can be explained as an attempt to gain popular support, but this would highlight only one piece of the puzzle. Discussions with South Korean scholars and officials reveal that the option of South Korea becoming a nuclear threshold state has become an issue that policy makers are no longer afraid to speak about in public, and this change opens up the possibility of questioning the alliance within the political arena, which was previously considered unacceptable.

If discussing the issue of the alliance previously led to tension between the two capitals (Joo 2006), the current nuclear debate is being seen as a sign of an incremental change in relations between Washington and Seoul, and of shifts in the boundaries of their alliance, without the need for it to be formally revised. This does not mean that South Korea will abolish the alliance with the United States, or that a dramatic change in the relations between the two states should be expected. Rather, it should be seen as an indicator that Seoul is looking for ways to become more independent in its security, by expanding the boundaries of the US alliance without abandoning it.

The command structure – ambivalent and cautious sounds of dependence

Public opinion polls in South Korea show that support for the US alliance is very high, including support for the deployment of US forces in South Korea. According to these polls, even following Korean unification, the South Korean public values the alliance and the presence of US forces (Asan Institute for Policy Studies Public Opinion Surveys).

The importance of the alliance and the US military presence highlights another element of the security relations between South Korea and the United States: the issue of command structure. Who will command the South Korean forces in Korea in times of war and peace, and who will command the US forces that are deployed in South Korea? One should remember that in the Korean Peninsula there are almost 1.8 million soldiers (North Korean, South Korean, and US) on alert.

The command issue has its origins in the Korean war, when South Korea voluntarily placed the operational control of its military under the US-led UN Command (Jung 2007). After the war, operational control was handed over to US forces in Korea (USFK) as part of the ROK–US Mutual Security Agreement. With the creation of the Combined Forces Command (CFC) in 1978, wartime command was placed under the authority of the CFC commander (Cha 2006, 488; Rich 1982, 18). In 1994, peacetime control of the Korean forces was transferred to South Korean hands, but wartime control still remained under the control of the CFC, which was led by a four-star US general (Bush and Bechtol 2006).

In the past, Washington was not willing to relinquish wartime command to Korea, because it was concerned that Seoul might drag it into a conflict with North Korea that did not serve Washington's interests (Hong 2000). Since the early 2000s, Washington has been openly willing to discuss this issue.

The command structure issue has three main elements: the financial cost; the impact on military capabilities; and the implications that restructuring the command might have for Korea–US relations.

The alliance with the United States and the presence of US forces in South Korea since the Korean war have allowed Seoul to develop its economy under the security umbrella provided by Washington. Without this alliance, Seoul would have had to increase its defense budget tremendously and upgrade its military forces in order to deter North Korea. The change of the command structure might force Seoul to increase its defense budget to compensate for diminished US forces in Korea.

The discussion of cost sharing between Seoul and Washington has been going on for a long time (Park 2013). As USFK Commander General B. B. Bell has said: "Defense burden-sharing is advantageous to both partners. For the United States, the Republic of Korea's willingness to equitably share appropriate defense costs is a clear indicator that the United States

Forces in Korea are welcome and wanted" (Jung 2008). Seoul understands that the cost-sharing burden of the US forces in Korea would be smaller than the cost of investing in upgrading its deterrent force without US forces.

The second element of the command structure issue is the question of whether the South Korean military forces have the military capabilities to deter North Korea without US command involvement. The military balance between North and South Korea reveals a quantitative advantage to the North (Cordesman and Hess 2013) and a qualitative advantage to the South. In any military scenario, the North would lose the war, but the damage to the South would be greater due to the enormous economic gap between North and South Korea.

Although South Korea might have a qualitative advantage over the North, the restructuring of the command was criticized by a group of former South Korean defense ministers and retired high-ranking South Korean officers, who opposed the acceleration of transferring wartime command that was pursued by President Roh Moo-hyun (Jung 2006). Opponents of the command change question the extent of South Korea's military command capabilities without US involvement.

Some of these concerns were refuted by President Roh, and even by US Secretary of Defense Leon Panetta on July 2012: "The Department of Defense is already drawing up numerous measures to ensure that there is no loss in the South Korea–US joint combat readiness in preparation for the handing over of wartime operational control" (Choi 2012).

The third element is the concern in South Korea about what might be the implications of the command change for the alliance and the possible withdrawal of US forces from Korea. Although President Roh Moo-hyun and US officials have stated that the command change will not undermine the alliance (Snyder 2006; Talev and Kim 2014), South Korean policy makers are concerned that the wartime command change will be the first step in the withdrawal of US forces from Korea, and will eventually herald the end of the alliance, leaving Korea defenseless (Park 2006).

It is likely that the transfer of wartime command will be postponed again from its current date in 2015. Although Seoul is testing the boundaries of the alliance on the nuclear issue, it appears to be more cautious regarding wartime command. While President Roh Moo-hyun pushed for the wartime command change, the subsequent two South Korean presidents have delayed its implementation. Every time North Korea initiates a military provocation in the Peninsula, the transfer of wartime command is delayed. This postponement is an indication of the alliance's importance to South Korea, and of South Korea's dependence on the presence of US forces.

The economic rise of China and other spheres

As an export-oriented economy that depends on foreign markets, the role of the economy in South Korea's foreign policy decision making is very important (Levkowitz 2014). United States–South Korea relations are based not only on security interests but on economic interests as well. A clear indicator of the importance of the economic sphere in the relations between Washington and Seoul was provided by the many years of negotiations between the two countries over the Free Trade Agreement (FTA). The negotiations included overcoming political and economic barriers on both sides, and eventually led to the signing (2007) and ratifying (2011) of the FTA between the two states (Brock *et al.* 2014). The ratification of the FTA demonstrates the importance of trade for both sides, and the huge economic incentives the agreement offers to both sides. Seoul even tried to include the Kaesong Korean industrial park in North Korea in the FTA, but Washington refused (Manyin and Nanto 2011).

Until 2003, the United States was South Korea's biggest trade partner (Korean Statistics Information Service). However, China became the largest trade partner with South Korea in 2004, and by 2008 trade between South Korea and China was double that between South Korea and the United States. (If Hong Kong is added to the trade balance, it might well be more than double.) This development has increased South Korea's dependence on the Chinese market for the long term. The declining volume of trade with the United States serves to reduce Washington's economic leverage on Seoul, although Washington still has leverage in other areas as well. The signing of a free trade agreement between South Korea and China will boost the trade between the two states even more, and may further decrease Washington's economic leverage on Seoul (Wright *et al.* 2014).

The increasing role of China in the Korean Peninsula can be seen in the comments made by South Korean political leaders and in South Korean public opinion polls. These show that South Korea currently attaches supreme importance to the relationship with the United States, even at the expense of China, but that in the long run, China's influence will increase, and Korea will have to maintain a delicate balance (Snyder and Byun 2014). For now, the majority of South Koreans (70.4 percent) think that South Korea should strengthen its alliance with the United States to keep China in check, and 53.4 percent think that South Korea should do so even if it makes China uncomfortable (Kang *et al.* 2014). This means that the South Korean government is expected, as it does, to balance its interests between Washington and Beijing.

But the Asan public opinion poll indicates a decline in the Korean perception of the United States' influence on Korea in the future, and the rise of Chinese influence (see Table 6.2). It appears that the South Korean public believes that, in the long run, Washington's role in the region will decline, not only in the economic sphere but also in the political sphere.

Table 6.2 Public appraisal of influence of China vs United States (in %)

	Economic current influence	Economic future influence	Political current influence	Political future influence
United States	64.7	22	81.8	44.8
China	25.2	66.7	5.2	39.3

Source: Kang *et al.* 2014.

South Korean public opinion concurs with the estimates of officials in the South Korean government, and even in the US government, that in the long run, China's influence in the region will increase (Snyder 2012). Seoul understands that it should find the delicate balance between Washington and Beijing, which will become more complex in the future with the rise of China (Park 2013).

President Xi Jinping of China visited South Korea in July 2014, symbolizing a turn of tides in Asia. For the first time, the Chinese leader did not visit North Korea prior to his visit to South Korea, thereby conveying to Kim Jong-un China's dissatisfaction with his policies (Page 2014). South Korea portrayed President Xi's visit to Seoul as a significant visit by Korea's biggest trade partner. Some analysts, however, viewed it as an attempt to tilt South Korea toward China in the grand Asia power game between Washington and Beijing (Perlez 2014), with South Korea seeking to explore how China's policy in the region might serve its own interests in establishing itself as a middle power.

Seoul understands China's increasing importance to its economy and the implications this might have for relations with Washington, and not just in economic terms. One example that has already surfaced is the issue of missile defense. Washington and Seoul negotiated the deployment of THAAD in South Korea (Song 2014), but Beijing is concerned that the missile defense system might change the strategic balance between the United States and China. This would explain Chinese President Xi's remark on this issue to President Park during his visit to Seoul, that China is displeased with this policy: "During the summit talks, President Xi told President Park that it needs to tread carefully over the issue of the THAAD deployment (to South Korea)" (*Korea Times* 2014).

Seoul sees Beijing as a counterweight to Japan in the regional balance (Glosserman 2014). South Korea is concerned that although Washington's "pivot to Asia" will increase the US presence in Asia, it might also mean that Tokyo will be allowed to pursue Prime Minister Shinzo Abe's plans to strengthen the Japan Self-Defense Forces and to lift the Japanese ban on collective self-defense policy. South Korea sees China as a balance to the rising military power of Japan, despite the discord this might cause with the United States (Chung 2014).

Seoul is aware that its increasing dependence on China's economy might affect other spheres, such as its relations with North Korea, where Beijing holds leverage on Pyongyang. South Korea is also aware that China will play an important role in any crisis that may erupt in North Korea, which is why one of Seoul's main goals is to maintain relations with China.

Conclusion

Although one can find cracks in the alliance between South Korea and the United States, there are no indications that Korea is contemplating making formal changes to it. The South Korean public support for the alliance, and even for US presence after the Korean unifications, demonstrates the importance of US–Korean relations to policy makers and to the public. However, the credibility of the alliance is being questioned by policy makers in South Korea, who have begun to discuss the nuclear option as a necessary deterrent against the North Korean threat.

The US "pivot to Asia" policy sends an important signal to its Asian allies that Washington will remain in Asia for a long time, and strengthens its commitment to its allies in the region. Yet South Korea is concerned that the pivot might threaten its security by allowing Japan to have a more active security policy, which Seoul opposes. In this case, Seoul sees China as a balance against Japan, which in turn might cause problems with Washington.

The rise of China is changing the regional and global balance of power between Washington and Beijing. Even South Korean public opinion indicates that, in the long run, the importance of China in Korea's economic and political spheres will increase, while that of the United States will decrease. The increasing trade volume between South Korea and China, and the parallel decline in trade with the United States, will influence the dominant role that Washington has played in Seoul throughout the years. Seoul will have to find a way to balance its relations with Beijing and Washington, and prevent China and the United States from using their leverage to force Seoul to tilt to one side only.

Bibliography

Asan Institute for Policy Studies Public Opinion Surveys. http://en.asaninst.org/contents/category/publications/public-opinion-surveys/.

Asan Institute for Policy Studies. 2012. *South Korea in a Changing World: Foreign Affairs Results of the Asan Institute's 2012 Annual Survey of South Korean Public Opinion*. Seoul: Asan Institute for Policy Studies.

Bandow, Doug. 2014. "Maybe US Should Defend South Korea by Letting it Develop Nuclear Weapons." Cato at Liberty. www.cato.org/blog/maybe-us-should-defend-south-korea-letting-it-develop-nuclear-weapons.

Brock, Williams R., Mark E. Manyin, Remy Jurenas, and Michaela D. Platzer. 2014. "The US–South Korea Free Trade Agreement (KORUS FTA): Provisions and Implementation." Congressional Research Service Report RL34330.

Bush, Richard C., and Bruce E. Bechtol. 2006. "Change of US–ROK Wartime Operational Command." Brookings Articles, September 14. www.brookings.edu/research/articles/2006/09/14southkorea-richard-c-bush-iii.

Cha, Du-hyeogn. 2006. "ROK–US Command Relations Adjustment: Issues and Prospects." *Korean and World Affairs* 30 (4): 488.

Cha, Victor. 2000. "Abandonment, Entrapment, and Neoclassical Realism in Asia: The United States, Japan and Korea." *International Studies Quarterly* 44 (2): 261–291.

Choi, He-suk. 2012. "US Reaffirms Wartime Command Transfer Plans to S. Korea." *Korea Herald*, July 30. www.asianewsnet.net/news-34160.html.

Chung, Min-uck. 2014. "US Pivot to Asia Corners Korea." *Korea Times*, April 25. www.koreatimes.co.kr/www/news/nation/2014/09/120_156107.html.

Colby, Elbridge. 2014. "Choose Geopolitics Over Nonproliferation." National Interest. http://nationalinterest.org/commentary/choose-geopolitics-over-nonproliferation-9969.

Cordesman, Anthony H., and Ashley Hess. 2013. *The Evolving Military Balance in the Korean Peninsula and Northeast Asia: Conventional Balance, Asymmetric Forces, and US Forces. Vol. II*. New York: Rowman & Littlefield.

Crabtree, Susan. 2013. "Obama Renews Commitment to Defend South Korea." *Washington Times*, May 7. www.washingtontimes.com/news/2013/may/7/obama-us-will-not-waver-protecting-south-korea/.

Dalton, Toby, and Yoon Ho Jin, 2013. "Reading into South Korea's Nuclear Debate." PacNet 20. http://csis.org/files/publication/Pac1320.pdf.

Demick, Barbara. 2013. "More South Koreans support developing nuclear weapons." *Los Angeles Times*, May 18. http://articles.latimes.com/2013/may/18/world/la-fg-south-korea-nuclear-20130519.

Dorell, Oren. 2013. "Some Suggest S. Korea Should Go Nuclear." *USA Today*, March 11. www.usatoday.com/story/news/world/2013/03/11/south-korea-thinks-nuclear/1979051/.

Fisher, Max. 2013. "Anti-American Countries Can Become Pro-American. Here's How South Korea Did It." *Washington Post*, May 7. www.washingtonpost.com/blogs/worldviews/wp/2013/05/07/anti-american-countries-can-become-pro-american-heres-how-south-korea-did-it/.

Glosserman, Brad. 2014. "Japan and Collective Self-Defense: Less Than Meets the Eye." PacNet 49.

Hayes, Peter, and Chung-in Moon. 2014. "Should South Korea Go Nuclear?" NAPSNet Policy Forum, July 28. http://nautilus.org/napsnet/napsnet-policy-forum/should-south-korea-go-nuclear/.

Hong, Sung Gul. 2011. "The Search for Deterrence: Park's Nuclear Option." In Byung-Kook Kim and Ezra F Vogel, eds., *The Park Chung Hee Era*. Cambridge: Harvard University Press, Chapter 17.

Hong, Yong-pyo. 2000. *State Security and Regime Security: President Syngman Rhee and the Insecurity Dilemma in South Korea*. London: St Martin's Press.

Joo, Seung-ho. 2006. "South Korea–US Relations in Turbulent Waters." *Pacific Focus* 21 (1): 59–104.

Jung, Sung-ki. 2006. "Ex-Defense Chiefs Oppose President." *Korea Times*, August 10. http://times.hankooki.com/lpage/nation/200608/kt2006081017180511950.htm.

Jung, Sung-ki. 2007. "Korea–US Alliance Will Grow Stronger." *Korea Times*, November 14. www.koreatimes.co.kr/www/news/nation/2009/07/205_13718.html.

Jung, Sung-ki. 2008. "Defense Cost-Sharing Talks to Test Korea–US Alliance." *Korea Times*, April 29. http://koreatimes.kr/www/news/issues/2015/01/242_23366.html.

Kang, Choi, Kim Jiyoon, Karl Friedhoff, Kang Chungku, and Lee Euicheol. 2014. *South Korean Attitudes on the Korea–US Alliance and Northeast Asia*. Seoul: Asan Institute for Policy Studies, 24.

Kim, Choong Nam. 2007. *The Korean Presidents*. Norwalk: EastBridge.

Kim, Dae-joong. 2012. "S. Korea Needs to Consider Acquiring Nuclear Weapons." *Chosun Ilbo*, July 10. http://english.chosun.com/site/data/html_dir/2012/07/10/2012071001459.html.

Kim, Jiyyoon. 2006. "National Identity under Transformation: New Challenges to South Korea." *Asan Forum* 3: 6.

Kim, Sangbae. 2014. "Roles of Middle Power in East Asia: A Korean Perspective." EAI MPDI Working Paper 2.

Korea Times. 2014. "China's Xi Asked Park to 'Tread Carefully' over US Missile-Defense System," August 26. http://koreatimes.co.kr/www/news/nation/2014/08/113_163578.html.

Korean Statistics Information Service (http://kosis.kr/).

Kwon, K.J. 2013. "Under Threat, South Koreans Mull Nuclear Weapons." CNN, March 19. http://edition.cnn.com/2013/03/18/world/asia/south-korea-nuclear/.

Lee, Joo-hee. 2013. "Park Says Korea–US Alliance Base for Reunited Korea Region." *Korea Herald*, May 8. www.koreaherald.com/view.php?ud=20130508000886.

Lee, Sook-Jong. 2012. "South Korea as New Middle Power Seeking Complex Diplomacy." EAI Asia Security Initiative Working Paper, 25.

Levkowitz, Alon. 2008. "The 7th Withdrawal – Has the US Forces' Journey Back Home from Korea Begun?" *International Relations of the Asia-Pacific* 8 (2): 131–148.

Levkowitz, Alon. 2014. "Upgrading Israeli–South Korean relations: Can Seoul Tilt in Favor of Jerusalem?" The Middle East–Asia Project. www.mei.edu/content/map/upgrading-israeli-south-korean-relations-can-seoul-tilt-favor-jerusalem.

Manyin, Mark E., and Dick K. Nanto. 2011. "The Kaesong North–South Korean Industrial Complex." Congressional Research Service Report RL34093.

Manyin, Mark E., Mary Beth D. Nikitin, Emma Chanlett-Avery, William H. Cooper, and Ian E. Rinehart. 2014. "US–South Korea Relations." Congressional Research Service Report RL41481.

Moon, Kyu-toi. 2011. "South Korean Public Opinion Trends and Effects on the ROK–US Alliance." http://asiafoundation.org/resources/pdfs/MoonPubilcOpinion.pdf.

Oberdorfer, Don. 1999. *The Two Koreas: A Contemporary History*. Reading, MA: Basic Books.

Oh, Chang Hun, and Celeste Arrington. 2007. "Democratization and Changing Anti-American Sentiments in South Korea." *Asian Survey* 47 (2): 327–350.

Page, Jeremy. 2014. "China President's Visit to South Korea Before North Seen as Telling." *Wall Street Journal*, June 27. http://online.wsj.com/articles/chinas-president-xi-to-visit-seoul-1403858327.

Park, Song-wu. 2006. "Korea Can Take Wartime Control Now." *Korea Times*, August 9.

Park, Won Gon. 2013. "A Challenge for the ROK–US Alliance: Defense Cost-Sharing." EAI Asia Security Initiative Working Paper 30.

Perlez, Jane. 2014. "Chinese President's Visit to South Korea is Seen as Way to Weaken US Alliances." *New York Times*, July 2. www.nytimes.com/2014/07/03/world/asia/chinas-president-to-visit-south-korea.html?_r=0.

Pew Research Center. 2014. "Global Opposition to U.S. Surveillance and Drones, but Limited Harm to America's Image." www.pewglobal.org/files/2014/07/2014-07-14-Balance-of-Power.pdf.

Pollack, Jonathan D. ed. 2006. *Korea: The East Asia Pivot*. Newport: Naval War College Press.

Poushter, Jacob. 2013. "South Koreans Remain Strongly Pro-American." Pew Research Center, May 6. www.pewresearch.org/fact-tank/2013/05/06/south-koreans-remain-strongly-pro-american/.

Rich, Robert G. 1982. *US Ground Force Withdrawal from Korea: A Case Study in National Security Decision Making*. Washington, DC: Foreign Service Institute.

Santoro, David. 2014. "Will America's Asian Allies Go Nuclear?" National Interest. http://nationalinterest.org/commentary/will-americas-asian-allies-go-nuclear-9794.

Snyder, Scott A. 2006. "A Comparison of the US and ROK National Security Strategies: Implications for Alliance Coordination toward North Korea." In Philip W. Yun and Gi Wook Shin, eds., *North Korea: 2005 and Beyond*. Stanford: Walter A. Shorenstein Asia Pacific Research Center, Chapter 8.

Snyder, Scott A. 2012. "South Korean Public Opinion and the US–ROK Alliance." *Council on Foreign Relations*, October 17. http://blogs.cfr.org/asia/2012/10/17/south-korean-public-opinion-and-the-u-s-rok-alliance/.

Snyder, Scott A., and See-won Byun. 2014. "China–Korea Relations: Balancing Acts by China and South Korea." Comparative Connections. http://csis.org/files/publication/1402qchina_korea.pdf.

Song, Sang-ho. 2014. "Korea, US to Discuss Missile Defense." *Korea Herald*, September 1. www.koreaherald.com/view.php?ud=20140901001150.

Talev, Margaret, and Sam Kim. 2014. "US Considers Delaying South Korea Wartime Command Handover." Bloomberg, April 26. www.bloomberg.com/news/2014-04-25/obama-considers-delaying-handover-of-south-korea-wartime-command.html.

The President's News Conference with President Park Geun-hye of South Korea. 2014. Seoul, South Korea, April 25. http://search.proquest.com/docview/1542019553?accountid=12994.

Waltz, Kenneth. 1981. "The Spread of Nuclear Weapons: More May Be Better." *Adelphi Papers* 171.

Wright, Tom, Kwanwoo Jun, and Mark Magnier. 2014. "South Korea, China Agree on Outline of Free-Trade Deal." *Wall Street Journal*, November 10. www.wsj.com/articles/south-korea-china-agree-on-free-trade-deal-1415588514.

7 Change and continuity in Russian perceptions of the United States

Dmitry (Dima) Adamsky

Introduction

This chapter offers a panoramic overview of change and continuity in Russian perceptions of the United States since the collapse of the Soviet Union. It also traces the evolution of Moscow's self-view in the context of US policies in the world, and specifically those toward Russia. It covers the main stages of this evolution: from euphoria and disillusionment in the 1990s; to the emergence of strategic competition in the 2000s; and to the current state of geopolitical confrontation.

This overview serves as a background for understanding the main components of current Russian threat perception with regards to the United States, in three main spheres: foreign and security; domestic; and energy. This outline of the threat perception enables a description and explanation of the logic behind Moscow's current responses to the West, and a separate section addresses current Russian countermeasures across several domains. The chapter is not confined to the level of the political elites, and also refers to the evolution of anti-US sentiment in Russian public opinion. The chapter compares and contrasts current Russian bottom-up anti-US opinion with its Soviet top-down analogue. The chapter concludes with a review of the main strategic issues on the Russian agenda vis-à-vis the United States, and outlines the main principles guiding Moscow's approach to the way ahead.

The chapter aims to deconstruct and represent the way in which Moscow has perceived Washington during the period under discussion. Some Russian perceptions may seem puzzling, counterintuitive, and illogical to Western observers. In addition to the unique characteristics of Russian strategic culture, which account for some of these peculiarities, three factors have strongly characterized Moscow's attitudes toward Washington during this period. First, Moscow's pragmatic-ideological zigzags, along the lines of its centuries-long alternating orientation between Slavophile and pro-Western approaches, have kept US–Russian relations in a mode of cooperation-competition. Second, as in many other periods of Russian history, conspiracy theories have significantly shaped elite and public perceptions of the United States. Finally, when dealing with the United States, Moscow has demonstrated a puzzling coexistence of contradictory views at the official policy level, which frequently reflect the bureaucratic dynamic within the Russian strategic community.

Evolution of Russia's geostrategic self-perception and its perception of the United States following the Soviet collapse[1]

During the decades since the Soviet collapse one can identify three stages in the evolution of the Russian geostrategic perception of itself and of the United States: *euphoria*, *disillusionment*, and *competition*, which recently transformed into occasional *confrontation*.

Pro-Western and pro-US *euphoria* characterized the final years of the USSR and the immediate post-collapse zeitgeist. Fascination with the Western way of life, and its social and political models, was evident both at the level of the mainstream political elite and also throughout society at large. The Kremlin promoted reforms to effect maximal democratization and liberalization of political and economic life. These efforts clearly emulated the US and Western ways of doing things, which were seen as a source of inspiration.

The overall optimism widespread in Russian society following the collapse of the Soviet Union in 1991 also provided a context for interpreting the end of the Cold War. The main narrative circulating among the political elites, one that had already emerged during the late Gorbachev era, glossed the termination of hostilities with the West not as a defeat to the United States but rather as a demonstration of the cool, pragmatic, and peace-loving attitudes that prevailed on both sides of the Atlantic, saving the world from nuclear catastrophe and from a mutually exhausting, irrational arms race. The United States was perceived and presented as an equal partner, and a co-winner in the Cold War, with whom the new Russia, a grand power, would now co-navigate the emerging international system. An alternative, and rather widespread, narrative did portray the end of the Cold War as a defeat. It attributed this outcome to internal treason, specifically that of Gorbachev and his cronies; under no circumstances was this defeat attributable to Soviet underperformance relative to the United States across the board. In any case, in their perceptions of the post-war future, proponents of both narratives were similar in assigning to Moscow its rightful and historical central role in world affairs, alongside Washington.

However, deep *disillusionment* began to gather momentum from the mid-1990s onward, displacing the euphoria of the early part of the decade, and marked by skepticism and the beginnings of anti-US ferment. According to the popular conceptions of the time, the rapid introduction of Western market economy models and the adoption of foreign economic approaches resulted in ineffective economic policies and privatization processes, increased corruption, concentration of capital in the hands of a small number of oligarchs, and severe poverty for the population, worse than anything experienced in Soviet times. A sense of political instability, distrust of the political process, lack of effective central power, and criminal chaos all augmented the above-mentioned social and economic insecurity. Following the initial fascination with the Western and US way of life, then, for Russian society and its elites alike, freedom and democracy became equated with chaos, instability, lawlessness, and utter social and personal insecurity – something that this last generation of Soviet people, then middle-aged and the most active mass of the population, had never experienced.

Until today, in the Russian collective memory, the US model of democracy is tainted with this highly negative connotation of having brought about a collapse of stability, and bringing Russia into the "times of trouble" (*smutnoe vremia*). Since, for significant portions of the population, what followed the collapse of the Soviet Union was indeed experienced as a geostrategic catastrophe, this term (used by Putin several times over the last decade) strongly resonates with contemporary Russian mass consciousness. Frustrated by their unfulfilled expectations of some kind of US-led "Marshall Plan," of trading privileges, and of a strategic partnership, from the mid-1990s Moscow felt that it was in a one-sided relationship of non-equals. This sense of Washington exploiting Russian weakness remained intact until the beginning of the mineral boom of the 2000s, and in some cases until even later.

Similar sentiments emerged about international relations. Russia became frustrated with the Unites States' international stance during the "unipolar moment," with the subordinate international role that Washington left for Moscow, and with the unilateral US policy, which took advantage of Russian weakness. This started in 1991 with the US invasion of Iraq, which excluded Moscow, and which targeted one of its main Middle Eastern allies. But the watershed was the 1999 Kosovo crisis, which made it clear to Moscow that the United States had no interest in showing it consideration in the international arena. According to the Russian perspective, the United States acted as a usurper of the unipolar moment: it manifested double standards and hypocrisy in foreign policy, and even gradually began to intervene in areas of privileged Russian interests, coming close to threatening Russian sovereignty itself. The current world order began to be seen not only as unfavorable and unjust, but also as dangerous.

A recurring motif of Russian foreign policy has been the understanding that after every great war there has been a congress of the great powers, which outlined new rules of the game to accommodate all the participants, both the winners and the losers. Examples include the Peace of Westphalia, the Congress of Vienna, the Treaty of Versailles, and the Potsdam

Conference. By contrast, according to this narrative, in 1991 no such international efforts were made to accommodate Russia. Since that time, Russia has been excluded from the great powers' table. The resulting frustration, often overlooked by the West, has been enormous. Moscow, which has traditionally perceived itself as a power (*derzhava*) with an indispensable and historical role in the international arena, has been sidelined in this new world, which instead is now led by the United States.

Following the disintegration of the Soviet Union, Russia developed responses characteristic of many empires after their collapse: feelings of national humiliation; and a revanchist quest for compensation, both individual (an improved quality of life for its citizens) and collective (restoration of the state's position in the global arena). Russian civilization had been at its highest point during the Soviet period, compared to other periods of its history, and now it found itself at the bottom. The West and the United States were often seen the source of this evil.

Moscow entered the twenty-first century irritated with what it saw as the United States' hypocrisy, double standards, and paternalistic and arrogant attitude. It felt that the Western, US way of life, with its democratic politics and its liberal-market economics, did not represent a universal truth or higher ideal, applicable in any place and under any circumstances, and it sought its right to differ. Russia at that time was seeking a new identity, self-determination, and a national leader who could save it from internal chaos, cope with international and internal humiliation, overcome the country's geopolitical catastrophe, and eventually restore national pride.

Economic stabilization, and the Kremlin's consolidation of political power, were the preconditions for *competition* and *confrontation* with the United States, a stage which Russia entered in the mid-2000s. The power vertical, rebuilt during the early 2000s and supported by revenues from the minerals boom on the world market, enabled the Kremlin to recentralize control over politics, align business and media with the government, reintroduce state control over the economy, and ensure social stability. Vladimir Putin's managed democracy steadily acclimatized following the financial crisis of the 1998, incrementally renationalized its largest economic assets with the biggest revenues (mainly energy companies), and transformed the wealthiest few of the previous epoch into "court oligarchs," also referred to as "managers of the state's wealth." This new Russia, a "petro-state" capitalizing on the unprecedented revenues from mineral exports, paid off its billions of foreign debt by 2003, and injected significant resources into pensions, salaries, social welfare, and infrastructure.

Internal political and economic stability brought strategic self-confidence and self-respect, and led to a quest for the restoration of the country's geopolitical glory, as befitting a great, if not super, power (*velikaia derzhava*). Even during the "times of trouble," Russia considered itself one of the leading countries in world politics, but at that stage it had no capacity to realize this self-view, partially due to what it saw as an American usurpation.

During the 1990s, although Moscow perceived itself as a big power (*derzhava*), it realized that its relationship with the United States, the superpower (*sverkhderzhava*), was not one of equality, and it was frustrated that its expectations of *derzhavnost'* were not being met.

From the early 2000s onward, the weakened Russia began to rise from its knees, aspiring to restore its status and to turn itself once more into a respected and indispensable force in international politics. Since then, Russian foreign policy has sought to be multi-vector and to promote the principles of multi-polarity. The straightforward logic of multi-polarity carries echoes of the nineteenth-century European notion of the "concert of powers": great powers respect each other's interests and zones of influence, and act accordingly in the international arena. While the principle of multi-polarity emphasizes Russia's sovereignty and great power status, the multi-vector approach aims to ensure more space for maneuver and bargaining vis-à-vis different actors, and primarily the United States.

Of all of the vectors of its foreign policy – US, European, Middle Eastern, Asian, and South American – the US vector has been the determining one. In a way, Russia's interests and actions in every vector were formulated in conjunction with its line of policy toward the United States. Relations with the United States define all other vectors of foreign policy. While for Moscow, from Soviet times without interruption, the United States has been the central reference point of Russian foreign and security policy, this does not work the other way around: Moscow played a relatively minor role in US foreign and security policy following the collapse of the Soviet Union. This situation continuously frustrated Russian decision makers, and Russian foreign policy has been making a consistent effort to revise this trend.

In Moscow's view, strategic competition with the United States worldwide, and counterbalancing it on the major issues of international politics, serves to upgrade Russia's international status, since competition with the hegemon implies the high-ranking status of the challenger. This became one of the main ways for Moscow to pursue its quest for *derzhavnost'* and to position itself as an indispensable actor in international relations. In part, its friction with Washington, whereby Moscow tries to become once more a compass of US foreign policy, was due to the above-mentioned Cold War legacy. That being said, significant portions of the Russian security elite and strategic community genuinely consider NATO as their main threat, and see the United States as being the source of many national security challenges. Moreover, competing with the United States has given Russia the opportunity to lead the "legitimate" anti-US camp worldwide. In regional conflicts in the Middle East and in Asia, Moscow has positioned itself as a "just broker," one who could mediate and talk to both sides; it has supported rogue actors, not because of any ideological identification with them, but due to its desire to spoil any US initiative; and it systematically tries to cultivate developing powers, especially China, in order to create a balancing triangle that will blunt the United States' edge.

According to the overall strategic perspective in Russia, which has been widespread since Moscow took control over Crimea and became a target of Western sanctions: the more Russia rose up from its knees, revived its geopolitical might, and increased its independence from the West, the more irritated Washington became by this new Russian independence, and the stronger it began to push back and compete. According to the Kremlin, while Moscow seeks to reverse the world order that emerged after the Soviet collapse, Washington endeavors to freeze the world order. Consequently, according to this zero-sum game view, the stronger Russia becomes, the more tensions with the United States will inevitably rise, regardless of which leaders happen to occupy the White House or the Kremlin. This view fully materialized during the second term of the Obama administration, when the "reset policy" evaporated, and it can be observed in current Russian threat perception, in Russia's current assessment of the United States' standing in the world, and in its subsequent countermeasures.

Sources of strategic irritation and threat perception[2]

What have been the main issues of concern and strategic irritation for Moscow during the last decade, and how are the United States and its allies in the European Union and NATO involved? When it comes to threat perception, Moscow feels that it is under attack on all fronts. The following is a summary of the main recurring themes and bones of contention, in three different spheres: *national security and foreign policy*; *energy*; and *internal politics*.

In the *national security and foreign policy* sphere Moscow has been continuously irritated by what it saw as the United States' unfair geopolitical exploitation of the unipolar moment. Despite the pledges that, according to Moscow's narrative, were given to it at the end of the Cold War, NATO did not reciprocate the Warsaw Pact and dismantle itself. Moreover, it continued to expand eastward, stretching during the 1990s to encompass most of the former pro-Soviet Warsaw Pact allies, and then in the early 2000s beginning to incorporate three former Soviet republics (Estonia, Latvia, and Lithuania). Moscow was disappointed and puzzled, and demanded to know the security reasons behind NATO's expansion. After receiving an answer related to the notion of collective security, it asked to join the alliance. But when its repeated attempts were rejected it eventually felt betrayed, exploited, and threatened.

The wake-up call for Moscow, which terminated the period of what it came to see as a naive illusion of US good intentions, came with the NATO operations in former Yugoslavia. By the mid-2000s, Moscow's operating assumption was that NATO was consolidating and expanding only because of its aggressive intentions toward Russia. This was seen as an extension of the West's Cold War aspirations to expand eastward, and of the traditional

US goal of containing Russia. In spite of NATO's reassuring rhetoric about its non-aggressive intentions, the expansion was not seen as a natural trend of twenty-first-century globalization, but rather as a clear anti-Russian démarche. From the mid-2000s on, Moscow was most seriously concerned about US and NATO military cooperation with, and influence on, the countries of its near abroad (especially Ukraine, Georgia, Azerbaijan, and Central Asia), that is, the states and regions that the Kremlin considers its "zone of privileged interests." A panoramic overview of US and NATO initiatives since the collapse of the Soviet Union presented to Moscow as the beginning of a new Western siege, and of an era of strategic competition with Russia. Subsequently, the current conflict in Ukraine is perceived not simply as a struggle with the Ukrainian armed forces, but as stopping the "Drang nach Osten" of the foreign legions of the United States and NATO.

Despite shared concerns regarding the global and regional Salafi jihad, and the Kremlin's initial support of the US-led global war on terror, the United States' policy since 9/11 has given Moscow more security concerns than solutions. Washington has deployed its forces and exerted its power in Central Asia and the Caucasus, and in Moscow's view has challenged and destroyed Russian alliance structures and spheres of influence in the post-Soviet space (in Uzbekistan, Kyrgyzstan, Azerbaijan, and Georgia). Similarly, US Middle Eastern policy over the last decade has dismantled Russia's Middle East alliance structure, which was based on Iraq, Libya, Iran, and Syria. In Moscow's view, Washington sought and carefully planned regime changes amongst all of these allies, with the subsequent subordination of their new governments into the US sphere of influence and reorientation away from Russia. For this reason the events of the Arab Spring and the colored revolutions in the post-Soviet space have been, from Moscow's point of view, links in the same chain. Both trends were instigated by the United States, as part of its strategic plan to turn these regional actors into US allies and support its aspirations of global dominance.

In line with the above, in Moscow's view the arms control initiatives led by the United States after the collapse of the Soviet Union, by design or by default, aimed for nothing less than the erosion of Russia's nuclear deterrence potential. Under the New Strategic Arms Reduction Treaty, Russia's problem has been not to reduce forces but to bring its shrinking arsenals up to the treaty ceilings, while the unilateral US withdrawal from the Anti-Ballistic Missile Treaty further downgraded the effectiveness of the Russian first and second-strike capabilities. In this context, Moscow began to see non-strategic nuclear weapons (NSNW) as a means of compensating for falling behind the US in strategic weapons, in addition to its traditional view of this capability as an equalizer of its conventional inferiority vis-à-vis NATO. Moscow did not take at face value US declarations that its Ballistic Missile Defense (BMD) and Prompt Global Strike (PGS) Programs were intended to counter terrorists and rogue states, considering this a smokescreen for the United States' main goal: degradation of Russian strategic nuclear deterrence. Moscow views BMD and PGS as a unified counterforce concept targeting its shrinking strategic forces, and consistently rejects every US initiative to downgrade NSNW arsenals.[3]

In the energy sphere, in which it was critical for the Kremlin to secure a state of uninterrupted demand and supply, Moscow observed a similar trend. The United States was competing with Russia in regional energy markets; was seeking to gain access to, and cultivate, non-Russian regional sources of energy, particularly in Azerbaijan and Kazakhstan; and was encouraging local actors to build energy pipelines and transit corridors outflanking and bypassing Russian territory, like the Baku-Tbilisi-Ceyhan and Nabucco pipelines, and in this way seeking to prevent Moscow from realizing its energy potential.

Last but certainly not least, there has been significant tension between the United States and Russia when it comes to the internal, ideological sphere: Russian domestic politics. Since the turn of the millennium, Washington has continuously criticized the Kremlin's return to an authoritarian political and economic course. It has also strongly criticized the renationalization of the country's energy riches, resulting in the state-owned Gazprom and Rosneft monopolies, as well as the curtailment of democratic principles and liberal freedoms, exemplified by the crackdowns on independent media, NGOs, political parties, and big business. Moscow considered this continuous critique from Washington to be an intervention into its own internal affairs, and assumed that it was driven only by the United States' desire to prevent the Kremlin gaining power at home, so as to limit its ability to compete in the international arena. Consequently, Moscow viewed the United States' funding and support for pro-democracy activities, and its backing and funding of opposition groups (including the protests that followed the last presidential election), as Western strategic and ideological subversion, not only against the ruling regime but against Russia as a strong state per se. In the same way, the Orange and Rose Revolutions (pro-Western regime changes) were seen by Russia as US subversion in its own backyard of former Soviet territories.

In summation, Moscow perceives the internal and external threats to its sovereignty from the United States as being interconnected, and addresses them all as an integrated whole. Its response to this gamut of threats is also holistic.

Moscow's correlation of forces assessment, and its competitive strategies vis-à-vis Washington[4]

How has the Kremlin viewed the United States' standing in the world during President Obama's second term? What have been the principles of Moscow's countermeasures and competitive strategy vis-à-vis Washington?

Overall, the tone of the discourse in the Russian strategic community over the last several years suggests that there has been a confusing net assessment of the correlation of forces. The United States is seen as very dangerous to Moscow's security interests, but at the same time as a relatively weak strategic actor. It is seen as dangerous not only because it is perceived as Russia's main competitor, one that tries to downgrade the latter's international status at every opportunity, and now to bring Moscow to heel using the sanctions regime, but primarily because Washington is viewed as the generator and disseminator of chaos, instability, and uncertainty in the Middle East (the Arab Spring) and in post-Soviet territory (Ukraine in particular), and also as a globally destabilizing power, deploying BMD and promoting PGS.

At the same time, this administration has been seen as inconsistent in its regional and global policies, lacking strategic vision and resolve, and frequently confused, especially in its management of the consequences of the Arab Spring, which according to Moscow was a direct result of US Middle Eastern policy. Lack of US strategic resolve to intervene militarily or to escalate in several Middle Eastern crises, especially in Syria and in Iraq against the Islamic State, transmitted an image of weakness. The failure of the United States' Middle Eastern policy in Iraq and Afghanistan, and in the Palestinian and Iranian negotiations, together with its pronouncements of withdrawal from the Middle East and the pivot to Asia, suggested to Moscow that Washington may be incrementally moving into a new era of isolationism. In Moscow's eyes, Washington reduced the credibility of its extended deterrence pledges by its actions during the crises in Egypt and Ukraine, which the Kremlin saw as an additional symptom of strategic weakness. In sum, the Kremlin seemed to conclude that the United States exploits the strategic weaknesses of other actors, as was the case with its invasions in Iraq and in Libya, but is deterred when it faces a significant strategic pushback, as was the case with Russia's support of Syria and its assertiveness in Ukraine.

When it comes to Russian countermeasures, it's important to keep in mind that the Kremlin perceives itself as operating under overall siege, and from within a long-lasting US encirclement. In its own eyes, Moscow's modus operandi is thus operational counter-offence in the context of strategic defense. This defensive counter-offence, in keeping with the principles of Russian operational art and strategic thought, is multidimensional, and merges soft and hard, military and non-military powers. The holistic nature of the current Russian operational approach, and its cross-domain deterrence and coercion, causes Western observers to qualify Moscow's modus operandi as hybrid warfare.

On the domestic front, to counter what it perceives as US ideological subversion, intrigues, and machinations, the Kremlin is injecting unprecedented resources into agitprop, in order to enhance patriotic education among Russian citizens. Under the logo of enhancing "spiritual staples,"

Moscow wages a battle of values and narratives, disseminating its interpretations of the Western siege, the reasons behind it, and its potential consequences. The aim is to promote traditional values unique to Russian culture, and to indoctrinate to the population toward a belief that Western (i.e., US) liberal values are not universal, and that the US approach to politics and life is hypocritical, foreign, and dangerous. This effort is also extended regionally. Among Russian-speaking communities of the former Soviet republics, which Moscow perceives as its zone of privileged interests, it promotes the idea of establishing a Eurasian union, some sort of a replica of the Soviet Empire. This vision of the "Russian world" implies not necessarily actual annexation of the independent states, but domesticating them and subordinating their foreign, security, and economic policy to the orbit of Russian influence.

Externally Moscow wages a cross-domain confrontation, dubbed in the West as asymmetrical, non-linear, or hybrid warfare, to promote its strategic interests vis-à-vis the United States and the West. Known in Russian professional discourse as "new-generation warfare/wars" (*voiny novogo pokoleniia*), this is an amalgamation of soft and hard power that is expressed across various domains through the skillful application of coordinated military, diplomatic, and economic tools.

Moscow flexes its nuclear muscles periodically. Every year it has conducted military exercises, including de-escalatory and deterrent first nuclear strikes against NATO conventional forces. Russian nuclear-armed strategic bombers, ships, or submarines regularly undertake aerial and naval patrols, sometimes in a rather aggressive manner, in the immediate proximity of NATO borders and forces, with occasional cross-border infiltrations. Moscow has also been signaling ceaselessly, via its statements and actions, both during and between crises, its willingness to brandish nuclear capabilities and limited nuclear strikes, both to coerce its adversaries into withdrawing from regional conflicts and as a deterrent to the escalation of economic sanctions.

The Ukrainian crisis, and particularly Russia's taking control of the Crimea by force, demonstrated that this muscle flexing could be skillfully choreographed with conventional and sub-conventional applications of military force. Special operations of unprecedented reach and scale were deployed in a clandestine manner in great operational depth, and were coordinated with information warfare, both technological (cyber and electronic warfare) and cognitive-psychological. These efforts in the theater of operations were synchronized with active political, diplomatic, and economic measures throughout the region and the world arena.

The operational logic of this approach demands that it is not escalated above a level that will activate traditional collective defense, as outlined in NATO Article 5, or that it maintains an opaqueness that clouds the nature and identity of the aggression and the aggressor, as was the case with the "little green and polite men" in Crimea. This enables the undermining of

NATO's collective security principle without the firing of a single bullet. Moreover, shifting the battle into the cognitive or psychological spheres serves to render irrelevant NATO's traditional military supremacy. Recent Russian military doctrine clearly takes the line that, in modern warfare, subversion against cultural, ideological, and patriotic values are to be conducted side by side with special ops, cyber warfare, and nuclear pressure.

Information warfare is Russia's way of striking back against what it sees as US abuses of soft power. It comprises technological and psychological components designed to manipulate the target's picture of reality, spread misinformation, and eventually interfere with the decision-making process of individuals, organizations, governments, and societies. Sometimes called "reflexive control," it forces the rival to act according to its false picture of reality in a predictable way, one which is favorable to the initiator of the attack. While digital sabotage aims to disorganize, disrupt, and destroy a state's administration capabilities, psychological subversion aims to deceive the victim, discredit the leadership, and disorient and demoralize the population.

Russia's approach to information warfare is *holistic*, that is, it merges digital-technological and cognitive-psychological attacks; *unified*, in that it synchronizes kinetic and non-kinetic military means and effects with other sources of power; and *hybrid*, in terms of co-opting and coordinating a spectrum of government and non-government actors, military, paramilitary, and non-military. The information campaign is waged simultaneously in local, regional, and international media, and in all spheres of the Internet and social media. The online "troll" armies wage battles on several fronts: informational; psychological; and probably digital-technological as well. This enables Moscow to create managed stability or managed instability in the territories for which it is competing with the United States.

This struggle extends to other non-military domains. Trade embargos on food products, and energy blackmails used as a tool of economic pressure on the EU, are also seen as channels of influence on the United States. Moreover, Moscow is steadily trying to expand its global influence and to cultivate the United States' allies and competitors worldwide: in the Middle East; in Asia; and in South America; and particularly in any place where US policy has left a vacuum or soured relations, such as President Sisi's Egypt. In part, this diplomatic activism seeks to contrast Moscow's image as a credible and responsible ally, which never leaves allies behind, with the low credibility of Washington, as the Kremlin has done in backing Syria and Iran over the last several years.

In the European arena the Kremlin's strategic goal is ambitious and straightforward: splitting Europeans on the issue of Russian policies, and sowing discord between them and Washington, while cultivating anti-US sentiment within the European Union. The overall goal in fracturing the alliance is to discredit the concept of collective defense, which if successful will bankrupt the whole notion of European security and crumble the alliance. Experts believe that, to this end, Moscow may extend its subversion beyond the Ukraine and cultivate the pro-Russian minority communities in Estonia, Latvia, and Lithuania through its "Russian world" policy. To further enlarge the differences between the United States and the European Union, Moscow is cultivating pro-Russian and anti-US political parties on Europe's far left and radical right, and co-opting senior European politicians and public figures into its active measures campaign. The aim is to promote the positive image of Russia and discredit the United States and its values. So far, as part of this trend, Moscow has achieved a significant improvement of its relations with Greece, Cyprus, Hungary, and Bulgaria, to which it provided a clear anti-US agenda, and has also been cultivating opposition parties and politicians in Germany, France, Britain, Belgium, and Austria.

Change and continuity in public opinion[5]

A discussion of Russian attitudes to the United States' standing in the world would not be complete without looking beyond the political elite, and exploring the views of broader society and ordinary Russians. Anti-US public sentiment in Russia today is much deeper and more genuine than during the Cold War. Back then, the Soviet agitprop messages barely resonated with the individual mindset of the mass of Soviet citizens. Certainly the United States was seen as a potential danger and as the possible enemy in the next war, and people carried these slogans during demonstrations and pronounced them from trade union tribunes. However, under the surface and in informal kitchen conversations, there was a certain admiration for the Western way of life and Western goods, clothes, and electronics, to the point that the United States and "Made in the US" were covertly idealized. Today, the situation is completely different, as the Kremlin's anti-West propaganda, especially since the Ukrainian crisis, resonates far more viscerally with large portions of the population. Thus much broader anti-US sentiment than ever before is evident in Russia today.

Current anti-US attitudes are clothed in a mixture of communism, imperialism, and religion. Public polls and sociological data reveal a growing social hostility that has accompanied political tensions. Antipathy, resentment, and even hatred are clearly evident. This has been an incremental process, beginning when post-Cold War euphoria evaporated during the "times of trouble" and soured into disillusionment with the idealized image of the United States. Subsequently, many tended to blame the United States for Russia's misfortunes at home and abroad. The United States was perceived as exploiting Russian weakness and refusing to accept Russia as an equal; it was felt that the time had come to take revenge for a half-century of geopolitical and social humiliations. Many Russians stereotypically perceive US citizens as superficial and blunt people who respect no one, who abuse their power across the globe, bomb whomever they please, and recognize no other views or interests but their own. According to reliable polls of Russian citizens, over 70 percent of respondents see the United States as a principle enemy. Moreover, this anti-US sentiment has itself become a foundation for Russian unity and identity, with Russian identity today often defined through opposition to the West. In short, in contrast to the Cold War, anti-US sentiment is not only indoctrinated from the top down, but is brewing from the bottom up.

In that context, the current sanctions regime, initiated by the United States, is seen as the moment of truth that reveals Washington's true anti-Russian face. The policy being pursued by the current US administration supports Russia's thesis that the West seeks to keep Russia down just when it is finally rising from its knees. It is a common belief that the United States is by default anti-Russian, and seeks to impose on Russia its values and way of life. This partially explains why the Kremlin continues to benefit from such a high level of public support despite the clear economic blows that the Russian population has recently suffered.

To some extent, Russia's ability to withstand sanctions is tied to its psychological orientation, its collective memory, and its strategic culture. For many Russians, this last decade of prosperity has been an exception to the historical rule. So the return of more difficult times is taken stoically, as another episode in Russia's centuries-long history, pockmarked by suffering. Also, the Kremlin promotes a concept of stability that resonates strongly with the population at large. It has sown the idea that adapting US values may produce similar chaos to that which has ravaged Ukraine, and could well return Russia to the times of trouble of the 1990s. In this context, Putin's continued leadership is seen not as a source of stagnation, but as a guarantee of stability.

The way ahead

Moscow perceives itself as being engaged in a continuous strategic competition with Washington, today and for the foreseeable future. It is mostly preoccupied with what it perceives as US political and economic subversion against Russia, particularly in Moscow's zones of privileged interests. It expects the United States to manipulate energy markets and oil prices further. It also sees that its asymmetrical countermeasures, outlined above, are bearing strategic fruit, and it will probably continue to apply them, with greater scope and rigor, against the United States and its allies regionally and elsewhere.

It seems that Moscow's responses and initiatives will continue to demonstrate contradictory characteristics, on a case-by-case basis. The basic operational assumption in Moscow is that the United States has turned modern international relations into a chaos in which countries act unilaterally, with US policies worldwide providing the prime examples. In this sense, Moscow is simply responding to the international reality that the United States has constructed: a manageable chaos, lacking agreed rules, where actors behave like the United States and promote their own interests. In response, if there are to be no rules for Washington, but only interests, there will be no rules for Moscow either. Comparing and contrasting Putin's speeches in Munich (a critique, but expressing readiness to work with partners) and Valdai (the same critique, but a suggestion that there is no partner) clearly demonstrate this. On the one hand, Moscow permanently signals its readiness to engage Washington in restoring the multi-polar game rules in international relations, as long as Russia receives its rightful place in modern international relations; and on the other hand, it continues a zero-sum game policy vis-à-vis the United States, as the recent S-300 deal demonstrates.

Moscow views the United States as a hegemon that is here to stay, at least for the foreseeable future. Consequently, the Kremlin is likely to preserve and maintain this competition-cooperation dynamic, in order to give itself room for strategic maneuver. For example, in terms of confrontation it is likely to continue seeking to separate the United States from the European Union, and to split the European Union (eastern/western) further, by exploiting differences over Ukraine; while also balancing with China and others against the Washington. At the same time, in terms of cooperation, Russia's significant concerns over the developments in the Middle East, close to its southern borders, may spur it to work with Washington, and even join forces, to fight IS and the Salafi jihad.

Overall, it seems that when evaluating the United States' standing in the world, as well as its own place with regards to Washington, Moscow feels under siege, but confident. Its confidence stems from its belief that, despite the difficulties, the constellation of forces is in its favor, and it possesses the necessary strategic strength to withstand US anti-Russian machinations. Confrontation abroad and authoritarianism at home, augmented by Putin's increasing popularity, is likely to continue. Moscow will continue to promote its interests, and will invest significant strategic energy in forcing Washington to recognize its domains. "The bear will not take orders from anyone; the bear does not intend to move into other climatic zones, but in his domain – the taiga – he will not give up" (Putin 2014).

The Kremlin believes that Russia has overcome the inertia of collapse and has begun to revive its power, while the West, and the United States in particular, is exhausted by its colonial wars, lacks strong values and backbone, and is losing momentum. In such a reality, Moscow now feels itself to be sufficiently powerful to stop dancing to the US fiddle, and to promote its own causes and courses in global politics.

Notes

1 For detailed analysis of this topic, see: Mankoff (2011); Donaldson and Nogee (2009); Tsygankov (2010); Legvold (2007); Goldman (2008); and Hoffman (2002).

2 Ibid. See also Van Herpern (2014); Lucas (2014); Pomerancev (2014); Dawisha (2014); Ermarth (2009); and Karaganov (2010).
3 For a discussion of current Russian strategic thought on nuclear weapons and strategy, see Adamsky (2014).
4 For an understanding of current Russian security policy and military thought, see: Jonsson and Seely (2014); McDermott and Blank (2014); Thomas (2014); Franke (2015); Heickero (2015); Pomerancev (2015); and Popescu (2015).
5 For detailed discussions of the topic, see: Social Trends and Public Opinion Polls of the Levada Analytical Center (www.levada.ru); Arbatov (2014); Borusiak and Levinson (2015); Urnov (2014); and Granina (2015).

Bibliography

Adamsky, Dmitry (Dima). 2014. "Deterrence Theory and Non-Strategic Nuclear Weapons in Russia." *Journal of Strategic Studies* 37 (1): 91–134.

Arbatov, Alexei. 2014. "Worse than the Cold War." *Moscow Carnegie Center Eurasia Outlook*, September 16.

Borusiak, Liubov, and Alexei Levinson. 2015. "Kak vozniklo post-Krymskoe edinstvo Rossiian?" *RBK*, March 18.

Dawisha, Karen. 2014. *Putin's Kleptocracy: Who Owns Russia*. New York: Simon & Schuster.

Donaldson, Robert, and Joseph Nogee. 2009. *The Foreign Policy of Russia: Changing Systems, Enduring Interests*. London: M. E. Sharpe.

Ermarth, Fritz. 2009. "Russian Strategic Culture in Flux: Back to the Future?" In Jeannie Johnson, Kerry Kartchner, and Jeffrey Larsen, eds, *Strategic Culture and WMD*. London: Palgrave Macmillan.

Franke, Ulrik. 2015. *War by Non-Military Means: Understanding Russian Information Warfare*. Helsinki: Finnish Ministry of Defense.

Goldman, Marshall. 2008. *Petrostate: Putin, Power and the New Russia*. Oxford: Oxford University Press.

Granina, Natalia. 2015. "Sploshnaia Pustota: Sotsiologu Rasskazali, Tchego Rossiiane Zhdut ot Novogo Goda." *Lenta.Ru*, January 11.

Heickero, Roland. 2015. *Emerging Cyber Threats and Russian Views on Information Warfare and Information Operations*. Helsinki: Finnish Ministry of Defense.

Hoffman, David. 2002. *The Oligarchs: Wealth and Power in the New Russia*. New York: PublicAffairs.

Jonsson, Oscar, and Robert Seely. 2014. "Russian Full Spectrum Conflict." *Journal of Slavic Military Studies* 28 (1): 1–22.

Karaganov, Sergei. 2010. "Russia's Choice." *Survival* 52 (1): 5–10.

Legvold, Robert. 2007. *Russian Foreign Policy in the Twenty-first Century and the Shadow of the Past*. New York: Columbia University Press.

Levada Analytical Center. Social Trends and Public Opinion Polls. www.levada.ru.

Lucas, Edward. 2014. *The New Cold War*. London: Palgrave Macmillan.

Mankoff, Jeffrey. 2011. *Russian Foreign Policy: The Return of Great Power Politics*. New York: Rowman & Littlefield.

McDermott, Roger, and Stephen Blank. 2014. "Special Issue: Russia's Armed Forces Transformation." *Journal of Slavic Military Studies* 27 (1): 1–188.

Pomerancev, Peter. 2014. *Nothing is True and Everything is Possible: The Surreal Heart of the New Russia*. New York: PublicAffairs.

Pomerancev, Peter. 2015. "Inside the Kremlin's Hall of Mirrors." *Guardian*, April 9.
Popescu, Nicu. 2015. "Hybrid Tactics: Neither New nor Only Russian." *EUISS*, January 30.
Putin, Vladimir. 2014. Speech on Valdai Eleventh Annual Meeting, Sochi, October 24.
Thomas, Timothy. 2014. "Russia's Information Warfare Strategy." *Journal of Slavic Military Studies* 27 (1): 101–130.
Tsygankov, Andrei. 2010. *Russia's Foreign Policy: Change and Continuity in National Identity*. New York: Rowman & Littlefield.
Urnov, Mark. 2014. "Great-Powerness as the Key Element of Russian Self-Consciousness Under Erosion." *Communist and Post-Communist Studies* 47: 305–322.
Van Herpern, Marcel. 2014. *Putin's Wars: The Rise of Russia's New Imperialism*. New York: Rowman & Littlefield.

8 India's perspective of US political leadership and foreign policy

C. Uday Bhaskar

At the end of September 2008, then Indian Prime Minister Manmohan Singh surprised his host at the White House, US President George Bush, when he told him: "The people of India deeply love you." Dr Singh added:

> In the last four and half years that I have been prime minister, I have been the recipient of your generosity, your affection, your friendship. It means a lot to me and to the people of India. When the history is written, I think it will be recorded that President George W. Bush played a historic role in bringing our two democracies closer to each other.
>
> (Khare 2008)

This adulation for a US president stood in sharp contrast to an earlier observation about the United States – almost 75 years before the Singh-Bush meeting. Jawaharlal Nehru (who would later become independent India's first prime minister), in his lucid survey of world history written from a prison cell, voiced his apprehension about the fundamental nature of the United States, and described the ambivalence it generated in the Indian political class. This unease remained deeply embedded in the collective Indian psyche for many decades, and it is the contention of this essay that it is at the core of the abiding Indian view of US political leadership and foreign policy.

In August 1933, in one of his many letters to his daughter Indira (who would later also become prime minister), Nehru (1985, 960), while acknowledging that the United States "is by far the most advanced capitalist country; she is the wealthiest, and her industrial technique is ahead of the others," expressed his reservations about the country's core ethos and values.

In March 1933, President Roosevelt assumed office and, as Nehru observed, the new US president was "immediately faced by a tremendous banking crisis in addition to the great depression that was going on." While tacitly endorsing Roosevelt's international orientation, which Nehru described as "a definite and more advanced attitude than that of England," it was the capitalist DNA of the United States that disturbed the Fabian socialist in him (Nehru 1985, 964). Ambivalence remained the predominant leitmotif, and the contrast between the perceptions that the two nations had of each other becomes even starker when we review two significant markers in the relationship between the world's oldest democracy and its largest democracy.

In 1971, Henry Kissinger, then US Secretary of State, was recorded (in a private conversation with President Nixon) deplorably referring to Indian Prime Minister Indira Gandhi as a "bitch," and going on to say, "The Indians are bastards." This vituperative outburst reveals something of the basis for Indian wariness of the US political leadership, although it should be noted that Mr Kissinger made amends in 2005 when the tapes were made public: "I regret that these words were used. I have extremely high regard for Mrs. Gandhi as a statesman," he said (BBC News 2005).

In the same interview, Mr Kissinger made what may be qualified as a central observation about why the United States and India had negative perceptions about each other at the time – and about the radical changes that have since taken place. About the estrangement in 1971, Kissinger says, "The fact that we were at cross purposes at that time was inherent in the situation"; and in the same interview, he adds, "The United States [now] recognizes that India is a global power that is a strategic partner of the United States on the big issues" (ibid.).

This new partnership between India and the United States in the post-Cold War era, and the radical manifestation it has taken, is reflected in the most recent development in the bilateral relationship – namely the invitation extended to US President Barak Obama to be the chief guest at the Indian Republic Day Parade on January 26, 2015. Until the surprise announcement was made by the Indian prime minister, Narendra Modi, most observers of the countries' relations would have deemed it highly improbable that a US president would be extended this honor. In many ways, the trajectory from Nehru through Indira Gandhi to Modi is reflective of the dramatic change that has taken place in India's perspective of the US political leadership – although the wariness about US foreign policy still persists.

Nehruvian influence

Post-1947, after independence, India's perspective of the United States was strongly shaped by the impressions and insights of Jawaharlal Nehru. He dominated policy making in the fledgling Indian state, and nowhere was his personal stamp more strongly felt than in the realm of foreign policy.

Nehru had an instinctive suspicion of the capitalist, big business, industrial complex, while he was enamored of the socialist ethos and aspiration. He first visited the Soviet Union in November 1927, and as historian Ramachandra Guha points out,

Nehru wrote out a travelogue on his trip; its tone is unfailingly gushing, whether speaking of peasant collectives, the constitution of the USSR, the presumed tolerance of minorities, or economic progress. It was, above all, the Soviet economic system which most appealed to Nehru. As a progressive intellectual of his time, he thought state ownership more just than private property, state planning more efficient than the market.

(Guha 2007, 162)

Nehru's formative years were spent in trying to understand the world of the early twentieth century and India's place in it. His views shaped Indian perspectives of the world outside for many decades. While Nehru had first-hand experience of the United Kingdom and some parts of Europe, he had never visited the United States, and whatever he gleaned was second hand.

The outbreak of World War II in 1939 resulted in the Congress Party, led by Mahatma Gandhi, and which spearheaded the struggle for independence, seeking greater concessions from the British in return for its support of the war effort. Prime Minister Churchill's antipathy for Indians in general, and Gandhi in particular, was well known, and a complex impasse ensued. India's contribution to the war effort was stupendous – both in terms of personnel and material resources – but Churchill was loath to offer any political concessions, and consequently in August 1942 Gandhi launched the famous "Quit India" movement.

This was when India first appeared on the political radar of the United States, with President Roosevelt at the helm. In 1942 Washington was deeply immersed in post-Pearl Harbor trauma and the related war effort. The Indian theater became relevant when the United States established the China–India–Burma command with its headquarters in Delhi. India began to receive the attention of the White House, although for the United States there was no question that the war effort was paramount, with Japan making steady advances through China and Southeast Asia toward the Indian subcontinent.

Yet President Roosevelt was troubled by the contrast between the commitment to freedom of the United States, itself a former British colony, and the stance of his closest ally, Churchill. A month before his death, Roosevelt observed that much of the Orient was "ruled by a handful of whites, and they resent it ... our goal must be to help them achieve independence – 1,100,000,000 potential enemies are dangerous. Churchill doesn't understand this" (Kux 1993, 37).

The foundation for the abiding ambivalence that was to characterize the political contours of the US–Indian relationship had been laid.

> If the US attitude toward Indian nationalism was ambivalent – support for independence, yet disappointment over the attitude of the (Indian)

nationalists toward the war effort – the Indian reaction to US policy was similarly ambiguous ... [they] appreciated the indications of US support for the nationalist cause ... but felt let down by the United States, especially after Roosevelt refused to intervene in August 1942 over the Quit India movement, and thereafter remained unwilling to press the British to make further political concessions.

(Ibid., 38)

In this early engagement between the United States and an India eagerly awaiting freedom from colonial rule, the two sides' core strategic priorities ultimately differed, foreshadowing what Kux describes as "the frustration that would follow during the next decades" (ibid., 38).

Independent India – the early decades

The ambivalence that characterized Indian attitudes toward the US political leadership turned into disappointment after India became independent in August 1947, as it became clear that the United States and India had greatly divergent objectives and priorities. For the United States, the primary objective was the containment of communism, as it struggled with the USSR for global dominance. Bipolarity was the dominant characteristic of the global strategic framework, and major nations were encouraged to be part of the emerging military alliances. In this context, Washington fully expected that a democratic India would be on the side of the forces of freedom, as represented by the US-led alliance.

However, India under Nehru was wary of being sucked into this vortex of superpower rivalry. Nehru wanted Delhi to remain neutral, and coined the term "non-entanglement" to describe his policy, which would later be better known as non-alignment. This policy infuriated the United States, and given that perspectives and perceptions in any dyadic relationship are mutually reinforcing to a large extent, the ambivalence that had until then characterized US–Indian relations was soon being leavened with steadily increasing frustration and disappointment.

By 1948, a year after India's independence, the Kashmir issue had been referred to the United Nations, and Nehru's conviction that the US–UK axis was unsupportive of the Indian position marked the beginning of the chasm that was to grow between India and the United States. For example, in a communication to Lord Mountbatten, then Viceroy of India, Nehru described the US and British attitude on Kashmir as "completely wrong." Nehru believed that "the motives of the United States were to get military and economic concessions in Pakistan." This charge of the United States being more supportive of Pakistan was to have an influence on the Indian assessment of US foreign policy toward South Asia for decades (ibid., 61).

In October 1949 Nehru made his first visit to the United States, and by that time, Kashmir apart, India and the United States were pursuing divergent or discordant foreign policies in relation to some of the more urgent matters of the time: the US–USSR rivalry; international control of atomic energy, nuclear weapons, and global disarmament; communist China and developments in East and Southeast Asia; the creation of Israel and the Palestine issue; and the pace of decolonization globally. Dean Acheson, US Secretary of State at that time, recalled: "I was convinced that Nehru and I were not destined to have a pleasant personal relationship ... he was one of the most difficult men I have ever had to deal with" (ibid., 70). After his first visit to the United States, during which he obtained a more informed, first-hand understanding of Washington's policies in South Asia, Nehru also voiced his disappointment about the United States and its lack of political perspicacity. He observed: "The Americans are either very naïve or singularly lacking in intelligence ... it does appear that there is a concerted attempt [by the United States] to build up Pakistan and build down, if I may say, India" (ibid., 72).

During the Korean war, Washington saw Nehru's attempts at peacemaking intervention as needless meddling. The discord was further compounded by India's advocacy for admitting Mao's communist China into the global community at a time when US policy was to ostracize it. The early Nehru years saw foundations being laid for a robust estrangement between the world's oldest democracy and its largest.

Indian vulnerabilities

In the early years after Indian independence it was clear that the nascent nation-state needed enormous resources for its internal consolidation, and for the improvement of the socioeconomic conditions of its teeming millions. A century of British rule (1857–1947) had resulted in a systematic de-industrialization of the country, and the ensuing trauma – one that was unmatched in the twentieth century in terms of the vast numbers dislocated and the blood spilt – of partition had taken its toll. India was impoverished, and while participative democracy had been embraced enthusiastically, the state had very limited resources to realize what had been promised in its constitution.

Nehru understood that the United States was the most prosperous and militarily powerful nation at the time, and while there were many disagreements on the political and diplomatic front, it was evident that assistance from foreign donors was urgently needed. The United States was already committed to a massive aid package for the reconstruction of Germany and Japan as part of the Marshall Plan, and while Washington was cognizant of India's vulnerabilities, it did not view it as a particularly high priority.

India under Nehru was facing a serious food shortage, and averting famine, or even near famine, was a political imperative. A high degree of self-pride, and the ignominy of having to seek food aid, perhaps prevented Nehru from seeking US assistance unambiguously, and a contradictory pattern emerged that became an abiding trait of the Indian perspective of Washington, and of its dealings with it. The contradictory pattern was this: through cloistered diplomatic exchanges and high-level political communication, India sought US assistance in core sectors of national inadequacy; while the dominant public discourse in India remained that of domestic autonomy (at least to a certain degree), couched in nuanced anti-US rhetoric.

In 1950 a poor monsoon meant a bad year for Indian agriculture, and food imports were essential. While the United States was inclined to provide this aid, as long as a formal request was made in the appropriate manner, it was not encouraged by the posture Nehru had adopted. Thus, the US Congress took its time to approve the aid to India. The symbolism of India with a "begging-bowl" was discomfiting to Nehru, and he was apprehensive that his request would be misconstrued as tacit acceptance of India's status as a political subordinate. Annoyed by Congressional foot-dragging and criticism of India, Nehru hit back: "We would be unworthy of the high responsibility with which we have been charged if we bartered away in the slightest degree our country's self-respect or freedom of action, even for something we badly need" (ibid., 80).

Yet the diplomatic channels were worked, and finally, in June 1951, President Truman signed the bill that enabled the provision of food to India as a long-term loan. This was the beginning of an extended period of US food and agricultural assistance to India, formalized as US Public Law 480 by the Eisenhower administration. This law remains as a symbol of tangible US aid to India at a crucial time, a reality that was internalized by the Indian political constituency and by the more objective spectrum of Indian intelligentsia.

It is the contention of this chapter that the ambiguous Indian assessment of the US political establishment and of its external policies shaped India's responses on major issues in the estranged bilateral relationship. This was most evident in the security and strategic arena – particularly the nuclear domain.

Strategic relations during the Cold War

While India was formally neutral in the Cold War, it began to develop close ties with the Soviet Union in the mid-1950s. The Soviets supported Indian sovereignty over disputed territory in Kashmir and they gave India substantial economic and military assistance. In 1971 India supported the secession of Bangladesh from Pakistan and, as a guarantee against possible Chinese intervention, signed the Indo-Soviet Treaty of Friendship and Cooperation.

In contrast, Kashmir and Pakistan had already become an issue of considerable disagreement between India and the United States between

1948 and 1962. Concurrently, India was becoming more concerned about its relations with China. While there had been an elusive aspiration that the two Asian giants could forge a degree of solidarity and meaningful cooperation, tension and conflict between Nehru and Mao was becoming part of the emerging political reality. Without digressing into the tangled complexity of Indian–Chinese relations, it is worth noting how the differing attitudes of Delhi and Washington toward Beijing over time provide an instructive example of the changing relations between them.

In the early years, independent India was an ardent advocate of admitting communist China into the global fold, despite US aversion to the Mao regime. India's attitude was summed up in the slogan of the time, "Hindi-Chini bhai-bhai" ("India–China brother–brother"), while in the United States there was growing anxiety about the looming "yellow threat." However, by the late 1950s tension was brewing between India and China over their unresolved territorial claims. This Sino-Indian tension progressively grew as the United States entered the period of the transition from the Eisenhower administration to the Kennedy years in the United States.

Concurrently, the Cold War rivalry between the US and the USSR was unspooling on its own trajectory. In October 1962, even as the superpowers were locked in the potentially apocalyptic Cuban missile crisis, China attacked India in response to Nehru's "forward policy," catching the country completely by surprise. India was militarily stunned, and Nehru, despite his commitment to non-alignment and his abhorrence of security alliances, turned to the United States for urgent military assistance.

The Indian government of the day was confident that Delhi could turn to Washington in times of dire distress – especially over sovereignty issues that related to China. President Kennedy, despite his preoccupation with the Cuban Missile Crisis, offered immediate military assistance, albeit modest from the Indian perspective. Kennedy wrote, "I want to give you support as well as sympathy," and Nehru acknowledged this help. In his reply to Kennedy, the Indian Prime Minister wrote: "I am deeply grateful to you for what you have written, and for your sympathy, and for the sympathy of the great nation whose head you are in a moment of difficulty and crisis for us" (ibid., 204).

The Indian perspective of the US government in the run-up to the 1971 war over Bangladesh has been alluded to at the outset, and marked one of the most bitter and near-hostile moments in the bilateral relationship. The political leadership on both sides had an extremely adversarial mutual perception. But an interesting aspect of how Indian perspectives were mediated emerged during that dark and bitter period.

President Nixon had his own (erroneous) perception of Indira Gandhi's grand design to attack West Pakistan, and saw India as a Russian satellite. Yet divisions within the US State Department over the Nixon–Kissinger policy in relation to Pakistan, and the genocide unleashed by the Pakistani army on the citizens of then East Pakistan, created an unprecedented backlash in the

United States. Many US diplomats publicly expressed their dismay at US policy, of which the starkest symbol was the deployment of the USS *Enterprise* aircraft carrier in the Bay of Bengal. In addition, influential sections of the US media supported the Indian position (Bass 2013). Indira Gandhi had already castigated the United States over its Pakistan policy, and accused it of abandoning the word and spirit of the US Declaration of Independence. Reaching out to US public opinion, she dwelt on the sanctity of human rights and liberty, which were being denied and trampled upon by the Pakistani army, with US support. For the average Indian who had experienced the 1962 China attack, the US military action was a shock. It appeared that India was now the target of US intimidation and military power.

With the Vietnam war and US military excesses still fresh in the collective Indian mind, the USS *Enterprise* incident only reinforced the image of the "ugly American" in India, and it is testimony to the resilience of the relationship that it was not irrevocably scarred by this experience, as significant as it was.

The nuclear issue during the Cold War

One area which came to define the contour and texture of India–US relations was what may be termed the nuclear nettle. China had conducted its own nuclear weapons test in October 1964 and this stoked Indian anxiety. The US-led Nuclear Non-Proliferation Treaty (NPT) sought to restrict the global nuclear weapons club to five countries, with China being the last to join. Indian objections that the NPT was inequitable and highly discriminatory were rejected. From the Indian perspective, the United States had imposed nuclear apartheid on the global strategic order. Furthermore, the rapprochement between the United States and China under Nixon aggravated Indian concerns and altered the Cold War alignment. Following these early divergences, the nuclear issue acquired high visibility in the aftermath of the Indian Peaceful Nuclear Explosion (PNE) of May 1974, during Indira Gandhi's term as prime minister. The United States perceived this action by India as a challenge to, and weakening of, Washington's nuclear non-proliferation effort.

Not long afterward, in 1978, the United States introduced the Nuclear Non-Proliferation Act. India saw itself as the target of this legislation, and remained steadfastly outside the NPT, although it remained committed to the spirit of nuclear disarmament and non-proliferation in a more earnest manner than some of the five members of the nuclear club. The NPT was seen in India as an imperial means of "disarming the unarmed." For President Carter, nuclear non-proliferation was a high priority, and the perception in India that the Democratic Party was more strident and evangelical about nuclear non-proliferation was not unfounded.

Thus the nuclear issue became a festering sore afflicting the bilateral relationship. An uneasy decade followed, and by the late 1980s India found itself in a strategic quandary. Pakistan, with opaque Chinese support, had acquired missile and nuclear weapon capability. The secret May 1990 nuclear test carried out by Pakistan is considered to have been enabled with active support from China, and India was now at a strategic disadvantage (*Wall Street Journal* 2010). It was the only country that had two adversarial, nuclear-armed neighbors, engaged in covert WMD cooperation with each other. India was greatly dismayed that the United States had tacitly turned a blind eye to this Sino-Pakistan WMD cooperation and had refused to acknowledge the strategic asymmetry in South Asia.

The post-Cold War era

When the Cold War ended in December 1991 with the dissolution of the USSR, which had been a staunch supporter of India, Delhi, like many capitals in the world, was in a state of strategic disarray. This was the extended unipolar moment for the United States, which in January 1991 had erased the ignominy of Vietnam with a victory over Iraq in the war for Kuwait. India felt very isolated in the "new world order" that the United States now straddled. Indian vulnerability was heightened by its balance-of-payment crisis and by a very frail domestic fiscal situation. The cautious economic liberalization initiated by Prime Minister Rao was still a work in progress, and this was a period in which India was at its wobbliest.

The Clinton administration's policy of "roll-back, cap, eliminate" all non-NWS (nuclear weapons state) WMD programs included the nascent Indian program, and was deeply resented in India. This only reiterated the perception noted earlier: that the United States was opposed to Indian security interests. Pressure mounted on India to join the Comprehensive Nuclear Test Ban Treaty (CTBT) and the Fissile Material Cut-off Treaty (FMCT), which was interpreted in Delhi as a roundabout manner of lassoing India and bringing it into the NPT fold as a permanent non-nuclear weapon state, even while it remained outside the NPT framework. Nevertheless, this did not prevent India from joining the United States in co-sponsoring the CTBT Resolution at the United Nations in late 1993. Yet India's discomfort became more pronounced following the United States' thwarting of its attempted nuclear test in December 1995.

One of the first major initiatives taken by the Vajpayee government, which returned to power in March 1998, was to conduct a series of five nuclear tests in May of that year, and to declare that India had now become a nuclear weapons state, albeit still outside the NPT. On May 12, 1998, a day after the nuclear tests, Vajpayee wrote a personal letter to Clinton in which he explained India's security rationale, and expressed his hope that it would be met with US understanding. While China was not mentioned explicitly, the reference was unambiguous. The letter merits quotation:

I have been deeply concerned at the deteriorating security environment, especially the nuclear environment, faced by India for some years past. We have an overt nuclear weapon state on our borders, a state which committed armed aggression against India in 1962. Although our relations with that country have improved in the last decade or so, an atmosphere of distrust persists mainly due to the unresolved border problem. To add to the distrust, that country has materially helped another neighbour of ours to become a covert nuclear weapons state. At the hands of this bitter neighbor we have suffered three aggressions in the last 50 years. And for the last ten years we have been the victim of unremitting terrorism and militancy sponsored by it in several parts of our country, especially Punjab and Jammu & Kashmir. Fortunately, the faith of the people in our democratic system, as also their patriotism, has enabled India to counter the activities of the terrorists and militants aided and abetted from abroad.

The series of tests are limited in number and pose no danger to any country which has no inimical intentions towards India. We value our friendship and cooperation with your country and you personally. We hope that you will show understanding of our concern for India's security.

(*New York Times* 1998)

But this was not October 1962, and the US response was very different. In an unprecedented protocol departure, the White House made the letter available to the *New York Times*, which published it the very next day. The United States, it was apparent, wanted not only to isolate India but also to "queer the pitch" for Delhi with Beijing. It would certainly seem that the Indian assessment of the US political leadership was overly optimistic, and perhaps naive. This episode reiterated the conviction in Delhi that Washington could not be trusted on such matters of grave national import.

The Clinton administration, now in its second term, was livid about India crossing the nuclear Rubicon. US–Indian relations were greatly damaged, and severe sanctions were imposed on India. But by this time the Indian economy was more robust, and the global response was mixed. In the UN Security Council, Russia and France were more sympathetic toward India's position, but the United States was determined to penalize India for its nuclear defiance. The Security Council passed a severe resolution (1172), and many US allies (Japan and Australia in particular) were zealous in their imposition of sanctions against India.

To the credit of both Vajpayee and Clinton, contact was maintained, and the Strobe Talbott – Jaswant Singh dialogue, sustained over many meetings, resurrected the relationship. The Indian strategic perspective was more successfully conveyed to the United States, and a modus vivendi arrived at. The India–Pakistan Kargil war of May 1999, and the restraint displayed by India in the face of Pakistan's blatant aggression, also led the Clinton administration to review its policy toward the Vajpayee government.

In March 2000, less than two years after the nuclear tests and US outrage, President Clinton made a very successful visit to Delhi, and the mutual respect at the political level was very much evident. C. Raja Mohan describes the impact of Clinton's address to the Indian Parliament:

> The Clinton magic was such that the entire Indian parliament, for long the deepest sceptic of American intentions towards India, was swooning over the American president. Clinton had transformed, in one speech, the atmospherics of Indo-US relations. The long accumulated bitterness in bilateral relations was a finally beginning to yield to a framework in which the two sides could engage each other despite strong differences.
>
> (Mohan 2006, 20)

After this rapprochement, the bilateral relationship acquired a more positive orientation, and while the nuclear conundrum was not satisfactorily resolved, the two country's perspectives of one another were more positive than in previous decades. This development was to be reinforced after the events of September 2001, when the trauma of 9/11 brought the challenge of global terrorism into sharp focus for the US establishment. With India having been a victim of such attacks for many years, a shared security perspective emerged.

The Bush administration that entered the White House in 2001 appeared more supportive of India, and Delhi was gratified that the hectoring on the nuclear issue, which had been a hallmark of earlier dialogues, was now a thing of the past. On the terror front, the swift US military action against the Taliban in Afghanistan in October 2001 mitigated some of the ignominy heaped on India in late December 1999, when an Indian civilian aircraft was hijacked by terrorists linked to the Taliban.

Gradually the Indian view of the US and its external policies was being transmuted, and this shift was being reciprocated by the Bush administration. The terror attack on the Indian Parliament in December 2001 removed the possibility of any serious movement in the bilateral relations, as the Vajpayee government, in 2002, embarked upon a tense military stand-off with Pakistan. Around the same time, the United States was also distracted as it moved the war effort from Afghanistan to Iraq in early 2003 – which from the Indian perspective marked the beginning of the loss of US institutional credibility, and the imprudent dissipation of its blood and wealth.

Radical breakthrough

From the Indian perspective, 2005 marks the beginning of a breakthrough in the bilateral relationship, and of an increasing correspondence between the two country's strategic orientations. President Bush, despite his insular, non-cerebral Texan image, was determined to radically re-orient the relationship with India, and found a mild-mannered but equally committed partner in Prime Minister Manmohan Singh.

In July 2005, the United States made a dramatic move when it announced a civilian nuclear agreement with India, which inter alia accepted India's status as a nuclear weapons state outside the NPT. The operative section of the announcement contained this key phrase: "President Bush ... stated that as a responsible state with advanced nuclear technology, India should acquire the same benefits and advantages as other such states" (Department of Atomic Energy, India 2005)

The nuclear nettle had been finally removed from the bilateral relationship thanks to the determination of President Bush, which was both radical and unexpected. India's relationship with the United States, and along with it Indian perspectives of the US political establishment, underwent a sea change. The United States was now seen as a natural partner, and this was reflected in Prime Minister Manmohan Singh's address to the US Congress on July 19, 2005. This seminal address by an Indian prime minister related to the entire spectrum of bilateral relations, and the essence of the change in Indian perspectives of the United States is contained in Singh's concluding remarks:

> As two democracies, we are natural partners in many respects. Partnerships can be of two kinds. There are partnerships based on principle and there are partnerships based on pragmatism. I believe we are at a juncture where we can embark on a partnership that can draw both on principle as well as pragmatism. We must build on this opportunity ... I believe that we have made a very good beginning.
>
> (Singh 2005)

After extensive and arduous negotiations, stretching from July 2005 to September 2008, India finally achieved the exceptional status in the nuclear domain that it had long sought, and which the Bush administration successfully enabled. The circle that metaphorically began with Nehru had been finally squared by the tenacity and perspicacity of the Bush–Singh combine. Their determination, which was severely tested to the last, ensured that the strategic interests and anxieties of both the United States and India were adroitly accommodated. This transformative initiative was impelled not by altruism, but by an objective appreciation of the existing global strategic framework, and of the trajectory it was most likely to take over the next few decades.

The past as a guide to the future

After the radical breakthrough on the nuclear issue which was concluded in late 2008 and could be termed a "game-changer," there was considerable hope that the bilateral would be infused with substantive content on the economic and trade front, particularly as far as civilian nuclear commerce and military technology trade were concerned. This was not to be, however. In the United States, a new president – Barack Obama – assumed office, and India applauded the election of the first African American to the White House. In India, the Congress-led UPA government won a second term in office (2009–2014) but was unable to sustain the momentum that had been hoped for in its relationship with the United States. Domestic politics constrained the Indian prime minister, and the unfortunate incident involving Devyani Khobragade – an Indian woman diplomat woman to the US who was charged with the violation of domestic labor law – led to yet another low in the relationship. Experts averred that the India–US relationship had gone as far south as possible for any two nations, without actually severing diplomatic relations. Yet on other matters, India was publicly restrained in its protestations – regarding the Snowden revelations about US cybersnooping, for example – in contrast to the furious reactions of major US allies. This shades-of-grey ambivalence is an abiding feature in US–India ties.

But a new phase in the bilateral relationship has commenced. While there is a global perception that the United States is now a declining power, India recognizes the United States' formidable prowess in hi tech, higher education, and research and development, as well as its abiding profile as the major international power, and seeks an increased level of engagement. The election of Prime Minister Narendra Modi in May 2014 has led to renewed hope that bilateral relations will soon gain renewed traction.

During Modi's September 2014 visit with Obama in Washington, the two leaders published a joint article, the first time that an Indian prime minister and a US president had co-authored an op-ed in a major US daily. The piece noted, *inter alia*:

> While our shared efforts will benefit our own people, our partnership aspires to be larger than merely the sum of its parts. As nations, as people, we aspire to a better future for all; one in which our strategic partnership also produces benefits for the world at large. While India benefits from the growth generated by US investment and technical partnerships, the United States benefits from a stronger, more prosperous India. In turn, the region and the world benefit from the greater stability and security that our friendship creates.
>
> (Modi and Obama 2014)

These are early days for the Modi government in India, and President Obama, in the last lap of his second term, is perceived to be on a weak political wicket, given the control of the US legislature that the Republican Party was able to secure in the 2014 mid-term elections. While there is a certain degree of political dynamism associated with Modi, there are structural and institutional limitations to the extent to which India and the United States are able to cooperate on major issues.

Looking ahead

If the past is any guide, it would be reasonable to expect that India will continue to be ambivalent toward, and wary of, US policies, having internalized the reality that US security and strategic interests are not necessarily convergent or congruent with its own. Whether Pakistan, China, Russia, Iran, Syria, Palestine, terrorism, climate change, or something else, there are many issues about which the political and security establishments of each country have strongly held views that are at variance with each another. However, it is likely that these differences will be managed with less prickliness than in the past.

The next decade is laden with many uncertainties and imponderables, but overall the considered perspective of India's political establishment, private sector, and intelligentsia is that a strategic partnership with the United States ought to be forged, regardless of the many anxieties and disappointments of previous decades.

On balance, it may be averred that for a quarter of a century – since the end of the Cold War in 1991 – the Indian elite and intelligentsia (with the exception of the far left) have been more favorably disposed towards the United States. A Pew Research Center (2014) survey found that 55 percent of Indians held a favorable view of the United States – a marked change from the less favorable perception of previous decades. This shift was enabled both by the economic liberalization that India embarked upon after five decades of socialist economics (often referred to as the "license-raj"), as well as the United States' standing as the sole superpower following the dissolution of the Soviet Union. A combination of the appeal of the capitalist mode of economic development, which benefited the middle classes, and a more pragmatic assessment of the post-Cold War reality, contributed to this gradual shift in public opinion and attitudes toward the United States.

India's overall strategy assessment of the US role is that a strong and militarily robust United States is in India's larger interests. In the immediate afterglow of the 1991 Kuwait war, the United States' stock was very high. Its swift victory over Iraq, along with the demonstration of US military hi tech and the potential of the RMA (revolution in military affairs), heightened the appreciation of the tangible benefits that could accrue to India by moving toward a more substantive relationship with the United States.

China remains an area of abiding anxiety for India, and here Indian perceptions of the United States are mixed. In the early Clinton years, when the United States was seeking to reach out to China, the concern in Delhi was the possibility of a G-2 being established that would be detrimental to Indian interests. However, the latent tension between a rising China and a status quo hegemon came into play, and from Clinton through to Obama it has been evident that the United States is seeking the right balance between engaging China while encouraging it to stay within the framework of global rules and norms. But as the United States knows only too well from its own experience, major powers that are confident in their comprehensive national power tend accept or flout the rule-based system depending on the issue at hand, and on the manner in which it affects its own core national interests.

China will thus remain an area of concern for both the United States and India, and the emergence of a critical strategic triangle that includes these three powers is the reality of the early part of the twenty-first century (Business Standard 2013). The Obama pivot or rebalance has been the subject of considerable discussion and assessment in India, and while a robust partnership with the United States is envisaged, India will not want to be part of a formal US military alliance in the way that either Japan or Australia is. Yet there has been some movement toward fostering closer military cooperation with these three nations (the United States, Japan, and Australia), particularly in the naval domain, and this remains a work in progress. The current political leaderships in India, Japan, and Australia are still refining the contours of their individual relationships with China, and a certain degree of hedging is inevitable.

Two other areas of dissonance will challenge the Indian–US bilateral relationship: Iran; and Islamist terrorism, with specific reference to Pakistan. Ever since the overthrow of the Shah of Iran in 1979 and that country's drastic subsequent transformation, US policy toward Iran has been adversarial. By contrast, India has a different perception of the clerical regime in Tehran. While India has voted against Iran in the International Atomic Energy Agency (IAEA) on the matter of Iran acquiring a nuclear weapon, it is reluctant to follow the United States' lead in severing its economic and trade links. As is the case with other major Asian economies, Iran remains a major source of hydrocarbons, and the growing energy demand in India indicates that this dependence on Iranian oil supplies is unlikely to change. Furthermore, Iran has a special relevance for India as a means to obtain transport access to Afghanistan and Central Asia, both of which are regions of strategic significance for India.

Iran and Pakistan offer an instructive contrast in relation to their linkage with radical Islamic ideologies, and to the complexities inherent in evolving effective national policies to counter state-sponsored terrorism. The United States has its own bleak assessment of Iran as a nation that supports terror, and it is determined that Tehran should not acquire nuclear weapons lest this apocalyptic capability be used to further destabilize the region.

A mirror image can be seen in the Indian assessment of Pakistan. The common wisdom in Delhi is that Pakistan acquired nuclear weapons in the late 1980s through covert means, and has been using this to enhance its capability to engage in terrorism against India since May 1990. In light of the Mumbai terror attack of November 2008 and its linkages with the Pakistani state, as well as the developments of the last five years, this remains a major challenge for the Indian security establishment.

The United States, however, has a more indulgent view of the role played by the Pakistani state in supporting terrorism. As far back as 1992, during the presidency of George Bush Senior, it had arrived at the conclusion that Pakistan was indeed a state sponsor of terrorism, but due to realpolitik and strategic security considerations it chose to make a Faustian pact and to engage with Rawalpindi, the GHQ of the Pakistan Army. This pact included the United States turning a blind eye to Pakistan's clandestine acquisition of nuclear weapons, and to Rawalpindi's recourse to NWET (nuclear weapon-enabled terror). The assessment in India is that this US indulgence is not likely to change in a hurry. In short, Pakistan's locus in the terror domain is the new "nettle" in the India–US relationship, and will test the political determination of Prime Minister Modi and President Obama.

Since the nuclear rapprochement that began in March 2000, there has been a gradual coalescing of what may be termed an Indian lobby in the United States, patiently nurtured by the Indian diaspora. Taking a leaf from the success of the US Jewish lobby, this effort saw the formation of an India caucus in the US Congress, which included senior representatives from both the Senate and the House of Representatives. The US private sector also supported this effort in a selective manner, although the actual growth in trade ties has been modest. Modi has identified the Indian diaspora as a bridge that can support bilateral cooperation, and in his first visit to the United States one of his objectives was to "consolidate the Indian Americans into a strong cohesive lobbying group, (which) is expected to be on the lines of the powerful Jewish lobby that considerably influences state policy in the US" (Chatterjee 2014).

Of more relevance than the Indian lobby in Washington, though, is the manner in which the Indian polity has slowly begun to accept the need for a broader and more substantive relationship with the United States. One of the anomalies of the bilateral relationship was the reluctance of the Indian government during the decade-long Congress Party-led UPA rule (from 2004 to 2014) to be visibly active in enhancing the relationship with Washington. No major political leader has ever endorsed the merits of a substantive engagement with the United States to a domestic Indian audience, and even the radical nuclear agreement was pursued in a very low-profile manner.

However, the Modi government has been more forthcoming. On his September 2014 visit to Washington, Prime Minister Modi and President Obama together declared that the bilateral relationship would be taken to "new levels," and Modi added that their conversation had strengthened his belief "that India and the US are 'natural partners'" (NDTV 2014). Politically, with the exception of the leftist parties, there is consensus among the major Indian political parties such as the BJP and the Congress Party that a more robust relationship with the United States is desirable. It was evident that the moribund Indian–US relations needed fresh political impetus, and this was provided by the unexpected announcement that President Barack Obama would be the chief guest at the Indian Republic Day Parade on January 26, 2015.

Obama's second visit

The formal announcement of the White House accepting Modi's invitation was conveyed first in a tweet: "President Obama looks forward to celebrating Republic Day in New Delhi with you" (White House 2014). This was a dramatic development, representing two firsts: the first time that a US president had been invited to grace the Indian Republic Day Parade as the chief guest – an unthinkable idea, until it actually happened; and also the first time that a White House incumbent would visit India twice during his tenure. President Obama had visited India for the first time in November 2010.

The context for this second Obama visit was remarkable. A year earlier, in early 2014, the bilateral relationship had soured considerably, due to the deplorable treatment meted out by the US Justice Department to an Indian woman diplomat in New York (the Devyani Khobragade case). Few could have imagined that within the year, India would invite the president for the equivalent of its national day in such a warm and enthusiastic manner. Moreover, the fact that Modi had previously been denied a visa by the United States, on the basis of the 2002 Gujarat violence, indicates just how radical a change was being wrought in the sluggish bilateral relationship.

A review of the Obama visit reveals a very rich mix of politico-diplomatic symbolism, as well as a measure of substantive content, which together served to reset and re-energize Indian–US ties. The symbolism that reflected the new comfort level between the two leaders was to be found in Modi's breaking of protocol in order to receive his friend "Barack" on his arrival at the airport, and this tone was continued throughout. The substantive content was announced in the resolution of the stalled civilian nuclear agreement, which had been stuck since late 2008. The liability clauses that India wanted, and the inspection arrangements sought by the United States, had become intractable obstacles. These were now cleared by the high-level political intervention of the two principals, Obama and

Modi. (It should be noted that although the road ahead has now been opened, its path still remains undefined, and a lot of detailed work will have to be completed before there can be any meaningful civilian nuclear commerce between the two countries.)

This breakthrough has had a cascading positive effect on other areas of potential bilateral cooperation and engagement, details of which were laid out in the three announcements made jointly during the visit: the Joint Statement; the Delhi Declaration of Friendship; and the Joint Strategic Vision for Asia-Pacific and the Indian Ocean Region. Predictably, the focus was on two areas of possible cooperation: clean energy, which is linked to the civilian nuclear sector, as well as to new technologies such as solar power, bio-mass, and so on; and the defense trade and technology sector.

India has an urgent need for an infusion of technology, investment, and know-how in these two areas, and they are a priority for the Modi government. If the Indian emphasis was on "made in India," the US president was exploring possibilities to enhance US economic and strategic interests, and a certain correspondence of interests can be identified.

India's development effort, and the improvement of the socioeconomic and human security indicators for millions who remain impoverished, is inexorably linked to the availability of affordable and environmentally sound energy options. Additionally, India's defense and military inventory is in dire need of modernization, which is not merely a case of importing foreign military hardware, at which pursuit India already leads the world. Broad trends indicate that over the next decade, India will allocate up to between $600 billion and 700 billion toward its overall defense expenditure. As much as 40 percent of this would be available for acquisitions and modernization, and the Modi government has indicated that it is determined to encourage the development of domestic manufacturing and (hopefully) design capabilities. While India has a traditionally robust military hardware relationship with Russia, and in niche areas with Israel, engaging with the US private sector offers a viable synergy that could animate the Indian manufacturing sector. There is huge potential for this kind of engagement in such fields as the space, cyber, and maritime domains.

The most significant areas of focus during the Obama visit were those of the Asia-Pacific and the Indian Ocean, and the Joint Strategic Vision document (White House 2015), though pithy, is laden with significant strategic import. Although these matters had been referred to in the past by Delhi, this was the most comprehensive articulation at summit level. The document provides some contours of a possible future framework for the partnership that India and the United States are seeking to forge, in order to improve their management of the uncertainties that have characterized the early decades of the twenty-first century.

Reiterating the common democratic ethos of the two countries, and dwelling on the maritime expanse from "Africa to East Asia," the key paragraph reads:

Regional prosperity depends on security. We affirm the importance of safeguarding maritime security and ensuring freedom of navigation and overflight throughout the region, *especially* [emphasis added] in the South China Sea. We call on all parties to avoid the threat or use of force, and to pursue resolution of territorial and maritime disputes through all peaceful means, in accordance with universally recognized principles of international law, including the United Nations Convention on the Law of the Sea.

(White House 2015)

While India has been consistent in supporting the resolution of potential conflicts in the East Asian region through peaceful dialogue and adherence to "recognized principles of international law" (which in global diplomatic semantics is the equivalent of the motherhood and apple-pie template), the inclusion of the word "especially" in relation to the South China Sea is extremely significant, because of the increasingly assertive manner in which China has been promoting its territorial claims in that area.

Prime Minister Modi has made what may be termed as an assertive move on the regional strategic chessboard, and this has clearly animated Beijing. The Chinese response has been to disparage the Obama visit, while also cautioning India not to roil the South China Sea disputes, which it is determined to address with the affected Association of Southeast Asian Nations (ASEAN) countries alone.

Paradoxically, while India does not wish to become an alliance partner with the United States, it is nonetheless wary of the rise of China and of the creeping assertiveness that has characterized Beijing in recent times. In the long run, ensuring that India maintains the appropriate degree of strategic equipoise and enabling it to realize its latent economic and military potential will benefit both the eagle and the elephant.

Bibliography

Bass, Gary J. 2013. *The Blood Telegram: India's Secret War in East Pakistan.* Gurgaon: Random House India.

BBC News. 2005. "Kissinger Regrets India Comments," July 1. http://news.bbc.co.uk/2/hi/south_asia/4640773.stm.

Business Standard. 2013. "India, China, US Will be in Uneasy Strategic Triangle," September 2. www.business-standard.com/article/news-ians/india-china-us-will-be-in-uneasy-strategic-triangle-113090200647_1.html.

Chatterjee, Mohua. 2014. "Push for India Lobby on Jewish Lines?" *Times of India*, September 25. http://timesofindia.indiatimes.com/india/Push-for-India-lobby-on-Jewish-lines/articleshow/43379057.cms.

Department of Atomic Energy, India. 2005. Joint Statement on India–USA Civil Nuclear Co-operation, July 18. www.dae.nic.in/?q=node/61.

Guha, Ramachandra. 2007. *India After Gandhi: The History of the World's Largest Democracy.* London: Macmillan.

Khare, Harish. 2008. "Manmohan to Bush: People of India Love You." *Hindu*, September 27. www.thehindu.com/todays-paper/manmohan-to-bush-people-of-india-love-you/article1346764.ece.

Kux, Dennis. 1993. *India and the US: Estranged Democracies, 1941–1991*. New Delhi: Sage Publications.

Modi, Narendra, and Barack Obama. 2014. "A Renewed US–India Partnership for the 21st Century." *Washington Post*, September 30. www.washingtonpost.com/opinions/narendra-modi-and-barack-obama-a-us-india-partnership-for-the-21st-century/2014/09/29/dac66812-4824-11e4-891d-713f052086a0_story.html.

Mohan, C. Raja. 2006. *Impossible Allies: Nuclear India, United States, and the Global Order*. New Delhi: India Research Press.

NDTV. 2014. "PM Modi, Obama Pledge to Take Indo-US Bilateral Relationship to New Levels," October 1. www.ndtv.com/article/india/pm-modi-obama-pledge-to-take-indo-us-bilateral-relationship-to-new-levels-600309.

Nehru, Jawaharlal. 1985. *Glimpses of World History*. New Delhi: Oxford University Press.

New York Times. 1998. "Nuclear Anxiety; Indian's Letter to Clinton On the Nuclear Testing," May 13. www.nytimes.com/1998/05/13/world/nuclear-anxiety-indian-s-letter-to-clinton-on-the-nuclear-testing.html?pagewanted=print.

Pew Research Center. 2014. "Global Opposition to US Surveillance and Drones, but Limited Harm to America's Image: Chapter 4, How Asians View Each Other." Pew Global Attitudes and Trends, July 14. www.pewglobal.org/2014/07/14/chapter-4-how-asians-view-each-other/.

Singh, Manmohan. 2005. "There is Much we can Accomplish Together." Address to a Joint Session of the United States Congress, July 19. www.rediff.com/news/2005/jul/19pmspeech.htm.

Wall Street Journal. 2010. "China Joins the Axis of Evil," December 7. http://online.wsj.com/articles/SB10001424052748704156304576003124111945808.

White House. 2014. "Statement by the Press Secretary on the President's Travel to India." Office of the Press Secretary, November 21. www.whitehouse.gov/the-press-office/2014/11/21/statement-press-secretary-president-s-travel-india.

White House. 2015. "US–India Joint Strategic Vision for the Asia-Pacific and Indian Ocean Region." Office of the Press Secretary, January 25. www.whitehouse.gov/the-press-office/2015/01/25/us-india-joint-strategic-vision-asia-pacific-and-indian-ocean-region.

9 US–Latin American relations and the role of the United States in the world
The view from Latin America[1]

Arie M. Kacowicz

Introduction

Latin America is a highly significant region for the United States, although the level of importance (and attention) afforded it has changed over time and across different areas of policy. It is the largest foreign supplier of oil to the United States, and an important partner in the development of alternative fuels, as well as being one of the United States' fastest-growing trading partners. However, it is also the largest source of illegal drugs imported to the United States. Relations between the United States and Latin America 25 years after the end of the Cold War are simultaneously characterized by both normalcy and a large degree of uncertainty (Haass 2008, xi; Smith 2008, 1).

Over the course of more than 200 years of sharing the Western Hemisphere, the relations between Latin America and the United States have seen long-term changes as well as continuities, in both perceptions and practices. A key parameter governing those relations has been that of inequalities and asymmetries of power between the two sides. By the mid-nineteenth century the United States had become stronger than any of the countries of Latin America – in economic, military, and political terms. And by the early twentieth century, the United States became more powerful than the region as a whole (Smith 2008, 405).

Latin America and the United States share a long historical relationship in which, from the Latin American perspective, the drawbacks often outweighed the benefits. The predominant metaphors for understanding the US relationship with Latin America, seen from south of the Rio Grande, have been either "the bull in the china shop," or Mexican Porfirio Díaz's lament: "so far from God, so near to the United States" (quoted in Mares 2015, 302). In the post-Cold War era, however, there has been a sense of fundamental change in the relationship, due to the combination of global challenges to US leadership stemming from the rise of China and other emerging powers, as well as to the diversification of Latin America's international relations in economic, political, and geopolitical terms toward extra-hemispheric actors (Lowenthal and Mostajo 2010; Domínguez and Covarrubias 2014; Mares 2015).

Nowadays there is a *perception* in both Latin America and the United States that there has been a significant decline of US hegemony in the region, to the extent that the United States may be "losing" Latin America to other powers, such as Europe, India, China, Russia, and Iran (Riggirozzi and Tussie 2012; Weeks 2014). Yet in fact, throughout Latin America it is possible to find only a few leaders, such as Argentine President Christina Fernandez de Kirchner, who have shown more than a superficial interest in copying the late Hugo Chávez's political or economic models of anti-Americanism and authoritarianism. Contrary to widely held beliefs, trade between Latin America and the United States is in fact still increasing annually, with the United States still the largest single source of foreign direct investment in the region. So it cannot really be claimed that the United States is "losing" Latin America, although it is true that Latin American countries today have more leverage and opportunities to diversify their international relations than in the past.

One would be hard pressed to find another region in the developing world with greater and more long-standing (and justified!) grievances about Washington's actions and interference, from the Monroe Doctrine, through the "dollar diplomacy" and the "gunboat diplomacy" of the early twentieth century, up to the coups and counter-revolutions associated with "Cold War containment." Thus, one would expect a typical (or stereotypical) sense of antipathy toward the United States among Latin American countries, with this intuitive expectation perhaps best expressed in an oversimplified narrative[2] that would read as follows: Latin Americans do resent the United States, and such resentment is richly deserved (Baker and Cupery 2014, 3).

And yet, after assessing the historical record, the relevant literature, and contemporary public opinion polls of Latin American perceptions of the United States, the real picture seems to be much more complex and multifaceted. Indeed, popular opinion of the United States in Latin America takes a loose form, in which negative and positive elements coexist with no apparent tension. Furthermore, in our analysis of Latin American perceptions of the United States, we should differentiate between the rhetoric of political elites and the public opinion of average citizens, as evident across different Latin American countries (Chiozza 2009, 4; Baker and Cupery 2013).

Over the following pages, I first conduct a brief review of the historical evolution of US–Latin American relations. The crux of the chapter focuses on the contemporary general regional perceptions of the United States, with some more detailed descriptions of attitudes in particular countries. In particular, I assess the Latin American views of the George W. Bush and Barack Obama administrations, as well as perceived Latin American and US roles in the contemporary world. Finally, I suggest some common themes and patterns, along with some conclusions regarding the relevance of the findings for policy.

The historical evolution of US–Latin American relations

In order to make sense of contemporary Latin American perceptions of the United States, we need to place them within the larger historical picture. To start with, we should be aware of the role of the United States in shaping Latin American identity and society.

The Latin American conception of an inter-American legal order has shown an obsession with the norms of sovereignty and independence in terms of its member states, with a concomitant emphasis on the principle of non-intervention. During the nineteenth century, Latin Americans in general (and Mexicans in particular) feared US land expansion. Mexico suffered the most from its northern neighbor, but outside of Mexico, it was Cuba's José Martí who best expressed the fear that the United States' desire for new land might reveal itself more subtly, through the Pan-Americanism movement for instance (McPherson 2007, 81). This suspicion subsequently proved well founded, in light of recurrent US interventions in Mexico, the Caribbean, and Central America, especially between 1904 and 1938.

By the turn of the twentieth century, the external European threat to Latin America had been replaced by the aggressive US foreign policy in the region. The behavior of the United States certainly provoked fear and hatred toward a coercive hegemon and predator. At the same time, the United States also garnered a certain amount of admiration for its actions in protecting its proxy leadership, acting as a kind of regional *caudillo* or even benevolent *patrón* (Ronnig 1963, 160; Ebel and Taras 1990, 200–201). For the region's liberal camp, admiration for the United States also had historical roots, related to the formation of the US constitution and republican presidential model, the American struggle against slavery, and the liberal tenets as embodied by US Presidents Woodrow Wilson and John F. Kennedy.

As a perceived external threat to the region, the United States has fulfilled an important, if unwitting, role in shaping Latin American identity (acting as the "other" in reaction to which identity can be formed) and in the development of a regional international society (Kacowicz 2005, 52–53). For instance, the constant US threat of intervention in the early twentieth century had the effect of inhibiting some Latin American states from using force to settle their international differences. Many precepts of international law developed by prominent South American jurists, such as the Calvo and Drago doctrines, defended the principles of non-intervention and peaceful settlement of disputes. These principles constituted the legal weapon and response of the weak Latin American states to the possibility of forcible interventions by extra-regional powers, first and foremost the United States.

In addition to these legal aspects, the concept of a Latin American international society evolved partially from a complex identity relationship with the United States that included both "negative" and "positive" elements.

The negative components developed as the result of the political and cultural shocks caused by the Spanish defeat in the 1898 Spanish–American War. Out of this "splendid little war" came the Platt Amendment of 1901, binding Cuba's foreign policy to the United States; the US drive to secure the Isthmus of Panama to build a canal; and Theodore Roosevelt's own declaration of the United States as a "police power" over the Caribbean in 1904. Later came the US Mariners, who landed repeatedly in Mexico, Central America, and the Caribbean (McPherson 2007, 83).

In the aftermath of the Spanish–American War and its accompanying soul-searching, some Latin American intellectuals redefined themselves partly in contrast to their North American counterparts, especially culturally and ideologically. For instance, José Enrique Rodó in the early part of the twentieth century epitomized the antinomies between Latin American and North American cultures and ideologies in his book *Ariel* (1922). Thus, *Arielismo*, as a form of Latin Americanism, expressed the cultural superiority of Latin America vis-à-vis the United States, alongside Hispanism and indigenism.

This ideological and cultural schism persisted during the Cold War throughout the late 1980s, when the Latin American countries as a whole (with the notable exception of Cuba) began to adopt the global tenets of political democracy and economic neoliberalism, marking a move toward the United States' own ideological and political culture. Following the Cold War, while the global arena moved toward complexity, the Western Hemisphere was marked by simplicity, at least until a decade ago, when the reassertion of US hegemony brought with it the prospect of geopolitical marginalization for many Latin American countries (Smith 2001, 38). This prospect was met with the emergence of the "new left" in the early 2000s, leading to frictions and fractures within the so-called Washington Consensus, and the rise of a persistent anti-Americanism that posed a challenge to the normalcy and stability of US–Latin American relations. The good news for Washington was that, with the end of the Cold War, anti-Americanism was no longer considered a military or security threat to the United States. Yet aversion and animosity to the United States contributed to the rise of the "pink tide" in the region, propelled by discontented majorities of Latin Americans who no longer accepted the tenets of the neoliberal model (McPherson 2007, 97–99).

Conversely, positive attitudes toward the United States usually derived from the identification of many ruling political elites in Latin America with US political and strategic interests in the Western Hemisphere in general, and in the region in particular. For instance, many analysts tend to attribute the normative consensus that has characterized Latin American international society, including its relatively peaceful international relations, to the potential positive influence of American exceptionalism in general, and US hegemony in particular. After all, the pacifying role of the United States seems to offer a plausible (yet not perfect) explanation for why Latin America, and especially South America, was more peaceful in the twentieth century than in the nineteenth century, with the United States having had both the motive and the capacity to deter wars between Latin American countries. However, it has been amply demonstrated that the "long peace" in the region is not necessarily linked to the United States, with a range of other factors being far more likely candidates (Kacowicz 1998, 2005). All the same, today many socialist leaders in the region are ready to adopt a more pragmatic approach toward normalized relations with the "colossus of the North," especially those of Brazil.

Contemporary perceptions of the United States: a regional approach

Do Latin American citizens admire the United States for its material wealth and the opportunities this creates for them, or do they resent the United States because of the enduring military and economic threat it has historically posed to the region? According to Baker and Cupery (2013), both narratives inform the contemporary perceptions of the United States in Latin America. From a regional perspective, we can probably group the Latin American countries into three different categories: 1 those who oppose the United States on ideological grounds, first and foremost Cuba and Venezuela, and the other countries that conform ALBA (the Bolivarian Alliance for the Peoples of Our America); 2 those who are close (geographically) and/or are aligned with the United States, such as Mexico, Colombia, Peru, and several Central American countries; and 3 the rest of the countries of the region, which maintain an ambiguous attitude toward the United States. In this context, we should differentiate between those who promote an active discourse against the United States and those who remain ambiguous, such as Argentina and Ecuador.

The view from the left

New left-wing movements and governments in the region reflect broader social processes in Latin America that reject neoliberalism and market versions of democracy, proposing instead a "new politics" based on a transformed understanding of democracy and inclusion. At the regional level, this has been translated into commitments to schemes for regional cooperation, such as ALBA (the Bolivarian Alliance for the Peoples of Our America) and CELAC (the Economic Community of Latin American and Caribbean countries, created in 2010), as a way of resisting US power and dominance in the region (Riggirozzi 2010).

Since the end of the Cold War and the disappearance of the Soviet Union, there has been no real or significant challenge to the US hegemony in the Western Hemisphere. The challenge posed by countries such as Cuba, Venezuela, Bolivia, Ecuador, Nicaragua, and perhaps Argentina to US dominance has been first and foremost rhetorical. These countries do not suggest a practical alternative to the existing security architecture, but rather a diluted form of "soft balancing," to redress to some extent the distribution of power in the international system in general, and in the Americas in particular (Lowenthal 2013, 6; Skidmore and Smith 1992, 376).

By launching ALBA in 2005, Venezuela and Cuba have attempted to develop an alternative regional scheme in opposition to neoliberalism and to economic globalization as sponsored by the United States. In particular, they have resisted the idea (one which never actually came to fruition) of establishing a Free Trade Area of the Americas (FTAA), and instead promoted a nationalistic and alternative regional path of integration. Thus, ALBA should be understood as a counter-hegemonic-globalization project that operates through international and transnational processes ranging from the local to the global (Muhr 2012, 768). According to this logic, member states of ALBA have established "strategic alliances" with Iran and Syria, as well as with powers such as China and Russia, in their opposition to the United States.

The Bolivarian Alliance Countries (Cuba, Venezuela, Bolivia, Ecuador, Nicaragua, and perhaps Argentina) are profoundly suspicious of globalization and market capitalism, and they prefer plebiscitary (illiberal, populist) forms of democracy to liberal representative institutions. At the level of their political elites, at least, there is a clear rhetoric of animosity toward the United States; however, this is not always reflected in their citizens' attitudes, which are often more positive.

ALBA and CELAC were heralded as indicators of significantly decreased US influence, since they both exclude the United States and use rhetoric attacking the United States and the liberal international order. It is not clear, however, what ALBA represents today, given that Hugo Chávez deceased and Venezuela's ability to finance ALBA has been destroyed by falling international oil prices and economic mismanagement at home (Mares 2015).

The view from the right

Conversely, the pro-US attitude that is reflected in the public opinion of vast sectors of the Latin American population is represented in the political writings of Mario Vargas Llosa, who identifies himself as a liberal thinker:

> Another positive sign in today's Latin American scenario filled with uncertainty is that the old anti-American sentiment pervading the

continent has diminished notably. The truth is that today, anti-Americanism is stronger in countries such as Spain and France than in Mexico or Peru. There are two reasons for the change in attitude toward the United States, one pragmatic and the other one of principle. Latin Americans who have retained their common sense understand that for geographic, economic, and political reasons, fluid, robust trade relations with the United States are indispensable for our development. In addition, US foreign policy, rather than backing dictatorships as it did in the past, now consistently supports democracies and rejects authoritarian tendencies.

(Vargas Llosa 2005, 3)

Furthermore, according to Vargas Llosa (2005, 4), and contrary to the view of Huntington (2004), the presence of about 40 million people of Latin American heritage in the United States bolsters the Untied States by contributing vitality and cultural capital, and forms a bridge between the two Americas.

Regional and national perceptions

Latin American citizens today are not overwhelmingly anti-American. On the contrary, recent polling data from the Pew Research Center suggests that on balance the opposite is true. Clear majorities of respondents in nearly every Latin American country (with the exception of Argentina) hold favorable perceptions of the United States, with some two-thirds of the public holding a favorable opinion of some description. Even a cursory look at public opinion data shows that the alleged anti-Americanism and "shared resentment" against the *yanqui* menace no longer exists, and has not done so since the 1990s. Data from the 18-country *Latinobarómetro* survey series shows that, on average, in every year between 1995 and 2010, Latin American respondents holding favorable views of the United States outnumbered those expressing negative views (Chiozza 2009, 19; Baker and Cupery 2014, 3). Still, the favorable collective positive perception of the United States might be related to "people-to-people interdependences," in the form of tourism, trade, student exchanges, and civil society exchanges across the divide between the two Americas.

Table 9.1 displays results from the Pew Research Global Attitude Project for 2013 and 2014; respondents were asked whether they had a favorable perception of, and attitude toward the United States.

The average percentage of Latin American respondents who expressed favorable opinions toward the United States (77 percent) was similar to those expressing favorable opinions toward China (77 percent), less than toward Europe (87 percent) and Japan (86 percent), but more than toward Cuba (55 percent) and Venezuela (51 percent). Interestingly, the average perception in the rest of the world is more unfavorable toward

Table 9.1 Proportion of population with a favorable perception of the United States (in %)

Country	2013	2014
Argentina	40	36
Bolivia	53	55
Brazil	73	65
Chile	68	72
El Salvador	79	80
Mexico	66	63
Venezuela	53	62

the United States than the average perception in Argentina, which is the most anti-US country in Latin America (Baker and Cupery 2014, 4).

Relative to other countries in other regions of the world, the United States receives mostly favorable ratings in the region, particularly in El Salvador, Brazil, Chile, and Mexico. Brazilians and Mexicans have become notably more positive toward the United States in recent years. Even in Bolivia and Venezuela, two countries whose national leaders have regularly engaged in vitriolic anti-US rhetoric over the past few years, the United States gets positive marks on balance, although in both countries ratings are higher among people situated on the political right than among those on the political left. Even more surprisingly, many of the countries that experienced US military interventions throughout the twentieth century (such as the Dominican Republic, El Salvador, Guatemala, Nicaragua, and Panama) are also the countries whose popular opinions about the United States are the most favorable (Baker and Cupery 2014, 2).

Contemporary perceptions of the United States: some country distinctions

In this section, I briefly review contemporary perceptions of the United States in Mexico, Venezuela, Brazil, Bolivia, and Argentina.

Mexico

Mexicans are surpassed only by the Argentines in their lack of goodwill toward the United States. But unlike Argentina, among other countries in the region, Mexico has very good reasons to detest the United States. And yet, Mexicans are on balance pro-American; about 60 percent of them had a favorable opinion of the United States between 1995 and 2010 (Baker and Cupery 2014, 7).

In the Mexican case, anti-American sentiments are intertwined with a long history of US interventions, ranging from the US–Mexican War of the mid-nineteenth century to the Mexican Revolution of 1910–1917. Still, under the influence of market-opening policies, adopted since the 1980s, and with the launching of the North American Free Trade Agreement (NAFTA) in 1994, Mexican sentiments toward the United States have become less antagonistic, if not pragmatic. The United States may well become more Hispanicized, *pace* the late Huntington. Furthermore, closer links with the United States may well bring about increased prosperity. Interestingly enough, geography and interdependence matter a lot: less interaction with the Americans seems to be associated with more anti-Americanism (Bow *et al.* 2007, 4, 33).

There is still a lingering feeling of deep and distrustful ambivalence toward the United States stemming from its refusal to recognize Mexico as an equal partner. There is also a clear divide between the political elites and the general public, which usually tends to be more pro-American (ibid., 33 and 39). In the Mexican case, US immigration policy has become the most important issue in their bilateral relations (Hakim 2006, 51).

Venezuela

The late Hugo Chávez was the first Latin American leader of the post-Cold War period to revive a consistently oppositional stance to the United States in both discourse and practices (McPherson 2007, 99). Among his many statements about the United States, one stands out: "In all history, there was never a government more terrorist than that of the US 'empire'" (Baker and Cupery 2014, 2). Chávez did not waste any opportunity to attack Bush personally, as he did most famously in a 2006 speech at the United Nations that referred to the US president as "the devil himself" and as a "world dictator" (quoted in Encarnación 2008).

From the beginning, it was clear that Chávez intended to take nationalistic and independent positions in international relations, even though there was some evidence that he was willing to accommodate US interests, such as continuing oil sales to the United States. His strategy for opposing the United States was rooted in the creation of both alliances and institutions that excluded the North Americans, such as ALBA (Vanderbush 2009, 343). At the rhetorical, declaratory level, Chávez, like Fidel Castro, regarded the United States and global capitalism as permanent adversaries (Crandall 2011, 92). And yet, despite the continuous tensions between Washington and Caracas, more than six in ten Venezuelans have a favorable opinion of the United States (Stokes 2014).

Challenging the United States has had a strong ideological component, as in practice it rests on the ability of the Venezuelan government (in connivance with Cuba), to mobilize political, economic or symbolic resources to resist direct US actions (Russell and Calle 2009). Moreover, some analysts perceive Venezuela as a security threat to the United States, due to its strong links with Iran and its prominent role as a primary transit country for cocaine flowing from Colombia to the United States, Europe, and West Africa. Venezuela has also had a significant effect on the foreign policy of countries like Argentina, leading to the latter's rapprochement with Iran and stance against the United States, and it has supported the FARC (the Revolutionary Armed Forces of Colombia) against the Colombian government (Walswer 2010, 2; Morales Solá 2013).

Brazil and Bolivia

Other elected heads of state in South America – such as Luiz Inácio Lula da Silva in Brazil, Néstor Kirchner in Argentina, Tabaré Vázquez in Uruguay, and Michelle Bachelet in Chile – soon joined Chávez in vociferously opposing US policies in the region. For instance, Lula's defiance of the US-promoted FTAA contributed to the failure of the 2003 WTO talks in Cancun and the 2004 FTAA negotiations in Miami (McPherson 2007, 100). In Bolivia, Evo Morales has explicitly spoken out on behalf of those long excluded from power because of their race. For this reason, his anti-US rhetoric has suggested a deep, perhaps irreconcilable cultural distance with the United States (McPherson 2007, 101). In a similar vein, the 2005 Summit of the Americas in Mar del Plata, Argentina, epitomized the consolidation of this anti-US rhetoric within ALBA, and against the possibility of an FTAA (Free Trade Area for the Americas).

In sum, the relative decline in US importance in the region, in terms of perception, is partly found in the successful challenges to the US hegemony made by Latin American leaders, including the late Hugo Chávez in Venezuela, Fidel and Raúl Castro in Cuba, and Evo Morales in Bolivia – the Latin American "axis of evil," as the Bolivian president is fond of describing the three countries (quoted in Vanderbush 2009, 342).

Argentina

Among all the countries of the region, Argentina stands out for its traditional aversion to the United States, rooted in historical and geopolitical circumstances. It is worth recalling that Argentina led the opposition against the United States during the first Pan-American Conference, held in Washington in 1889. Argentina had always regarded itself as an alternative to and a potential competitor with the United States in the Western Hemisphere, with the possible exception of the 1990s, when, under the administration of Carlos Menem, the two countries sustained very close relations. Thus, over the two countries' long history of more than 200 years, Argentina has generally sustained a "Gaullist" attitude toward the US hegemony in the Western Hemisphere.

In 2014 Wonder Consultants published the following results from a poll of 3,089 Argentines regarding their opinion of the United States: "Very good," 514; "good," 1,295; "regular/fair," 794; "bad," 292; and "very bad,"

194. In comparative terms, Argentines rated Brazil, Uruguay, France, and Chile in better terms than the United States, whereas the United Kingdom, Spain, Israel, Ecuador, Bolivia, Venezuela, Nicaragua, and Iran received worse scores. Currently the relations between the two countries are in crisis, due to Argentina's sovereign debt being litigated in US courts, as well as to the recent Argentine rapprochement toward Iran, conducted in spite of the terrorist attacks perpetrated in 1992 and 1994 against the Israeli Embassy and the local Jewish community in Buenos Aires. Moreover, Argentines still resent the shocking indifference – even obliviousness – of the Bush administration toward the severe Argentine economic crisis of 2001–2002 (Encarnación 2008).

Latin American perceptions of the Bush (2001–2009) and Obama (2009–2014) administrations

In this section, I refer to the Latin American perceptions of US global standing under the two George W. Bush administrations (2001–2009), as well as the six years of the Obama administrations (2009–2014). In particular, I assess how these perceptions affect overall Latin American foreign policy orientation in general, and policy toward the United States in particular. I relate this to Latin American countries' perceptions of their own role in the world, as well as of the role of the United States.

Latin American perceptions of the Bush administrations, 2001–2009

From the standpoint of the Latin American countries, the Bush era is likely to be remembered with a profound sense of disappointment. In Latin America, there were no parallel examples of Bush's AIDS and malaria initiatives in Africa, or the tsunami relief in Asia, which generated significant goodwill for the United States. Indeed, one is hard pressed to find a bright spot in the bilateral relations after September 2001 (Encarnación 2008).

When George W. Bush took office in January 2001 there were expectations that he would prioritize the relationship with Latin America in general and Mexico in particular. And indeed, he managed to maintain this commitment for seven and a half months, until 9/11, after which the United States focused attention on its "War on Terror" against Afghanistan, al-Qaeda, and Iraq (Castañeda 2008, 126; and Shifter 2004). The subsequent lack of attention to Latin America led to the redefinition of the US–Latin American relationship as the "forgotten relationship" (Castañeda 2003). Issues such as an immigration agreement with Mexico, fighting poverty and inequality, strengthening democracy and the rule of law, and promoting economic development were abandoned or marginalized in the US agenda. Instead, the United States led a process of securitization (or militarization) of its relations with countries such as Mexico and Colombia as part of its struggle against terrorism, guerrillas, and narco-traffic.

Perhaps the only positive note in the relations between Latin America and the United States in this period can be found in trade, with the creation of the Central American Free Trade Area (CAFTA), ratified by the US Senate in June 2005. At the same time, that success was eclipsed by the final collapse of the trade talks about the creation of a hemispheric free trade area (FTAA) in Mar del Plata in November 2005.

In more general, international terms, people in the region resented the Bush administration's aggressive unilateralism and condemned Washington's disregard for international institutions and norms, naming and shaming the US actions as "unilateralism," "hegemony," and "empire" (Hakim 2006, 47; Shifter 2004). For many Latin Americans, the US practice of preventive military action has a long history in the region, especially vis-à-vis Central American and Caribbean countries, such as Grenada (1983) and Panama (1989). Thus, US actions in Afghanistan and Iraq touched a raw nerve among Latin Americans, who viewed them as a blatant disregard for the precepts of international law (Shifter 2004).

More disturbing still were the Bush administration's coercive tactics when pressuring Latin American governments to support the war in Iraq in 2003, as the main focus of its global war on terror. A case in point was the discussion at the United Nations regarding possible military action against Iraq in 2003. Mexico and Chile, in addition to Cuba and Venezuela, opposed the US invasion at the United Nations Security Council. Several Central American countries (including Honduras, El Salvador, Nicaragua, Costa Rica, Panama, and the Dominican Republic), as well as Colombia, supported the United States, whereas most of the South American countries adopted an intermediate, ambiguous, and reluctant position. The unilateral and coercive approach adopted by the United States backfired, as many governments, including traditional US partners such as Chile and Mexico, refused to cooperate. This explains why in his second term President Bush attempted a more conciliatory approach toward Latin America, for instance, cultivating a pragmatic and even personal relationship with the Brazilian leftist president Lula (Crandall 2011, 92–93).

Ordinary Latin Americans have shown themselves openly contemptuous of President Bush on a personal level, arguably one of the most unpopular US presidents in Latin America ever. Bush's 2007 tour of the region (taking in Brazil, Colombia, Uruguay, Guatemala, and Mexico) provided ample evidence of the Latin American dislike of the US president (Encarnación 2008). The dissatisfaction with Bush reflected a widespread opposition to specific US policies, including the invasion of Iraq and the ideological insistence on the benefits of the "Washington Consensus" (Lowenthal 2010). For instance, according to a BBC poll conducted in Brazil in 2007, more than four in five Brazilians disapproved of the United States' handling of the war in Iraq (85 percent), of the war between Israel and Hezbollah in Lebanon in 2006 (82 percent), and of the US policy toward the Iranian nuclear program (80 percent) (Pew 2007). According to 83 percent, the US military presence in the Middle East provoked conflict, rather than preventing it. Also highly unpopular in Brazil (and in Latin America in general) was the United States' treatment of the detainees at Guantanamo (76 percent), as well as US policies on global warming (73 percent).

Latin American perceptions of the Obama administrations, 2009–2014

Following his election in November 2008, President Obama came to office with a real opportunity to repair Washington's tattered relationship with Latin America. He began with the advantage of not being George W. Bush, and all 33 countries in the region, including Cuba and Venezuela, broadly welcomed Obama's election as the forty-fourth president of the United States (LeoGrande 2011; Erikson 2008, 102–103; and Whitehead and Nolte 2012, 3).

As part of his general approach to international relations, characterized by cooperation and diplomatic engagement, President Obama promised a new partnership with Latin America based on equality and multilateralism. He participated in the Fifth Summit of the Americas at Port of Spain, Trinidad and Tobago, in April 2009, where he engaged in a civil dialogue with the late Hugo Chávez. A few months later, at the OAS (Organization of American States) General Assembly, the United States agreed to repeal the 1962 resolution that suspended Cuba's membership, although it made the return of Cuba to the OAS conditional on its adoption of the 2011 Democratic Charter.

And yet, as with his predecessor, Latin Americans became disappointed with Obama's policies toward the region, due to the relative inattention and lack of innovation in US policies toward the rest of the Western Hemisphere, at least until December 17, 2014 (Whitehead and Nolte 2012, 4). This sense of disappointment reflected how few of Obama's initial promises of change had been realized. Criticism came not only from the predictable sources – the Castro brothers in Cuba, the late Hugo Chávez in Venezuela, Evo Morales in Bolivia, and the Kirchners in Argentina – but also from President Lula in Brazil, and from many experienced analysts in Latin America and the Caribbean (Lowenthal 2010). "The truth is that nothing has changed, and I view that with sadness," remarked President Lula as he left office (quoted in LeoGrande 2011). As with the Bush administrations, the encouraging news related only to trade, specifically the ratification of trade agreements with Colombia and Panama.

Then, on December 17, 2014, the US and Cuban presidents, Barack Obama and Raúl Castro, simultaneously announced a historical breakthrough in US–Cuba relations, including the restoration of full diplomatic relations between the two countries after a hiatus of 53 years, along with a series of reconciliatory actions. Obama said the United States and Cuba had chosen "to cut loose the shackles of the past," and Castro called for the embargo to end.

From the Latin American perspective, there has been widespread agreement about the need for normalizing relations between Cuba and the United States. Policy toward Cuba has long divided the United States from the rest of the hemisphere. There is a consensus among the other nations of the hemisphere (including Canada) that Washington's 53-year-old embargo has not worked and, in fact, may have been counterproductive, prolonging Cuba's non-democratic rule rather than ending it. Bringing Cuba back into the hemispheric fold was one of the main reasons for the creation of CELAC in 2010, which excluded the United States but included Cuba. Thus, by deciding to normalize relations with Cuba, Obama regained respect, if not admiration, from the Latin American countries and peoples.

Latin American perceptions of its role in the world, and of the US role

The relationship between Latin America and the United States has been influenced not only by the power asymmetry between the parties, but also by the changing global context (Mares 2015). Yet the participation of Latin American countries in world politics has traditionally been a function of the intertwining dynamics of US–Latin American relations and the continental hegemony of the United States. Since the United States has been the paramount power (at least until recently), to some extent the participation of Latin America in world politics has been perceived as relatively minor if not insignificant.

Latin American views on global security are very much affected by the states' strong adherence to norms of sovereignty and non-intervention (Kacowicz 2005). There is a common perception in Latin America that the region is far away from the most pressing global security issues and hotspots, including terrorism, rogue states, failed states, and the proliferation of weapons of mass destruction. Therefore, it seems that Latin American countries are reluctant to take upon themselves international responsibilities "out of their area" in the more general context of global or international security (Merke 2011, 4; Heine 2006, 485–487). This reluctance has a strong ideological basis, with most of the Latin American nations opposed to active cooperation with the United States, and preferring a more multilateral and multi-polar world to the "unipolar moment" under the aegis of the United States.

As mostly small or middle-sized powers in a region generally considered as being on the margins of global security, Latin America has historically placed a strong emphasis on the legal international order, and on its participation in international organizations such as the United Nations (Heine 2006, 481). Traditionally, Latin American countries always favored the strategy of binding multilateralism, using global institutions to restrain the power of the United States and to persuade Washington to comply, or at least to adhere to international laws and rules (Russell and Tokatlian 2011, 138). This also explains the tendency of many Latin American countries (with the exceptions of Colombia and Panama) to vote with other developing countries at international forums and against the United States.

By and large, Latin American nations have adopted a rather passive role in the world security architecture. A case in point is the US invasion of Iraq in 2003, as mentioned above. Similarly, in the case of Libya (2011 onward), despite their rhetorical support for the new humanitarian intervention doctrine of "Responsibility to Protect," many Latin American countries also opposed the UN and US actions in Libya.

In the new world architecture, with the increased presence of such external actors as Russia, China, and Iran in Latin America, there is a widespread perception of a kind of "hegemonic vacuum" on the part of the United States. Thus, several Latin American countries – notably Brazil, Chile, Mexico, Peru, and Venezuela – have been vigorously building bridges and ties beyond the Americas, with countries of the European Union, the Asia-Pacific Economic Cooperation forum, and China, India, Iran, and Russia (Lowenthal 2010; and Vanderbush 2009). In particular, many people in the region look to China as an economic and political alternative to US hegemony, though the involvement of China in the region has been so far mostly in the economic realm (Hakim 2006, 45; Tokatlian 2007; and Arnson and Davidow 2011).

Explaining Latin American perceptions of the United States: looking for common patterns and themes

What are the variables that might explain, in general terms, the diversity of Latin American attitudes toward the United States? Here is a tentative list:

1 *The realities of asymmetrical distribution of power between the parties*: Because of Latin America's particularly long-lived, diverse, and unequal interactions with the United States, the region's realities contribute significantly to discounting claims that anti-Americanism is either a recent phenomenon or one that is primarily an irrational rejection of US models of civilization (McPherson 2007, 77).
2 *The realities of economic interdependence*: The polling data indicates that the stronger the economic ties between a Latin American country and the United States – whether through trade, aid, migration, remittances, or investment – the more favorable are its citizens' opinions toward the United States. In a nutshell, economic interdependence trumps historical legacies of American imperialism and exploitation (see Baker and Cupery 2014).

3 *Geography matters*: It is within the countries that are geographically closest to the United States (such as Mexico, and the Central American and Caribbean states) that we can identify the most favorable perceptions of the United States. Conversely, Argentina keeps its distance from the United States, in both geopolitical and ideological terms.

Conclusions

There is important policy relevance to these findings and explanations, since Latin American attitudes and perceptions toward the United States can shape trade and policy preferences in Latin American countries, such as in Mexico and the Central American countries (Kocher and Minushkin 2007). In other words, most of the region's leaders are well aware of the overwhelming political and economic strength of the United States, so they are pragmatic enough to work hard in order to maintain good relations with the United States. Thus, what the majority of Latin American countries most want and need from the United States are productive and efficient economic ties, such as the free trade agreements concluded during the Bush and Obama administrations (see Hakim 2006, 48).

It is time to move beyond the caricature that depicts Latin America as a self-perceived helpless victim of oppressive US imperialism, which uses and abuses the tools of globalization in order to continue its neo-colonial exploitation of the region. (One could in fact argue that today China uses more neo-colonial economic tools in the region than the United States.) Even though there are genuine sentiments of anti-Americanism, rooted in a long and tragic shared history, and fed by certain decisions and acts in US foreign policy (such as the wars in Iraq), overall it seems that globalization, trade, and economic opportunities attract more than they repel.

On average, then, the region's citizens are favorable toward the United States, and they are more likely to view the United States through the lens of economic opportunity than of threat (Baker and Cupery 2013, 126). Thus, Latin American perceptions of the United States are tinted today by a more mundane and pragmatic view that brings the region much closer to the United States than one might expect from reading Galeano's *Open Veins of Latin America* (1971).

This state of affairs is wittily summarized by my colleague Professor Robert Lieber (2007), who argues, in characterizing the complex relations between developing countries (including those of Latin America) and the United States, that the slogan "Yankees go Home!" should be complemented by the addendum: "...But take me with you!"[3] There might still be a lingering cultural clash and innate tension between the two Americas, but their shared need for the economic and political benefits of practical cooperation bridges their cultural and historical schisms.

Notes

1 This chapter is based upon a paper presented at the international conference "America's Stand in the World: Image and Reality," held at the BESA Center, Bar-Ilan University, on December 8, 2014. I would like to thank Galia Press-Barnathan, Keren Sasson, Exequiel Lacovsky, David Mares, Robert Lieber, Rut Diamint, Daniel Wajner, and the editors of this book for their comments and suggestions.
2 See Baker and Cupery (2014), and McPherson (2007, 77).
3 The original quote is from "Yankee Go Home, But Take Me With You," the title of a paper by Jairam Ramesh, Secretary, Economic Affairs Department, All-India Congress Committee, presented to the Roundtable on India–US Relations organized by the Council on Foreign Relations and the Asia Society, New York, November 1, 1999. www.jaimram-ramesh.com/publications/yankee.htm.

Bibliography

Arnson, Cynthia J., and Jeffrey Davidow, eds. 2011. *China, Latin America, and the United States: The New Triangle*. Washington, DC: Woodrow Wilson International Center for Scholars.

Baker, Andy, and David Cupery. 2013. "Anti-Americanism in Latin America: Economic Exchange, Foreign Policy Legacies, and Mass Attitudes toward the Collossus of the North." *Latin American Research Review* 48 (2): 106–130.

Baker, Andy, and David Cupery. 2014. "Gringo Stay Here!" *Americas*, March 23: 1–13. www.americasquarterly.org/gringo-stay-here.

Bow, Brian, Peter Katzenstein, and Arturo Santa-Cruz. 2007. "Anti-Americanism in North America: Canada and Mexico." Paper presented at the Forty-Eighth Annual Meeting of the International Studies Association, Chicago, February 28 to March 3.

Castañeda, Jorge G. 2003. "The Forgotten Relationship." *Foreign Affairs*, May/June.

Castañeda, Jorge G. 2008. "Morning in Latin America: The Chance for a New Beginning." *Foreign Affairs* 87 (5): 126–139.

Chiozza, Giacomo. 2009. *Anti-Americanism and the American World Order*. Baltimore, MD: Johns Hopkins University Press.

Crandall, Russell. 2011. "The Post-American Hemisphere: Power and Politics in an Autonomous Latin America." *Foreign Affairs* 90 (3): 83–95.

Domínguez, Jorge I., and Ana Covarrubias, eds. 2014. *Routledge Handbook of Latin America and the World*. New York: Routledge.

Ebel, Roland H., and Raymond Taras. 1990. "Cultural Style and International Policy-Making: The Latin American Tradition." In Jongsuk Chay, ed., *Culture and International Relations*. New York: Praeger, 191–206.

Encarnación, Omar G. 2008. "The Cost of Indifference: Latin America and the Bush Era." *Global Dialogue* 10. www.world.dialogue.org/content.php?id=432.

Erikson, Daniel P. 2008. "Obama and Latin America: Magic or Realism?" *World Policy Journal* 25 (4): 101–107.

Galeano, Eduardo. 1971. *Open Veins of Latin America: Five Centuries of the Pillage of a Continent*. New York: Monthly Review Press.

Hakim, Peter. 2006. "Is Washington Losing Latin America?" *Foreign Affairs* 85 (1): 39–53.

Haass, Richard N. 2008. "Foreword." In Shannon K. O'Neill, ed., *U.S.-Latin American Relations: A New Direction for a New Reality*. New York: Council on Foreign Relations, xi–xii.

Heine, Jorge. 2006. "Between a Rock and a Hard Place: Latin America and Multilateralism after 9.11." In Edward Newman, Ramesh Thakur, and John Triman, eds., *Multilateralism under Challenge? Power, International Order, and Structural Change*. Tokyo: United Nations University Press.

Huntington, Samuel P. 2004. *Who are We? The Challenges to America's National Identity*. New York: Simon & Schuster.

Kacowicz, Arie M. 1998. *Zones of Peace in the Third World: South America and West Africa in Comparative Perspective*. Albany, NY: SUNY Press.

Kacowicz, Arie M. 2005. *The Impact of Norms in International Society: The Latin American Experience, 1881–2001*. Notre Dame, IN: University of Notre Dame Press.

Kocher, Matthew A., and Susan Minushkin. 2007. "Antiamericanismo y Globalizacion Economica: Libre Comercio, Apertura de Mercados y Opinion Publica en Mexico." *Politica y Gobierno* 14 (1): 77–115.

LeoGrande, William M. 2011. "Latin American Policy in the Next Two Years: The Obama Administration and the New Congress." *WOLA: Washington Office in Latin America*, March 7. www.wola.org/event/latin_american_policy_in_the_next_two_years_the_Obama_administration_and_the_new_congress.

Lieber, Robert J. 2007. *The America Era: Power and Strategy for the 21st Century*. New York: Cambridge University Press.

Lowenthal, Abraham F. 2010. "Obama and the Americas: Promise, Disappointment, Opportunity." *Foreign Affairs*, August 2010: 110–124.

Lowenthal, Abraham F. 2013. "Rethinking US–Latin American Relations: Thirty Years of Transformations." In *The Americas in Motion: Looking Ahead*. Washington, DC: Inter-American Dialogue, 1–7.

Lowenthal, Abraham F., and Felix G. Mostajo. 2010. "Estados Unidos y América Latina, 1960–2010: De la Pretensión Hegemónica a las Relaciones Diversas y Complejas." *Foro Internacional* 50 (3/4): 552–626.

Mares, David R. 2015. "United States' Impact on Latin America's Security Environment: The Complexities of Power Disparity." In David R. Mares and Arie M. Kacowicz, eds., *Routledge Handbook of Latin American Security*. London: Routledge.

McPherson, Alan. 2007. "Anti-Americanism in Latin America." In Brendon O'Connor, ed., *Anti-Americanism: Comparative Perspectives*. Portsmouth, NH: Greenwood, 77–102.

Merke, Federico. 2011. "Framing Global Security in South America." Paper presented at the workshop on "Global Security Regimes in the Making," Rio de Janeiro, Brazil.

Morales Solá, Joaquin. 2013. "Una Foto del Aislamiento Argentino." *La Nación*, February 3. www.lanacion.com.ar/1551395-una-foto-del-aislamiento-argentino.

Muhr, Thomas. 2012. "The Politics of Space in the Bolivarian Alliance for the Peoples of Our America – Peoples' Trade Agreement (ALBA-TCP): Transnationalism, the Organized Society, and Counter-Hegemonic Governance." *Globalizations* 9 (6): 767–782.

Pew Research Center. 2007. "Latin America." www.pewresearch.org/topics/latin-america/.

Riggirozzi, Pia. 2010. "Region, Regionness and Regionalism in Latin America: Towards a New Synthesis." Latin American Trade Network, Working Paper 130, April: 1–17.

Riggirozzi, Pia, and Diana Tussie. 2012. "The Rise of Post-Hegemonic Regionalism in Latin America." In Pia Riggirozzi and Diana Tussie, eds., *The Rise of Post-Hegemonic Regionalism*. Dordrecht: Springer, 1–16.

Rodó, Jose Enrique. 1922. *Ariel*. Translated by Frederic J. Stimson. Boston: Houghton Mifflin.

Ronning, C. Neale. 1963. *Law and Politics in Inter-American Diplomacy*. New York: John Wiley & Sons.

Russell, Roberto, and Fabian Calle. 2009. "La Periferia Turbulenta como Factor de la Expansión de los Intereses de Seguridad de EEUU en América Latina." In Monica Hirst, ed., *Crisis de Estado e Intervención Internacional: Una Mirada desde el Sur*. Buenos Aires: Edhasa.

Russell, Roberto, and Juan Gabriel Tokatlian. 2008. "Resistencia y Cooperacion: Opciones Estrategicas de America Latina frente a Estados Unidos." In Ricardo Lagos, ed., *America Latina: Integración o Fragmentación*. Buenos Aires: Editorial Edhasa, 209–238.

Russell, Roberto, and Juan Gabriel Tokatlian. 2011. "Beyond Orthodoxy: Asserting Latin America's New Strategic Options toward the United States." *Latin American Politics and Society* 53 (4): 127–146.

Shifter, Michael. 2004. "The United States and Latin America through the Lens of Empire." *Current History*, February 1. www.thedialogue.org/page.cfm?pageID=32&pubID=1044.

Skidmore, Thomas E., and Peter H. Smith. 1992. *Modern Latin America*. New York: Oxford University Press.

Smith, Peter H. 2001. "Strategic Options for Latin America." In Joseph S. Tulchin and Ralph H. Espach, eds., *Latin America in the New International System*. Boulder, CO: Lynne Rienner, 35–72.

Smith, Peter H. 2008. *Talons of the Eagle: Latin America, the United States, and the World*. Third edn. New York: Oxford University Press.

Stokes, Bruce. 2014. "Which Countries Don't Like America and Which Do." Pew Research Center, July 15.

The Economist, 2010. "A Latin American Decade: Special Report on Latin America," September 9.

Tokatlian, Juan Gabriel. 2007. "Las relaciones entre Latinoamerica y China: un enfoque para su aproximación." *Análisis Político* 59 (Enero-Abril): 46–56.

Vanderbush, Walt. 2009. "The Bush Administration Record in Latin America: Sins of Omission and Commission." *New Political Science* 313 (3): 337–359.

Vargas Llosa, Mario. 2005. "Confessions of a Liberal." Address at Kristol Lecture AEI Annual Dinner, Washington DC.

Walswer, Ray. 2010. "State Sponsors of Terrorism: Time to Add Venezuela to the List." *Heritage Foundation*, January 20. www.heritage.org/research/reports/2010/01/state-sponsors-of-terrorism-time-to-add-venezuela-to-the-list.

Weeks, Gregory. 2014. "Is the United States 'Losing' Latin America? Is Growing Anxiety that the United States is Losing its Positions in Latin America Justified?" Al-Jazeera, September 4. www.aljazeera.com/indepth/opinion/2014/09/us-losing-latin-america-20149411713646156.html.

Whitehead, Laurence, and Detlef Nolte. 2012. "The Obama Administration and Latin America: A Disappointing First Term." *GIGA Focus* 6: 1–8.

Part III
The Middle East

10 Obama and the Middle East
Illusions and delusions

Efraim Karsh

It is a historical irony that, as the first US president to proclaim the "fight against negative stereotypes of Islam wherever they appear" an integral part of his presidential responsibilities (White House 2009b), Barack Obama has done more than any of his predecessors to foster sterile stereotypes of Arabs and Muslims that have little to do with reality. Worse, his attempt to translate these misconceptions into actual policies has resulted in a string of disasters – from the failure to contain Tehran's quest for nuclear weapons, to the disruption of Washington's relations with key regional allies, to the surge of Islamist terrorism, to the fragmentation of the Iraqi state, to the collapse of the Palestinian–Israeli peace talks – that have plunged the United States' regional standing to its lowest ebb in decades (see, for example, Pew Research Center 2012).

Misrepresenting Islam

Having long downplayed his Muslim roots (*Newsweek* 2008), Obama embraced them after taking office in an attempt to underscore his (supposed) intimate familiarity with Islam. As he explained in his celebrated June 2009 address to the Muslim World in Cairo:

> I'm a Christian, but my father came from a Kenyan family that includes generations of Muslims. As a boy, I spent several years in Indonesia and heard the call of the *azaan* at the break of dawn and at the fall of dusk. As a young man, I worked in Chicago communities where many found dignity and peace in their Muslim faith ... So I have known Islam on three continents before coming to the region where it was first revealed. That experience guides my conviction that partnership between America and Islam must be based on what Islam is, not what it isn't.
>
> (White House 2009b)

By way of educating Americans on "what Islam isn't," the Obama administration went out of its way to deny, ignore, euphemize, and whitewash anything smacking of Islamic violence, radicalism, or expansionism. Federal agencies purged counterterrorism training materials of references to Islam (Daily Caller 2011), presidential advisers extricated such terms as "jihad" and "Islamic extremism" from the central document outlining the US national security strategy (Haaretz 2010), and NASA was instructed "to reach out to the Muslim world and engage much more with dominantly Muslim nations to help them feel good about their historic contribution to science, math and engineering" (Space.Com 2010).

At the same time, Obama spared no effort to dismiss the religious credentials of radical leaders and groups operating in the name of Islam and to disassociate their actions from that faith. Osama bin Laden "was not a Muslim leader" but "a mass murderer of Muslims" whose demise "should be welcomed by all who believe in peace and human dignity" (White House 2011c); the jihadist group Islamic State (IS, also known as ISIS, the Islamic State of Iraq and Greater Syria, or ISIL, the Islamic State of the Levant) was un-Islamic since "no religion condones the killing of innocents, and the vast majority of [its] victims have been Muslim" (CNN 2014a). Even the Muslim Brotherhood – the world's foremost Islamist organization committed to the creation of a worldwide caliphate and the bedrock of some of today's most murderous terror groups – was described as "largely secular" (ABC News 2011). As such, these groups' extremism was presented as having nothing to do with the faith they pretended to represent, but instead as a misguided (if not wholly inexplicable) overreaction to arrogant and self-serving Western policies. "The relationship between Islam and the West includes centuries of coexistence and cooperation, but also conflict and religious wars," Obama argued in his Cairo speech.

> More recently, tension has been fed by colonialism that denied rights and opportunities to many Muslims, and a Cold War in which Muslim-majority countries were too often treated as proxies without regard to their own aspirations.... Violent extremists have exploited these tensions in a small but potent minority of Muslims ... [culminating in] the attacks of September 11, 2001 and the continued efforts of these extremists to engage in violence against civilians.
>
> (White House 2009b)

This depiction of Muslims as hapless victims of the aggressive encroachments of others is not only patronizing in the worst tradition of the "white man's burden," which dismissed regional players as half-witted creatures too dim to be accountable for their own fate, but is the inverse of the truth. Far from a function of its unhappy interaction with the West, the story of Islam has been the story of the rise and fall of an often-astonishing imperial aggressiveness and, no less important, of never-quiescent imperialist dreams that have survived the fall of the Ottoman Empire to haunt

Islamic and Middle Eastern politics into the twenty-first century. And even as these dreams have repeatedly frustrated any possibility for the peaceful social and political development of the Arab-Muslim world, they have no less repeatedly given rise to fantasies of revenge and restoration, and to murderous efforts to transform fantasy into fact. If, today, the United States is reviled in the Muslim world, it is not because of its specific policies but because, as the preeminent world power, it blocks the final realization of this same age-old dream of regaining the lost glory of the caliphate.

This in turn means that, contrary to Obama's wishful thinking, in the historical imaginations of many Arabs and Muslims bin Laden was not a "mass murderer," but the new incarnation of Saladin, defeater of the Crusaders and conqueror of Jerusalem – a true believer who courageously stood up to today's neo-Crusaders. That much is clear from the overwhelming support for the 9/11 attacks throughout the Arab and Islamic worlds, the admiring evocations of these murderous acts during the 2006 crisis over the Danish cartoons, and the glaring lack of enthusiasm about his demise. In the words of then Palestinian Prime Minister Ismail Haniyeh:

> We condemn the assassination and the killing of an Arab holy warrior. We ask God to offer him mercy with the true believers and the martyrs. We regard this as a continuation of the American policy based on oppression and the shedding of Muslim and Arab blood.
> (Al-Jazeera 2011)

Nor has IS' extroverted brutality detracted one iota from its religious credentials, as evidenced by the influx of thousands of young Muslim men (and women) from all over the world to participate in its self-proclaimed jihad. With far more Muslims killed throughout history by their co-religionists than by non-Muslims, these volunteers see no doctrinal or moral impediments to fighting their "deviant" co-religionists, let alone local "infidels," not least since the group's bloodletting has thus far been insignificant by regional standards (suffice it to mention the 250,000 fatalities of the ongoing Syrian civil war, where most of the killing has been done by the "infidel" Alawite regime).

It is the failure to recognize this state of affairs that accounts for the total breakdown of Obama's Islamic and Middle Eastern policies. For all his appeasing outreach to Arabs and Muslims, the president's professions of humility were viewed not as the goodwill gestures they purported to be but as signs of weakness leading to a steady decline in his – and the United States' – prestige from his first days in office. So much so that by the time of his 2012 re-election campaign most Middle Easterners who favored a strong United States had come to oppose his return to the White House (Pew Research Center 2012).

Duped by the mullahs

Take Iran's quest for nuclear weapons, perhaps the foremost threat to Middle Eastern stability, if not to world peace, in the foreseeable future. In a sharp break from the Bush administration Obama opted for the road of "engagement that is honest and grounded in mutual respect" (*Washington Post* 2009) – only to be cast as weak and indecisive by his eagerness to placate a regime committed to the world-conquering agenda of its founding father, Ayatollah Ruhollah Khomeini.

This image was further reinforced by the administration's knee-jerk response to the Islamist regime's brutal suppression of popular protest over the rigging of the June 2009 presidential elections. That the US president, who had made a point in his inaugural address (*New York Times* 2009) to dismiss "those who cling to power through corruption and deceit and the silencing of dissent" as being "on the wrong side of history," and who lectured Muslim regimes throughout the world of the duty to rule "through consent, not coercion" (White House 2009b), remained conspicuously aloof in the face of the flagrant violation of these principles did not pass unnoticed by the mullahs. President Mahmoud Ahmadinejad demanded an apology from the United States for its supposed meddling in the elections, while Iran's supreme leader, Ayatollah Ali Khamenei, ridiculed Obama for privately courting Tehran while censuring it in public (CBS News 2009).

It is true that at the end of December 2011, following Tehran's persistent rebuff of UN resolutions and the voicing of "serious concerns regarding possible military dimensions to Iran's nuclear program" by the International Atomic Energy Agency (IAEA), Obama authorized harsh sanctions that effectively crippled Tehran's oil-exporting capabilities. Yet he did this with the utmost reluctance, under heavy congressional pressure, and with the Damocles sword of a preventive Israeli strike on Iran's nuclear facilities hovering over his head (International Crisis Group 2012). And although the European Union followed suit with similar measures that further damaged the Iranian economy, Obama refrained from carrying the sanctions to their logical conclusion, instead capitalizing on the election of the (supposedly) moderate Hassan Rouhani as president to offer the mullahs an olive branch. With his proposal to meet Rouhani at the UN General Assembly's annual session declined, the two presidents held a 15-minute phone conversation on September 27, 2013 – the first such high level contact since the 1979 Islamic revolution – which was described by Obama as laying the "basis for resolution" of the Iranian nuclear problem (Solomon and Lee 2013; Mason and Charbonneau 2013).

The nuclear talks between Iran and the great powers – France, Germany, Britain, Russia, China, and the United States (or P5+1 as they are commonly known) – were thus resumed in Geneva. On November 24, 2013 the two sides reached an interim nuclear agreement known as the Joint Plan of Action (JPOA), whereby Tehran agreed to curb some of its nuclear activities (such as ceasing to enrich uranium beyond 5 percent) for a period of six months, so as to facilitate "a mutually-agreed long-term comprehensive solution that would ensure [that] Iran's nuclear program will be exclusively peaceful," in return for some $7 billion of sanctions relief (IAEA 2013).

No sooner had the ink dried on the accord than it transpired that for the Islamist regime it was but a clever ploy to loosen the economic noose around Iran while holding fast to its nuclear ambitions. "In this agreement, the right of [the] Iranian nation to enrich uranium was accepted by [the] world powers," Rouhani told his subjects in a nationwide television broadcast. "With this agreement ... the architecture of sanctions will begin to break down" (BBC News 2013; Kamali Dehgan 2013). Two months later, as the JPOA was about to come into effect after two more months of haggling, Rouhani described the accord as a "big-power surrender to the great Iranian nation" and pledged to defend Iranian rights and interests in the ensuing negotiations over the country's nuclear future (Mansharof et al. 2014; Shinkman 2014). And while Western commentators and diplomats whitewashed this assertion as a ploy to deflect domestic criticism, Tehran did not moderate its stance regarding the permanent settlement, thus forcing the extension of the designated negotiating period by another four months – to November 24, 2014.

And why should it have acted differently at a time when the Western powers were bending over backward to reach an agreement, even if this failed to address the problem it was designed to solve? This was evidenced inter alia by the administration's undisguised aversion to the military option, despite its lip service about leaving "all options on the table"; by its blocking of congressional legislation authorizing new sanctions in the event of noncompliance with the JPOA; by the rapid breakdown of Tehran's diplomatic isolation and economic strangulation;[1] and by the apparent readiness to leave substantial parts of Iran's nuclear infrastructure intact, thus allowing it to resume its nuclear weapons drive at will (Heinonen 2014). Above all, in mid-October 2014, at a time when the IAEA's director general warned that "we cannot provide assurance that *all* material in Iran is for peaceful purposes" (Amano 2014, 4), Obama wrote a secret letter to Supreme Leader Khamenei proposing US–Iranian military collaboration against IS after the conclusion of a nuclear agreement – only to be peremptorily told that "Iran will not accept having an [uranium] enrichment program that is nominal or decorative" (Solomon and Lee 2014; Goodenough 2014). Small wonder then that when the Joint Comprehensive Plan of Action (JCPOA) was eventually pronounced on July 14, 2015, thousands of jubilant Iranians took to the streets to celebrate the event while Rouhani triumphantly declared that "this is the day on which all the large countries and the superpowers in the world have officially recognized Iran's nuclear activities" (MEMRI 2015).

Destabilizing Iraq

In fairness to Obama, the Iranian impasse was not wholly of his own making. Rather, it was largely a corollary of the United States' ongoing entanglement in Iraq, which diminished its appetite for fresh foreign adventures. Yet the president's deep aversion to the use of force in pursuit of foreign policy goals undoubtedly made a bad situation worse, not merely by effectively eliminating the military option – the ultimate deterrent to Tehran's nuclear quest – but by creating a power vacuum in Iraq that brought the country to the verge of disintegration. For although it was President Bush who had laid the groundwork for departure in his November 2008 status of forces agreement (SOFA) with the Iraqi government, Obama's eagerness to make good his electoral promise to leave Iraq within 18 months led to a rushed extrication with extremely detrimental consequences.

Indeed, as the August 31, 2010 deadline for the completion of the first stage of the plan – the removal of all fighting brigades from Iraq – loomed large (White House 2009a), it had become evident that the country was beset by renewed anarchy, with Parliament failing to form a government in the wake of the latest elections, near-daily terror attacks exacting scores of fatalities, and dilapidated public services stirring widespread restiveness. "Right now, if you ask any Iraqi, 'What do you think of democracy?' they will say it's blood, stagnation, unemployment, refugees, cheating," lamented the former (Shi'ite) prime minister, Ayad Allawi (Londofi 2010), whose Sunni-backed, predominantly-Shi'ite Iraqiya coalition beat Prime Minister Nouri Maliki's ruling party by a slim margin to become Iraq's largest parliamentary bloc. "If democracy does not succeed in Iraq and tyranny is replaced by another tyranny, there will be no legacy."

Ignoring this grim reality, Obama presented the withdrawal as a "powerful reminder" of the "renewed American leadership in the world," boasting of "leaving behind a sovereign, stable and self-reliant Iraq," ruled by "a representative government that was elected by its people" (White House 2009a).

In fact, the Iraq that was left behind was anything but a "sovereign, stable and self-reliant" state. Rather, it was a hopelessly polarized society oppressed by a sectarian and brutal Shi'ite regime that retained power through underhand methods, in the face of an electoral defeat, and used it to restore the all-too-familiar pattern of one-man rule characterizing Iraq since its inception.

Matters came to a head on July 23, 2012 when over 100 people were killed and another 250 injured in Iraq's worst day of violence since 2010. A similar number of people were murdered on September 9 in retribution for the death sentencing of exiled Sunni Vice President Tariq Hashemi (tried and convicted in absentia of operating death squads), and by March 2013, most of the country's Sunni areas were mired in protest. Meanwhile, the president of the Kurdistan Regional Government (KRG), Massoud Barzani, implemented a series of measures (such as passing a separate budget, separating the region from the national electricity grid, independently exporting oil through Turkey, and intensifying relations with foreign countries) that significantly enhanced Kurdistan's autonomy and edged it toward statehood (SIGIR 2012).

To make matters worse, a number of jihadist groups, notably the Islamic State (or the Islamic State of Iraq, ISI, as it was initially known), capitalized on the swelling protest to style themselves as protectors of the oppressed Sunnis. When on April 23, 2013 Iraqi security forces killed some 50 Sunni protestors near the northern town of Kirkuk, ISI retaliated with a string of car bombings and suicide attacks that killed dozens of people (SIGIR 2013a, 5–6). With Shi'ite militias responding in kind, 963 civilians were killed and another 2,191 were injured in May alone – the deadliest month since 2008; and this grizzly record was quickly broken when more than 1,000 people were murdered during the holy month of Ramadan in July–August (SIGIR 2013b, 66–67). By the end of 2013, some 7,800 civilians had been murdered and another 18,000 wounded, making it Iraq's bloodiest year since 2008 (United Nations Iraq 2014; see also: Dodge 2013; Laub and Masters 2014).

By January 2014 ISI had captured Ramadi, capital of the Anbar province (though parts of it were subsequently retaken by the government) and the key city of Fallujah, where US forces had fought two bitter battles a decade earlier. Five months later it launched a major offensive in northern and western Iraq. On June 9 the group conquered Mosul, Iraq's second-largest city, and two days later it captured Tikrit, Saddam Hussein's hometown. By the end of the month ISI had established control over much of Iraq's Sunni areas and the northeastern Syrian province of Deir Ezzour, proclaimed a caliphate headed by ISI leader Abu Bakr Baghdadi, and changed the group's name to the Islamic State (IS) to reflect its claim to leadership of the worldwide Muslim community (*Ummah*) (Al-Ansari 2014; Al-Jazeera 2014; McElroy 2014).

When in August 2014 US fighters bombed IS targets in northern Iraq, the organization responded by posting YouTube videos showing the decapitation of two captured US journalists and a British aid worker. Yet while this ghastly PR exercise enticed further European Muslims into IS' ranks, and drove the CIA to concede that the group "mustered between 20,000 and 31,500 fighters across Iraq and Syria" (rather than the 10,000 as previously believed) (CNN 2014b), it failed to achieve its intended deterrent goal, as the international revulsion sparked by the beheadings drove the grudging administration to declare that "the US is at war with ISIL in the same way the US is at war with al-Qaeda" (White House 2014; NBC News 2014).

Thus, three years after announcing the end of the Iraq war, the president who had made disengagement from the conflict a key electoral promise and the hallmark of his first term in office found himself sucked again into the Iraqi quagmire. And while Obama has thus far managed to avoid deploying US ground forces while somewhat degrading IS' military capabilities (killing some of its top leaders and apparently wounding Baghdadi), the air campaign has neither dimmed the group's appeal to Western Muslims nor prevented it from making substantial gains in Iraq, gains that may well force Washington to deepen its military intervention.

Springtime delusions

The rise of IS was indicative of the wider failure of the administration (and Western governments more generally) to grasp the nature of the tidal revolutionary wave that cascaded across the region from December 2010 onward, toppling in rapid succession the long-reigning Tunisian and Egyptian autocrats, Zine El Abidine Ben Ali and Hosni Mubarak, and kindling euphoric talk in the West of an "Arab Spring" that would usher in an era of regional democratization.

While Obama claimed (White House 2011d) that these events "should not have come as a surprise," the truth is that Washington was totally overwhelmed by their occurrence and was reduced from the outset to the role of a hapless spectator. By the time Obama condemned (on January 14, 2011) "the use of violence against citizens peacefully voicing their opinion in Tunisia," and urged "all parties to maintain calm and avoid violence" (White House 2011a) the crisis had blown over and Ben Ali had fled the country.

Obama's impact on the subsequent Egyptian crisis was not much greater. To be sure, in an abrupt U-turn from his earlier position he prodded Mubarak to step down so as to initiate a "meaningful" and "peaceful" transition process (White House 2011b). Yet this public betrayal of one of the United States' staunchest regional allies was typical Obama grandstanding, aimed at taking credit for events he had not set in train and over which he had no control. As Zbigniew Brzezinski, President Carter's national security adviser and a former Obama foreign affairs mentor, put it: "The rhetoric is always terribly imperative and categorical: 'You must do this,' 'He must do that,' 'This is unacceptable' ... [But] he doesn't strategize. He sermonizes" (Lizza 2011, 34).

Sermonizing was very much in evidence in Obama's May 19, 2011 speech (White House 2011d) enunciating his vision of the "Arab Spring," where he had no qualms about telling local leaders how to conduct themselves in the face of the regional turbulence. "The Syrian people have shown their courage in demanding a transition to democracy," he categorically stated, as if the Syrian dictator was taking his marching orders from Washington. "President Assad now has a choice: He can lead that transition, or get out of the way."

In the coming years Obama was to reiterate this refrain while at the same time shunning real measures to facilitate its implementation. Time and again he warned Assad that the use of chemical weapons against the civilian population would constitute a "red line" that could trigger a US military response, only to be repeatedly rebuffed (White House 2012b). Even after the regime's gassing to death of over 1,000 of its rebellious subjects forced Obama to announce (White House 2013) his intention to launch a punitive air strike, he went out of his way to clarify that "this would not be an open-ended intervention" and that the US "would not put boots on the ground." And while Assad's acceptance of a Russian proposal for the dismantling of Syria's chemical weapons arsenal allowed Obama to call off the strike while claiming victory, the incident not only ensured the survival of the Syrian regime for as long as it feigned compliance with the Russian deal, but effectively gave it *carte blanche* to continue slaughtering its citizens, provided this was done with conventional weapons. Indeed, following the deterioration of US–Russian relations over the Ukraine crisis, the regime has apparently resumed chemical attacks on its subjects (Limor 2015).

Even the Libyan intervention – the first and only Western military attempt to sway the "Arab Spring" in its desired direction – exposed the dissonance between Obama's categorical rhetoric and its timid implementation, as the president left it to Paris and London to orchestrate the international intervention on behalf of the fledgling uprising, with Washington "leading from behind." While the intervention overthrew Libya's long-reigning dictator Muammar Qadaffi (albeit at a far greater effort and cost than expected), the emergent "new Libya" has been a far cry from the democratized society it was supposed to become. Indeed, whereas the Qadaffi regime had kept the country's disparate components intact for 42 years, his overthrow gave rise to general anarchy, with a multitude of (mainly Islamist) militias controlling various parts of the country and vying for power with the central government. Even in the unlikely event of the government's success in enforcing its authority, this will hardly mean a shift to democracy; even the National Forces Alliance, which defeated the Islamist Justice and Construction Party in the February 2012 elections to become the largest parliamentary faction (before being eclipsed by the Islamists a year later), promised to make Shari'a "the main inspiration for legislation," and went out of its way to rebut the liberal label attached to it by Western observers. In the words of its spokesman: "The concepts of 'liberal' and 'secular' simply don't exist in Libyan society" (Norris-Trent 2012).

Reluctant to concede that the regional upheavals had never been the liberal awakening they were taken for, Western leaders and observers downplayed the significance of the Islamist surge they unleashed, whether by denying its very occurrence (as with the US administration's astounding characterization of the Muslim Brothers as "largely secular" (ABC News 2011), which helps explain its warm embrace of their short-lived rule in Egypt); or by attributing it to the Islamists' organizational superiority and the secularists' failure to provide compelling alternatives at both the ideological and personal levels; or by predicting the Islamists' inevitable moderation due to their newly assumed governing responsibilities.[2]

In his May 19 speech, Obama portrayed the "Arab Spring" as a regional antithesis to Islamism in general, and the militant brand offered by Osama bin Laden and his ilk in particular. "Bin Laden and his murderous vision won some adherents," he argued.

> But even before his death, al-Qaeda was losing its struggle for relevance, as the overwhelming majority of people saw that the slaughter of innocents did not answer their cries for a better life. By the time we found bin Laden, al-Qaeda's agenda had come to be seen by the vast majority of the region as a dead end, and the people of the Middle East and North Africa had taken their future into their own hands.
> (White House 2011d)

When al-Qaeda affiliates attacked the US Consulate in the Libyan city of Benghazi a year later, on the eleventh anniversary of 9/11, killing Ambassador J. Christopher Stevens and three other US citizens, the administration responded with customary obfuscation, ignoring both the attack's deliberate timing and a Libyan forewarning of its imminence (*Independent* 2012). UN Ambassador Susan Rice described the incident as a spontaneous protest over a US-made anti-Muslim video clip that spun out of control (CBS 2012), while White House press secretary Jay Carney argued that "we don't have and did not have concrete evidence to suggest that [the attack] was not in reaction to the film" (White House 2012c). Obama tacitly amplified this misrepresentation a day after the attack ("We reject all efforts to denigrate the religious beliefs of others. But there is absolutely no justification to this type of senseless violence" (White House 2012c; Fox News 2012)), and became more explicit in a UN address a fortnight later: "I have made it clear that the United States government had nothing to do with this video ... [Yet] there is no video justifying an attack on an Embassy" (ABC News 2012). After all, wasn't al-Qaeda supposed to fade into oblivion after the killing of its founding leader?

Exacerbating the Arab–Israeli conflict

No less disastrous was Obama's handling of the Israeli–Palestinian conflict. By the time he took office in January 2009, Israel and the PLO had been engaged in 15 years of negotiations within the framework of the Oslo "peace" process. Within months of his inauguration the Palestinian leadership, buoyed by his sustained pressure on Israel, dropped all pretense of seeking a negotiated settlement in favor of bringing about a complete Israeli withdrawal from the disputed territories without a peace agreement.

On June 14, 2009 Prime Minister Benjamin Netanyahu broke with Likud ideology and agreed to the establishment of a Palestinian state, provided it recognized Israel's Jewish identity. Yet Washington did nothing to shift the Palestinian leadership from its adamant rejection of Jewish statehood – the root cause of the decades-long failure of the two-state solution – and instead pressured the Israeli government for a complete freeze of building activities in the West Bank and East Jerusalem. This culminated in Israel agreeing to a ten-month construction freeze, with a view to launching "meaningful negotiations to reach a historic peace agreement that would finally end the conflict between Israel and the Palestinians" (*Haaretz* 2009).

Nor did Palestinian Authority President Mahmoud Abbas have any qualms about walking away from the negotiations table upon the expiry of the construction moratorium in September 2010, in defiance of Obama's buoyant prediction earlier that month that peace could be achieved within a year. Asked by Netanyahu to reconsider, in return for a renewed settlement freeze and recognition of Israel as a national home for the Jewish people (*Jerusalem Post* 2010a), Abbas reiterated his rejection of ever signing "an agreement recognizing a Jewish state" and threatened a unilateral declaration of statehood were the peace process to remain stalled (*Jerusalem Post* 2010b).

He made good his threat in September 2011 when, in open rebuff of Jerusalem and Washington, and in flagrant violation of the 1990s PLO–Israel accords that envisaged the attainment of peace through direct negotiations between the two parties, he sought to face Israel with a *fait accompli* by gaining UN recognition of Palestinian statehood. Having failed to garner sufficient support at the Security Council, in November 2012 Abbas obtained a General Assembly recognition of Palestine as a "non-member observer state," to the dismay of the administration, which condemned the move as "counterproductive" and an obstacle "in the path [to] peace" (CBS News 2012).

The stark warning by Secretary of State John Kerry that "the window for a two-state solution is shutting" (JTA 2013) made no impression on the Palestinians. To be sure, in apparent deference to the secretary's tireless efforts to jumpstart the stalemated talks they agreed to return to the negotiating table at the end of July 2013; yet this was merely a ploy to drive a wedge between Israel and the administration – which temporarily seemed to have recognized the futility of its first-term strategy and adopted a more conciliatory tone toward Jerusalem – and to lay the groundwork for a renewed unilateral drive for UN recognition of Palestinian statehood.

This strategy bore the desired fruit before too long. When at the end of April 2014 Abbas walked out of the talks yet again, having rallied the Arab League behind his "absolute and decisive rejection to recognizing Israel as a Jewish state," and formed a "unity government" with the Islamist Hamas (*Haaretz* 2014), the administration blamed Israel for the debacle (*Times of*

Israel 2014), while the EU indicated the possible boycott of Israeli entities that operated beyond the 1967 lines (see Birnbaum and Tibon 2014).

Netanyahu's acceptance of Kerry's proposal to free another 400 convicted terrorists and halt new construction activities in the West Bank, as a quid pro quo for the extension of the talks for another nine months, did little to redeem his tarnished image in Washington. When in July 2014 he was grudgingly drawn into a new war with Hamas that subjected most of Israel's population to constant rocket and missile attacks for seven full weeks, he was cold shouldered by the administration. Over the course of the conflict, the administration collaborated with Hamas' foremost patrons – Turkey and Qatar – in an attempt to organize a ceasefire amenable to the terror group; endorsed the suspension of US flights to Israel, triggering an avalanche of suspensions that left the Jewish state briefly cut off from the rest of the world (*US Today* 2014); and withheld certain weapons supplies in an attempt to rein in Israel's military operations (*Washington Post* 2014). "The thing about Bibi is, he's a chickenshit," complained an anonymous senior White House official.

> [H]e won't do anything to reach an accommodation with the Palestinians or with the Sunni Arab states. The only thing he's interested in is protecting himself from political defeat. He's not [Yitzhak] Rabin, he's not [Ariel] Sharon, he's certainly no [Menachem] Begin. He's got no guts.
>
> (Goldberg 2014)

Appeasement of one's enemies at the expense of friends, whose loyalty can be taken for granted, is a common – if unsavory – human trait, and Obama has been no exception to this rule. Yet while his persistent snub of the United States' longest and most loyal Middle Eastern ally bought him the distrust of most Israelis (at the end of the 2014 Gaza war only 4 percent of them found the president more pro-Israel than pro-Palestinian, compared to 31 percent upon his 2008 election (*Jerusalem Post* 2014)), his constant attempts to satisfy the Palestinians ("You will never have an administration as committed … as this one," he told Abbas (Birnbaum and Tibon 2014)) failed to buy him their appreciation. On the eve of the 2012 US elections a mere 9 percent of Palestinians viewed his re-election favorably, and nearly four times as many thought it would have adverse implications (Palestinian Center for Policy and Survey Research 2012). As if to add insult to injury, a comprehensive 2013 survey found Palestinians more hostile to the United States than any other national group, with 76 percent considering it an enemy (compared to 1 percent of Israelis) and only 4 percent viewing it as a partner (Pew Research Center 2013, 2014).

So much for the "new beginning between the United States and Muslims around the world" heralded by Obama's Cairo speech.

Conclusion

As the only person to have won the Nobel Peace Prize on the basis of sheer hope rather than actual achievement, Barack Obama could be expected to do everything within his power to vindicate this unprecedented show of trust. Instead he has not only exacerbated ongoing regional conflicts but made the world a far more dangerous place; and nowhere has this phenomenon been more starkly demonstrated than in the Middle East, where the Nobel laureate brought the mullahs in Tehran to within a stone's throw of nuclear weapons; drove Iraq to the verge of disintegration; expedited the surge of Islamist terrorism; facilitated the survival of a genocidal Syrian regime; paved the road for the Taliban's return to power; made the intractable Palestinian–Israeli conflict almost irresolvable; and plunged the United States' regional influence and prestige to new depths.

In order to salvage whatever he can of this catastrophic legacy, Obama will need to shed his perceptions of Muslims and Arabs, acknowledge the irreconcilable nature of the challenge posed by the United States' Islamist adversaries, and substitute containment and counterattack for appeasement and self-abnegation. Anything short of this is a recipe for continued failure.

Notes

1 See, for example, United States Institute of Peace 2014; Katzman 2014, 57–58; Smith 2013.
2 See, for example: National Endowment for Democracy 2012; Tadros 2012; Lynch 2012; Gause 2012.

Bibliography

ABC News. 2011. "Director of National Intelligence James Clapper: Muslim Brotherhood 'Largely Secular,'" February 10.
ABC News. 2012. "Transcript: President Obama Talks to the UN about Mideast Peace, Iran," September 25.
Ahren, Raphael. 2014. "Kerry Focuses Blame on Israel for Collapse of Talks." *Times of Israel*, April 8.
Al-Ansari, Abdelwahed. 2014. "How did 'Islamic State' Proclaim Caliphate?" *Almonitor*, July 7.
Al-Jazeera. 2011. "Reactions: Bin Laden's Death," May 2.
Al-Jazeera. 2014. "Sunni Rebels Declare 'Islamic Caliphate'," June 30.
Amano, Yukiya. 2014. "Challenges in Nuclear Verification: The IAEA's Role on the Iranian Nuclear Issue." Speech to the Brookings Institution, Washington, DC, October 31.
Baker, Peter. 2010. "In Speech on Iraq, Obama Reaffirms Drawdown," *Washington Post*, August 2.
BBC News. 2013. "Iran Agrees to Curb Nuclear Activity in Geneva Talks," November 24.

Birnbaum, Ben, and Amir Tibon. 2014. "The Explosive, Inside Story of How John Kerry Built an Israel–Palestine Peace Plan – and Watched It Crumble." *New Republic*, July 20.
CBS. 2012. "Face the Nation," September 16.
CBS News. 2009. "Ayatollah Mocks US Pre-election Overture," June 24. www.cbsnews.com/stories/2009/06/24/world/main5109744.shtml.
CBS News. 2012. "UN General Assembly Votes to Recognize Palestinian State," November 30. www.cbsnews.com/news/un-general-assembly-votes-to-recognize-palestinian-state/.
CNN. 2014a. "Transcript: President Obama's Speech on Combating ISIS and Terrorism," September 11. www.aljazeera.com/news/asia/2011/05/20115241936984209.html.
CNN. 2014b. "How Foreign Fighters are Swelling ISIS Ranks in Startling Numbers," September 14.
Daily Caller. 2011. "Obama Administration Pulls References to Islam from Terror Training Materials, Official Says," October 21.
Dodge, Toby. 2013. "Iraq's Renewed Political Violence – Is the Country Heading Back into Civil War?" International Institute for Strategic Studies: Manama Voices, December 7.
Fox News. 2012. "As Carney Labels Libya Strike Terrorism, Obama Continues to Cite Anti-Islam Film," September 21.
Gause, Gregory III. 2012. "The Year the Arab Spring Went Bad." *Foreign Policy*, December 31.
Goldberg, Jeffrey. 2014. "The Crisis in US–Israel Relations is Officially Here." *Atlantic*, October 28.
Goodenough, Patrick. 2014. "Iran: 'Hypocritical' Obama Adopts Friendly Tone in Secret Letters, Tough Tone in Public." cnsnnws.com, November 13.
Haaretz. 2009. "Netanyahu Declares 10-Month Settlement Freeze 'to Restart Peace Talks,'" November 25.
Haaretz. 2010. "Obama Bans Terms 'Islam' and 'Jihad' from US Security Document," April 7.
Haaretz. 2014. "Arab League Rejects Israel as Jewish State," March 26.
Heinonen, Olli. 2014. "The Iranian Nuclear Programme: Practical Parameters for a Credible Long-Term Agreement." Henry Jackson Society, November: 6–7, 17–18. http://henryjacksonsociety.org/wp-content/uploads/2014/11/The-Iranian-Nuclear-Programme-online.pdf.
IAEA. 2013. Communication dated 27 November 2013 received from the EU High Representative concerning the text of the Joint Plan of Action. INFCIRC/855.
Independent. 2012. "Libya: We Gave US Three-Day Warning of Benghazi Attack," September 18.
Independent Online. 2009. "Palestinians Reject Netanyahu Speech," June 14.
International Crisis Group. 2012. "In Heavy Water: Iran's Nuclear Program, the Risk of War and Lessons from Turkey." Middle East and Europe Report No. 116–23: 12.
Jerusalem Post. 2010a. "At Knesset Winter Session Opening Netanyahu says Palestinian State may be a Source of Continued Conflict if Irresponsibly Handled," November 10.
Jerusalem Post. 2010b. "Both Sides must Take Steps for Negotiations to Continue," and "Abbas to Arab League: Israel has Violated All Agreements," December 10.

Jerusalem Post. 2014. "Only 16% of Israeli Public Believe US President's Administration is More Pro-Israel than Pro-Palestinian," October 30.
JTA. 2013. "Kerry: Two-Year Window is Maximum for Two States," April 18.
Kamali Dehgan, Saeed. 2013. "Iran's Leaders and Public Celebrate Geneva Deal." *Guardian*, November 24.
Katzman, Kenneth. 2014. "Iran Sanction." Congressional Research Service, October 23: 57–58. www.cbsnews.com/news/ayatollah-mocks-us-pre-election-overture/.
Laub, Zachary, and Jonathan Masters. 2014. "Islamic State in Iraq and Syria." Council on Foreign Relations, August 8.
Limor, Yoav. 2015. "Turbulence Expected to Continue in 2015." Interview with Brig. Gen. Itai Bron, outgoing head of the IDF's intelligence research department. *Israel Hayom*, January 15 (Hebrew).
Lizza, Ryan. 2011. "The Consequentialist: How the Arab Spring Remade Obama's Foreign Policy." *New Yorker*, May 2.
Londofi, Ernesto. 2010. "Iraqis Don't Expect Political Impasse to be Resolved by Fall." *Washington Post*, August 1.
Lynch, Marc. 2012. "Islamists in a Changing Middle East." *Foreign Policy*, July 8.
Mansharof, Y., E. Kharrazi, and Y. Lahatet. 2014 "The Geneva Joint Plan of Action: How Iran Sees It (1)." MEMRI – Inquiry & Analysis Series Report, No. 1,050, January 13.
Mason, Jeff, and Louis Charbonneau. 2013. "Obama, Iran's Rouhani Hold Historic Phone Call." Reuters, September 28.
McElroy, Damien. 2014. "Rome will be Conquered Next, says Leader of 'Islamic State.'" *Telegraph*, July 1.
MEMRI. 2009. "Fatah's Sixth General Conference Resolutions: Pursuing Peace Options Without Relinquishing Resistance or Right to Armed Struggle," August 13.
MEMRI. 2015. "Iranian President Rouhani Describes Nuclear Deal, says: The Superpowers Have Officially Recognized a Nuclear Iran," July 21.
National Endowment for Democracy. 2012. "Democratic Transition in the Middle East: Between Authoritarianism and Islamism," July 12.
NBC News. 2014. "Obama Administration says US is 'At War' with ISIS," September 12.
New York Times. 2009. "Text of Barack Obama's Inaugural Address," January 20.
Newsweek. 2008. "When Barry Became Barack," March 22.
Norris-Trent, C. 2012. "Who Are Libya's Liberals?" France 24, July 11.
Palestinian Center for Policy and Survey Research. 2012. Palestinian Public Opinion Poll No. 45, September 13–15.
Pew Research Center. 2012. "Global Opinion of Obama Slips, International Policies Faulted." Pew Research Global Attitudes Project, June 13. www.pewglobal.org/2012/06/13/global-opinion-of-obama-slips-international-policies-faulted/.
Pew Research Center. 2013. "America's Global Image Remains More Positive than China's. Chapter 1: Attitudes Toward the United States." Pew Research Global Attitudes Project, May 18.
Pew Research Center. 2014. "Global Opposition to US Surveillance and Drones, but Limited Harm to America's Image." Pew Research Global Attitudes Project, May 14.
Poniewozik, James. 2011. "The Banality of Bin Laden." *Time*, December 13. www.time.com/time/nation/article/0,8599,188329,00.html.

Shear, Michael D., and William Branigin. 2010. "Obama Speaks with Vets on Iraq Drawdown." *Washington Post*, August 2.

Shinkman, Paul D. 2014. "Iranian President Hassan Rouhani Says Nuclear Deal Marks US 'Surrender.' " *U.S. News & World Report*, January 14.

SIGIR (Special Inspector General for Iraq Reconstruction). 2012. Quarterly Report to the United States Congress, October 30.

SIGIR (Special Inspector General for Iraq Reconstruction). 2013a. Quarterly Report to the United States Congress, April 30.

SIGIR (Special Inspector General for Iraq Reconstruction). 2013b. Final Report to the United States Congress, September 9.

Smith, Lee. 2013. The Collapse of Sanctions on Iran. *Weekly Standard*, March 3.

Solomon, Jay, and Carole E. Lee. 2013. "Historic Call for Obama, Rouhani." *Wall Street Journal*, September 27.

Solomon, Jay, and Carole E. Lee. 2014. "Obama Wrote Secret Letter to Iran's Khamenei about fighting Islamic State." *Wall Street Journal*, November 6.

Space.com. 2010. "NASA Chief Bolden's Muslim Remarks to Aljazeera Causes Stir," July 7.

Tadros, Samuel. 2012. "Egypt's Elections: Why the Islamists Won." *World Affairs*, March/April.

United Nations Iraq. 2014. "UN Casualty Figures for December, 2013 Deadliest Since 2008 in Iraq." Civilian Casualties, January 2. www.uniraq.org/index.php?option=com_k2&view=item&id=1499:un-casualty-figures-for-december-2013-deadliest-since-2008-in-iraq&Itemid=633&lang=en.

United States Institute of Peace. 2014. "Western Countries Flood Tehran." The Iran Primer, April 29. http://iranprimer.usip.org/blog/2014/apr/29/western-countries-flood-tehran.

US Department of State. 2012. "President Obama on Death of US Embassy Staff in Libya," September 12.

USA Today. 2014. "Obama: FAA took 'Prudent Action' in Israel," July 25.

Washington Post. 2009. "Obama's Tone in Iran Message Differs Sharply from Bush's," March 21.

Washington Post. 2014. "In Deaths of Civilians in Gaza, US Weapons Sales to Israel Come Under Scrutiny," August 23.

White House. 2009a. Remarks of President Barack Obama, as prepared for delivery: "Responsibly Ending the War in Iraq; Camp Lejeune, North Carolina." Office of the Press Secretary, February 27.

White House. 2009b. "Remarks by the President on a New Beginning, Cairo University." Office of the Press Secretary, June 4.

White House. 2011a. "Osama Bin Laden Dead." White House Blog, May 2.

White House. 2011b. "Statement by the President on Events in Tunisia." Office of the Press Secretary, January 14.

White House. 2011c. "President Obama on Transition in Egypt." Office of the Press Secretary, February 1.

White House. 2011d. "Remarks by the President on the Middle East and North Africa." Office of the Press Secretary, May 19.

White House. 2011e. "Weekly Address: Renewing America's Global Leadership." Office of the Press Secretary, October 22.

White House. 2011f. "Remarks by the President and First Lady on the End of the War in Iraq." Office of the Press Secretary, December 14.

White House. 2012a. "Remarks by the President on the Middle East and North Africa." Office of the Press Secretary, May 19.

White House. 2012b. "Remarks by the President to the White House Press Corps." Office of the Press Secretary, August 20.

White House. 2012c. "Press Briefing by Press Secretary Jay Carney 9/18/2012." Office of the Press Secretary, September 18.

White House. 2013. "Statement by the President on Syria." Office of the Press Secretary, August 31.

White House. 2014. "Statement by the President on Isil." Office of the Press Secretary, September 10.

11 US counter-proliferation policy
The case of Iran*

Emily B. Landau

Introduction

Since the end of the Cold War, the United States has pursued various nuclear counter-proliferation policies. Iran and North Korea stand out as prime case studies for examining the difficulties that are faced when seeking to confront a determined proliferator through peaceful means. Whether efforts focus on an attempt to alter such proliferators' motivation through offers of inducements ("carrots") or application of pressure ("sticks"), international negotiators have found that the proliferator tends to gain the upper hand in negotiations, due to its determination at the strategic level and its ability to play a primarily tactical game at the negotiating table (Landau 2012a).

The relevant international negotiators – the P5+1 group in the case of Iran, and five regional powers in the case of North Korea – are structurally hampered in this dynamic. The political context within which their efforts are carried out has a crippling effect on their ability to garner the kind of unified and determined stance necessary to compel a nuclear proliferator, in a tough bargaining situation, to back away from its military aspirations and uphold its commitment to remaining non-nuclear.

This article will focus on the major constraints that have hobbled efforts to halt Iran's nuclear development, even though these efforts have been ongoing for close to a dozen years, in different forms and formats.

The significance of the NPT framework

Any informed assessment of US policy in confronting determined proliferators must begin with the Nuclear Non-Proliferation Treaty (NPT), as the states in question are all members of the treaty, holding the status of non-nuclear weapons states (NNWS).[1] As such, the NPT has become the major source of *legitimacy* for the international community to respond with determination to states attempting to acquire military nuclear capability, as that represents a violation of their NPT commitment. The US was a major architect of the NPT, and is strongly committed to upholding it as the centerpiece of the non-proliferation regime (see FAS 2014).

But the NPT has also – albeit not intentionally – proven to be a serious *constraint* to counter-proliferation efforts. Article IV of the treaty – intended to provide compensation to the NNWS for their willingness to forgo nuclear weapons by allowing them access to nuclear energy for peace purposes[2] – has ended up enabling today's determined proliferators to advance a military nuclear program under the guise of a civilian program. The treaty's support for civilian nuclear programs does not exclude the NNWS from enriching uranium to produce fuel for reactors, but uranium enrichment is dangerous dual-use technology: uranium enriched to 5 percent is suitable for civilian uses, but enrichment of over 90 percent produces fissile material for a nuclear device. In this manner, states that have strived to acquire military nuclear capability in recent decades, such as Iran, Iraq (in the 1980s), Syria, and North Korea, have all abused the terms of the NPT to do so: they all worked clandestinely on military capabilities while claiming that their activities were carried out in the framework of a civilian nuclear program.

The fact that the architects of the NPT knowingly enabled the NNWS access to dual-use technology is testimony to the fact that they were not envisioning that states would purposely cheat on their commitment, and abuse the treaty as a cover for military programs. Indeed, when formulated in the late 1960s, states of concern included Sweden, Japan, West Germany, Israel, India, and perhaps Canada and Australia,[3] and the NPT was viewed as a means of creating a positive *collective security system* for these states and the entire international community. The overriding assumption was that states joining the treaty would have an interest in upholding their commitment over time.

So the provisions of the NPT were never intended to provide the tools for seeking out state violations and acts of deception, or the means to deal with them in a quick and decisive manner. Rather, the safeguard agreements that each NNWS signed with the IAEA were designed with the goal of ensuring that everything was running smoothly and according to plan, with the overriding assumption that they *were*. Because the provisions were not tailored toward seeking out and confronting violations, the result is that in today's world, confronting states that cheat on their commitments has proven to be a very complex, lengthy, and cumbersome process. It is a process that Iran in particular has proven very adept at (ab)using to its best advantage. The loopholes in the NPT explain, in a nutshell, how Iran has been able to advance its program from several hundred centrifuges to 19,000 of these machines, including more and more advanced generations and models; and from a very small stockpile of low-enriched uranium (LEU) to an amount that – if enriched to levels of over 90 percent – could provide fissile material for six or seven nuclear devices. No doubt the international community is unhappy with the situation, and Iran has been paying a price in the form of sanctions; however, for all its unhappiness, the international community has proven powerless to stop Iran's advances.

Shadow of the Iraq war: embracing negotiations to stop determined proliferators

All of this does not mean that the United States has been averse to considering, and sometimes employing, military force as a counter-proliferation policy, as was certainly the case in the Iraq war of 2003. However, in the case of the Iraq war, not only did use of force prove to be unnecessary because weapons of mass destruction (WMD) were not found, but its use had serious negative ramifications in terms of overall counter-proliferation efforts.

In fact, the common assessment that developed rather quickly after the US invasion was that the war was a failure. It had been justified by the necessity of destroying Iraq's WMD, but no WMD were found – and this led the international community to conclude that the rush to a devastating war based on faulty intelligence was a mistake that must not be repeated. This atmosphere of caution engendered the sense that diplomacy, not war, should now be the "strategy of choice" for dealing with proliferation threats (Landau 2012a, 26–31). Certainly, the thinking went, diplomacy should be embraced as the strategy for dealing with the two cases that came prominently onto the international agenda over the course of 2003: North Korea and Iran. This has put the world on the course of ongoing negotiations with each of these proliferators since 2003. So far there is very little, if anything, to show by way of successful counter-proliferation in either case, with North Korea having achieved nuclear status. The lack of success in dealing with Iran even includes the Interim Deal (or Joint Plan of Action, JPOA) that was concluded in late November 2013. This deal was part of a strategy of buying time in order to negotiate a comprehensive nuclear deal, but has not fundamentally altered the situation as regards Iran's breakout capability (an issue to be revisited below).

Why has it been so hard to stop Iran?

Once the commitment to diplomacy and negotiations as the strategy of choice for pursuing counter-proliferation in the case of Iran is understood (with, it seems, some efforts at sabotage as well (Ynet 2014), but more as a sideshow to the major diplomatic initiative), the question is why it has proven so difficult to bring these negotiations to a successful conclusion.

As already mentioned, the problems begin with the spirit and provisions of the NPT itself – in particular Article IV, which created the dual-use technology loophole. This has enabled states to accumulate a stockpile of low-enriched uranium ostensibly for civilian purposes, which can later be quickly enriched to the higher levels needed for a nuclear explosive device. The fact that the same technology is used for both legitimate and illegitimate purposes means it is more difficult to make the case that the state is harboring military ambitions.

Additionally, the treaty lacks clear criteria and/or benchmarks for ruling that a violation of a member state's treaty obligations has occurred, as well as lacking any guidelines for following through with an effective decision-making process in response to a violation. Each decision along the way – from initial detection of a violation to action to bringing the violator back into line – has become fraught with potential constraints, due to the fact that the process takes place in the context of international politics, with a full array of cross-cutting and conflicting state interests affecting state positions and policies.

Simply put, not all the relevant actors, at every moment along the way, are driven primarily by their shared desire to stop the potential proliferator. Rather, the economic and geopolitical interests of the different parties – vis-à-vis the proliferator as well as toward their own partners in the negotiation – also intervene, and can weaken their collective resolve to act in a unified and determined manner. Prominent examples include the impact of Russian economic and military interests regarding Iran; Russia's interest in increasing its role in the Middle East, which pits it against the United States; and its general strategic rivalry with the United States, which makes it somewhat less inclined to be perceived as being on board a US-led agenda. China's interest in buying oil from Iran has almost always trumped determination on the nuclear front, and European states' strong economic interests connected to Iran have strained their ability to sustain economic sanctions over time. The impact of these different interests was apparent in the UN Security Council resolutions on sanctions from 2006 to 2010: each resolution was watered down to the lowest common denominator, in line with other interests that were influencing the decision making of the permanent members. The US approach has also been affected by additional interests: one can argue that the United States' negotiation strategy in the nuclear talks over the course of 2013–2014 was influenced by political considerations regarding the nature of US–Iran bilateral relations, and by the president's desire to secure some form of détente with Iran.

A second factor to note is that this negotiation is not a "normal" one, in the sense that the two sides do not have a shared interest in reaching a negotiated solution. Rather, the P5+1 are interested in a negotiated deal, and are even dependent on one to achieve their goal of stopping Iran (because they do not want to have to resort to more coercive measures). Iran, on the other hand, has absolutely no interest in a negotiated deal that would mean giving up the nuclear capability it has worked so hard to create and paid such a high price to maintain. More importantly, Iran can reach its goal on its own, and has no need for cooperation with international powers.[4] All of this has played to the disadvantage of the international negotiators at the table.

What this means is that in terms of the negotiations dynamic, Iran has had the upper hand. Since 2003, it has been playing a tactical game of buying time in order to push its program forward, while never seriously considering steps that would undermine or harm its program and plans. Iran is a single, very determined state that speaks with one voice (literally, that of the supreme leader). Iran also has a clear idea of what it wants to achieve in the nuclear realm: to push its program forward at maximum speed while paying a minimal price in terms of sanctions and other forms of pressure. By contrast, the P5+1 is a group of states that lack unity and a common position on many of the relevant issues, which undermines their ability to communicate resolve.

Iran became very adept over the years at exploiting the lack of clarity in the NPT – its negotiators would haggle over interpretations of the treaty (for example, regarding its "right to enrich") and the terms of its safeguard agreement signed with the IAEA, and would often refuse to grant visas to specific inspectors whom Iran disliked. It consistently played for time using a variety of delay tactics, which included the "divide and conquer" game vis-à-vis the P5+1 states (attempting to deepen the divide it knew existed between the United States with its European allies on one side, and Russia and China on the other), and stalling for months at a time before responding to any proposal presented by the international negotiators. Two examples of Iran's tendency to vacillate (using a "yes, no, maybe" tactic) with regard to proposals presented to it are the late 2005 Russian proposal and the fuel deal proposal of October 2009 (Landau 2012a, 53–58). In fact, Iran learned that ambiguity served its interests well, and enabled it to play a game of crisis avoidance that it was difficult for the other side to counter with force and determination; indeed, it has continued to exploit unclear language in the Interim Deal of November 2013, and haggles over interpretations in order to improve its position with regard to the constraining provisions. All the while, Iran uses whatever time it gains in order to push its nuclear program forward and build up its nuclear infrastructure. The more Iran is able to advance its program, the harder it will be for the international community to roll it back.

The Iraq war also cast a long shadow over future non-proliferation efforts, and produced two notable constraints as far as the negotiations with Iran were concerned. First, it weakened the West's determination by keeping open the question of whether Iran was truly working on a military nuclear capability. Negotiators and diplomats kept asking themselves – especially in the first eight years – whether they might not be making the same intelligence estimate mistake regarding Iran as they had in Iraq (Jervis 2010). A second detrimental result of the Iraq war was the decreased US appetite for military intervention. As such, an important potential source of leverage at the negotiating table – namely, a credible threat of military consequences for Iran's lack of seriousness in the negotiations – was squandered.

After attempting to alter Iran's calculation regarding cooperation with the international community in the early years through offers of inducements, by 2006 the negotiators' disappointment with Iran's lack of cooperation set them on the course of pressure, through sanctions. However, the process was slow, as it proved very difficult to garner support in the Security Council for robust sanctions. Effective economic pressure on Iran came only very late in the game – in 2012 – with a series of financial and economic sanctions led by the United States and the European Union, outside the framework of the Security Council.

Finally, it is worth mentioning that the specific nature of negotiations with Iran was often incorrectly characterized over the years. Due to the zero-sum nature of the two sides' interests, the logic of this negotiation is that of a very tough bargaining process, with the international community attempting to compel Iran to accept its stance. Yet the international negotiators have often mistakenly referred to it as a "normal" negotiation in which both sides share interest in a deal, and both understand the importance of, and are willing to make, difficult compromises for the sake of reaching a mutually desirable agreement. That is not the case, nor is it the game that Iran has been playing.[5] Through its reluctance to play hardball, the P5+1 has failed to maximize its (in any case limited) leverage.

Did anything change for the better after Rouhani was elected?

Following the June 2013 election of Hassan Rouhani – a candidate who ran on the ticket of improving the internal situation in Iran, both in terms of the economy and of reforms and civil rights – international hopes were running high for a new Iranian approach to the nuclear negotiations, due to the importance for the regime of lifting the crippling sanctions.

However, since the latest round of negotiations began in October 2013 there has been no indication of any fundamental change in Iran's strategic nuclear goals. Iran still seeks to advance its nuclear program, and still harbors the same desire to achieve and maintain a breakout capability that will enable it to move quickly to nuclear weapons at a time of its choosing.

That nothing fundamental had changed was evident from the dynamic surrounding the Interim Deal of November 24, 2013. While the official US narrative plays up the JPOA as a great success – for freezing and even rolling back some aspects of Iran's nuclear activities (White House 2014) – the JPOA should be assessed in terms of what it has meant for Iran's *breakout capability*, because this is what matters to Iran. In this respect Iran did not really give any ground: it maintained its vast stockpile of uranium enriched to 3.5–5 percent (an amount that could produce six or seven nuclear devices with further enrichment). The achievement of getting Iran to suspend its enrichment at 20 percent, and to dilute or oxidize the stockpile it had accumulated, is much less striking when put in the perspective of Iran's breakout capability. This is because, in breakout terms, the role of 20 percent enriched uranium is simply to enable Iran to move very quickly to the 90 percent level needed for nuclear weapons. However, this goal can be realized by other means – specifically, by using more advanced centrifuges. Iran made sure that the JPOA safeguarded its ability to continue research and development work on increasingly advanced generations of centrifuges, which spin many times faster than the current ones. These centrifuges, when ultimately installed and operational, will also be able to support a quick move to breakout at a time of Iran's choosing. Indeed, in the context of Iran's breakout capability, 20 percent enriched uranium and advanced models of centrifuges are *functional equivalents*.

What changed, then, over the course of 2013–2014? The only change that can be discerned is in Iran's *tactics*. Iran came back to the negotiating table in a more serious manner in the fall of 2013 due to the effects of the biting sanctions that were put in place by the United States, the European Union, and several additional countries over the course of 2012. There is no indication of any substantial change of direction initiated by the "more moderate" Rouhani; rather, Rouhani was elected (at least in part) because of the effect of the sanctions. Rouhani was most likely allowed to run because the supreme leader decided that there was a need for a candidate who was part and parcel of the regime, but whose election platform addressed the population's growing resentment, caused by worsening economic conditions, and its demand for reforms. There is reason to believe that Khamenei was concerned about the possibility of another round of mass demonstrations following the 2013 elections, potentially more difficult to control, after the 2009 post-election demonstrations, and the waves of uprisings in the ensuing years amongst Arab populations fed up with repressive regimes. For the disgruntled in Iran, Rouhani would be an easy choice.

Regarding the balance that Iran has traditionally sought between "nuclear progress," on the one hand, and "paying a low price in sanctions and other pressure," on the other, in the Ahmadinejad years Iran had moved too far in the direction of "progress," while not paying enough attention to the price it was paying in sanctions. Over the course of late 2012 and early 2013, the sanctions had begun to really bite. This was the situation that Rouhani's nuclear strategy was set to rectify. In order to neutralize the effects of the high price the regime was paying in sanctions, there was a shift in tactics: from "maximum nuclear progress for minimal price," the focus in the negotiation moved toward lowering the cost, i.e., "maximum sanctions relief in return for only minimal nuclear concessions." While this new approach sought to restore the balance between the two goals, it was no more than a tactical shift: there is nothing to indicate that Iran had made a strategic U-turn in terms of its nuclear aspirations.

For their part, the challenge for the international negotiators vis-à-vis sanctions was to use their new and hard-earned leverage to compel Iran to finally accept the deal that they wanted. But very early on it became clear that the P5+1 members seemed not to trust their own leverage, certainly not as a means to compel Iran to comply. Rather, they began expressing concern that if they pressed too hard, Iran would walk away from the table, although there was little evidence to support this concern – indeed, quite the opposite: over the years it had become apparent that Iran responded to pressure by demonstrating a more cooperative stance. The introduction of more severe sanctions had caused many pundits to predict in late 2011 that Iran would "go crazy" in the face of this escalation in pressure, possibly exiting the NPT. In fact, Iran did nothing of the sort, and instead returned to the negotiating table in 2013.

Once negotiations began in late 2013 there was a notable change, particularly in the US approach. Rather than communicating to Iran that America was "in the driver's seat" and set to drive a hard bargain, the Obama administration began working on its stance regarding issues on which it believed there would be no chance of compromise from Iran. Indeed, there was a sense at times that the United States was more focused on what might be acceptable to Iran – and adjusting its positions accordingly – than in setting its own bottom lines. Moreover, the administration confronted Congress on pending sanctions legislation in late 2013, with the president threatening to use his veto power to topple the legislation and accusing senators who supported it of being "warmongers." And throughout the months of negotiation in 2014 there were offers of concessions to Iran. Although Barack Obama has said quite clearly on a number of occasions that no deal is better than a bad deal, at no stage did he define what would constitute a bad (and thus unacceptable) deal.

The United States also took great pains to prove that it was negotiating in good faith and was not showing any disrespect toward the regime. This initiated a new dynamic whereby the Obama administration was virtually bending over backwards in its efforts not to do anything that might be construed as lacking in respect toward this dangerous proliferator, even though Iran was certainly not responding in kind. In fact, the supreme leader continued to hurl accusations, while expressing great disdain and contempt, as well as deep hatred, toward the United States (see for example Walker 2014).

These trends were exacerbated by attitudes displayed by the Obama administration over the course of 2014 in reaction to worsening regional conditions in the Middle East – such as ISIS taking over vast expanses of territory in Syria and Iraq – that the superpower signaled might be better confronted if the United States and Iran were to work together. The combined effect was that the United States increasingly advertised to Iran its eagerness for a deal, which obviously had the effect of weakening its hand at the negotiation table.

It is not clear what accounts for this change in the US approach, but some insight can be gained from the exposure in late 2013 of the fact that the United States had been secretly conducting bilateral talks with Iran since early 2013, before Rouhani was elected (Ravid 2013). Together with the evidence noted above, this could support the view that Obama was keen to change the nature of US–Iranian relations, perhaps looking toward his legacy. This would render the nuclear issue one piece of that broader foreign policy goal, rather than primarily a non-proliferation challenge that must be confronted with absolute determination in and of itself. Couched in this broader political context, the United States was perhaps wary of presenting a hardline approach that might be regarded by Iran as overly harsh, threatening what the administration hoped was a budding détente dynamic.

Coming full circle to the NPT: Iran's weaponization activities and the offer on the table

There are a range of issues related to Iran's nuclear program that are under discussion in the negotiations over a comprehensive nuclear deal. These include: the number and type of centrifuges Iran must dismantle and/or reconfigure; the fates of Iran's vast stockpile of low-enriched uranium (LEU), of the Fordow uranium enrichment facility, and of the Arak heavy-water reactor; how long Iran will have to abide by the terms of the comprehensive deal ("sunset provision"); the rate of sanctions relief; and the question of Iran's ballistic missile program. But probably the most important aspect of Iran's program that must be clarified in the context of a comprehensive deal is its past work on weaponization – what the IAEA has called the possible military dimensions (PMD) of Iran's nuclear program (IAEA 2011).

This issue of weaponization brings us full circle to the NPT, because it is Iran's work on a military nuclear program that constitutes its clearest violation of the NPT, and it is what legitimizes all of the demands that the international community is making of Iran. Letting Iran off the hook in this regard would be tantamount to enabling Iran to continue with its deceitful narrative according to which it "has done no wrong in the nuclear realm": that no evidence has been produced of Iran's wrongdoing, and therefore all the measures that have been taken against it, first and foremost the sanctions, are illegal and unjust (for an example of this narrative see Fars News Agency 2014; Stein and Landau 2015). Confronting Iran on this issue would make it crystal clear why Iran cannot be trusted not to lie and deceive (after cheating on its NPT commitment for decades while building up its nuclear infrastructure) and why massive dismantlement of its nuclear program is therefore essential.

As of the time of writing, and even after the announcements of April 2, 2015, it is still not clear what degree of agreement exists between the P5+1 and Iran about the different aspects of Iran's nuclear program that are under review. It is clear, however, that the goal of the P5+1 in these negotiations is to keep Iran at about 12 months from breakout, and that they have put such a proposal – relating to the full range of relevant technical issues – on the table. The international negotiators seem to believe that this is enough of a window to ensure that Iran is kept at a "safe" distance from the ability to produce a first nuclear device. Their hope is that within this time frame they will be able to detect and stop any Iranian violation; to ensure this, a key component of their plan is a strong verification regime.

Two issues deserve mention in this regard. First, this 2014 goal is a watered-down version of what the international negotiators were hoping to secure only a few years earlier, when the stated goal was more generally to prevent Iran from producing a nuclear weapon, and there were more far-reaching demands regarding dismantlement of Iran's nuclear program.[6] If the goal has been redefined as that of keeping Iran at a certain distance from breakout, then the implicit assumption is that Iran is likely to cheat; and indeed, if nothing has been done to influence Iran's motivation in this regard, it is safe to assume that it will continue to aspire to a military capability. The second issue, which follows from the first, is that this downgraded goal puts all the attendant provisions of a prospective deal in a problematic light. If the goal is physically to prevent Iran from moving to weapons capability, with the accompanying assumption that Iran's strategy remains to maintain the ability to move to weapons capability at a time of its choosing, then the time frame for effective counter-proliferation measures to be decided upon and executed would have to be much longer than one year.

The reason why 12 months is not enough time to deal with a possible Iranian breakout to a nuclear device lies first of all in the extent of Iran's nuclear infrastructure, possibly with clandestine elements still in place.[7] But an even more problematic issue for enacting swift counter-proliferation measures is the fact that, as noted above, every step along the way – from detecting a violation, declaring it to be significant enough to confront Iran, deciding what to do about it, and who should do it – will have to be made within a rich political context, where a full array of state, institution, and bureaucratic interests will come into play, significantly complicating the process (Landau 2014). For almost a dozen years Iran has made slow, careful, and incremental advances in its nuclear program, in the face of the demonstrated inability of international actors to make quick, determined, and effective decisions to counter or prevent these advances. It can safely be assumed that future decisions will not be any less politically complex or time consuming.

Two incidents in the latter months of 2014 are poignant illustrations of the kind of problems that will be faced, and the degree to which the "detection, decision, action" process will be anything but problem free. The first regards information reported by the IAEA in its early November 2014 report, according to which Iran had injected gas into the IR-5 centrifuge at the Natanz pilot plant. When the Washington-based Institute for Science and International Security (ISIS) raised the question of whether this was not a violation of the JPOA, an involved debate ensued in official and unofficial circles (see Albright and Stricker 2014). The answer to the question was not a clear yes or no, although the United States felt that this activity did indeed violate its understanding of the Interim Deal, and demanded that Iran desist. For its part, Iran claimed that it would continue working on all research and development aspects of advanced centrifuges.

The second issue regarded Iran's illicit procurement of components for its Arak heavy-water reactor, as reported in a foreign policy article (Lynch 2014). While clearly a violation of sanctions on Iran, again the question was raised as to the JPOA. In this case, the answer was easier – it was not a violation of the JPOA – but this incident brought into sharp relief the dilemma of sanctions vs any nuclear deal with Iran. Moreover, if procurement of these components was not a violation of the JPOA, then clearly the JPOA contained a dangerous loophole. These examples highlight the contentiousness of even claiming that a violation has occurred (see Greenberg 2014), as every such claim is likely to be accompanied by debates over interpretations of what has been decided, and which international decisions carry more weight. They also highlight the implications of dangerous loopholes that will inevitably surface down the line.

Military force: any role?

An analysis of US counter-proliferation policy cannot be complete without relating to the question of military force. As noted, the Bush administration decided to go to war as a means of confronting Iraq's suspected WMD program, but with very problematic results, both for Iraq itself and for dealing with the nuclear aspirations of Iran and North Korea.

What role, if any, has the threat of military force played in the overall dynamic of confronting Iran's nuclear aspirations? Once it became clear that negotiations had been chosen as the policy for dealing with Iran, the regime in Tehran breathed a sigh of relief; its fear in 2003 had been that Iran would be next in line for attack after Iraq. In the ensuing years, the United States could still have issued a credible threat of military consequences were Iran not to cooperate, and this could have been an important lever of pressure on Iran in the framework of the ongoing negotiations.[8] But while a loose threat of "all options are on the table" has been a constant in US rhetoric over the years, the threat has not been strong and/or credible enough to alter Iran's behavior. Instead the United States has projected a sense of war-weariness that took the sting out of any threat; moreover, at times US officials themselves would undermine the administration's deterrence attempts. If the president says all options are on the table, but the chairman of the Joint Chiefs of Staff says an attack on Iran's nuclear facilities could have disastrous consequences, then clearly there is a lack of unified commitment to a possible use of force.

Iran also made a concerted effort to empty the US military threat of any credibility by not only working to fortify its nuclear facilities against attack but also by issuing its own deterrent threats. Iran's leaders said loud and clear what would happen to any country that dared attack Iran, and if there were Western voices warning against such an attack, this was the best proof that Iranian – not US – deterrence was proving effective. Indeed, in recent years the threat of military consequences has receded so far into the background that it is virtually nonexistent, even though the US administration has not officially removed it from the table.

Conclusion

Generally speaking, the experience of the past few decades has demonstrated that the international community as a whole – and particularly the United States, as a leading power on the global scene and a strong proponent of nuclear non-proliferation – has proven ill-equipped to stop a determined NPT member-state proliferator from using the NPT as a cover for illicit clandestine nuclear activities aimed at achieving the status of a threshold (or actual) nuclear weapons state. The prospect of successful counter-proliferation efforts has been proven to be dim if the choice is made to rely on diplomacy and negotiations. As the Iranian case has highlighted, embracing diplomacy has involved going through a long and arduous process of referring the case to the IAEA for an ongoing investigation, attempting to secure clear-cut smoking-gun evidence of wrongdoing and confronting the proliferator with the findings, and finally, on this basis, attempting to compel the suspected proliferator, by means of negotiations, to back away from its military aspirations. All the while the proliferator will be using the time to advance its nuclear program, hoping to thwart any prospect of being stopped by more coercive means.

One could go further and argue that international norms of arms control and non-proliferation are currently in such dire straits that the single most successful act of counter-proliferation over the past decade was not the result of diplomacy and negotiations but rather of the use of targeted force: the bombing of the nuclear facility in Syria in September 2007 (Gartenstein-Ross and Goodman 2009). There is little doubt that had evidence of the initial construction of a covert Yongbyon-type nuclear facility in al-Kibar been referred to the IAEA for investigation, this would have initiated a process that would most likely have ended with Syria presenting a challenge to the international community – and to states in the Middle East – similar to the one faced with Iran.

The Syrian case demonstrated that using military force as a counter-proliferation policy can work, but its effectiveness depends on the stage at which it is employed. In the very earliest stages of a proliferator's nuclear program it can cause a long-term delay. But once a proliferator's nuclear infrastructure is built up, perhaps with more clandestine facilities than we imagine, force as a counter-proliferation strategy is less potent, and carries the risk of drawing the state employing force into a more massive and possibly longer-term military engagement. Specifically with regard to Iran, from the start there was a keen lack of political will to employ or even forcefully threaten military force, which was very much the result of the Iraq war, as laid out above. Although the military option is still analyzed (see, for example, Kroenig 2014 and Pollack 2013), it seems no longer to be on the table as far as the United States is concerned; rather, commitment to diplomacy is near absolute.

Notes

* A few months after this article was completed, the Joint Comprehensive Plan of Action (JCPOA) was announced on July 14, 2015. While the deal is the culmination of twelve years of negotiations discussed in this chapter, it does not fundamentally alter the analysis. Although hailed by its supporters – first and foremost the Obama administration – as an historic achievement, the nuclear deal is the result of major concessions that the P5+1 made to Iran. It suffers from holes and weaknesses, especially regarding the verification regime, as well as ambiguous formulations that Iran is likely to abuse in order to advance its interests. Most disturbingly, the agreement sunsets after 10–15 years, regardless of indications that Iran has given up its nuclear ambitions. In short, the JCPOA is not a success story for diplomacy and negotiations. It is a far cry from the original goal set out by the negotiators, which was to ensure that Iran would never be able to acquire nuclear weapons. At the very best it might delay this scenario for 10 years, but even that is not assured due to the weaknesses of the deal, as well as the questionable political will of the P5+1 to hold Iran accountable if it cheats.

1 With the caveat that North Korea left the NPT in 2003, although it was a member in the years in which it began proliferating.
2 From Article IV of the NPT:

> 1. Nothing in this Treaty shall be interpreted as affecting the inalienable right of all the Parties to the Treaty to develop research, production and use of nuclear energy for peaceful purposes without discrimination and in conformity with Articles I and II of this Treaty.
>
> (www.un.org/en/conf/npt/2005/npttreaty.html)

3 For one historical review of the situation in the 1960s, see Gavin (2004, 104–107). These pages give an overview of the countries of concern at that time, although I disagree with the conclusions drawn by the author as far as current-day proliferation challenges. Indeed, understanding the Iranian nuclear challenge necessitates a keen understanding of how nuclear issues and other threat perceptions have unfolded and played out in Middle East politics over the last four decades (see Landau 2012b).
4 This situation changed only in 2013, when the effect of harsh sanctions brought Iran back to the negotiating table, looking for a deal to ease the pressure of sanctions. There was finally something that it needed from the international negotiators, which granted them some leverage. Still, Iran's goal was to obtain economic relief (lifting sanctions) in return for an absolute minimum of nuclear concessions.
5 See, for example, US Vice-President Joseph Biden's speech at the December 2014 Saban Forum (White House 2014), when (as part of a much longer analysis of the negotiations) he summed up that "A good deal exists that would benefit America, Iran, Israel and the world – if Iran is willing to take the deal." But this win–win solution clearly does not exist, at least not yet. Iran does not view the

proposed deal in this way; rather, it believes a better deal from its perspective – one much closer to its basic interest in maintaining a short breakout to nuclear weapons while still getting sanctions relief – is possible. The basis for this belief is that in the final weeks of bargaining in the fall of 2014, the P5+1 members exposed how dependent they are on securing a negotiated deal, when they started offering concessions to Iran (namely, moving toward its position) even though Iran remained steadfast and defiant on the critical nuclear issues. This highlights the true nature of this tough bargaining situation, with no mutually desired outcome.

6 In 2012, the P5+1 demand for "stop, shut, ship" was only considered a first step at the time, and even these demands (shut and ship) are no longer on the table (see Barry and Gladstone 2012).

7 Iran has hidden facilities in the past (Natanz, Arak, Fordow), so there is no reason to assume that it would not have additional hidden facilities now, or attempt to develop them in the future.

8 Significantly, the deterrent threat should have focused specifically on *targeted use of military force against a few nuclear facilities*, and not a general threat of war or invasion (see Yadlin *et al.* 2013).

Bibliography

Albright, David, and Andrea Stricker. 2014. "A Note on Iran's IR-5 Centrifuge Feeding." ISIS Reports, November 20. http://isis-online.org/isis-reports/detail/a-note-on-irans-ir-5-centrifuge-feeding/.

Barry, Ellen, and Rick Gladstone. 2012. "Setback in Talks on Iran's Nuclear Program in a 'Gulf of Mistrust.'" *New York Times*, June 19. www.nytimes.com/2012/06/20/world/middleeast/tense-iran-nuclear-talks-resume-in-moscow.html?pagewanted=all&_r=0.

FAS (Federation of American Scientists). 2014. "Nuclear Non-Proliferation Treaty – Background." www.fas.org/nuke/control/npt/back.htm.

Fars News Agency. 2014. "Presidential Aide: Iran-Powers Talks Cannot Continue Forever." Fars News, December 27. http://english.farsnews.com/newstext.aspx?nn=13931006001502.

Gartenstein-Ross, Daveed, and Joshua D. Goodman. 2009. "The Attack on Syria's al-Kibar Nuclear Facility." *inFocus Quarterly* 3 (1).

Gavin, Francis J. 2004. "Blasts from the Past: Proliferation Lessons from the 1960s." *International Security* 29 (3): 104–107.

Greenberg, Jon. 2014. "Stephen Hayes: Iran Cheated on the Interim Nuclear Deal." *Tampa Bay Times*, December 31. www.politifact.com/punditfact/statements/2014/dec/31/stephen-hayes/hayes-iran-cheated-interim-nuclear-deal/.

IAEA. 2011. "Implementation of the NPT Safeguards Agreement and Relevant Provisions of Security Council Resolutions in the Islamic Republic of Iran." http://isis-online.org/uploads/isis-reports/documents/IAEA_Iran_8Nov2011.pdf.

Jervis, Robert. 2010. *Why Intelligence Fails: Lessons from the Iranian Revolution and the Iraq War*. Isthaca, NY: Cornell University Press.

Kroenig, Matthew. 2014. *A Time to Attack: The Looming Iranian Nuclear Threat*. New York: Palgrave Macmillan.

Landau, Emily B. 2012a. *Decade of Diplomacy: Negotiations with Iran and North Korea and the Future of Nuclear Nonproliferation*. INSS Memorandum 115 (March). www.inss.org.il/uploadimages/Import/(FILE)1333022628.pdf.

Landau, Emily B. 2012b. "When Neorealism Meets the Middle East: Iran's Pursuit of Nuclear Weapons in (Regional) Context." *Strategic Assessment* 15 (3). www.inss.org.il/uploadImages/systemFiles/adkan15_3cENG3%20(2)_Landau.pdf.

Landau, Emily B. 2014. "12 Months is Not Enough Time to Stop an Iranian Nuclear Breakout." *National Interest*, December 17.

Lynch, Colum. 2014. "US Accuses Iran of Secretly Breaching UN Nuclear Sanctions." *Foreign Policy*, December 8. http://foreignpolicy.com/2014/12/08/us-accuses-iran-of-secretly-breaking-un-nuclear-sanctions-exclusive/.

Pollack, Kenneth M. 2013. *Unthinkable: Iran, the Bomb, and American Strategy*. New York: Simon & Schuster.

Ravid, Barak. 2013. "Israeli Intel Revealed Secret US–Iran Talks, Months Before Obama Briefed Netanyahu." *Haaretz*, November 24. www.haaretz.com/news/diplomacy-defense/.premium-1.559964.

Stein, Shimon, and Emily B. Landau. 2015. "Iran's Nuclear Fairy Tale." *INSS Insight* 672 (March 10). www.inss.org.il/index.aspx?id=4538&articleid=8947.

Walker, Hunter. 2014. "Iran's Supreme Leader says Ferguson Shows What's Wrong with America." *Business Insider*, November 27. www.businessinsider.com/ayatollah-ali-khamenei-weighs-in-on-ferguson-2014-11.

White House. 2014. "Remarks by Vice President Joe Biden to the 2014 Saban Forum." www.whitehouse.gov/the-press-office/2014/12/07/remarks-vice-president-joe-biden-2014-saban-forum.

Yadlin, Amos, Emily B. Landau, and Avner Golov. 2013. "If it Comes to Force: A Credible Cost-Benefit Analysis of the Military Option Against Iran." *Strategic Assessment* 16 (1): 95–112.

Ynet. 2014. "Senior Iranian Official: US has been Sabotaging our Nuclear Program." Ynet news, April 17. www.ynetnews.com/articles/0,7340,L-4510946,00.html.

12 Erdoğan's Turkey and Obama's United States

Efrat Aviv

Introduction

On November 3, 2002, an earthquake took place in Turkish politics with the election victory of the AK Party. The party (henceforth AKP), which during the campaign had stressed its anti-corruption agenda and its "Islamic Conservatism" agenda, proposed a balance between a commitment to Turkey's secular constitution and a Muslim world view (Walker 2007, 94). The rise of the AKP as a dominant force in Turkish politics, as demonstrated by its successful passage of the constitutional referendum on September 12, 2010, and by the party's third consecutive electoral victory 11 months later, has heightened fears among many that Ankara has turned its back on its historical alliance with Washington, especially in light of the weakening of the military and secular elites in Turkey (Walker 2012, 144). The main concern has been that Turkey, an important Islamic actor, will adopt a more radical brand of Islam with undemocratic, anti-Semitic, and anti-Western dimensions (see, for example, Rubin 2006). Scholars labeled the AKP's new foreign policy, especially in the Middle East, as "neo-Ottomanism," "re-Islamization," or even as a "Middle Easternization of Turkey." According to Turkey's current prime minister, Ahmet Davutoğlu, Turkey needs to combine its rich Ottoman past and culture with contemporary republican values. His famous "strategic depth" notion means tapping into the historical and geographical features of Turkey as sources of political capital, with the aim of developing Turkey into a global actor (Türkmen 2009, 119).

The Islamic background of the AKP (an offshoot of the Islamist and anti-US Welfare Party), and the party's relative lack of foreign policy experience, made the United States suspicious (Walker 2007, 95). However, given Turkey's status as an important strategic partner, the US administration decided to overcome its apprehensions. US Deputy Secretary of Defense Paul Wolfowitz and Under Secretary of State Marc Grossman visited Ankara in 2002 to request Turkish cooperation in the Iraq war planning efforts. The Turks responded by underscoring the importance of "international legitimacy," meaning the securing of a UN mandate before any action in Iraq. From this point on, the term "cooperation" became understood differently in the eyes of the Turkish and US negotiators (Walker 2012, 148).

The AKP government signaled that it would not follow the US lead under all conditions, and positioned Turkey as a rising soft power. Turkey, a non-permanent member of the UN Security Council, held the position of Secretary General of the Organization of Islamic Cooperation (OIC), as a member of the G-20 group of nations. Turkey has the world's eighth-strongest military, is a NATO member, has multilateral relations with various political actors, and sees itself as an emerging soft power in the regions extending from the Balkans to the Middle East and Central Asia (Kalın 2010, 98). While Turkey's image in the Middle East has deteriorated somewhat, the Turks still attribute growing influence to their country: in 2013, 64 percent of Turks believed that their country's political role in the Middle East was becoming more important (Mensur and Gündoğar 2013).

This article examines Turkish–US relations over the last decade, and surveys attitudes in Turkish public opinion toward the United States. The article first analyzes the impact of the 2003 US invasion of Iraq on bilateral relations, as well as on several other foreign policy issues. Subsequently, the Turkish domestic scene is reviewed, assessing attitudes toward the United States.

Invasion of Iraq

The US invasion of Iraq was a benchmark in the relations between Ankara and Washington. On March 1, 2003, the Turkish Parliament decided to deny the US military permission to launch a ground offensive into Iraq using Turkish soil (Rubin 2005; Copson 2003; Yetkin 2004). This decision was popular in Turkey, reflecting widespread anti-Americanism in Turkish society (Grigoriadis 2010). The vote was preceded by a Turkish demand for $30 billion from the United States, which angered Washington. After the vote the United States felt betrayed, and consequently Turkey was left out of the decision-making process on Iraq – an area critical for Turkey's national security. The invasion of Iraq determined the tone of the US–Turkish relationship for the first decade of the twenty-first century (Walker 2012, 149).

The US invasion of Iraq touched upon the Kurdish problem – one of the most sensitive issues in Turkey. A Kurdish autonomous zone was established in northern Iraq when the country was under US tutelage. Back during the 1991 Gulf war, US policies in Iraq were perceived as failing to consider Turkish security concerns. Moreover, rumors regarding US assistance to the PKK (Kurdistan Workers' Party) strongly fueled anti-US sentiments in Turkey. Despite Erdoğan's "democratic initiative" policy regarding the Kurdish issue, which displayed some openness to Kurdish cultural aspirations in Turkey, the struggle against the PKK has continued. US clarifications that it does not favor a break-up of Iraq or an independent Kurdish state have not been sufficient to eliminate suspiciousness toward the United States (Lesser 2006, 88).

Another event triggering a major crisis between the two countries came on July 4, 2003, when the US military arrested 11 Turkish special forces officers in Sulaymania in northern Iraq, suspected of planning the assassination of a local Kurdish politician. The Turkish officers were taken away hooded and cuffed. Although they were released two days later, this act led to loud protests, during which US flags were burned in front of the US Embassy in Ankara. The Sulaymania incident was seen as a national insult. The fact that those arrested were soldiers made things even worse, as the military has traditionally been popular within Turkish society, and was one of the most pro-US actors in Turkey (Grigoriadis 2010, 58). This incident marked the beginning of a more vocal anti-Americanism in Turkey, which was supported by various political groups, including nationalists, leftists, radical Islamists, and even mainstream secularists.

These anti-US sentiments received notable expression in the entertainment sphere: *The Valley of the Wolves*, a movie based on a successful TV series, was a blockbuster in Turkey in early 2006. The movie concerns US activities in Iraq, and portrays the United States as a perpetrator of atrocities against Iraqi civilians, with US soldiers shown as particularly brutal. The movie also creates linkage between the United States, the Jews, and Israel: one of the characters in the movie is a Jewish doctor who removes kidneys from Iraqi soldiers killed in the war and ships them to Tel Aviv, New York, and London to implant them in Jewish patients. In one of the scenes, a Hassidic Jew eats dinner in an expensive US hotel in northern Iraq and then leaves the building only a few minutes before a bomb destroys the hotel, implying the Jews were forewarned. This echoes the conspiracy theory that the Israeli Mossad was responsible for 9/11, and that only a few Jews died in that attack (Hoff 2013, 185). The film's premiere in Ankara was attended by the country's most powerful politicians, including the prime minister's wife Emine Erdoğan, Istanbul Mayor Kadir Topbaş, and Vice Premiere Bülent Arınç, who described the film as "absolutely magnificent" (ibid., 187–188).

Foreign policy issues of discord

The Iraq war aside, there are number of other foreign affairs issues that negatively affect Turkish–US relations: Iran, Israel, Syria, and the Armenian issue have all created tensions.

Washington has been concerned by Turkey's policy on Iran. At the UN Security Council in 2010, Turkey voted against US-backed proposals for additional sanctions against Iran. And in fact, Turkey acted to circumvent the sanctions imposed upon Iran because of its nuclear program, paying

Iran for natural gas sales in Turkish liras, and allowing Iran to convert the Turkish currency into gold in Turkey ("gas for gold"). In August 2012, nearly $2 billion worth of gold was sent from Turkey to Dubai on behalf of Iranian buyers (Arbell 2014, 30–31). As Turkey largely relies on Iran's oil and gas for its economy, Ankara sees it as critical to maintain its economic alliance with Tehran and its access to Iran's oil and gas reserves (Rafizadeh 2014). In addition, Erdoğan has sharply criticized the Obama administration's policy on Iran, and instead has proposed diplomatic efforts to resolve the nuclear crisis.

The tensions between Turkey and Israel during this period have also strained US–Turkish relations. In the 1990s Turkey became closer to Israel, which was welcomed in Washington. However, the Iraq war produced tensions between the two countries. Rumors of Israel's cooperation with the Iraqi Kurds (such as training Kurdish militias and preparation of the Kurds for independence) were denied by Israel, but clouded the relationship. The growing Turkish–Israeli animosity from 2006 onward was a source of discomfort for Washington, which would have preferred its two strong allies in the Middle East to continue their strategic partnership.

Israel and the United States have been criticized in Turkey for their stance on the Palestinian issue. For example, on May 20, 2004, Erdoğan accused Israel and the United States of "state terror" (Cagaptay 2004). In response, neoconservatives in the United States, who were previously strong advocates of good relations with Turkey and great supporters of Israel, have instead become vocal critics of Turkey. This rift was accompanied by anti-Turkish stories reported in the US news media (Galen Carpenter 2010, 33). Tensions peaked in the summer of 2010 due to the Mavi Marmara incident, and to Erdoğan's referring to Zionism as a "crime against humanity" (*Radikal* 2014a; 2014b).[1] Turkey's harsh rhetoric against Israel, and its decision to terminate diplomatic relations at ambassador level until the Israeli government apologized, was not well received in the United States.[2]

The Israeli apology of March 2013, mediated by President Obama, did not end the crisis in Israel–Turkey relations.[3] Indeed, the widespread anti-Americanism within Turkish society has been associated to an extent with US support of Israel, while Turkey instinctively sides with the Palestinians. Turkey, of course, has paid a price in US opinion for its consistent siding with Hamas, classed in the United States (and elsewhere) as a terrorist organization. It also lost the support of the US "Jewish lobby,"[4] which has been a traditional supporter of the Turkish position in Washington.

The increasingly hostile divergence of views between Turkey and the United States over Syria has also tested the 60-year alliance. Turkey's refusal to allow the United States to use its bases to launch attacks against the Islamic State (ISIS) in the Syrian border town Kobane, and the harsh anti-US rhetoric by top Turkish officials denouncing US policy, have worried US policy makers. "If Turkey is not an ally, then we and Turkey are in trouble. It is probably the most important ally," said Francis Ricciardone who served as US ambassador to Turkey until summer of 2014 (Sly 2014).

At the end of October 2014, Erdoğan attacked Obama for ordering three C-130s to airdrop weapons and supplies to Kobane immediately after a conversation they held. US officials sought to reassure Turkey that the airdrop was a one-time action, and the two countries have agreed on a plan to reinforce the Syrian Kurds with Kurdish Peshmerga fighters from Iraq. Yet the US actions humiliated Erdoğan, who refused to agree on the necessity of handling the Kobane problem: when Washington requested the use of the US base in İncirlik, which is in close proximity to ISIS targets inside Iraq and Syria, Erdoğan demanded that the anti-ISIS coalition set up a no-fly zone over Syria before taking a more active military role. Erdoğan has made it clear that he considers Syrian President Assad to be a bigger threat than ISIS. Erdoğan attacked US "impertinence" on Syria, claiming that the West's only concern in the region is oil (*Daily Mail* 2014).

The United States finds it difficult to understand Turkey's "obsession," as an unnamed US official has described it, with removing the Assad regime in Syria. So far, Turkey has accepted the role of training the Syrian opposition, including Kurdish militias in Turkey, but negotiations over allowing military operations against ISIS have not ended. The insistence on removing Assad probably stems from Assad's 2011 refusal to accept Turkish demands to incorporate the Muslim Brotherhood into his government. Since then, he has become an "arch enemy" (Arslan 2014). During Erdoğan's May 2013 visit to Washington he tried to enlist US support for Assad's removal; Assad's political survival indicates a Turkish failure, yet this is something that Ankara refuses to admit. The costs incurred by Ankara's intransigence continue to mount; refugees flee to Turkey and there are problems with the Kurds. Yet Turkey appears ready to pay the price of tense relations with the United States (ibid.).

According to a US government official, the United States believes that Turkey has been playing a double game in Syria, lending covert support to ISIS (Hogg 2014). Erdoğan has denied this, and labeled ISIS a "terrorist organization." When US Vice President Joe Biden claimed, at the beginning of October 2014, that Turkey was among other countries that had backed extremists and inflamed sectarian conflict, he was obliged to apologize to Erdoğan (*Milliyet* 2014). Despite Turkey's refusal to allow the United States to use the İncirlik base, Secretary of State John Kerry declared, "Turkey has agreed to host and train and equip people. It certainly has allowed the use of certain facilities" (Ergan 2014). Obama's national security adviser, Susan Rice, made clear that the United States has not asked the Turks to send ground forces of their own into Syria (Tanış 2014b).

The Kobane dispute reflects basic differences that are hard to bridge. The Turks often claim that the United States struggles to understand the

Middle East, as it does not, unlike Turkey, border Syria. Moreover, located far away from the Middle East, the United States, unlike Turkey, is less likely to suffer from its foreign policy failures.

A constant irritant in the relations between Ankara and Washington is the role played by the Greek and Armenian lobbies in the United States, seeking to influence US policy on Turkey. Obama's election to president raised concerns in Turkey because Obama, as a senator, was among those who had endorsed an "Armenian genocide" resolution in Congress. Yet President Obama avoided using the term "Armenian genocide" in his message to the Armenian-American community on the Armenian commemoration day, April 24, 2009. Instead, he used the Armenian term "great catastrophe" (Grigoriadis 2010, 64). When the House Foreign Relations Subcommittee voted to pass the Armenian Genocide Resolution (March 10, 2010), Ankara responded in great anger. If the US Congress were to vote favorably on the "Armenian genocide," that would certainly poison relations between Turkey and the United States (Kalın 2010, 104; Grigoriadis 2010, 64).

It is important to note that, in addition to the above-mentioned foreign affairs issues, which cast a shadow over US–Turkish relations, some other minor issues also contribute to the ongoing rift, such as Turkish–China, Turkish–Russia, Turkish–EU relations, and of course Turkey's support for Hamas.

Attitudes toward the United States in Turkish politics

As noted, the invasion of Iraq negatively affected Turkish perceptions of the United States. Occasionally not only the Turkish military (see below) but also the government is seen by the Turkish public as the United States' puppet (see, for instance, Poyraz 2007a, 2007b; Akgül 2014). This criticism has even come, surprisingly, from pro-government journalists such as Abdurrahman Dilipak, who writes for the Islamist, pro-AKP *Yeni Akit*. According to Dilipak, the AKP is "a project" established by the United States, Britain, and Israel;[5] these being the exact same accusations that AKP supporters level toward the republican opposition party, the CHP.

The view of the MHP (Milliyetçi Hareket Partisi – Nationalist Movement Party) toward the United States is very negative, especially because of the Kurdish problem. The main concern of the MHP is that the Kurdish issue will lead to the disintegration or partition of Turkey. According to MHP's leaders, the Kurds have replaced Turkey as the United States' main strategic partner in the region, due to the latter's interests in oil (*Rudaw* 2014). The MHP sees the United States as the puppeteer who pulls the strings of Turkey in general, and of the AKP government in particular (*Bugün* 2014). The MHP and other nationalists generally support ties with the United States only if the latter shows some "gratitude" by combating Kurdish terrorism, and only if the relations are based on equality and mutual trust.

Suspicion of the United States has also been expressed by the CHP (*Cumhuriyet Halk Partisi* – the Republican People's Party) and by the Democratic Party (DP).[6] Onur Öymen, CHP deputy chairperson, has claimed that the United States has been insensitive toward Turkey's fight against PKK terrorism (ibid.). However, since becoming leader of the CHP, Kılıçdaroğlu has begun to transform it into a dynamic, social democratic movement. In the process, he has pushed the party toward adopting a strong pro-Western stance, in contrast to the AKP's foreign policy, which is focused largely on religiously based alliances in the Middle East (Unver and Cagaptay 2011). As part of that, and as an attempt to create a proper opposition to the AKP's Eastern focus, the CHP has strengthened relations with the West and especially with the United States. Unlike the older version of the CHP, the new one is positive toward religion, but opposes the AKP's religion-based conservatism; the CHP is open to Islam, but not to its social conservativeness. In other words, the CHP's tendency to favor close relations with the United States, Israel, and the European Union is part of its domestic battle with the AKP. Indeed, the CHP's vice chairperson is Faruk Logoğlu, a retired ambassador who served in Washington between 2001 and 2005. Logoğlu believes that there is a great need for a strong connection to the United States, and moreover that there is no chance of Turkey having a good relationship with the United States unless it maintains cordial relations with Israel.

The CHP's opponents highlight the fact that it is closely identified with good relations with Washington. According to Levent Baştürk, a scholar and one of the opponents of the CHP, the relations between the CHP and the United States are so strong that Western media, such as the *New York Times*, Reuters, and *The Economist*, called on Turks to vote for the CHP, and thus assisted it in the 2011 elections. It is no secret, claims Baştürk, that the United States, Israel, and the European Union have sought to topple the AKP government in Turkey, and this is the reason why Turkey's relations with these actors has deteriorated. This complements Erdoğan's accusations that the CHP is not only a Turkish project but "an international one." Dr Canan Arıtman of the CHP has even concurred, saying that "CHP is an American project." Baştürk also claims that, just like the United States, the CHP is not interested in toppling Assad, and instead seeks to blame the AKP for helping radical elements in Syria to fight Assad. The CHP's representatives are always welcome in the United States, he claims, and are always invited to formal meetings with high-ranking US representatives in Turkey (Baştürk 2013).

The radical left in Turkey strongly opposes the United States for being a "colonialist," "imperialist," and "capitalist" power. In their eyes, the Obama administration is not that different from the Bush administration. US support for Israel (allegedly at the expense of the Palestinians), US policy toward Afghanistan and Iraq, and "threatening messages" to Iran and North Korea all strengthen the anti-US stand of the radical left in Turkey. Yet in the eyes of the radical left, the worst United States' deed is its support for Armenian rhetoric about the "Turkish genocide," and its support for the Kurds and PKK. In other words, the United States is believed to be planning to divide Turkey along the lines of its minorities' interests, and even to create a second Treaty of Sèvres (Erdem 2009).[7]

During the first years of the Obama administration, the AKP was very supportive of the United States. Egemen Bağış, an AKP Member of Parliament, said in 2007 that not only does the AKP not oppose the United States but in fact it is the "self-appointed guardians of Kemalism who have shown themselves to be the most radical anti-US, anti-EU and anti-free market groups" (*Today's Zaman* 2007). The Islamists and the supporters of AKP regarded the United States positively until the Gülen affair exploded on December 17, 2013 (see below).

Obsessed with the idea that "foreign powers" are interested in toppling the Turkish government, every expression of criticism is taken as the former's intervention within Turkish domestic politics. This tendency has become so extreme that even the famous novelist and Nobel laureate Orhan Pamuk, as well as the novelist Elif Şafak, were accused by the pro-government press. After being charged with criticizing the state and Turkish identity, under Article 301 of the criminal code, both Şafak and Pamuk were eventually acquitted in court. According to the accusations, both novelists were "projects" of an "international literature lobby" developed by Western powers to criticize the Turkish government (Yüksel 2014). AKP supporters are particularly sensitive to critical voices against the ruling party. In the controversial attack on media affiliated with the exiled US-based cleric Fethullah Gülen, during which prominent journalists and media people were arrested, a mystery Turkish Twitter user named Fuat Avni correctly predicted the raids against Gülen's people. As Avni's identity is still unknown, parts of the Turkish press accused him of being a CIA spy attempting to stir up the country.

Yet the AKP cannot allow itself cold relations with the United States, and as a consequence Turkey's prime minister and other ministers visit Washington as often as possible.

Turkish public opinion toward the United States

Anti-US sentiments in Turkey are well documented by several leading research centers, such as Pew and TESEV. According to a TESEV poll from 2011, only 26 percent of Turks believed that the United States is a friend of Turkey, while 53 percent believed that it is not a friend. The same poll found that 73 percent of Turks were certain that Turkey behaves in a friendly way toward the United States, while 53 percent saw US–Turkish relations in a positive, promising way (*Sabah* 2011).

A Pew Research Center (2013) poll found that 70 percent of the Turkish public had unfavorable views of the United States, while only 20 percent were favorably disposed. Since 2000, the proportion of those favorably disposed toward the United States had dramatically decreased from 52 percent to 19 percent. Younger people (ages 18–29) tended to be more ill disposed toward the United States than older ages; only 8 percent of Turks over 50 had unfavorable views of the United States. Some 49 percent of the Turks claimed that the United States was "the enemy," compared to 14 percent who saw it as a partner; 75 percent of Turks felt that the United States did not take the interests of Turkey into consideration, while only 18 percent believed that the United States did consider Turkey's interests a great deal or to some extent. The 75 percent figure is one of the highest in the world, and expresses great mistrust of the United States. Therefore it is no surprise that 82 percent of the Turkish society opposed deployment of US drones on Turkish territory, whereas only 7 percent approved. In 2014, 73 percent of the Turkish public were found to have unfavorable views of the United States, while only 19 percent were favorably disposed (Poushter 2014).

These Turkish attitudes display a paradox: on the one hand, US culture enjoys great popularity and Turkey is a US ally through NATO. On the other hand, there are strong anti-US sentiments and a tendency to see "CIA fingerprints" everywhere. This contradiction represents "Komplocu mantığı," a "conspiracy logic" (Taşpınar 2014). The conspiracy theories have such a strong hold on the Turkish imagination that it is felt that an international operation may be launched in Turkey at any given moment. One example is the claim that the United States supports the Kurds in Iraq, while it is the AKP that provides the greatest economic and political support to the local Kurdish administration in Iraqi Kurdistan (ibid.). Thus anti-Americanism persists in Turkey despite its irrationality.

The election of President Obama in 2008 nurtured hopes for turning a new page in the United States' relations with its key allies, which helped both Turkey and the United States overcome Bush's policies in the Middle East.[8] Obama's visit to Turkey in 2009, his Cairo speech in the same year, and his visits to Europe and Russia confirmed his determination to make a clean foreign affairs break with the Bush administration (Kalın 2010, 93). Obama made Turkey his first overseas visit, and in his speech to Turkish Parliament on April 6, 2009, he emphasized Turkey's importance, and used the terms "partner" and "partnership." Obama also initiated the term "model partnership" during a joint news conference with his Turkish counterpart Gül, replacing "strategic" with "model." Obama meant that the alliance with Turkey was no longer based on mutual interests only, but was also based on shared values and democratic principles (Walker 2012, 151). The Obama administration hailed Turkey as an example of "moderate Islam," stressing its positive influence throughout the region. The motto accompanying these efforts was, "Islam is compatible with democracy" (Özçelik 2014, 31).

Obama's positive perspective of Turkey complemented the eagerness of Erdoğan and Davutoğlu to prove Turkey's importance as a rising regional power. This led to the highest number of bilateral visits by US and Turkish officials in the history of Turkey (Walker 2012, 152). Obama later listed Erdoğan among the five world leaders with whom he has the closest personal ties (Getegüncel 2012). According to Pew Research Center (2013) polls, the Turkish public's confidence in Obama was 33 percent in 2009, 23 percent in 2010, 12 percent in 2011, 24 percent in 2012, and 29 percent in 2013. Only 27 percent of the Turks had an unfavorable opinion of the United States after the re-election of Obama. According to a 2011 TESEV poll, 67 percent of Turks believed that the Obama administration made a positive contribution to Turkish–US relations. This is also the reason why 53 percent of the Turks were optimistic regarding the future relations of both states (*Sabah* 2011).

Yet, the general image of the United States in Turkish eyes remains basically unchanged (Taşpınar 2014). The Turks believe that the United States continues to fail in military interventions, such as in Iraq and Afghanistan, and although the United States is unlikely to lose its superpower superiority to other powers such as Russia or China, it will still pay a costly price for their aggressive policy. The decline in the belief of the uniqueness of US power is coupled with a search for a new distribution of global power (Kalın 2010, 95–97). The changes in US standing in the world appear beneficial for Turkey. The US emphasis on soft power and regional allies suits Turkey's new foreign policy toward the Middle East, the Caucasus, and Central Asia. It will make Turkey more influential and involved, especially in the regions where Turkey feels "at home" (ibid. 101).

Domestic affairs and their influence on US–Turkish relations

Turkish domestic events also have a negative impact on the relations between Turkey and the United States. One example is the Ergenkon affair, an alleged clandestine, secularist, ultra-nationalist organization in Turkey with ties to members of the country's military and security forces, which was accused of planning terrorist activities to undermine the AKP's democratic rule (Walker 2012, 150–151). Military officers (in service and retired) were arrested and charged with a coup attempt. Washington's mute reaction to the Ergenkon affair, a clear attempt on the part of the AKP to neutralize the political power of the Kemalist military, was seen by the secularists in Turkey as hypocritical and in contrast to US rhetoric in support of democracy. Some Turks believed that the United States was interested in keeping the Turkish military weak so that it can pursue its agenda in the region without any resistance (Voice of America 2010).

A similar example is that of the Gezi Park protests. In May 2013, two weeks after he was feted at a White House dinner, Erdoğan was confronted by massive street demonstrations that were violently suppressed by the police.[9] The remarkable discourse that subsequently emanated from Erdoğan, AKP ministers, and elements of the media abounded with conspiracy theories. It blamed the demonstrations on foreign plots, interest lobbies, Americans, Jews, and the foreign press. Erdoğan claimed that an "interest-rate lobby" was responsible for orchestrating the protests, a thinly veiled attack on Jews (Goodman 2013). He furthermore implied that the flames of dissent had been fanned by Western powers who do not want a strong Turkey (Deliveli 2013).[10]

The Obama administration was frustrated with Erdoğan's handling of the Gezi protests, and has repeatedly cautioned Turkish authorities against the use of force to end demonstrations (*Hürriyet Daily News* 2013). Six months after Gezi Park, in an unprecedented move, Erdoğan directly criticized the US ambassador in Turkey, while his spokesmen accused embassy officials of plotting against Turkey. One conspiracy theory even mentioned a CIA allocation of $24 billion to overthrow the AKP government (Barkey 2014).

Turkey, for its part, complains that Washington describes Ankara as a trusted ally in public, while hundreds of thousands of leaked State Department documents show a different picture. It seems that US diplomats have cast doubts on Turkey's reliability, portraying its leadership as divided, and controlled by Islamists (Voice of America 2010).

For many Turks the reasons behind the increased criticism of Turkey in the United States, and the shift in US depictions of Erdoğan from Obama's best friend to a dictator who has ties with al-Qaeda, lie in Turkey's rapid economic and political growth, as well as in its increasingly independent (and popular) international policy. The word in Turkey is that "when Erdoğan no longer plays the puppet, his rule has no legitimacy in the eyes of the Americans" (Time Türk 2014). Many newspapers supported Erdoğan's condemnation of foreign organizations for attempting to topple the AKP government. For a great number of media outlets in Turkey, the economic success of the AKP and its success in stabilizing Turkish politics could not have been achieved by any other party (ibid.).

The clash between the Gülen movement and the AKP was another domestic incident that soured relations between Ankara and Washington.[11] Despite differences in approach, the AKP and the Gülen movement had had a "symbiotic relationship" that elicited much concern in secular sectors in Turkey (Yavuz 2013, 217). Then Erdoğan accused Gülen's followers, for a long time partners in the AKP government, of infiltrating state institutions to gain control of state mechanisms, perpetrating illegal wiretapping, forging official documents, and spying. This rift between the AKP and the Gülenists surfaced in December 2013, at a time when the police, under the influence of the Gülenists, were accused of orchestrating a corruption probe against Erdoğan's inner circle. In response the government purged thousands of police officers and hundreds of judges and prosecutors. (On Gülen links to AKP, see Jenkins 2007 and Kuru 2007.)

Erdoğan signaled in April 2014 that Turkey would ask the United States to extradite Gülen, but this request was probably denied by President Obama (Tanıs 2014a). Erdoğan expressed hope that the Turkish and US governments would cooperate in the struggle against the Gülen movement, which he portrayed as a threat to both of them. He claimed that certain media outlets and think tanks in the United States were being adversely affected by the smear campaign of the Gülen movement (*Daily Sabah* 2014).

For many years the rumor in Turkey was that Gülen, in self-exile in the United States, was supported by the CIA.[12] Harsh rhetoric against the US "Jewish lobby" sought to reinforce the idea that the Gülen movement received assistance from both the CIA and US Jewish organizations (Time Türk 2014). The AKP reinvoked the idea that Turkey's three external enemies were the Jews (and Israel), the United States, and the Gülen movement, partly to divert the attention from AKP corruption and to provide a specific target against which to agitate the masses.[13] Eventually, Turkey's national security council (MGK) declared the Gülen movement, once the government's most powerful political ally, to be a "threat to national security." The Gülenists were labeled by an AKP spokesman as perpetrators of a "postmodern coup d'état" and builders of a "parallel (state) structure," which has become the government's preferred term for it (*Sözcü* 2014). The struggle against the Gülen movement was accompanied by anti-US statements.

Conclusion

The image of the United States in Turkish eyes has been deteriorating since the 2003 Iraq war. The war strengthened widespread anti-US sentiments, and changed views in those parts of the Turkish political map that were previously supportive of the United States. Anti-US feeling now exists to some extent among all political groups, and the uniting theme behind it is national pride: the United States is not entitled to interfere in domestic Turkish politics and should not drag Turkey into US attempts to promote its regional interests. The election of Obama nurtured hopes for a more positive relationship, especially in the AKP, whose foreign policy seemed to coincide with Obama's foreign preferences. But these hopes very quickly changed into mutual suspicion, and the harshest criticism from Turkey has been expressed when the United States is suspected of getting involved in Turkey's domestic affairs, something the Turks find impossible to forgive. Domestic issues and inflammatory rhetoric, especially from Erdoğan, have banished the initial optimism attached to the Obama administration, particularly since 2013. Erdoğan has been successful in gaining greater freedom of action in the domestic political arena due to timid responses from the United States.

It seems that there is growing suspicion between the two countries. In the United States, Turkey is viewed as playing a double game. For their part the Turks see the United States as duplicitous, supporting Erdoğan's Turkey on the one hand and holding up its moderate Islam agenda as a model for the world, but on the other hand undermining Erdoğan's regime. Turkey nurtures ambitions to lead, not only to obey. Erdoğan aspires to a level of status and influence similar to Obama's, and seeks to become the leading figure in Turkey, the Middle East, and Central Asia. When it comes to bones of contention such as Iran and Israel, it appears that the United States has come closer to the Turkish position, if not with the same intensity: the US–Israeli rift has been growing slowly, and US negotiations with Iran get warmer. Turkey's economic growth has led to a desire on its part to upgrade its role in the American–Turkish alliance. Ankara seeks more equality and reciprocity, and does not want be taken for granted any longer.

Both sides believe that their foreign policy is moral and that they are on the right side of history. It is hard, however, to avoid the impression that Turkey and the United States are moving on separate, parallel tracks.

Notes

1 The Mavi Marmara incident is the name given to the Israeli military raid on a Turkish-led aid flotilla to Gaza in May 2010, which resulted in the death of nine Turks and shattered the once-close ties between Ankara and Jerusalem.
2 On Israeli–Turkish relations under AKP rule, see: Uzer (2013); Inbar (2010); Bengio (2004); Altunışık (2000); and Oğuzlu (2010).
3 According to Arbell (2014, 15), the US administration was concerned with the Palestinian Authority's pursuit of an upgraded status in the UN, and thus Washington was eager for Israel to issue its apology.
4 There is a great confusion within Turkish society between legitimate pro-Israel lobbying and conspiracy theories about "Jewish domination" of the world in general (and the United States in particular), which constitute classical anti-Semitism (see, for instance, Bali 2013).
5 Ali Bulaç (2014) from *Zaman* has confirmed that he heard these claims from Dilipak.
6 The DP (Demokrat Parti) is a center-right, conservative party, established by Süleyman Demirel in 1983 as the True Path Party (Doğru Yol Partisi). It succeeded the historical Democratic Party and the Justice Party.
7 The Treaty of Sèvres partitioned the Ottoman Empire between Armenia, Greece, Britain, France, and Italy in 1920, leaving a small unaffected area around Ankara under Turkish rule. Accordingly, in Turkey "Sèvres Syndrome" is the perception of being encircled by enemies (especially Western ones) that are attempting the destruction of the Turkish state.
8 On Bush's policy in the Middle East, see: Elridge (2013); Carothers (2007); and Stewart (2005).
9 On the Gezi Park events, see a report prepared by CHP's Research and Policy Development Department (CHP 2014); and Turan (2013).
10 According to Deliveli, these accusations of foreign investors are ridiculous, as almost two-thirds of shares on Turkey's stock market are owned by foreign investors.
11 The Gülen movement is a transnational religious and social movement led by Turkish Islamic scholar and preacher Fethullah Gülen, a moderate Turkish

Muslim scholar, prolific writer, and philosopher, who resides in the United States.
12 Among many other accusations, see, for instance, those of Osman Nuri Gündeş, former head of the national intelligence organization MIT, who claimed that at least 130 CIA agents serve as teachers in the movement's schools in Central Asia (SoL 2011). Others claim that Gülen was obliged to cooperate with the CIA in order to receive a residency permit for the United States (AHBR 2014).
13 Author interview in Istanbul, February 4, 2013.

Bibliography

AHBR. 2014. "Fethullah Gülen CIA'e mi çalışıyor?" January 22. www.ahaber.com.tr/gundem/2014/01/22/fethullah-gulen-ciae-mi-calisiyor-338586753764.

Akgül, Ahmet. 2014. *ABD'li Siyonistlerin AKP'li Piyonistleri*. Istanbul: Togan.

Akgün, Mensur, and Sabiha Senyücel Gündoğar. 2013. *Perceptions of Turkey in the Middle East 2013*. Istanbul: TESEV. www.tesev.org.tr/assets/publications/file/03122013120651.pdf.

Altunışık, Meliha. 2000. "The Turkish–Israeli Rapprochement in the Post-Cold War Era." *Middle Eastern Studies* 36 (2): 172–191.

Arbell, Dan. 2014. "The US–Turkey–Israel triangle." *Brookings: Center for Middle East Policy* 24: 15. www.brookings.edu/~/media/research/files/papers/2014/10/09%20Turkey%20us%20Israel%20arbell/usTurkeyIsrael%20trianglefinal.pdf.

Arslan, Deniz. 2014. "Turkey's 'Obsession' with Removing Assad Hurts Turkish Interests." *Today's Zaman*, October 19. www.todayszaman.com/national_Turkeys-obsession-with-removing-assad-hurts-turkish-interests_362010.html.

Bali, Rıfat. 2013. *Antisemitism and Conspiracy Theories in Turkey*. Istanbul: Libra Kitap.

Barkey, Henri. 2014. "Obama's new problem: Turkey." *Al-Monitor*, January 23. www.al-monitor.com/pulse/originals/2014/01/Turkey-united-states-obama-pronlem.html#.

Baştürk, Levent. 2013. "Yeni CHP'nin Amerika gezisinin şifreleri." *Dünya Bülteni*, December 6. www.dunyabulteni.net/haber-analiz/282371/yeni-chpnin-amerika-gezisinin-sifreleri.

Bengio, Ofra. 2004. *The Turkish–Israeli Relationship. Changing Ties of Middle Eastern Outsiders*. New York: Palgrave Macmillan.

Bugün. 2014. "Oktay Vural: Türkiye'yi Washington mu yönetiyor Ankara mı?" October 22. http://gundem.bugun.com.tr/turk-milleti-bunu-kabul-etmez-haberi/1311259.

Bulaç, Ali. 2014. "AK Parti bir proje miydi?" *Zaman*, December 22. www.zaman.com.tr/ali-bulac/ak-parti-bir-proje-miydi_2265819.html.

Cagaptay, Soner. 2004. "Where Goes the US–Turkish Relationship?" *Middle East Quarterly*, Fall: 43.

Carothers, Thomas. 2007. "US Democracy Promotion During and After Bush." http://carnegieendowment.org/files/democracy_promotion_after_bush_final.pdf.

CHP. 2014. *Gezi Hareketi*. https://chpbxl.files.wordpress.com/2014/06/chp-ve-gezi-hareketi-tr.pdf.

Copson, Raymond W. 2003. *Iraq War: Background and Issues Overview – Report for Congress*. Washington, DC: Congressional Research Service. www.fas.org/man/crs/RL31715.pdf.

Daily Mail. 2014. "Turkey's Erdogan Attacks US 'Impertinence' on Syria," November 26. www.dailymail.co.uk/wires/afp/article-2850311/Turkeys-Erdogan-attacks-US-impertinence-Syria.html.

Daily Sabah. 2014. "Red Notice Likely to be Issued Against Gülen, Says Erdoğan," September 24. www.dailysabah.com/politics/2014/09/24/red-notice-likely-to-be-issued-against-gulen-says-erdogan.

Deliveli, Emre. 2013. "The Chapull-Jew (Çapulcu) Interest Rate Lobby." *Hürriyet Daily News,* June 10. www.hurriyetdailynews.com/the-chapull-jew-capulcu-interest-rate-lobby.aspx?pageID=449&nID=48497&NewsCatID=430.

Deutsche Welle. 2013. "Erdoğan'a 'siyonizm' tepkisi," March 1. www.dw.de/erdo%C4%9Fana-siyonizm-tepkisi/a-16639265.

Elridge, Alyssa. 2013. "No Exit: The Bush Doctrine and Continuity in US Middle East Policy." *Avicenna: The Stanford Journal on Muslim Affairs* 3 (2): 26–32.

Erdem, Özgür. 2009. "Sevres Syndrome." *Türk Solu,* April 13. www.Turksolu.com.tr/232/erdem232.htm.

Ergan, Uğur. 2014. "US Military Team in Ankara for ISIL Talks." *Hürriyet Daily News,* October 16. www.hurriyetdailynews.com/us-military-team-in-ankara-for-isil-talks.aspx?PageID=238&NID=73041&NewsCatID=510.

Galen Carpenter, Ted. 2010. "Estrangement: The United States and Turkey in a Multipolar Era." *Mediterranean Quarterly* 21 (4): 27–37.

Getegüncel. 2012. "Obama'nın En Sevdiği 5 Lider," January 20. [Turkish] www.gazeteguncel.com/haber-Obamanin-En-Sevdigi-5-Lider-25128/.

Goodman, Alana. 2013. "Turkish Politician Links Jews to Unrest in Turkey." *Washington Free Beacon,* July 3. http://freebeacon.com/turkish-politician-links-Jews-to-unrest-in-Turkey/.

Grigoriadis, Ioannis N. 2010. "Friends No More? The Rise of Anti-American Nationalism in Turkey." *Middle East Journal* 64 (1): 51–66.

Hoff, Anne-Cristine. 2013. "Normalizing Anti-Semitism in Turkey." *Journal for the Study of Antisemitism* 5 (1): 185.

Hogg, Jonny. 2014. "Stubborn Streak Leaves Turkey Increasingly Isolated." *Daily Star,* October 24. www.dailystar.com.lb/News/Middle-East/2014/Oct-24/275161-stubborn-streak-leaves-Turkey-increasingly-isolated.ashx#axzz3K5CUUKiB.

Hürriyet Daily News. 2013. "Turkish Deputy Prime Minister Denies Remarks on 'Jewish Diaspora'," July 2. www.hurriyetdailynews.com/Jewish-diaspora-behind-gezi-protests-turkish-deputy-prime-minister-says.aspx?pageID=238&nID=49858&NewsCatID=338#.UdK96Re4HbM.twitter.

Hürriyet Daily News. 2013. "US Senate Discusses Gezi Park Protests," August 1. www.hurriyetdailynews.com/us-senate-discusses-gezi-park-protests.aspx?PageID=238&NID=51815&NewsCatID=358.

Inbar, Efraim. 2010. "Israeli–Turkish Tensions and Beyond." *Israel Journal of Foreign Affairs* 4 (1): 27–35.

Jenkins, Gareth. 2007. "AKP Forming Closer Links With the Gülen Movement." *Eurasia Daily Monitor* 4 (217). www.jamestown.org/single/?no_cache=1&tx_ttnews[tt_news]=33187.

Kalın, Ibrahim. 2010. "US–Turkish Relations Under Obama: Promise, Challenge and Opportunity in the 21st Century." *Journal of Balkan and Near Eastern Studies* 12 (1): 98.

Kuru, Ahmet. 2007. "Changing Perspectives on Islamism and Secularism in Turkey: The Gülen Movement and the AK Party." In Ihsan Yilmaz, ed., *Muslim World in*

Transition: Contributions of the Gülen Movement. London: Leeds Metropolitan University Press, 140–151.

Lesser, Ian O. 2006. "Turkey, the United States and Delusion of Geopolitics." *Survival* 48 (3): 88.

Milliyet. 2014. "Biden Erdoğan'dan özür diledi," October 4. www.milliyet.com.tr/biden-erdogan-dan-ozur-diledi/dunya/detay/1950274/default.htm.

Oğuzlu, Tarik. 2010. "The Changing Dynamics of Turkey–Israel Relations: A Structural Realist Account." *Mediterranean Politics* 15 (2): 273–288.

Özçelik, Murat. 2014. "Turkish Foreign Policy in the Middle East." *Turkish Policy Quarterly* 13 (3).

Pew Research Center. 2013. "Global Opinion of Barack Obama." In "America's Global Image Remains More Positive than China's, Chapter 2." Pew Global Attitudes and Trends website. www.pewglobal.org/2013/07/18/chapter-2-global-opinion-of-barack-obama/.

Poushter, Jacob. 2014. "The Turkish People Don't Look Favorably upon the U.S., or Any Other Country, Really." Pew Research Center, October 31. www.pewresearch.org/fact-tank/2014/10/31/the-turkish-people-dont-look-favorably-upon-the-u-s-or-any-other-country-really/.

Poyraz, Ergün. 2007a. *Musa'nın Gül'ü*. Istanbul: Togan.

Poyraz, Ergün. 2007b. *Musa'nın çocukları: Tayyip ve Emine*. Istanbul: Togan.

Radikal. 2014a. "Başbakan Erdoğan: İslamofobi insanlık suçu görülmeli," February 27. www.radikal.com.tr/dunya/basbakan_erdogan_Islamofobi_insanlik_sucu_gorulmeli-1123152.

Radikal. 2014b. "Erdoğan'a 'Siyonizm' tepkisi," March 1. www.radikal.com.tr/dunya/erdogana_siyonizm_tepkisi-1123458.

Rafizadeh, Majid. 2014. "What's Behind Turkey and Iran's Strategic Friendship?" *Al-Arabia*, June 13. http://english.alarabiya.net/en/views/news/middle-east/2014/06/13/What-s-behind-Turkey-and-Iran-s-strategic-friendship-.html.

Rubin, Michael. 2005. "A Comedy of Errors: American–Turkish Diplomacy and the Iraq War." *Turkish Policy Quarterly* 4 (1). www.turkishpolicy.com/default.asp?show=spr_2005_Rubin.

Rubin, Michael. 2006. "Mr. Erdoğan's Turkey." *Wall Street Journal*, October 19. www.meforum.org/1036/mr-erdogans-turkey.

Rudaw. 2014. "MHP: ABD'nin stratejik müttefiki artık Kürtler," December 15. http://rudaw.net/turkish/middleeast/turkey/151220143.

Sabah. 2011. "Türklerin % kaçına göre ABD dostumuz!" March 25. www.sabah.com.tr/gundem/2011/03/25/turklerin__kacina_gore_abd_dostumuz.

Sly, Liz. 2014. "For Turkey and US, At Odds Over Syria, a 60-Year Alliance Shows Signs of Crumbling." *Stars and Stripes*, October 30. www.stripes.com/news/us/for-Turkey-and-us-at-odds-over-syria-a-60-year-alliance-shows-signs-of-crumbling-1.311102.

SoL. 2011. "Gülen okullarında CIA ajanları mı çalışıyor?" January 14. http://haber.sol.org.tr/devlet-ve-siyaset/gulen-okullarinda-cia-ajanlari-mi-calisiyor-haberi-38030.

Sözcü. 2014. "Tarihin En Uzun MGK Toplantısı," October 31. http://sozcu.com.tr/2014/gundem/mgk-sona-erdi-2-635561/.

Stewart, Dona J. 2005. "The Greater Middle East and Reform in the Bush Administration's Ideological Imagination." *Geographical Review* 95 (3): 400–424.

Tanış, Toga. 2014a. "Erdoğan'ın ABD'den 'Gülen' beklentisi." *Hürriyet Daily News*, April 29. www.hurriyet.com.tr/dunya/26315034.asp.

Tanış, Tolga. 2014b. "US Says Turkey Agreed Use of Bases Against ISIL Militants." *Hürriyet Daily News*, October 13. www.hurriyetdailynews.com/us-says-Turkey-agreed-use-of-bases-against-isil-militants.aspx?pageID=238&nID=72881&NewsCatID=359.
Taşpınar, Ömer 2014. "Türkiye'nin ABD'ye değişmeyen komplocu bakışı." *T24*, May 2. http://t24.com.tr/yazarlar/omer-taspinar/turkiyenin-abdye-degismeyen-komplocu-bakisi,9168.
Time Türk. 2014. "CIA Erdoğan'ı neden hedef aldı?" February 24. www.timeturk.com/tr/2014/02/27/cia-erdogan-i-neden-hedef-aldi.html#.VHrqKbdxljo.
Today's Zaman. 2007. "What do Parties Promise on Turkey–US Relations?" July 9. www.todayszaman.com/national_what-do-parties-promise-on-turkey-us-relations_116097.html.
Turan, Ömer. 2013. "Gezi Parkı Direnişi ve Armağan Dünyası." *Toplumsal Tarih* 238: 62–73.
Türkmen, Füsun. 2009. "Turkish–American Relations: A Challenging Transition." *Turkish Studies* 10 (1): 119.
Unver, H. Akin, and Soner Cagaptay. 2011. "Turkey's Opposition Turns Social Democratic: Will the Turks Follow?" *Washington Institute Policy Analysis* 1,792, April 4. www.washingtoninstitute.org/policy-analysis/view/turkeys-opposition-turns-social-democratic-will-the-Turks-follow.
Uzer, Umut. 2013. "Turkish–Israeli Relations: Their Rise and Fall." *Middle East Policy* 20 (1): 97–100.
Voice of America. 2010. "WikiLeak Documents Question Turkey's Relationship with US," November 28. www.voanews.com/content/wikileak-documents-question-Turkeys-relationship-with-us-110978699/170350.html.
Walker, Joshua W. 2007. "Reexamining the US–Turkish Alliance." *Washington Quarterly* (Winter 07/08): 94.
Walker, Joshua W. 2012. "The United States and Turkey in a Changing World." In Kerem Öktem, eds., *Another Empire: A Decade of Turkey's Foreign Policy Under the Justice and Developement* Party. Istanbul: Istanbul Bilgi University Press, 144.
Yavuz, M. Hakan. 2013. *Toward an Islamic Enlightenment: The Gülen Movement.* New York: Oxford University Press.
Yeni Şafak. 2013. "Siyonizm insanlık suçudur," March 20. http://yenisafak.com.tr/politika-haber/siyonizm-insanlik-sucudur-20.03.2013-501927.
Yetkin, Murat. 2004. *Tezkere: Irak Krizi'nin Gerşek Öyküsü.* Istanbul: Remzi.
Yüksel, Mevlüt. 2014. "Pamuk projesi." *Takvim*, December 9. www.takvim.com.tr/Guncel/2014/12/09/pamuk-projesi.

13 Vultures over the Nile

US–Egypt relations between Hosni Mubarak to Abdel-Fatteh al-Sisi

Yehuda U. Balanga

Introduction

Since 1979, for close to four decades, Egypt has been considered one of the main pillars of US foreign policy in the Middle East, alongside Saudi Arabia. In the words of Martin Indyk, "Egypt is the strategic cornerstone of all American involvement in the Middle East" (Indyk 2009, 52). The strategic significance of this relationship for the United States stems from Egypt's control of the Suez Canal, as well as of the land bridge that connects the Middle East, North Africa, and Asia. Furthermore, Egypt acts as a mediator in the peace process between Israel and the Arab world, serves as a counterweight to radical Islam, and provides security support for US troops stationed in the region.[1]

Yet throughout a period of rapid regime change in Egypt, during which the country was in greater need than ever of US support, it seemed that Washington was cooling its relations with Cairo. The United States displayed a hesitant policy toward the "Lotus Revolution" of early 2011, supported the Muslim Brotherhood, alienated Cairo following the military coup of July 2012, and reduced US military aid to Egypt.

This chapter looks at US policy toward Egypt from the collapse of the Mubarak regime with the events of January and February 2011; through the Muslim Brotherhood regime and its overthrow by military coup in July 2013; to the rise of the regime headed by General Abdel Fatah al-Sisi. The lack of consistency shown by the United States has been interpreted by its allies as a lack of foreign policy direction, forcing them to seek support from other countries, or alternatively to create local alliances that serve their interests, principally against the backdrop of the rise of radical Islam.

The fall of the Sphinx

Over the 30 years of Hosni Mubarak's rule, during which he successfully maintained stability in Egypt, the Egyptian president enjoyed the support of US presidents, Democrats and Republicans alike, who saw him as a faithful ally providing a moderating influence in the Arab arena and in the Middle East, and as a partner in defending US interests in the region. However, Egypt's citizens were less enamored of the United States and its actions, as became very clear following the election of Barack Obama to the White House.

The Obama administration sought to establish relations with the Arab world that would be built on trust and openness. In June 2009 Obama visited Cairo University and gave a speech that brought him much admiration in Egypt and throughout the Arab world. But this credit began to run dry very quickly in light of his hesitant and clumsy handling of the Arab Spring, which erupted in 2010. At the beginning of the uprising, the US leadership continued to support the Mubarak regime, but as the mood on the streets became more and more extreme, the United States changed direction, and called on Mubarak to resign. This demand from the White House was seen as proof of the United States' disloyalty toward its Egyptian ally (Gilboa 2013; Blanga 2014).

In March 2011, US Secretary of State Hillary Clinton traveled to Cairo. The visit was intended to repair relations with the transitional Egyptian government, but the hesitant and confusing line taken by the US administration two months previously had created great suspicion of the United States, among both the general population and the military leadership, headed by General Muhammad Hussein Tantawi. Clinton praised the political developments in Egypt, and refrained from taking any stance regarding the reforms. "We don't have an opinion," she said (Myers 2014). "We have a clear message of support for what the Egyptians decide is in their own best interest."

But at such an important crossroads it was vital that the United States adopt a clear position: first, because the young revolutionaries expected a formal response from the US administration, especially given its support for the Mubarak regime in the early days of the Tahrir Square demonstrations; and second, because many of the young leaders of the protests, as well as others in the West, feared that the old regime or the Muslim Brotherhood would assume positions of power. Indeed, in the 2011–2012 parliamentary elections it was the Islamists who emerged victorious, and in June 2012 the Muslim Brotherhood completed its political advance, when Muhammad Morsi won 51.7 percent of the vote in the second round of the presidential elections (Al-Jazeera 2011; Essam al-Din 2012).

The rise and fall of the Muslim Brotherhood

The Muslim Brotherhood's short period of rule was characterized by fear and mistrust toward the United States, which had supported Mubarak's dictatorship for decades. The Americans, for their part, were wary of the new regime's religious ideology, which they perceived might undermine the peace treaty between Egypt and Israel, and might delay the advent of democracy in Egypt, which had sought the end of a dictatorial regime

(Kirkpatrick 2012). The attack on the US Embassy by an angry mob on September 11, 2012 left a very unfavorable impression on US decision makers. Washington understood that it could expect disagreement with Cairo, but it had hoped that, in core areas, the Muslim Brotherhood would continue the diplomatic line that characterized the Mubarak years: maintaining peace with Israel; fighting terror groups in the Sinai Peninsula; mediation between Israel and the Palestinians; and military-security cooperation with the United States (Sharp 2012; Elyan 2012).

In July 2012, Secretary of State Clinton arrived for a first formal meeting with the elected president, Morsi, and with the minister of defense, General Muhammad Hussein Tantawi. The visit took place against a backdrop of tension between the High Council of the Egyptian Armed Forces and Morsi over the transfer of powers from the army to the civil authorities. The High Council was insistent that the order for the dispersal of Parliament (which had just been elected), issued by the Constitutional Court in June 2012, should now be followed. Clinton expressed her support for the civil authority and for Morsi, and added that the US administration expected the army to return to its original role of protecting Egypt's national security (Kirkpatrick 2012). Clinton basically repeated the message relayed by various State Department spokespeople, according to which there would be consequences for US–Egyptian relations if the army were not to fulfill its obligations toward the Egyptian people. And indeed, Congress sought to delay the annual aid to Egypt of $1.3 billion, including special assistance of $1 billion that Obama had requested back in 2011 (Kirkpatrick 2012).

These events brought hundreds of secular demonstrators onto the streets, as well as other opponents of the Muslim Brotherhood, who called Clinton "devil woman," and demanded that the United States cease interfering in Egypt's internal affairs. Others even claimed a conspiracy between the United States and the Muslim Brotherhood, due to a perception that US officials were backing the Brotherhood's ascension to positions of power. The State Department tried to make it clear that the US administration did not support any specific candidate for president in Egypt, and was not interested in becoming involved in a dispute between the army and the civilian government, or in the question of the design of Egypt's new constitution (Al-Meshad 2012; *Al-Youm al-Sabea* 2012; Kirkpatrick 2012).

On August 12, 2012, with the support of the Egyptian masses, Morsi removed the upper echelons of the military from their governing roles, including Minister of Defense Tantawi and the chief of general staff, Sami Anan. In their place he appointed as minister of defense the former head of military intelligence, General Abdel Fatah al-Sisi, and as chief of general staff the commander of the Sixth Army, Zadki Zabahi. Concurrently, Morsi also repealed the constitutional amendments that the High Council had passed prior to the presidential elections, which gave the Council supreme authority over military and security issues, and which had also restricted presidential powers (Al-Jazeera 2012a; Bader al-Din 2012). This sudden change at the top of Egypt's ruling echelon did not rouse the United States from its passivity. The US administration declared that this was nothing more than a generational handover of military leadership, which was in any case mostly old, unpopular, and identified with the previous regime. It also stated that the new position holders had good relations with the United States, and that the cooperation between the two countries would continue as before.

After taking control of the political and military apparatuses, Morsi faced the challenge of addressing the social unrest that threatened Egypt's stability, but also sought to focus attention on the Palestinian–Israeli conflict (Blanga 2012; Ignatius 2012; SpiegelOnline International 2012). "Pillar of Defense," the Israeli military operation in Gaza lasting eight days in November 2012, was the first test of Morsi's loyalty to Hamas, the ruling faction in Gaza that is also considered part of the Muslim Brotherhood movement. And indeed, in contrast to Mubarak, who disagreed with Hamas and its actions, Morsi stood by the organization unreservedly: he denounced the Israeli air strikes on Gaza, recalled the Egyptian ambassador from Tel Aviv, called an emergency meeting of the National Security Council, and warned that "Today's Egypt is different from yesterday's Egypt," and that if "Israeli aggression continues, the price to pay will be high." As an act of Egyptian solidarity with the Palestinian population, senior Egyptian officials were dispatched to visit Gaza, among them Prime Minister Hasham Kandil and Minister of Health Abd al-Manam Abu al-Fatuh. Egypt also opened the Rafiah border crossing for humanitarian aid to pass to Gaza, and allowed casualties to be treated at the El-Arish hospital (Al-Rahman Abu al-Ala 2012; Awad 2012).

Yet all these actions, including also tempestuous demonstrations against Israel that called for the revocation of the peace treaty with it, can be seen as nothing more than letting off steam. Egypt was not really capable of taking actions that might jeopardize its relations with the United States and with the West in general. The severe financial crisis which had enveloped the country since the 2011 uprising necessitated the continuation of financial assistance, including approval of loan requests from the International Monetary Fund. For this reason Egypt was constrained to keep the (cold) peace with Israel, and quietly to restrain the more extremist voices that called for Egyptian military intervention in Gaza. All told, Egypt took no real action to aid Hamas in Gaza, and in this way Cairo retained its status as a potential mediator between Israel and the Palestinians. During "Pillar of Defense," Morsi was forced to choose between ideology and realism: if the Egyptians failed to act to get Hamas to stand down, they were liable to pay a major price in terms of assistance from the outside.

Morsi chose realism. His principle achievement was to prevent an Israeli ground operation in Gaza, which served his interests in two ways: first, a ground incursion would have caused the Egyptian street to demand Egyptian military intervention in Gaza, bringing the regime to face a dilemma of whether to stand off or become involved militarily; and second, an Israeli ground operation would have resulted in significant damage to Gaza's civilian infrastructure, leading to increased internal criticism of the Hamas regime in the Strip. The rapid achievement of a ceasefire maintained Hamas' status as a regime capable of surviving repeated rounds of warfare with Israel, while Egypt's diplomatic involvement, in particular vis-à-vis the United States, maintained its status as a key player in the Middle East.

However, despite the foreign policy successes – including improved relations with Turkey and Qatar, as relations with Saudi Arabia weakened – Egypt's economic problems, together with Morsi's political errors, dragged the country into a whirlpool of regime instability for the second time in two years.

The US response to the overthrow of Morsi

For many in Egypt, particularly among the younger generation that had led the "Lotus Revolution," Morsi's rise to power was not the political change that they had sought (Hellyer 2013; *Al-Ahram* 2012). In May 2013, the Kefaya movement, which had also been prominent as an outspoken opponent during the Mubarak era, launched a campaign called "Tamarud" (rebellion). The success of the Tamarud campaign encouraged other opposition movements and parties to join demonstrations against the Muslim Brotherhood (Al-Alam 2013; Srur 2013). On June 30, 2013, after Morsi's "100 day plan" had met with failure, the youngsters of the "January 25 Revolution" took to the streets in mass demonstrations, drunk on power and demanding the president's resignation (Al-Jazeera 2012b). Unlike during the events that led to the fall of Mubarak, this time the Egyptian army (which for many weeks had been aware of the general state of unrest) made it clear that it would not stand by while Egypt slid into internal conflict or civil war (Al-Miyani 2013; Al-Behairy 2013).

Thus on July 1 the army issued a 48-hour ultimatum to President Morsi, calling on him to open talks with representatives of the demonstrators and with the opposition, and to agree to their demands. Should he refuse, the army would take responsibility for protecting the Egyptian people. In response, Morsi addressed the populace directly in a speech in which he admitted his mistakes and his failures, but refused to bow to the army's ultimatum. After hundreds of thousands thronged the streets of Cairo once more, Minister of Defence al-Sisi made good on the ultimatum's threat: on July 3, troops arrested Morsi, other members of his administration, and hundreds of Muslim Brotherhood activists. With mass support, the army reassumed control of the state; and so ended the brief period of rule of the Muslim Brotherhood (YouTube 2013; Al-Quds 2013; *Elaph* 2013).

The United States' initial reaction to Morsi's overthrow was to freeze defense aid to Egypt. US distaste for military coups is expressed in a federal law, the Consolidated Appropriations Act (2010), which forbids the transfer of financial aid "to the government of any country whose duly elected head of government is deposed by military coup or decree." The Obama administration refrained at first from labeling the removal of Morsi as a coup, as it was less the involvement of the military that provoked US opposition, than the violence used by the Egyptian army to supress support for the Muslim Brotherhood. The United States denounced the violent means used to disperse the demonstrations at the Rabaa al-Adawiya mosque and in Al-Nahda Square on August 14, canceled the "Bright Star" joint US–Egyptian maneuvers planned for September, and froze the delivery of four F-16s to Egypt (Holland and Mason 2013).

Since 1981, every two years, Egypt and the United States have held large-scale joint exercises, which over the years have also been joined by other countries. "Bright Star" is one of the largest multinational exercises in the Middle East, and apart from the fact that it provides the Egyptian army with an opportunity to work with Western armies (lending it significant prestige and pride), the exercise also serves as a platform for the activities of the US Central Command Forces (CENTCOM) in the Middle East. In addition to canceling "Bright Star," the United States also halted the transfer of annual aid, in the form of $250 million of economic support funds. According to a source in the US administration: "We have stopped spending money in areas that would be prevented if it were determined to be a coup.... We'll put a pause on those programs, because we don't want to flout the law" (Sharp 2013).

Every year since 1986, the US Congress has approved military aid to Egypt to the amount of $1.3 billion, the largest aid package provided by the US after that to Israel. However, this does not mean that the Egyptian military receives this sum in liquid funds; rather, the money is transferred to the Federal Reserve Bank of New York, then to trust funds at the Treasury, and finally to US contractors, who produce the tanks and warplanes that are sent to Egypt (Simon 2013). In this context, we should note that a cornerstone of US–Egyptian relations in general, and of US military aid to Egypt in particular, has been the joint production of Abrams tanks at the Abu Zaabal Tank Repair Factory 200, in Helwan. Clearly the importance of this collaboration for the Egyptian military lies not only in the security aspect, that is, joint production of US tanks, but also in the fact that the factory provides employment for thousands of local workers (Sharp 2012). In this way, since 1986 the United States has delivered to Egypt, as part of its military aid package, some 221 F-16 warplanes, worth $8 billion, and over 1,000 Abrams tanks, at a total cost of $3.9 billion. This, despite the fact that for years US military attachés in Cairo have claimed that the Egyptian army already possesses more than sufficient numbers of planes and tanks (ibid.). Indeed, of 1,000 tanks delivered to Egypt since 1992, around

200 have been kept in storage and never used (Institute for National Security Studies 2013).

The response of the heads of the Egyptian army and interim regime to what appeared to be a lack of US backing was swift. Minister of Defense al-Sisi, now set to become Egypt's next president, gave an interview to the *Washington Post* (Weymouth 2013) in which he attacked the US administration: "You [the United States] left the Egyptians. You turned your back on the Egyptians, and they won't forget that." In a subsequent interview with ABC, on August 20, he said that "we need the United States as much as the United States needs us." But according to al-Sisi, although suspending military aid would be a bad thing, and would even temporarily affect the Egyptian army, Egypt would survive and adapt to the new situation. He reminded his interviewer that Egypt had for years received military aid from Russia, and therefore he was not troubled (ABC News 2013; for more on the possibility of forging ties with Russia, see *Trik al-Akhbar* 2013).

There may have been harsh outbursts against the United States from Egypt's political and military leadership, but overall the criticism was restrained. The Egyptian masses, on the other hand, gave full vent to the nation's feelings, and on August 1 a protest campaign was launched, called "Ban the Aid," which was also joined by the Tamarud movement (Ma'an News Agency 2013). On August 17, Tamarud launched another protest campaign called "Reviving Sovereignty," which its leaders claimed was aimed at US attempts to interfere in internal Egyptian policy, at Egyptian aspirations toward democracy, and at attempts to undermine the outcome of the "June 30 Revolution." Through the movement's website, Tamarud launched a petition calling for the end of US aid and for the annulment of the peace treaty with Israel (*Al-Ahram* 2013a; *El-Balad* 2013).

In an interview with Reuters (2013), Mahmoud Bader, one of the founders of Tamarud, fiercely attacked President Obama for denouncing the "June 30 Revolution." Bader called on the United States not to meddle in Egypt's internal affairs, in particular in the struggles of the army and demonstrators against "the terrorism of the Brotherhood," and declared that Egypt had no need of US aid: "I tell you President Obama, why don't you, and your small meaningless aid go to hell?" For Bader and his colleagues in the protest movement, the violent struggle and the bloodshed had been essential in order to save Egypt from the Muslim Brotherhood.

Prior to this, Hassam al-Handi, another Tamarud leader, had accused the United States of signing a deal with the Brotherhood in order to return it to power. He called on people to take to the streets and "defend the revolution" from the Muslim Brotherhood, who he claimed were collaborating with the United States to undermine the legality of the revolution, and to present it as a military coup. Al-Handi also claimed that the United States and the Muslim Brotherhood had a long history of shared relationships, since "it's perfectly clear that the Muslim Brotherhood and President Morsi played a major role in pressurising Hamas into a ceasefire during the recent Israeli aggression against Gaza ["Defense Pillar"]." He added that the United States protected Morsi more than it had protected Mubarak (Elaph 2013).

A couple of months later, the US administration hardened its position against the interim Egyptian government, and on October 9 a State Department spokesperson announced President Obama's decision "to maintain our relationship with the Egyptian government, while recalibrating our assistance to Egypt to best advance our interests." The State Department took pains to emphasize that Egypt would continue to receive US aid in the areas of health, education, business, border security, fighting terror, and security in the Sinai Peninsula. Similarly, the United States would continue to provide military training for Egyptian soldiers and officers, and to supply spare parts for US military equipment already in Egyptian hands. However, the United States would be suspending the transfer of large military systems and funds to the Egyptian government, until the establishment of a democratic civil regime elected via free and fair elections (US Department of State 2013).

In response, the Egyptian Foreign Ministry spokesperson Badr Abdel Aati described the US decision as flawed, in terms of both its content and its timing. He added that it raised serious doubts as to the willingness of the United States to provide permanent strategic support for the Egyptian defense plans. Aati pointed out that Egypt was interested in the continuation of good relations with the United States, but that in terms of its internal affairs and national security needs it would act independently of any outside influence. For many observers, including those in the military, this was a clear hint at the possibility of Egypt turning to alternative sources of military arms and equipment (*Al-Wafd* 2013).

Similar sentiments were expressed by Egyptian Foreign Minister Nabil Fahmi (*Al-Ahram* 2013b) on October 16. Fahmi described the tension between the United States and Egypt as having an influence on the Middle East as a whole, and on US interests in the region. At the same time, he was not worried by the suspension of aid, which he described as a mistake by the United States, and said that the Egyptian people would be able to cope successfully with the situation "in order to preserve their freedom of choice after two revolutions." He also thought that the US decision had an upside, as it would lead to a re-evaluation of the relations between the two countries. Fahmi made clear that he saw the United States as having an interest in maintaining ties with Egypt, "the heart and mind of the Arab world," while Egypt similarly understood the importance of the United States as a global power. Yet he stated that Egypt should also open its gates to other powers, such as Russia and China, which also hold influence over world politics and the global economy.

In essence, the Egyptian declarations were about defending Egyptian national honor. The various US threats, including the October 2013 state department announcement about recalibrating relations with Egypt, were seen as insults and as attacks on national pride. The most strident response was the popular call to break off relations with the United States, as the Egyptian public perceived the United States as "buying" their country, using military aid to leverage influence over internal politics. Thus many felt that ending the aid would significantly reduce dependence on the United States, and return Egypt its sovereignty. Yet in spite of these echoes from the street, the leadership echelon showed restraint in its dealings with the United States. Defense Minister al-Sisi and Foreign Minister Fahmi may have emphasized Egypt's honor, but their pronouncements mainly reflected their desire to maintain strategic ties with the United States.

Operation "Protective Edge" as a test case for Egyptian–US relations

The rise of the al-Sisi regime completely reversed Egypt's attitude toward Hamas in Gaza. While Egyptian–Gazan relations under Morsi had been about support and identification, al-Sisi's Egypt saw Hamas as a security threat, because of its assistance for the Muslim Brotherhood and for terrorist groups in the Sinai Peninsula operating against Egyptian targets. Al-Sisi forbade Hamas from operating on Egyptian soil, and enabled the courts to freeze the organization's assets. Similarly, the Egyptian army began to act aggressively against terrorist organizations in Sinai and their infrastructure, including tunnels that served Hamas in Gaza and enabled it to bring in supplies.

In spite of its continued desire to support the Palestinian cause, al-Sisi's Egypt sought to reduce Hamas' power and to isolate it. And indeed, according to several assessments, it was the Egyptian pressure that encouraged Hamas leaders in Gaza to reconcile with Fatah and to form a unity government with Palestinian Authority Chairman Abu Mazen. Egypt and Fatah both viewed this development favorably, as it promised to reduce Hamas' terrorist activity. But Hamas had other plans: it saw the establishment of a unity government as an opportunity to broaden its influence in the West Bank, and even to conspire against Abu Mazen. Furthermore, the renewal of rocket fire from Gaza, the encouragement of terror attacks against Israel from the West Bank, and the kidnap and murder of three Israeli youths on June 12, 2014 all led to a serious deterioration in relations between Gaza and Israel. On July 8, 2014 Israel launched another campaign in Gaza, operation "Protective Edge."

As it had during "Defensive Pillar," so now did Hamas expect backing from Egypt. Khaled Mashal, chairman of the Hamas Political Bureau, blamed Israel for the outbreak of this new round of hostilities. He called on the international community to "stop the bloodshed ... and the aggression of the Netanyahu government in Gaza, the West Bank, and the Occupied Territories." He also addressed Egypt: "The Movement [Hamas] expects the courage of the mighty Egyptian armed forces for the sake of the Arab nation" (Ramchan 2014). But now new winds were blowing in Cairo, and they were not favorable for the Hamas regime; instead, they were even supportive of Israel. The Egyptian media attacked Mashal, portraying him as living a life of luxury in Qatari hotels while the Palestinians struggled under harsh conditions. Hamas was accused of trading in the blood of the Palestinian people, of agitation, and of plotting with the Muslim Brotherhood to destabilize the Egyptian regime. The criticism in Egypt grew to such an extent that there were calls for Egyptian military action against the "nest of terror" in Gaza, "to destroy Hamas with a forceful military operation" (YouTube 2014a, 2014b, 2014c).

On July 14, Egypt devised a framework for a ceasefire that would begin at 9 a.m. the following day, but Hamas rejected this initiative, and continued firing rockets at Israel (*Haaretz* 2014). This rejection of the Egyptian proposal drew intense international criticism of Hamas, particularly from the United States. On July 15, and again on August 1, President Obama and Secretary of State John Kerry condemned the continued rocket fire against Israel, reiterated Israel's right to defend itself, and voiced support for Egypt's efforts to achieve a ceasefire. Kerry also expressed concern at the possibility of a further escalation (US Department of State 2014a), which duly arrived two days later in the form of an IDF ground incursion into Gaza.

After the failure of the Egyptian mediation attempt, the United States turned to Turkey and Qatar, competing powers with Egypt, inviting them to join efforts to broker a ceasefire. These contacts with the Turks and the Qataris, which had begun even before Egypt's failure, surprised many of the United States' allies in the Middle East, in particular Jordan, Saudi Arabia, Egypt, and Israel. In Israel this maneuvre of Kerry's was seen as support for Hamas, and as ignoring the interests of the United States' most loyal friends in the region. Egypt struggled to understand why the United States had opened talks with countries supportive of Hamas at a time when the Egyptian military was fighting terror groups in Sinai that were supported by Hamas and the Muslim Brotherhood. Even worse, while the Egyptian proposal had called for a ceasefire with no preconditions, the Hamas leadership sought to prolong the fighting, and had set conditions for any deal with the Israelis: removing the blockade of Gaza, opening the border crossings (including into Egypt), transfer of tax funds from Israel to Gaza, construction of a sea port and an airport, and release of prisoners. Turkey and Qatar both supported the Hamas demands, for which they were roundly criticized in the Arab world, and even in Palestinian quarters. In many eyes, the Qatari-Turkish support gave Hamas fresh impetus and encouraged it to continue the fighting with Israel, despite the awful situation of the Gazan population (Avni 2014).

Egyptian Foreign Minister Sameh Shoukry accused the "Hamas–Qatar–Turkey axis" of trying to undermine Egypt, in spite of its role as "a defensive wall against a plan to break up the entire region," as had happened in Libya, Iraq, Syria, and Sudan. He added that this tripartite axis was harming efforts to bring about a ceasefire, and was attempting to damage Egypt's status in the Middle East (*Al-Hayat* 2014a). A similar claim was made several days earlier in the Egyptian media. The TV broadcaster Hiya al-Dardiri said:

> It's clear that Hamas, America, Qatar, Turkey, and other states are first and foremost set against Egypt returning to a leading role in the region. Similarly, the aim of Hamas is to drag Arab states such Egypt, Jordan, and Saudi Arabia into a war with Israel.
>
> (YouTube 2014c)

She added that it was on Qatari orders that Hamas had rejected President al-Sisi's ceasefire proposal, with the aim of embarrassing him.

Against this backdrop, on July 22 al-Sisi announced that he had no intention of attending a US–African summit in Washington, planned for the beginning of August, at which he was due to meet with Obama. In his place, he would be sending the prime minister, Ibrahim Mahlab, and Foreign Minister Shoukry (El-Shahed 2014; *Al-Hayat* 2014b). The al-Sisi announcement was made just before a visit of Secretary of State Kerry to Cairo, and revealed how chilly the atmosphere between the two states was. At the same time, Egyptian commentators saw positive signs in the impending visit: recognition of the legitimacy of al-Sisi's presidency; recognition of the importance of Egypt's role in maintaining stability in the Middle East; and strengthening of the ties between the two countries (Freij 2014; *Al-Dostor* 2014).

And indeed, the closing address delivered by Kerry in Cairo, flanked by Shoukry, gave a sense of a return to healthy relations between Egypt and the United States.[2] Kerry expressed his admiration of the Egyptian people for the transition to a democratic regime, and for the difficult decisions (including economic) that they had had to take for the sake of their future. He expressed his condolences for the murder of 21 Egyptians in a terror attack in the Wadi al-Jadid region on July 20, and highlighted the need for cooperation in the war on terror. On the subject of Gaza, the Secretary of State thanked his counterpart for the efforts of the Egyptian leadership to broker a ceasefire, and emphasized that "there is a framework available to end the violence, and that framework is the Egyptian initiative that has been put forward." Kerry called on Hamas to accept the Egyptian initiative, to end the crisis with Israel, and to prevent any further harm to the people of Gaza (Abd al-Hafith 2014; US Department of State 2014b).

Nevertheless, the United States continued negotiations with actors in the Middle East who were obviously unacceptable to both Israel and Egypt. On July 25, Kerry met at the US Embassy in Paris with Turkish Foreign Minister Ahmet Davutoglu and with Qatari Foreign Minister Khalid Bin

Mohamed al-Attiyah, two of Hamas' biggest supporters. (Egypt boycotted the Paris discussions.) In a joint summary address, al-Attiyah placed the responsibility for Gaza's economic plight firmly on Israel and on Egypt, which had blockaded Gaza, and linked the achievement of any ceasefire with removing the blockade. Davutoglu claimed that it was Israel that had rejected a permanent ceasefire, and ignored Hamas' responsibility for the outbreak of the current round of violence (US Department of State 2014c).

This support for Hamas from Turkey and Qatar did not deter the Americans. On the contrary, Martin Indyk, formerly the White House special envoy to the Middle East, said: "I don't think one should dismiss anybody who has influence in this situation. The challenge is to get Hamas to stop its firing of rockets" (Solomon 2014). The US State Department also began voicing harsh criticism of Israel. In his summarizing statement in Paris, Kerry said:

> I want everybody in Israel to understand: we clearly understand ... that Palestinians need to live with dignity, with some freedom, with goods that can come in and out, and they need a life that is free from the current restraints that they feel on a daily basis, and obviously free from violence.
>
> (US Department of State 2014c)

Moreover, Kerry also stated that it was Gazans' lack of hope for a better life that drove them to continue the conflict with Israel (Ravid 2014a, 2014b). This declaration was a slap in the face not just for Israel but also for the other countries seeking to curtail the power of Hamas: Egypt, Jordan, and Saudi Arabia, as well as the Palestinian Authority. The headline in the Hebrew daily *Haaretz* referred to Kerry as "the UFO from Washington," because of the unfamiliarity he showed with internal Arab relations between rival camps in the Middle East, and because of his complete lack of identification with the interests of the United States' allies.

The United States' transferral of its support from the Egyptian initiative to the Turkish–Qatari initiative sharpened the rivalry between these power blocs, and in effect sabotaged the efforts to achieve a ceasefire. Israel rejected any proposal for a cessation of hostilities based on the Turkish–Qatari initiative, and was even supported in this by Egypt. At the end of July, President Obama and the UN Security Council called on Israel and Hamas to agree to a humanitarian ceasefire, which would lead eventually to a full ceasefire based on the Egyptian initiative. The final ceasefire was achieved on August 26, 2014, and was in line with the Egyptian proposals, which were eventually adopted by the United States (Avni 2014; United Nations 2014). By the end of the conflict, Egypt had positioned itself as the only power able to bring about a ceasefire.

Conclusion

It seems that the US administration has lacked a clear and well-defined strategy for the Middle East in general, and for relations with Egypt in particular. In the summer of 2013, Washington froze a portion of its military aid to Egypt, and then partially relented in December 2014, delivering ten Apache helicopters. At the same time, Cairo is still awaiting the delivery of additional weaponry it needs in its fight against terror based in Sinai. This issue is a raw nerve in relations between the two countries. Egypt sees the delivery of military aid as a declaration of US support, and views the corollary to be true as well. Claims along these lines were made by al-Sisi in March 2015, when he said that delaying military aid gives "a negative indication to the public, that the United States is not standing by the Egyptians ... [The Egyptian people] would like to feel that the United States is standing by them." With these words, al-Sisi expressed the dissatisfaction of the Egyptian people with its US ally, which after decades of support had now left Egypt to stand alone in its most difficult hour (Fox News 2015).

The weakness shown by the United States in the Middle East has brought Egypt to search for another power with which it might cooperate on the basis of shared strategic interests. Enter Russia, which has always sought to find footholds in the Middle East, and to constrain US hegemony. Since the Arab Spring, Russia has invested in maintaining its position in Syria by defending the Assad regime from rebel forces, thus also preventing the overspill of radical Islam from the Middle East into Russia's neighbors, and even into Russia itself (Shama 2013; Orlov 2012).

Following the "June 30 Revolution" and the removal of Morsi, relations between Moscow and Cairo began to improve. In September 2013 the Egyptian foreign minister visited Moscow, and in October the head of Russian intelligence, Viackeslav Kondraskou, visited Cairo. A month later a delegation of diplomats, parliamentarians, public figures, journalists, and artists traveled to Moscow, to show appreciation for Moscow's support of the "Glorious June 30 Revolution." On November 13, for the first time since the mid-1970s, the Russian foreign and defense ministers, Sergei Lavrov and Sergei Shoigu, visited Egypt together. In February 2014 al-Sisi and Foreign Minister Fahmi visited Moscow for meetings with their Russian counterparts, including a meeting between al-Sisi and President Putin. A year later it was Putin's turn to visit Cairo: on February 9, 2015 he arrived in the Egyptian capital for a two-day visit that included a successful meeting with al-Sisi (State Information Service 2013).

The subjects of the discussions between the Egyptian and Russian political and military leaderships included strengthening relations between the two countries, economic cooperation, and cooperation on agriculture, culture, tourism, and energy (including nuclear energy). The Egyptians saw these meetings as an attempt to create "strategic cooperation" between

Cairo and Moscow, against the backdrop of deteriorating relations with the United States. In addition, Egypt sought to show the United States that it had no monopoly over arms supplies to the Egyptian army. The crowning achievement of the discussions with Russia was an agreement on military cooperation and on a large arms deal, according to reports estimated at between two and three billion dollars. Under the terms of the deal, to be funded by Saudi Arabia and the United Arab Emirates, Russia will supply Egypt with MiG-29 planes, Mi-35 helicopters, air defense missile complexes, and coastal anti-ship complexes, as well as light arms and ammunition (*Al-Ahram* 2013c; *Daily News Egypt* 2013; RIA Novosti 2014). In return, Egypt will provide the Russian fleet with docking facilities at Alexandria, and will increase cooperation with it throughout the Mediterranean. Syria currently provides a port for the Russian fleet at Tartus, and the fall of the Assad regime would critically damage Russia's ability to use the Syrian port's facilities. Thus the upgrading of relations with Cairo is a significant step for Russia and for its continued naval presence in the Mediterranean (*Al-Ahram* 2013c).

For the last three years Egypt has been engaged in a growing struggle with terror groups based in the Sinai Peninsula and in the Libyan desert. Al-Sisi has identified this as a severe threat to the country, and is pursuing all available means to fight it. He seeks economic and military support, now more than ever, including from the United States. In the absence of a clear US strategy or strategic vision, Egypt will be forced to explore other regional and global partnerships, some with competitors of the United States, in order to achieve its goals.

Notes

1 It should be noted that the US Navy passes through the Suez Canal, with the permission of the Egyptian authorities, in order to travel quickly from the Mediterranean to the Persian Gulf. Any delay or restriction imposed on the US Navy would require it to deploy naval forces in the Cape of Good Hope region, in South Africa, and to go around the Cape in order to reach the Persian Gulf and the Indian Ocean.
2 Although it is worth noting that, on its way to the meeting with President al-Sisi in the Presidential Palace, the US delegation was forced to undergo an unprecedented and highly unusual security check, with Kerry himself passing through a metal detector. This incident more than anything else indicated the tense atmosphere between Egypt and the United States.

Bibliography

ABC News. 2013. "Egyptian PM: 'Bad Sign' if America Cuts Military Aid," August 20.

Abd al-Hafith, Zabari. 2014. "A Security Self-Check for John Kerry before Meeting al-Sisi." *Elaph*, July 25. [In Arabic.] www.elaph.com/Web/News/2014/7/925546.html.

Al-Ahram. 2012. "Morsi's First 100 Days: A Report Card," October 9. http://english.ahram.org.eg/NewsContent/1/140/55089/Egypt/The-Balance-Sheet/Morsis-first-days-A-report-card.aspx.

Al-Ahram. 2013a. "Egypt's Rebel Campaign Launches Petition to Cancel US Aid, Israel Peace Treaty," August 18. http://english.ahram.org.eg/NewsContent/1/64/79334/Egypt/Politics-/Egypts-Rebel-Campaign-launches-petition-to-cancel-.aspx.

Al-Ahram. 2013b. "Egypt–US Tension Crucial for Middle East: Foreign Minister," October 16. http://english.ahram.org.eg/NewsContent/1/64/84072/Egypt/Politics-/EgyptUS-tension-crucial-for-Middle-East-Foreign-Mi.aspx.

Al-Ahram. 2013c. "Foreign Minister Lavrov Declares Russia's Willingness to Fund the Egyptian Nuclear Energy Project," November 19. [In Arabic.] http://gate.ahram.org.eg/News/420528.aspx.

Al-Alam, Kanat. 2013. "Protests in Egypt: 'Tamarud' is Collecting 22 Million Signatures in Order to Fire Morsi." Al-Alam, June 29. [In Arabic.] www.alalam.ir/news/1489271.

Al-Behairy, Nouran. 2013. "President Morsi to Address Nation on Wednesday." *Daily News Egypt,* June 25. www.dailynewsegypt.com/2013/06/25/president-morsi-to-address-nation-on-wednesday/.

Al-Dostor. 2014. "Shibana: Kerry's Visit Confirms American Recognition of President al-Sisi," July 22. [In Arabic.] www.dostor.org/632702.

Al-Hayat. 2014a. "Shoukry Accuses the 'Hamas-Qatar-Turkey Axis' of Trying to Sabotage the Egyptian Role," July 18. [In Arabic.] www.alhayat-j.com/newsite/details.php?opt=2&id=240210&cid=3365.

Al-Hayat. 2014b. "Al-Sisi Declines Obama's Invitation," July 22. [In Arabic.] http://alhayat.com/Articles/3721208/%D8%A7%D9%84%D8%B3%D9%8A%D8%B3%D9%8A-%D9%8A%D8%B1%D9%81%D8%B6-%D8%AF%D8%B9%D9%88%D8%A9-%D8%A3%D9%88%D8%A8%D8%A7%D9%85%D8%A7.

Al-Jazeera. 2011. "Clinton Tours Cairo's Tahrir Square," March 16. www.aljazeera.com/news/middleeast/2011/03/20113167497706160.html.

Al-Jazeera. 2012a. "Crowds in Cairo Praise Morsi's Army Overhaul," August 13. www.aljazeera.com/news/middleeast/2012/08/201281215511142445.html.

Al-Jazeera. 2012b. "Have Morsi's First 100 Days been a Success?" October 9. www.aljazeera.com/programmes/insidestory/2012/10/201210952026585832.html.

Al-Meshad, Sarah. 2012. "Sunday's Papers: Egypt's Future is Debated and Clinton Makes Waves." *Egypt Independent,* July 15. www.egyptindependent.com/news/sunday-s-papers-egypt-s-future-debated-and-clinton-makes-waves.

Al-Miyani, Hasham. 2013. "Amar: 'The Army Knows its Job Very Well.'" *Al-Ahram,* June 24. [In Arabic.] http://gate.ahram.org.eg/News/363504.aspx.

Al-Quds. 2013. "Fateful Day for President Morsi with the Expiry of the Egyptian Armed Forces Ultimatum," July 3. [In Arabic.] www.alquds.com/news/article/view/id/448025.

Al-Rahman Abu al-Ala, Abd. 2012. "Gaza Between Mubarak and Morsi." Al-Jazeera, November 20. [In Arabic.] www.aljazeera.net/news/reportsandinterviews/2012/11/20/غزة-بين-مبارك-ومرسي.

Al-Wafd. 2013. "Egypt Reacts Harshly to the Decision to Reduce American Aid," October 10. [In Arabic.] www.alwafd.org.

Al-Youm al-Sabea. 2012. "Demonstration opposite the Presidential Palace protests Clinton's visit to Egypt," July 14. [In Arabic.] www.youm7.com/#.VP1sUtKsWhs.

Avni, Benny. 2014. "Kerry's Ceasefire Pivot Angers Egypt, Israel – Even the Palestinian Authority." *Newsweek*, July 28. www.newsweek.com/kerrys-ceasefire-pivot-angers-egypt-israel-even-palestinian-authority-261834.

Awad, Marwa. 2012. "Egypt's Morsi Condemns Israel, Orders Prime Minister to Gaza." Reuters, November 15. www.reuters.com/article/2012/11/15/us-palestinians-israel-egypt-mursi-idUSBRE8AE1MN20121115.

Bader al-Din, Hani. 2012. "Changes in the Command of the Armed Forces. New Changes by an Old Method. The End of the Army's Political Role." *Al-Ahram*, August 18. [In Arabic.] http://digital.ahram.org.eg/articles.aspx?Serial=995618&eid=859.

Blanga, Yehuda. 2012. "The Revolutionary: A Special Profile of the Egyptian Leader." *NRG*, August 18. [In Hebrew.] www.nrg.co.il/online/1/ART2/395/965.html.

Blanga, Yehuda. 2014. "Turmoil in Egypt 1968–2011: The Status of the Armed Forces in Citizen Uprisings in Egypt." *Contemporary Politics* 20 (3): 371–377.

Consolidated Appropriations Act, Public Law 111–117, 111th Congress. 2010. www.gpo.gov/fdsys/pkg/PLAW-111publ117/html/PLAW-111publ117.htm.

Daily News Egypt. 2013. "Russia Prepared to invest in Egyptian Nuclear Energy: Lavrov," November 20.

El-Balad. 2013. "Tamarud Launches Campaign to Gather Signatures to End American Aid and Revoke the Peace Treaty [with Israel]," August 17. [In Arabic.] www.el-balad.com/587048.

El-Shahed, Salma. 2014. "Why did al-Sisi Decline Obama's Invitation to Washington?" *Al-Arabiya*, July 23. http://english.alarabiya.net/en/perspective/analysis/2014/07/23/Why-did-Sisi-decline-Obama-s-invitation-to-Washington-.html.

Elaph. 2013a. "House Arrest is a Reasonable Outcome for Morsi with the Expiry of the Army's Deadline and Morsi's Refusal to Resign." July 3. [In Arabic.] www.elaph.com/Web/news/2013/7/821634.html.

Elaph. 2013b. "Tamarud Leader: The Brotherhood Conspired with the United States to Regain Power," July 6. [In Arabic.] www.elaph.com/Web/news/2013/7/822281.html.

Elyan, Tamin. 2012. "Egyptians Angry at Film Scale US Embassy Walls." Reuters, September 11. www.reuters.com/article/2012/09/11/us-egypt-usa-protest-idUSBRE88A11N20120911.

Essam al-Din, Gamal. 2012. "Egypt's Post-Mubarak Legislative Life Begins Amid Tension and Divisions." Al-Ahram Online, January 23. http://english.ahram.org.eg/NewsContent/33/100/32384/Elections-/News/Egypts-postMubarak-legislative-life-begins-amid-te.aspx.

Fox News. 2015. "Exclusive: El-Sisi Urges 'Arab Ready Force' to Confront ISIS, Questions If US 'Standing by' Egypt," March 9. www.foxnews.com/politics/2015/03/09/exclusive-el-sisi-urges-arab-ready-force-to-confront-isis-questions-if-us/.

Freij, Shimaa. 2014. "Foreign Minister: The Kerry Visit is Proof of Egypt's Role in the Region." *Al-Dostor*, July 22. [In Arabic.] www.dostor.org/632679.

Gilboa, Eytan. 2013. "The United States and the Arab Spring." In Efraim Inbar, ed., *Arab Spring? Israel, the World, and Regional Changes*. Tel Aviv: Yediot Aharonot. [In Hebrew.]

Haaretz. 2014. "The Full Text of the Egyptian Cease-Fire Proposal," July 15. www.haaretz.com/news/diplomacy-defense/1.605165.

Hellyer, H. A. 2013. "How Morsi Let Egyptian Down." *Foreign Policy*, August 2. http://foreignpolicy.com/2013/08/02/how-morsi-let-egyptians-down/.

Holland, Steve, and Jeff Mason. 2013. "Obama Cancels Military Exercises, Condemns Violence in Egypt." Reuters, August 15.

Ignatius, David. 2012. "US Officials Warily Endorse New Egyptian Defense Minister." *Washington Post*, August 12.

Indyk, Martin. 2009. *Innocent Abroad*. New York: Simon & Schuster.

Institute for National Security Studies. 2013. "Military Balance Files – Egypt." http://inss.web2.moonsite.co.il/uploadimages/SystemFiles/Egypt.pdf.

Kirkpatrick, David D. 2012. "Clinton Visits Egypt, Carrying a Muted Pledge of Support." *New York Times*, July 14. www.nytimes.com/2012/07/15/world/middleeast/clinton-arrives-in-egypt-for-meeting-with-new-president.html?_r=0.

Ma'an News Agency. 2013. "Egypt's Tamarud Movement Joins Campaign to Boycott US Aid," August 17. www.maannews.net/eng/ViewDetails.aspx?ID=621524.

Morsimeter website. http://morsimeter.com/ar. [In Arabic.]

Myers, Steven L. 2014. "Clinton, in Cairo's Tahrir Square, Embraces a Revolt She Once Discouraged." *New York Times*, March 16. www.nytimes.com/2011/03/17/world/middleeast/17clinton.html?_r=0.

Orlov, Alexander, ed. 2012. *The Middle East: Options and Transformation Processes*. Moscow: Moscow State Institute of International Studies.

Ramchan, Bassam. 2014. "Khaled Mashal: We Expect the Courage of the Mighty Egyptian Army for the Sake of the Arab Nation." *Al-Masry Al-Youm*, July 9. [In Arabic.] www.almasryalyoum.com/news/details/479594.

Ravid, Barak. 2014a. "Kerry's Latest Cease-Fire Plan: What Was He Thinking?" *Haaretz*, July 27. www.haaretz.com/blogs/diplomania/.premium-1.607332.

Ravid, Barak. 2014b. "Kerry's Cease-Fire Draft Revealed: US Plan Would Let Hamas Keep its Rockets." *Haaretz*, July 27. www.haaretz.com/news/diplomacy-defense/.premium-1.607379.

Reuters. 2013. "Egyptian Youth Leader Backs Army in Battle with Brotherhood," August 17. www.reuters.com/article/2013/08/17/us-egypt-protests-tamarud-idUSBRE97G07220130817.

RIA Novosti. 2014. "Russia, Egypt Reach Initial $3 Billion Arms Deal," February 14.

Shama, Nael. 2013. "Cairo and Moscow: Limits of Alliance." Middle East Institute, December 16. www.mei.edu/content/cairo-and-moscow-limits-alliance.

Sharp, Jeremy M. 2012. "Egypt: Background and US Relations." Congressional Research Service, December 6. http://fpc.state.gov/documents/organization/201971.pdf.

Sharp, Jeremy M. 2013. "Egypt in Crisis: Issues for Congress." Congressional Research Service, September 12.

Simon, Julia. 2013. "Egypt May Not Need Fighter Jets, But the US Keeps Sending Them Anyway." NPR, August 3. www.npr.org/sections/money/2013/08/08/209878158/egypt-may-not-need-fighter-jets-but-u-s-keeps-sending-them-anyway.

Solomon, Jay. 2014. "Diplomatic Divide Saps US Push for Mideast Cease-Fire." *Wall Street Journal*, July 18. www.wsj.com/articles/diplomatic-divide-saps-u-s-push-for-mideast-cease-fire-1405723920.

SpiegelOnline International. 2012. "The World from Berlin: Egypt's Moment of Truth has Arrived," August 14.

Srur, Zafa'a. 2013. "The Founders of 'Tamarud' Commit to Ending Morsi's Rule." *Al-Masry Al-Youm*, June 30. [In Arabic.] www.almasryalyoum.com/news/details/228340.

State Information Service. 2013. November 13. [In Arabic.] www.sis.gov.eg/Ar/Templates/Articles/tmpArticles.aspx?CatID=4711#.UyAX9D9_uhs.

Trik al-Akhbar. 2013. "Egypt Turns the Page on American Armament. Welcome Russia and China," October 12 [In Arabic].

United Nations. 2014. "Expressing Concern over Deteriorating Situation in Gaza, Civilian Casualties, Security Council Calls for Full Respect of International Humanitarian Law," July 28. www.un.org/press/en/2014/sc11494.doc.htm.

US Department of State. 2013. "US Assistance to Egypt," October 9. www.state.gov/r/pa/prs/ps/2013/10/215258.htm.

US Department of State. 2014a. "Press Availability in Vienna, Austria," July 15. www.state.gov/secretary/remarks/2014/07/229275.htm.

US Department of State. 2014b. "Secretary of State John Kerry and Egyptian Foreign Minister Shoukry's Joint Statements after Meeting with Egyptian President al-Sisi," July 22. www.state.gov/secretary/remarks/2014/07/229626.htm.

US Department of State. 2014c. "Remarks with Turkish Foreign Minister Ahmet Davutoglu and Qatari Foreign Minister Khalid al-Attiyah after Their Meeting," July 26. www.state.gov/secretary/remarks/2014/07/229811.htm.

Weymouth, Lally. 2013. "Rare Interview with Egyptian Gen. Abdel Fatah al-Sisi." *Washington Post*, August 3.

White House. 2014. "Press Conference by the President," August 1. www.whitehouse.gov/the-press-office/2014/08/01/press-conference-president.

YouTube. 2013. "Armed Forces declaration of July 1, 2013, giving Morsi 48 hours to resign." www.youtube.com/watch?v=p3uTLb9K-iI.

YouTube. 2014a. "Hiya al-Dardiri on 'Egypt Today'," July 12. www.youtube.com/watch?v=lcDT5j416zc.

YouTube. 2014b. "Tawfiz Akaasha on 'Egypt Today'," July 13. www.youtube.com/watch?v=23jeXD5ichA.

YouTube. 2014c. "Hiya al-Dardiri on 'Egypt Today'," July 15. www.youtube.com/watch?v=REFV7h-eVd8.

14 Israeli attitudes to the Obama administration

Yaeli Bloch-Elkon and Jonathan Rynhold

Introduction

Israel is a rumbustious democracy in which the public takes a keen interest in foreign and security policy. Foreign and security policy is usually the number-one issue on the political agenda, and it often plays a critical role in determining the results of elections (Rynhold and Steinberg 2004; Rynhold 2007, 2010a, 2010b). Consequently, Israeli public opinion is regularly and systematically surveyed on issues related to the peace process and security threats emanating from the Middle East (Arian 1995; Shamir and Shikaki 2010; Israel Democracy Institute 2015; Institute for National Security Studies 2015). Surprisingly, however, given the centrality of the United States to Israeli foreign and security policy, there has been little systematic polling of Israeli attitudes toward the United States. This chapter aims to fill that gap by presenting and analyzing several ongoing comprehensive surveys of Israeli opinion toward the United States during the Obama era, conducted by the Begin-Sadat Center for Strategic Studies, including a recent wide-ranging survey taken in November 2014.

Overall, the polls show that Israelis strongly support the United States, while also being very critical of the Obama administration's Middle East policies. More specifically, the findings are that Israelis overwhelmingly view the relationship with the United States as vital to Israeli security. Indeed, they rank it as more important than any factor other than Israel's own military capabilities. They also clearly view the United States in general as a reliable ally of Israel. However, Israelis are evenly divided as to whether Obama's approach to Israel is a positive one and, even more significantly, a clear majority of Israelis view Obama's policies in the Middle East in a negative light. This is true for the administration's policies toward the Islamic State in Syria and Iraq (ISIS), the Iranian nuclear issue, and the Israeli–Palestinian peace process.

The chapter begins by exploring the role of the United States in Israeli strategy and Israeli politics. It then discusses the standing of the United States in general, and more specifically as regards Middle East policy issues, in the eyes of the Israeli public, as reflected in various polls conducted from 2009 through 2014.

The United States in Israeli strategy and politics

Prior to discussing the standing of the United States in Israeli public opinion, it is necessary to understand the context in which opinions have been formed by briefly reviewing the strategic and diplomatic relationship between the United States and Israel.

Traditionally, Israeli strategy has placed a major emphasis on self-reliance, deterrence, and military power. Yet Israeli strategy has always recognized that Israel is a small country that requires the assistance of a great power patron; the importance of such a patron in Israeli strategy increased during the period following the Yom Kippur war in 1973 (Inbar 1983). While the United States was always the preferred patron, France played that role from the mid-1950s until 1967. Subsequently, in the 1970s, the strategic relationship with the United States grew, and the United States emerged as Israel's most important strategic partner. The most dramatic display of US support came when the United States resupplied Israel with military equipment during the Yom Kippur war, in the largest airlift of military supplies between allies during a conflict since World War II (Levey 2008; Boyne 2002). The fact that many Western countries refused to assist the US in this effort, and that many other countries broke off diplomatic relations with Israel or shifted their policy in a pro-Arab direction in the wake of the Arab oil embargo, brought home to the Israeli public the importance of relations with the United States. Whether or not the airlift made a substantial difference on the battlefield is debatable, but as far as the public was concerned the United States had been alone in its willingness to stand by Israel at a time when it faced severe danger.

In any case, by the 1970s the United States was Israel's principle arms supplier, and was committed to preserving Israel's "qualitative edge" over Arab states' armies. It defended Israel diplomatically at the UN, where Arab states sought to isolate and delegitimize the Jewish state, and it helped broker peace agreements and peace negotiations, notably between Israel and Egypt. It has also provided Israel with billions of dollars' worth of military aid since the 1970s. However, this is much less significant than it used to be. In 1988, US aid to Israel constituted 6.5 percent of Israel's GNP; by 2009 that had shrunk to 1.1 percent – about 20 percent of the defense budget (Nathanson and Mandelbaum 2012). In any case, since the 1970s the countries have signed a string of memoranda that have upgraded their strategic relationship, for example in 1983 and 1987, and since the 1980s the IDF has been involved in regular exercises with the US armed forces. Until the 1990s Israeli–US cooperation was mainly directed against the Soviet Union's allies in the Middle East. Since the end of the

Cold War, cooperation has focused on opposing radical actors and terrorism in the Middle East, especially so since 9/11, including intelligence cooperation directed against the Iranian nuclear program.

None of this means that there have not been numerous crises in the relations between US administrations and Israeli governments; in fact there have been many, from the very foundation of the State of Israel down to the Obama administration. But the existence of a "special relationship" means that following any specific crisis the relationship recovers (Feldman 1984). It also means that, even when there are strained relations between the president and the prime minister at the political level, it is quite possible that broader cooperation remains robust. Indeed, this has been the case during the Obama era, when despite the poor relationship between Netanyahu and Obama, professionals on both sides have hailed the unprecedented depth of strategic cooperation.[1]

Nonetheless, it is during political crises that the Israeli public plays an especially important role in the relationship. As Robert Putnam recognized (1988), international politics is a "two level game," in which each side negotiates not only with the other side, but also internally within its own polity. Naturally, each side tries to influence the other government's position by appealing to their public as a means of pressuring their interlocutor. In the context of US–Israeli relations, Ben-Zvi refers to this as the "balance of legitimacy," that is, "the domestic social and political context which constrains actors" (Ben-Zvi 1993, 10). This is usually taken as referring to the way in which the pro-Israel lobby and the pro-Israel orientation of US public opinion constrain the US administration from pressuring Israel.[2]

Less talked about is the way the United States seeks to influence Israeli policy by appealing to the Israeli electorate. On several occasions the United States has deliberately sought to affect Israeli public opinion as a means of promoting its policies regarding the peace process, especially in terms of pressuring or seeking to remove Israeli right-wing governments; examples include the 1992 and 1996 election campaigns (Weinberg 2011, 2012). In a similar vein, President Obama's visit to Israel in 2013 was designed to push forward the US-sponsored peace process in the face of a skeptical Israeli prime minister. In an attempt to get Israel to be more amenable to US policy, Obama decided to engage directly with the Israeli public. He recognized that majority of Israelis were skeptical of the peace process, but he calculated that he could take advantage of the fact that Israelis are very pro-United States. By making a good impression and showcasing his pro-Israel credentials, the president hoped to make it more difficult for Netanyahu to be uncooperative. It was one thing to say no to the Palestinians; it would be quite another to say no to Israel's best friend and ally in the middle of a charm offensive.[3] As it turns out, the trip failed to achieve its political objective, as will be discussed below.

The United States in Israeli public opinion

Public opinion is a significant political force. Polls and surveys have become the preferred tools for measuring public opinion. Although polls are open to manipulation, they still constitute the most common and accurate measure of public attitudes, and have thus become considered an important tool for decision makers, especially in democracies. Poll results play a significant role in the political calculations of elites concerning both domestic and foreign policy (Nacos *et al.* 2011). Indeed, they help to set the boundaries of the policy debate.

Specifically, broad and constant public support has been a key factor in the founding and continuation of the special relationship between Israel and the United States. Yet despite that fact, there has been no research project – other than the Begin-Sadat Center project discussed here[4] – that has focused exclusively on Israeli attitudes toward the United States. Other research projects, such as the Israel Democracy Institute's monthly Peace Index, occasionally ask questions related to US–Israeli relations if the issue has been in the news during the particular month in question.[5] However, they do not ask a set of consistent questions concerning relations with the United States, as this is not their central focus.

In addition, the INSS (Institute for National Security Studies, formerly the Jaffee Center for Strategic Studies) has been surveying Israeli public opinion toward peace and security since the 1980s. As such, it has produced the most comprehensive studies on this subject, usually on an annual basis.[6] While Israel's relations with the United States have not been the central concern of these studies, they have asked several questions over the years that are relevant to this topic. Some of these questions, as well as some of the questions asked by the Peace Index, have been incorporated into this study. The bulk of the data, however, comes from the BESA surveys.

The most prominent issue touched upon by previous INSS studies concerns the relative importance of relations with the United States to Israeli security. While this issue was addressed over a long period, the question was not asked directly or in a consistent manner. For example, between 1990 and 1994 about 80 percent of Israelis thought that Israel could contend successfully with a war against the Arab countries of the "Eastern Front" (Syria, Jordan, Iraq), while between 55 percent and 60 percent thought that Israel could contend successfully with UN sanctions. However, only a minority, approximately 40 percent, thought that Israel could contend with the ending of US aid (Arian 1995, 46–47). Again, between 2004 and 2009 the public was asked to assess the ability of Israel to cope with a variety of threats. Of the ten threats listed, the possibility that the US might reduce support for Israel ranked as one of the three most severe, along with all-out war with Arab countries and the threat of nuclear attack. The exact order varied from year to year (Ben Meir and

Bagno-Moldavsky 2010, 58). Clearly, these results indicate the great value placed by Israelis on US support for Israeli security.

We now turn to the surveys of Israeli public opinion on US–Israeli relations conducted by the Maagar Mochot polling agency for the BESA Center at three points during the Obama presidency: 2009, 2012, and 2014.[7] The 2009 poll coincided with Obama's election entry into office; the 2012 poll was at the end of his first term; and the 2014 poll was conducted immediately following the mid-term elections during President Obama's second term in the White House. This wide time frame allows for the polls to reveal a full and accurate picture of trends in Israeli opinion throughout the Obama presidency.

As we can see, Figure 14.1 clearly shows an overwhelming appreciation of the United States. In 2014, good relations between Israel and the United States were perceived by almost all Israelis (96 percent) as highly important, while a huge majority of 90 percent or more consistently believed that close relations with the United States are vital to Israeli security.

In the same vein, as is apparent in Figure 14.2, in 2014 approximately three-quarters of the public (73 percent) considered the United States a

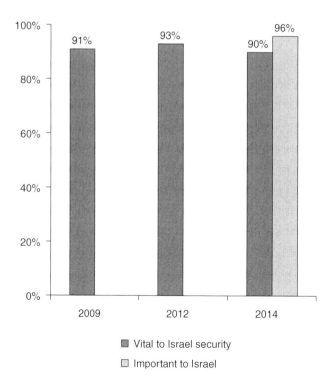

Figure 14.1 The importance of close relations with the United States to Israeli security.

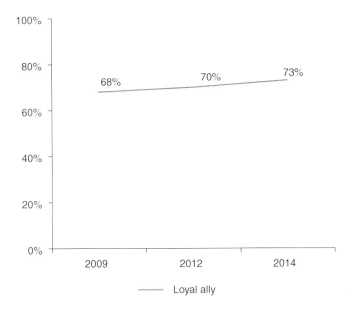

Figure 14.2 The United States: a loyal ally of Israel.

loyal ally of Israel. This percentage has increased steadily from just over two-thirds in 2009. As such, it is higher than in the late 1980s and early 1990s, when roughly between a half and two-thirds thought that the United States' commitment to ensuring Israel's security was reliable (Arian 1995, 169–170). In addition, in 2014, about three-quarters of the public continued to believe that in an existential crisis, with Israel facing a so-called "moment of truth," the United States would come to its defense (Figure 14.3).[8]

Thus, the standing of the United States in a general sense could not be much higher. Indeed, by any comparative measure, Israelis are extremely pro-United States. Back in the late 1980s and early 1990s, more than 80 percent of Israelis had a good opinion of the United States, a far higher percentage than that found among the United States' European allies (Arian 1995, 169–170). According to a survey of 39 countries conducted by the Pew Research Center (2013), 90 percent of Israelis viewed the United States as a partner, while only 1 percent viewed it as an enemy. Indeed, the percentage of the Israeli population viewing the United States as a partner was higher than for any other country in the world. Moreover, in the Middle East, Israel stood out as the only country where a majority viewed the United States as a partner. In the other Middle Eastern countries surveyed – Lebanon, Tunisia, Egypt Jordan, Turkey, and the Palestinian Authority – more people viewed the United States an as enemy than as

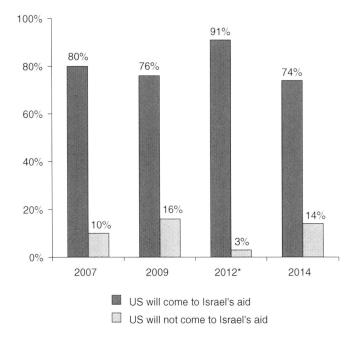

Figure 14.3 US willingness to aid Israel in the event it is faced with an existential crisis.

a partner. In the same survey, 83 percent of Israelis held favorable attitudes toward the United States. Once again, this was the highest percentage of favorability of all the countries surveyed, and Israel was the only country in the Middle East where a majority held favorable attitudes toward the United States.

The high standing of the United States is also demonstrated by the fact that the Israeli public ranks relations with the US as more important to Israeli security than any factor other than the military power of Israel itself. This includes those factors valued more by the right, such as settlements, and those valued more by the left, such as peace with the Palestinians, as well as other more consensual factors, such as the peace agreements with Jordan and Egypt and an Israeli security presence in the Jordan Valley.

In turn, this demonstrates the potential importance of the United States as an influential factor in Israeli politics. Because the relationship with the United States ranks above all these factors, it means that the standing of an Israeli government which is perceived by the public to be damaging the relationship with the United States could face wide-ranging disapproval across the political spectrum. Indeed, in October 2014 a clear majority of the public defined the relationship between the Netanyahu government and the Obama administration as poor (Israel Democracy

Israeli attitudes: the Obama administration 255

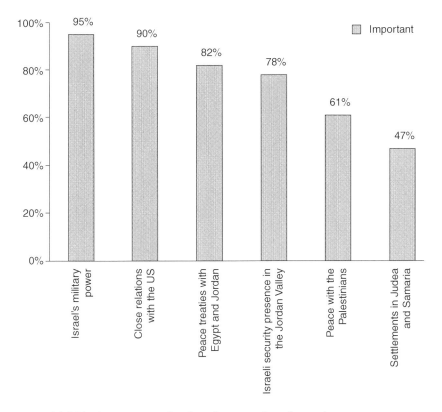

Figure 14.4 The importance of various factors to Israeli security.

Institute 2014). One might deduce from this that the Netanyahu government would be blamed by the public for damaging the relationship. In fact, a plurality blamed the Obama administration (47 percent) rather than Netanyahu (30 percent) (Israel Democracy Institute 2014).

Israeli public opinion toward the Obama administration and its policies

As is apparent from Figure 14.5, in 2014 Israelis were evenly divided in their assessment of President Obama's approach toward Israel, with 37 percent holding the opinion that he had a positive approach, and 37 percent that he had a negative approach. About a quarter of the public attributed to President Obama a neutral attitude toward Israel. In other words, the majority of the Israeli public did not believe that Obama had a positive approach toward Israel. On this question, Obama's personal standing with Israelis has clearly declined. In 2012, a majority (51 percent) believed he had a positive approach, while only 15 percent believed he

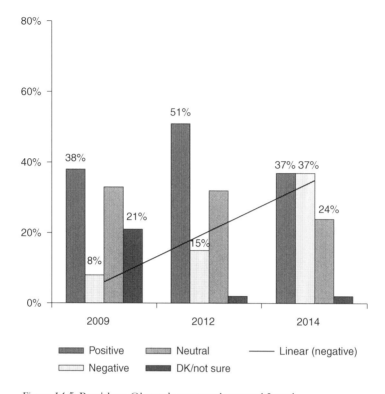

Figure 14.5 President Obama's approach toward Israel.

had a negative approach. Back in 2009, only 8 percent thought he had a negative approach.

Thus, as Figure 14.5 indicates, a shift appears to have taken place between 2009 and 2014, with a decline in the number of respondents who were unsure of Obama's approach to Israel and a rise in the number of respondents who felt that Obama had a negative approach to Israel. Although there is no consensus regarding the question, it is clear that Obama's personal standing on this issue is in decline – in stark contrast to the consistently high standing of the United States in general in the eyes of Israelis.

The reason for this decline in Obama's personal standing is related to the fact that the Israeli public took a negative view of the Obama administration's policies toward the Middle East. Around three-quarters of Israelis (Figure 14.6) perceive radical Islamism, Iran's development of nuclear weapons, and the Israeli–Palestinian conflict as constituting threats to Israel's existential interests. In parallel, as we can see in Figure 14.7, in 2014 about half the Israeli public viewed the Obama administration's policies toward the Israeli–Palestinian conflict, Iran, and the confrontation with

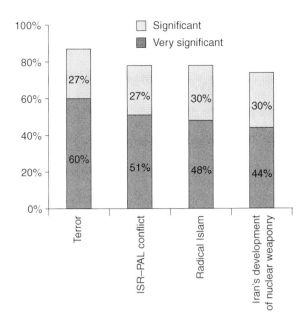

Figure 14.6 Threats to Israel's existential interests.

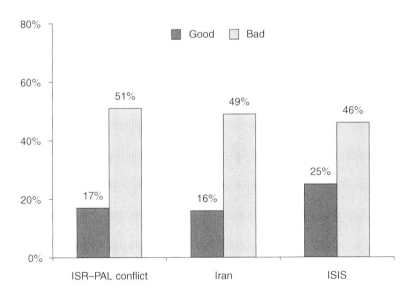

Figure 14.7 President Obama's policies toward the Middle East.

ISIS (the Islamic State of Iraq and Syria) to be "bad." Barely 20 percent of the public believed Obama's policies were "good," meaning that only one in five Israelis thinks Obama is pursing the correct policy toward the major security and foreign policy challenges facing both Israel and the United States in the Middle East.

On the Israeli–Palestinian conflict, the gap between those who thought Obama's policy was bad (51 percent) and those who thought it was good (17 percent) was at its widest. In addition, it should be noted that this gap has widened since 2012, when "only" 41 percent of the public was dissatisfied with Obama's policies on the Israeli–Palestinian conflict, meaning the dissatisfaction had increased by ten percentage points in only two years. Why should this be so? Two factors are worth examining: first, the United States' failed attempt to broker a breakthrough in the peace process by mediating between the Netanyahu government and the Palestinian Authority, led by Mahmoud Abbas. Israelis were deeply skeptical regarding the possibility that negotiations would succeed, so they may well have viewed Secretary of State John Kerry's efforts to reach an accord as naive. On the other hand, Israelis are generally supportive of negotiations in principle, even as they remain highly skeptical, so this factor is unlikely be the main explanation. The second, much more likely explanation for the particularly high level of negative attitudes found in November 2014 has to do with perceptions of US policy during the Gaza conflict in the summer of 2014. Specifically, there was widespread consternation in Israel when the United States was perceived as favoring the ceasefire proposal proffered by Turkey and Qatar, who were supportive of Hamas and other Islamists, as opposed to that put forward by Egypt, a staunch US ally. Even the left-wing liberal Israeli newspaper *Ha'aretz* was highly critical of this move (Ravid 2014).

In the case of Iran, a survey from November 2013 – when the negotiations between Iran and the P5+1 led by the United States commenced – found that three-quarters of Israelis believed that the negotiations between the United States and Iran would not prevent Iran obtaining nuclear weapons capability (Israel Democracy Institute 2013). This probably explains the significant decline (of 17 percent) in the percentage of Israelis who believe that the United States would stand by Israel "if Israel is faced with a serious crisis involving a threat to its very existence, a so-called 'moment of truth'" (Figure 14.3, above). Still, the fact remains that around three-quarters of Israelis continued to believe that the United States nonetheless remains a reliable ally. This may be related to the fact that 82 percent of Israelis believe that relations between the Israeli and US peoples are good (only 11 percent think they are bad). In turn, this could indicate that Israelis believe that widespread public support for Israel in the United States would have a major impact on administration policy in a crunch (Israel Democracy Institute 2014).

Regarding US policy toward ISIS, the size of the plurality holding a negative view of US policy (46 percent bad : 25 percent good) was smaller

Israeli attitudes: the Obama administration 259

than that for US policy toward Iran (49 percent bad : 16 percent good). This is probably because the administration had begun to take active military measures to counter ISIS in Iraq (though not in Syria) prior to the BESA survey. So that even while Israelis remained unimpressed overall, this limited display of active involvement in countering threats in the region appeared to positively affect Israeli public opinion.

Taken together then, the Obama administration's policies were perceived by almost two-thirds of the public as weakening the standing of the United States in the Middle East in 2014; only 11 percent thought that Obama's overall approach strengthened the United States' standing, as shown in Figure 14.8. This represents a major decline from 2012, when about one-third thought the Obama administration's approach to the Middle East weakened the standing of the United States in the region, compared to about a fifth who thought the opposite. The growth of this negative trend in opinion is illustrated in Figure 14.8, with the difference between negative and positive attitudes growing from 17 percentage points in 2012 to a huge 53 percentage points in 2014.

As a result, it is not surprising to see in Figure 14.9 that only about a third of the Israeli public rate the United States' current position in the Middle East as "strong," meaning that more than 60 percent think otherwise.

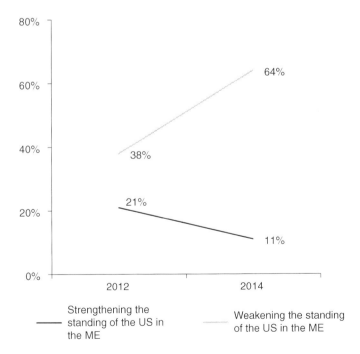

Figure 14.8 Obama's policies and US standing in the Middle East.

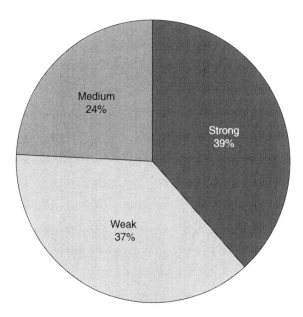

Figure 14.9 The United States' standing in the Middle East.

As far as the Israeli public is concerned, the decline in US standing has serious implications for Israel. This is because two-thirds of Israelis believe that Israel's position in the Middle East is heavily influenced by the United States' standing in the region (Figure 14.10). In addition, about three-quarters of Israelis view US and Israeli interests in the Middle East as similar or complementary (Figure 14.11).[9] Indeed, both Israelis and US citizens rank terrorism and the Iranian nuclear threat as major threats to their countries' security (Chicago Council on Global Affairs 2010).

In other words, most Israelis think that Obama's approach to the Middle East damages the standing of *both* Israel and the United States. This is probably connected to the fact that a clear majority of Israelis believe that reduced US involvement in the region is bad for Israel (Figure 14.10). In this vein, the Obama administration's strategy toward the Middle East has been a cautious one of retrenchment, aimed at reducing assertive, forceful US interventions abroad. Indeed, the administration has been very cautious about using military force abroad, as it fears getting bogged down. It perceives the wars in Afghanistan and Iraq to have been costly failures, and in the wake of economic crises it sought to focus its efforts on a domestic agenda (Dueck 2015; Drezner 2011).

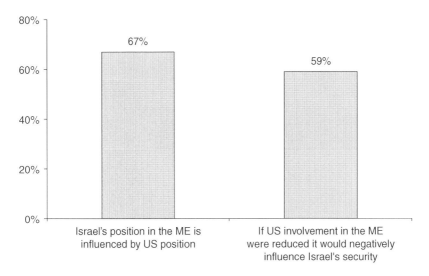

Figure 14.10 Israeli security and the United States' standing in the Middle East.

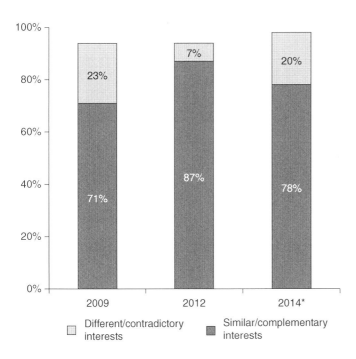

Figure 14.11 US and Israeli interests in the Middle East.

An Israeli attack on Iran: the impact of US opposition

Back in 2002 and 2003, the public was asked what should be done if Israel determined that a (hostile) country in the region had nuclear capacity. The most popular response by far was that Israel should seek to remove that capacity by any means available; around half of respondents favored this option. Only 16–20 percent favored asking for US protection (Arian 2002, 34, 2003, 15). However, the 2014 BESA survey indicates that Israeli public opinion has shifted on this issue since then.

Indeed, perhaps the most significant and surprising results from the 2014 BESA survey concern attitudes toward an Israeli military strike on Iran in the event that diplomacy fails to prevent Iran obtaining nuclear weapons. Only a narrow plurality thought that Israel should attack in such circumstances, by a margin of 41 percent to 37 percent (Figure 14.12). This represents a dramatic change from previous BESA survey results. In 2009 and 2012 a large majority of around two-thirds thought that Israeli should attack in such circumstances. Even more significantly, for the first time, a narrow plurality (42 percent vs 35 percent) thought that Israel should *not* attack Iran in such circumstances if the United States opposed such an attack (Figure 14.13). In other words, even when the public is unhappy with US policy, relations with the United States remain a central component in determining the public's approach to critical security issues. Furthermore, the case of Iran is particularly important because it is viewed as an existential security scenario which pits the number-one security value of Israelis, Israeli military power, against their number-two value, the relationship with the United

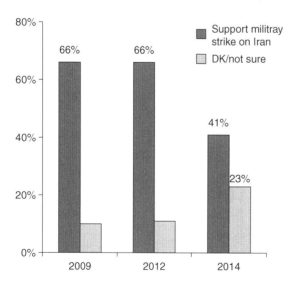

Figure 14.12 Support for Israeli military action if diplomacy fails to halt Iran's drive for nuclear weapons.

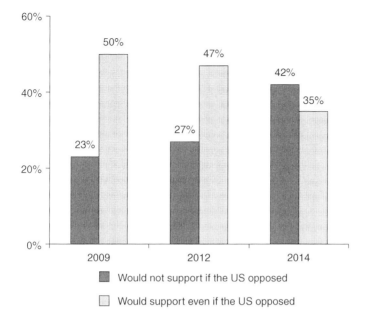

Figure 14.13 Support for Israeli military action in the event that diplomacy fails to halt Iran's drive for nuclear weapons and the United States opposes an Israeli air strike.

States. Despite this general ranking, in this specific instance, the US relationship narrowly trumps an Israeli military strike. The question is: what explains this discrepancy and the shift in Israeli attitudes?

For many years there was little public debate about the Iranian nuclear issue. There was a consensus that Iran needed to be stopped, and that Israel should be prepared to act militarily in the last resort if necessary. But as long as Iran was still considered to be some distance from the bomb, this debate remained largely theoretical and considered in tone. In any case, the public seemed willing to leave the issues for the elites to deal with (Rynhold 2010a). Around 2012, as the window for an effective Israeli strike was perceived by some to be shrinking, the debate among the elites became much more vociferous. The former head of the Mossad, Meir Dagan, the president, Shimon Peres, and several members of the security cabinet, all preferred to focus on working closely with the United States, and they were critical of Prime Minister Netanyahu and then defense minister Ehud Barak, who were widely believed to favor a strike (see, e.g., Goldberg 2012). However, as of 2012 Israeli public opinion still favored a strike to stop Iran going nuclear.

What changed between 2012 and 2014 was the advent of formal negotiations between Iran and the P5+1, led by the US. It would seem that, while Israelis were overwhelmingly skeptical of these talks, an increasing number came to believe that an Israeli strike during these negotiations would harm Israel without providing a clear-cut solution to the Iranian nuclear program. In the best case, an Israeli military operation could only delay the Iranian nuclear program by somewhere between six months and two years. Moreover, even a successful Israeli strike during negotiations would lead to the collapse of the sanctions regime, which has been surprisingly successful, while embroiling Israel in a crisis with its number-one ally, which was sponsoring the negotiations. Nonetheless, it is important to point out that Israelis oppose a strike in the face of US opposition only by a narrow margin. If Iran is perceived to be cheating, it is likely that the Israeli public would come to support an Israeli military strike as a last resort.

Conclusion

At the heart of Israeli attitudes toward the United States under Obama is a dichotomy. On the one hand, Israelis are consistently very positive about US leadership, they trust the United States as a loyal ally, and believe that US involvement in the Middle East is of vital importance to Israel's security. Indeed, the Israeli public remains one of the most pro-US publics in the world. On the other hand, Israelis are very critical and apprehensive about President Obama's Middle East policies, and their approach became increasingly negative during 2012–2014, including on the Iranian nuclear issue. Despite this, and the fact that Israelis rank Israeli military power as the most important determinant of Israeli security, a slim plurality of Israelis in 2014 believed that Israel should not attack Iran in the event that diplomacy fails and the United States opposes an Israeli military strike. Events may lead the public to change this assessment. Nonetheless, it is a testament to the fact that the Israeli public appreciates the strategic significance of close relations with the United States, even when it believes US policies in the region to be seriously mistaken.

Notes

1 Author discussions with US and Israeli officials, 2012–2013.
2 For the case that the pro-Israel lobby plays a major role in determining US policy, see Mearsheimer and Walt (2007). For rebuttals of this thesis, see Rynhold (2010b) and Lieberman (2009).
3 Author discussions with members of the Obama administration in late 2012 and early 2013.
4 Analysis of the results from an earlier BESA survey, conducted in 2007, is presented in Gilboa (2009).
5 The Israel Democracy Institute "Peace Index" surveys have been overseen by Ephraim Ya'ar and Tamar Hermann.
6 The surveys of Israeli public opinion were originally overseen by Asher Arian, but in the mid-2000s Yehuda Ben-Meir took over the running of the project.

7 The 2014 poll covered the Israeli public at large, including the Arab sector (about 13 percent of respondents), while the previous polls surveyed only the Jewish sector.
8 In 2012 the answer "would help" was divided into two categories: "would help" (53 percent) and "would help conditionally" (38 percent).
9 In 2014 there was a slight change in the wording of the answer categories, so that the scale included five categories: very different; different; more or less similar; similar; very similar. In 2012 and 2009 the scale included only three categories: different; complementary; similar.

Bibliography

Arian, Asher. 1995. *Security Threatened*. Cambridge: Cambridge University Press.
Arian, Asher. 2002. *Israel Public Opinion on National Security 2002*. Tel Aviv: JCSS.
Arian, Asher. 2003. *Israel Public Opinion on National Security 2003*. Tel Aviv: JCSS.
Ben Meir, Yehuda, and Olena Bagno-Moldavsky. 2010. *Vox Populi: Trends in Israeli Public Opinion on National Security 2004–2009*. Tel Aviv: INSS.
Ben-Zvi, Abraham. 1993. *The United States and Israel*. New York: Columbia University Press.
Boyne, W. 2002. *Two O'Clock War: The 1973 Yom Kippur Conflict and the Airlift that Saved Israel*. New York: St Martin's Press.
Chicago Council on Global Affairs. 2010. "Constrained Internationalism: Adapting to New Realities: Results of a 2010 National Survey of Public Opinion." The Chicago Council on Global Affairs, Chicago. www.thechicagocouncil.org/UserFiles/File/POS_Topline%20Reports/POS%202010/Global%20Views%202010.pdf.
Dueck, Colin. 2015. *The Obama Doctrine: American Grand Strategy Today*. Oxford: Oxford University Press.
Drezner, Daniel. 2011. "Does Obama Have a Grand Strategy?" *Foreign Affairs*, July/August: 57–68.
Feldman, Lilian. 1984. *The Special Relationship between West Germany and Israel*. Winchester, MA: Allen & Unwin.
Gilboa, Eytan. 2009. "The Public Dimension of US–Israel Relations: A Comparative Analysis." In Efraim Inbar and Eytan Gilboa, eds., *US–Israeli Relations in a New Era*. London: Routledge, 53–75.
Goldberg, Jeffrey. 2012. "Ex-Mossad Chief: Israeli Attack Would Help Iran Go Nuclear." *The Atlantic*, June 13. www.theatlantic.com/international/archive/2012/06/ex-mossad-chief-israeli-attack-would-help-iran-go-nuclear/ 258434/.
Inbar, Efraim. 1983. "Israeli Strategic Thinking After 1973." *Journal of Strategic Studies* 6 (March): 36–59.
Institute for National Security Studies. 2015. *Israeli Society and Public Opinion*. Accessed January 4. www.inss.org.il/index.aspx?id=4414.
Israel Democracy Institute. 2013. The Peace Index, November 2013. www.peaceindex.org/indexMonthEng.aspx?mark1=&mark2=&num=258.
Israel Democracy Institute. 2014. The Peace Index, October 2014. http://peaceindex.org/indexMonthEng.aspx?num=285#.VLOXJyuUcXA.
Israel Democracy Institute. 2015. "Peace Index" Surveys. Accessed January 4. http://en.idi.org.il/tools-and-data/guttman-center-for-surveys/the-peace-index.
Jones, Jeffrey. 2010. "In US, 6 in 10 View Iran as Critical Threat to US Interests." Gallup, February 16. www.gallup.com/poll/125996/View-Iran-Critical-Threat-Interests.aspx?CSTS=alert.

Levey, Zach. 2008. "Anatomy of An Airlift: United States Military Assistance to Israel During the 1973 War," Cold War History. www.informaworld.com/smpp/title~content=t713634851~db=all~tab=issueslist~branches=8 – v88 (4): 481–501.

Lieberman, Robert. 2009. "The 'Israel Lobby' & American Politics." *Perspectives on Politics* 7 (2): 235–257.

Mearsheimer, John, and Stephen Walt. 2007. *The Israel Lobby and US Foreign Policy*. New York: Farrar, Straus and Giroux.

Nacos, Brigitte L., Yaeli Bloch-Elkon, and Robert Y. Shapiro. 2011. *Selling Fear: Counterterrorism, The Media and Public Opinion*. Chicago, IL: University of Chicago Press.

Nathanson, Roby, and Ron Mandlebaum. 2012. "Aid and Trade: Economic Relations between Israel and the US." In Robert O. Freedman, ed., *The United States and Israel*. Boulder, CO: Westview, 124–140.

Pew Research Center. 2009. "US Seen as Less Important, China as More Powerful." Pew Research Center for the People and the Press, December 3. http://people-press.org/2009/12/03/us-seen-asless-important-china-as-more-powerful/.

Pew Research Center. 2013. "America's Global Image Remains More Positive than China's." Pew Research Center, July 18. www.pewglobal.org/files/2013/07/Pew-Research-Global-Attitudes-Project-Balance-of-Power-Report-FINAL-July-18-2013.pdf.

Putnam, Robert. 1988. "Diplomacy and Domestic Politics: The Logic of Two-Level Games." *International Organization* 42 (3): 427–460.

Ravid, Barak. 2014. "Kerry's Latest Cease-Fire Plan: What was he Thinking?" *Ha'aretz*, July 27. www.haaretz.com/blogs/diplomania/.premium-1.607332.

Rynhold, Jonathan. 2010a. "Peace and Security in the 2009 Election," *Israel Affairs* 16 (1): 142–164.

Rynhold, Jonathan. 2010b. "Is the Pro-Israel Lobby a Block on Reaching a Comprehensive Peace Settlement in the Middle East?" *Israel Studies Forum* 25 (1): 29–49.

Rynhold, Jonathan, and Gerald Steinberg. 2004. "The Peace Process and the Israeli Elections." *Israel Affairs* 10 (4): 181–204.

Shamir, Jacob, and Khalil Shikaki. 2010. *The Public Imperative: Palestinian and Israeli Public Opinion in the Second Intifada*. Bloomington, IN: Indiana University Press.

Weinberg, David A. 2011. "American Intervention in Israeli Politics: Past Experience, Future Prospects." *Strategic Assessment* 14 (3): 91–103.

Weinberg, David A. 2012. "Playing Favorites: Washington's Meddling for Peace in the Politics of Israel and the Palestinian Authority." Doctoral dissertation, MIT.

15 The impact of a transformed US global stance on Israel's national security strategy

Shmuel Sandler

Introduction

Israeli security is currently based on four pillars: conventional deterrence; strategic depth; strategic deterrence; and above all a US–Israeli strategic partnership, complemented by an Israeli inclination toward self-reliance. Despite pressures for dilution of one or more of the pillars, or even a trade-off between two or more elements, this network has been sustained successfully for over four decades. The US role is essential for the other three elements, and a change in the role of the United States in the Middle East would have severe implications for the other pillars of Israeli security. The purpose of this essay is to evaluate the implications of a reduction in the United States' role at the global level, and in the Middle East in particular, on Israel's national security doctrine and strategy. Attention is given to the impact on each element of the national security strategy of the Jewish state.

Prior to starting our discussion of the strategic implications of a reduced US role in Middle Eastern affairs, a note of caution is in order. This chapter does not argue for the desirability of US withdrawal from the affairs of the Middle East; on the contrary, it is this author's belief that the United States most certainly should not turn its back to the Middle East in favor of other interests. The United States cannot afford to be indifferent to nuclear proliferation, especially in unstable regions like the Middle East, as the prevention of proliferation touches upon the United States' own national security. In the Middle East, proliferation could mean the acquisition of nuclear devices not only by religious fundamentalist regimes, but even worse, by anti-Western terror organizations. Similarly, even an energy-independent United States cannot allow for the Middle East, with its tremendous oil reserves and terror threats, to be either controlled by one hegemonic nuclear power or subject to a power struggle among terrorist regimes. Ultimately, the United States should not consider abandoning the Middle East to be managed by imperial Islamic regimes like Shi'ite Tehran and Islamic Ankara. However, given the current approach of the Obama administration, a scenario of relinquishment is plausible, and hence the implications of such a road for Israel must be explored.

The four pillars of Israeli national security strategy

Conventional deterrence

The first pillar of Israeli security is conventional deterrence. It requires that Israel maintains a conventional military force able to overcome any combination of forces aimed at conquering Israeli territory or destroying the Jewish state. Given that the Arab states could repeat such an attempt indeterminately, it became axiomatic that Israel's war potential would not be limited to preventing the other side from accomplishing its goal, but must also have the capacity to punish the aggressor to an extent that would deter similar attempts in the near future. This is the essence of Israel's deterrence doctrine (Rabin 1996, 4–5).

Strategic depth

In the 1967 Six Day war Israel acquired borders that provided the strategic depth it had previously lacked. Israeli presence on the Jordan River, and control of the Golan Heights and the Sinai Desert, allowed the Jewish state to abandon its preventive war and preemptive strike doctrine that resulted in the 1956 and the 1967 wars. Indeed the Israeli–Egyptian 1979 peace treaty assured demilitarization of the Sinai, accompanied by guarantees regarding free navigation via the Tiran Straits. These clauses in the peace treaty, backed by US assurances, removed two red lines that had been responsible for the two above-mentioned wars between Israel and Egypt. It became a consensual principle among Israel's national security elite that any peace treaty to be made on its eastern and northeastern borders would require similar arrangements (Allon 1970; Dayan 2010, 22–32).

Strategic deterrence

Both the 1967 and the 1973 wars were influenced by Israel's developing nuclear option. The implicit knowledge of Israel's strategic capacity has been an important element in the winding down of the general war option in the Arab–Israeli conflict. This implicit acceptance has been facilitated by Israel's strategy of opacity, by which it did not reveal its nuclear capability either by conducting a test or by a declaration (Cohen 1998, 277–293). Following the 1981 Osirak strike in Iraq a new element in Israel's approach to nuclear weapons emerged: while Israel would not be the first in the Middle East to declare a nuclear capability, it would also try to stop other states in the region to acquire one. The current Iranian nuclear ambitions challenge that doctrine.

The composite US–Israeli strategic relationship

The US–Israeli relationship has been defined as a special relationship. It started gaining momentum after the Six Day war, although its first real test came when the United States moved to nuclear alert during the final stages of the 1973 Yom Kippur war. It has now also been seriously tested during the Obama administration. Despite the unfriendly relations between the White House and Prime Minister Netanyahu, both sides insist that the military cooperation between the two sides has not been hampered, and has even been upgraded.

This multifaceted relationship is described in Figure 15.1 below:

The US–Israeli relationship is a central pillar of Israel's security by its contribution to the deterrence of potential aggressors. In addition, it influences the other strategic pillars. A short description will unveil this multidimensional relationship:

1   The United States is the main supplier of Israel's conventional weapons. Washington has stated repeatedly that it will continue to maintain Israel's technological-military edge over its regional rivals. It became a US interest to maintain this military superiority, as it exempts the United States from direct involvement in protection of an ally. In addition, the United States assists the Israeli military budget by injecting, since 1974, $2–3 billion annually (Reich 1995, 5–9).
2   In contrast to Dwight D. Eisenhower, who in 1956 forced Israel to withdraw from all conquered territory, the Johnson administration in 1967 was active in passing UN Security Council Resolution 242, which required an Israeli withdrawal from territories (not all) acquired in the Six Day war only after

> termination of all claims or states of belligerency and respect for and acknowledgment of the sovereignty, territorial integrity and political independence of every state in the area and their right to

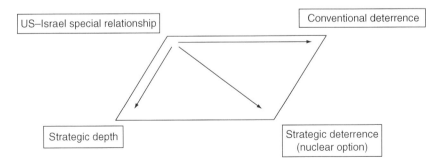

Figure 15.1 US–Israel parallelogram of forces.

> live in peace within secure and recognized boundaries, free from threats or acts of force.
>
> (Gold 2010, 34–51)

Washington has vetoed all attempts in the UN Security Council to alter this resolution.

3   It seems that, in contrast to previous harassment from US presidents (Eisenhower and J. F. Kennedy), from the Johnson presidency onward, and more concretely during the Nixon–Kissinger era, a tacit understanding was reached: Washington will tolerate Jerusalem's nuclear option as long as Israel does not cross the testing threshold and makes no nuclear threats (Israeli nuclear opacity). US policy allowed Israel to ignore pressures to join the Non-Proliferation Treaty (NPT) (Cohen 1998, 315–338). The only exception has been the Obama administration, as in a statement to the May 2009 preparatory meeting for the 2010 NPT Review Conference, the US delegation reiterated the long-standing US support for "universal adherence to the NPT," but uncharacteristically named Israel among the four countries that have failed to comply. But even the Obama administration has learned very quickly that US pressure on Israel regarding its joining the NPT was a non-starter. However, this incident does serve as an omen with regard to the importance for the US of maintaining a nuclear-free Middle East, with the exception of Israel.

The Iranian attempt to develop nuclear weapons challenges Israel's nuclear doctrine. Netanyahu's repeated threats to attack the Iranian nuclear facilities resulted in a comprehensive international regime of economic sanctions against Tehran. The ongoing negotiations between Iran and the six powers (the five members of the Security Council plus Germany) have so far failed to reach any final agreement. The role of the United States, especially Secretary of State John Kerry, has been crucial in deciding the future of the Iranian nuclear program. The US role is also of cardinal importance for Israeli preemption strategy options, should the negotiations fail to assure a non-nuclear Iran (David 1996, 33–36).

US impact on the other pillars of Israeli security was recognized as early as the 1970s, via proposals for a trade-off between the pillars. Senator William Fulbright, then chairman of the US Senate Foreign Relations Committee, and a critic of the special relations between the United States and Israel, suggested that in order to achieve an Israeli withdrawal from the territories the United States should provide guarantees for Israel's existence. Similarly, Under Secretary of State George Ball (1977, 453–471) also proposed a US–Israel formal alliance in exchange for Israeli withdrawal from territories acquired in 1967. In another vein, Robert W. Tucker (1975) suggested that if Israel were to give up territories it should demand in exchange US and international recognition of Israel as a nuclear power.

Ultimately, despite recurrent attempts to find substitutes for one or more of the pillars, in particular the territorial strategic depth pillar, or to carry out trade-offs between two or more elements, this network has been sustained successfully for over four decades.

The implications of a US role contraction in the Middle East

While the Bush presidency was characterized by over-extension of US responsibilities, the Obama presidency is perceived as narrowing US global commitments and responsibilities, especially in the Middle East. The question that is being raised in capitals around the world is whether the Obama strategy indicates a trend, or is just a reaction to his predecessor's track. It is problematic to predict the future course of US foreign policy and degree of involvement in the Middle East. Yet there are several realistic assumptions regarding a possible US scaling back and subsequent implications for Israel's national security.

First, a return to the Bush international approach is not expected even if a Republican administration comes to power. Nor is it anticipated that, after Obama, US appeasement of political Islam will continue, even under a Democratic White House. We may presume a more balanced grand strategy that would position itself between the approaches of the last two presidents. In any case, the next administration will have to assess US standing in the Middle East and restore at least some US credibility.

Should a policy of retrenchment be adopted, it would be felt in the global presence of the United States. In the Middle East, the size of the US navies in the Mediterranean and the Gulf would be vastly reduced. These strategic forces would be restationed in the United States. Such a move could signal to local leaders a potential US isolationism. Similarly, the United States would abstain from committing ground troops unaided by its allies. Alternatively, it would not act to defend Middle Eastern allies without the umbrella of collective security.

However, even a more limited US role in the Middle East does not mean a total divestment of US responsibilities. US interests in the region are too abundant to allow neo-isolationism, especially with regard to Israel, the Gulf States, and the Eastern Mediterranean countries. Nevertheless, a retrenching the United States might create the impression of withdrawal from the region, and hence implications must be studied.

Implications for Israel's national security doctrine

A lower profile of US presence in the Middle East does not contribute to stability in the Arab-Israeli arena. After over a century of Zionist presence in the region and almost seven decades of Israeli independence, the Jewish state is still perceived in the Arab, Iranian, and increasingly in the

Turkish narratives, as a Western colonial entity. Hence Israel's survival is seen in large parts of the Middle East as being dependent on US support. Consequently, a reduced US presence might bolster the belief that the existence of the State of Israel is reversible. On the other hand, the animosity to the Jewish state was also instilled by enmity toward an imperialist United States. A reduced US presence may somewhat lower the objection to Israel in some quarters of the Arab and Muslim worlds. Nevertheless, on balance, Jerusalem prefers a visible US presence in the region.

How would a reduced US presence influence the other elements of Israel's national security doctrine?

1 Conventional deterrence doctrine

Israel's deterrence doctrine emphasizes the punishment rationale rather than denial of Arab objectives vis-à-vis the Jewish state. To some extent, the rationale is similar to US deterrence strategy of the 1950s that called for massive retaliation if attacked by the Soviet Union. Both schools of thinking hold that the enemy must be punished disproportionately in order to prevent repeated aggressions or a war of attrition (Schelling 1972, 198–204).

The fact that since 1973 no major war with an Arab state has taken place increases confidence that, on the inter-state level at least, deterrence has been stable. The United States' involvement in resupplying Israel's military needs in 1973 and its readiness for a nuclear confrontation with Moscow at the end of the war (Kissinger, 2003: 258–353) were important components in the conviction that the destruction of Israel was inconceivable. The peace with Egypt, followed 15 years later with peace with Jordan, further relaxed Israeli threat perceptions. Consequently, at the inter-state conventional level, Israeli thinking began to change informally, from a doctrine of punishment toward a doctrine of denial strategy. Thus the IDF attacked on the inter-state level to deny the other side an offensive nuclear option – against Iraq in 1981, and against Syria in 2007. Another arena in which the Arab–Israeli conflict has been transformed is the sub-state level, as described below (Ben-Yehuda and Sandler 2002, 110–116).

A reduced US presence in the region might resurrect Jerusalem's old threat perception and thus revive the doctrine of disproportional punishment. This process would depend on two factors: the technological ability to deny a strike on Israel's strategic sites, and a revival of Israel's eastern front. The latter has been dismantled during the last decade with the disintegration of Iraq and Syria, but it might be rejuvenated by an Iranian takeover of Syria or by an expansion of the Islamic State to the borders of Israel. A combination of the above factors would generate a shift from denial to the punishment component in Jerusalem's deterrence thinking.

Strengthening the punishment component would imply a return to the "decisive victory" requirement in Israel's deterrence strategy (Kober 1995, 473–478). In the absence of inter-state wars, Israel in effect did not seek a decisive victory in its confrontations, and these have thus been limited and primarily sub-conventional. A less secure Israel would require the return to a decisive victory in order to deter recurrent confrontations.

Finally, the destabilization of the current balance of power, resulting from a US withdrawal, might reinstate the preventive war rationale into Israel's national security doctrine. The preventive mode of action has been absent on the conventional level during the last several decades. The last time the fear of a deteriorating balance of power triggered a war was in 1956. Then, supplies of modern Soviet arms to Egypt without equivalent assistance from Washington to Israel generated the perception that led to a preventive strike by Israel, in coordination with France and Britain (Dayan 1966, 3–19).

A variation of the preventive mode has been the preemptive strike. The Jewish state during its early years of independence adopted a doctrine of striking first against a forthcoming attack in order to escape the worse choice of having to fight on its own territory. This was the rationale for the preemptive air strike on June 5, 1967 (Horowitz 1984, 104–148). Nevertheless, all available evidence shows that Jerusalem waited over three weeks to convince Washington that it had no other choice but to preempt (Oren 2002, 163–212). In October 1973, the Golda Meir government abstained from a preemptive strike lest it be accused of aggression.

In short, a reduced US role might compel the revival of the pre-1967 deterrence doctrine that resulted in recurring wars. The stable balance of power backed by the United States has resulted in no major conventional, inter-state confrontations since 1973. Instead, violence moved to the sub-state level.

Violence at the sub-state level

Since the 1973 Yom Kippur war, the Arab–Israeli conflict has been transformed. Almost all of the violence moved from the inter-state to the sub-state level. Conventional deterrence, which occasionally succeeds in preventing violence between states, is less effective at the sub-state level. Thus the improved eastern Israeli borders following the Six Day war resulted in a guerrilla war against Israel in the West Bank. Israeli military strength, accompanied by US strategic support, as demonstrated during the last stages of the 1973 war, convinced Egypt to make peace with the Jewish state in exchange for Sinai. Syria and Jordan did not join President Anwar Sadat's peace initiative, but did keep the ceasefire agreements with Israel. In contrast, even after being expelled from the West Bank in 1968, the Palestine Liberation Organization (PLO) continued its struggle against the Jewish state. Its belligerence moved to the sub-conventional level in Lebanon, and to a worldwide war of terror. Similarly, most of Israel's combat during the two Lebanon wars in 1982 and 2006 was against non-state actors (NSAs): the PLO and Hezbollah respectively. In addition, the Palestinian–Israeli conflict has found expression in two intifadas (1987–1991; 2000–2003), and in three confrontations with Hamas since the latter's takeover of the Gaza Strip in 2007. Another indication of the caution displayed by Israel's enemies is the Israeli–Iranian confrontation; it has been conducted by proxy via Tehran's military support for Hezbollah and Hamas.

The movement from inter-state conflicts toward sub-state conflicts was also a feature of the Cold War, when nuclear deterrence strategies prevented the expression of violence at the state level. The US–USSR balance of terror did not eliminate, and in fact probably induced, sub-state warfare (Kissinger 1984; Osgood 1957). One can expect that this phenomenon of war will continue to be a central feature for which Israel must prepare itself.

Indeed, in the wake of the 2003 Iraq war and the "Arab Spring," the current Middle East is full of sub-state actors. The recent disintegration of territorial states such as Syria and Iraq may spread throughout the Middle East. Sub-state actors such as the Palestinians and Hezbollah in Lebanon, and the Kurds in Iraq, are joined by Islamic trans-state actors like al-Qaeda and its linked organizations such as Jabhat al-Nusra or ISIS, as well as its branches in Libya and in Europe. The awakening of political Islam produced transnational forces, such as the Muslim Brothers in Egypt and its outgrowth organization among the Palestinians, Hamas (Toft, Philpott, and Shah 2011, 147–173). Another example of transnational relations is the region-wide conflict between the Shi'ites and the Sunnis. All of this promises proliferation of sub-state warfare, or low-intensity conflicts as they are known (Hoffman 1992, 25–37).

A US contraction in the Middle East would probably allow the continuation of the process of state disintegration and encourage the propagation of NSAs in the Middle East. The dissemination of subnational or transnational ideologies and violence would be influenced, especially if the current policies of President Obama – "no boots on the ground" or "leading from behind" – take hold. Although President Obama is trying to pass a law allowing him to deploy ground forces, it is not expected in the foreseeable future that the United States will intervene in the Middle East with large ground forces to halt the current wave of state disintegration.

At the same time, the reality of hostile and potentially hostile states with large conventional armies, such as Iran, Turkey, and Egypt, will not disappear. The implications for Israel of this "compound threat" can be divided into two major arenas: the conventional and the sub-conventional. Accordingly, the Jewish state would have to prepare two forms of military response:

1 Continue strengthening its conventional military strength (armored and air power), and adopt a suitable conventional military doctrine.
2 Prepare special forces trained to intervene against non-state actors when preemption would be needed.

Both dimensions of Israeli strength must be accompanied by a robust intelligence capability, alert to potential threats, and a strong and flexible air force that can also hit non-conventional armies.

The Israeli strategy of deterrence in the twenty-first century has recently been termed "mowing the grass" (Inbar and Shamir 2015, 69–90). This refers to "a strategy of attrition designed primarily to debilitate the enemy capabilities" – in other words, a strategy of denial. While designed to destroy the capabilities of the opposing terror actor, it is accompanied by policy of restraint. Although this policy is dictated by domestic considerations and the growth of military capabilities and weapons accumulated over time, the approval of Washington is also a factor. In general, a low US profile in the Middle East would release the existing constraints on all belligerent parties, and especially on Israeli military activity when it feels threatened by its enemies. Mowing the grass may turn into an attempt to uproot the grass.

At the same time, Israel would have to look for a new network of regional alliances that would reflect the new realities in the Middle East. A low-key US role would not only upset the balance of power between Israel and its neighbors; should such a process take place, other Middle East regimes would also have to look for partners with an interest in maintaining the regional international order. The traditional conflict between Shi'ite and Sunni Islam that has re-emerged with the ascendance of Iran, and the evolving conflicts between radical and conservative Sunni Islam, provide new opportunities for realignment in the Middle East. Iranian presence in Yemen and on the Golan Heights, supported by Hezbollah, indicates an imperial drive.

Jerusalem must look for such openings, even if they are temporary ones. Just as previous alliances with non-Arab Iran and Turkey were ad hoc arrangements, alliances with conservative states, who share a fear of imperial powers activating radical forces as proxies both on the state and substate levels, could be a solid basis for realignment.[1] Diplomatic initiatives will be needed to form regional alignments to prevent the collapse of the regional international order. Ironically, yet in accord with the tenets of realism, Israel must look for new regional partners to deter Iran and Turkey, its former cohorts.

2 *The strategic depth factor*

Another pillar of stability on the inter-state level has been the defensible geostrategic borders that Israel has enjoyed since 1967.

It was Yigal Allon (1970, 58–59), one of Israel's greatest military thinkers and foreign minister in the first Yitzhak Rabin government (1974–1977), who outlined the importance of Israeli control of the Golan Heights, the Jordan River, and a demilitarized Sinai Peninsula as defensible borders needed for its survival. While some argued that in an age of rockets the value of strategic depth is on decline, the recurrent rocket and mortar attacks from Hamas-controlled Gaza Strip on the Israeli south have reaffirmed the importance of Israeli control of the West Bank (Judea and Samaria). The West Bank is adjacent to Israel's heartland, Haifa-Tel Aviv-Jerusalem, where 70 percent of Israel's population lives and where its business community and hi-tech industry are concentrated. The civil war in Syria, and the involvement of al-Qaeda and DAESH (The Islamic State in Iraq and as-Shām, commonly known as ISIS) forces in Syria, as well as their growing presence to the east of Israel, further strengthen the importance of Israeli control of the Golan Heights.

The US position with regard to Israel's demand for secure borders has not been unambiguous. As mentioned, the United States has always backed the Israeli interpretation of UN Resolution 242, that the resolution did not require a full withdrawal to the 1967 borders. And Israel and the United States have always stressed the sentence in UN Resolution 242 that every peace treaty must entail defensible borders for Israel.

At the same time, different organs in US administrations and government have interpreted differently the demand for defensible borders. The State Department usually interpreted the resolution as not requiring substantial changes in the pre-1967 borders, while Congress stressed the secure borders dimension. The White House in most years accepted the importance of defensible borders, but with varying interpretations. The last two administrations' readings are a good example of these variations. President George W. Bush clarified that defensible borders implied the ability of Israel to defend itself. In other words, the "secure borders" mentioned in 242 would not be accomplished by foreign forces, but through the IDF. The Obama administration stood behind the traditional US commitment to secure borders, but refused to confirm the 2004 Bush declaration and letter. The Obama White House hinted at the possibility of NATO forces stationed along the Jordan River (Gold 2010, 43–44).

Overall though, while pressuring Israel to exchange territory for peace, Washington has consistently supported Israel's demand for secure and recognized borders. Israel's insistence on continued control over the Jordan as its security border in the east and over the Golan Heights in the northeast, and on maintaining Sinai as buffer zone between Israel and Egypt, has to a large extent been backed by the United States, as long as peace treaties were signed.

Washington's position on borders is important to Jerusalem. So is its contribution to Israel's political, economic, and strategic sustainability. But in the Arab approach to the US–Israel relationship, Washington's role goes beyond the tangible, and has much to do with perception. In general, the Arab world has yet to internalize that Zionism is a genuine national movement, and is still engrossed in the myth of Israel being a Western creation. Since Europe has abandoned Israel (at least in Arab eyes), some Arab states, the Palestinians, Iran, and increasingly Turkey see the United States as the last bastion of Zionism. In contrast to President Sadat, who understood ultimately that he must negotiate directly with Jerusalem, the Palestinians still hope that someone else will provide them with a Palestinian state without satisfying Israel's basic security needs. This is particularly relevant when it comes to the borders issue. President Obama's declaration of May 19, 2011, recognizing the 1967 borders as the basis for final boundaries between Israel and a Palestinian state, was the statement the Palestinians had long been waiting for. It restored their hopes of receiving a state without having to negotiate directly with Israel over the latter's territorial requirements.

Robust US support for defensible borders is decisive for ensuring the balance of power between Israel and its neighbors. A wavering stance on this issue would also inflict damage on the possibility of a negotiated settlement of the territorial issue. But most importantly, a reduced US presence in the Middle East would raise the need of Jerusalem for even more strategic depth. Without US backing, the temptation to attack the Jewish state from the east or the northeast would grow, and with it Israel's need to control the West Bank.

A Palestinian state in the West Bank could revive the eastern front that was active in both 1967 and 1973. A sovereign Palestinian state controlling Tulkarm, only 14 kilometers from the Mediterranean, would revive the option of cutting the Jewish state into two. Without US influence on Ramallah (adjacent to Jerusalem), the Palestinians could invite radical regimes in from the east to "assure" its existence vis-à-vis the Jewish state. To prevent the entrance of foreign armies from the east, the IDF would need a forceful presence on the Jordan River. The IDF would also need to control roads leading eastward in order to be able to move reinforcements to the Jordan River front (Inbar and Sandler 1997, 23–41).

The possible emergence of a Palestinian state also requires a reevaluation of the argument that in the age of missiles territory has lost its prominence. This claim does not hold water. At a time of a coordinated missile attack on Israeli population centers, a Palestinian militia could obstruct Israeli capabilities to move forces against the sources of the missile attack in Lebanon or Syria, or any other political entity on its northeast border (Eiland 2009).

Since the Gulf War, Israel's enemies have concluded that the answer to Israel's technological superiority was missile warfare. The terror inflicted in 1991 on Israeli cities by Iraqi Scud missiles did not elicit an Israeli response. Israel's restraint was misinterpreted, eroding deterrence (Inbar and Sandler 1993, 330–58). The Second Lebanon War confirmed this belief in Israel's vulnerability to missile attacks. The minimal damage caused by Hamas missiles during the Operation Protective Edge round of hostilities in the summer of 2014, thanks to Israel's successful Iron Dome anti-missile system, has undermined the hypothesis that Israel is vulnerable to missiles. At the same time, part of Israel's ability to limit its strikes on Gaza was due to its control of the West Bank. Moreover, that conflict demonstrated the limitations of air strikes and missile attacks. Even in the era of missiles, only a territorial conquest can decide the outcome of a war.

Finally, Israeli ability to resist pressures from the international community on the territorial issue is to a large extent dependent on Washington's support in international forums and institutions, as well as on US standing in the world. Ultimately, should the United States show signs of watering down its commitments in the Middle East, Israel will have to reevaluate its "territory for peace" position. In such a case Israel may decide upon a unilateral annexation of strategic areas in the West Bank. The other option would be enhance deterrence by abandoning its traditional implicit nuclear deterrence.

3 The strategic deterrence dimension

Israel's possession of the nuclear option reduced the likelihood of its destruction, and the destruction of Iraq's prospective nuclear capabilities in 1981 eliminated that possibility for a while. However, while the focus was on Iraq, a new emerging threat came from a non-Arab state: Iran. A nuclear Iran, or indeed Arab or adjacent Muslim state, could revive the destruction option. The US role in this realm is critical.

In his January 29, 2002 "axis of evil" speech, President George W. Bush warned that the proliferation of long-range missiles developed by Iraq and Iran constituted terrorism and threatened the United States (White House 2002). Consequently, following the United States' sweeping military victory in Iraq, Tehran halted its nuclear project for a while; but once the US involvement in Iraq began showing problems, the Iranians resumed their nuclear efforts. As a state that enjoys enormous gas and oil reserves, Iran's enrichment program, which began in 2007 and was accompanied by the production of ballistic missiles and design of nuclear warheads, indicated that its nuclear efforts were not energy oriented. Israel was the main target for Tehran's threats.

Bush's United States, involved in wars in Iraq and Afghanistan, was too exhausted to stop Iran from continuing its nuclear project. It did however allow the Olmert government to eliminate the beginning of a nuclear reactor in Syria (*Haaretz* 2010). It would be difficult to imagine the consequences of an active reactor in Syria during the civil war that broke out four years later. The Obama administration's approach to the mounting Iranian threat was different.

Undoubtedly, there was US–Israeli cooperation against a nuclear Iran, and it was multifaceted. The preoccupation of Prime Minister Netanyahu with the Iranian threat, which started before his 2009 electoral victory, intensified with the progress of the nuclear project. Since entering office he has pressed the international community, and especially the United States, to take a harsher stance on Iran, and particularly its nuclear program, warning that a lack of international action would compel Israel to act unilaterally. In 2010, a wave of assassinations targeting Iranian nuclear scientists started. In June 2010, an advanced computer worm ("Stuxnet") was discovered in Tehran's nuclear laboratories. It is believed that it had been developed by the United States and Israel to obstruct Iran's nuclear program (Sanger 2012).

Netanyahu's warnings resulted in a strict international economic sanctions regime against Tehran, led by Washington. The devastating effects of the economic sanctions, accompanied by continued preventive strike threats by Israel, ultimately resulted in Tehran's consent to enter into negotiations with six major powers (the five permanent UN Security Council members, plus Germany – the P5+1). On November 24, 2013 an interim agreement was reached that freezes key parts of Iran's nuclear program in exchange for temporary relief on some economic sanctions. While the results of the diplomatic process are still not clear, the combination of Israeli threats and US international prowess has at least forced Tehran to slow down the nuclear race in the Middle East (see Gladstone 2011 on the effects of the sanctions).

The US opposition during the Obama presidency to an Israeli strike against Iran probably prevented it. The trade-off was instituting severe economic sanctions, which were followed by negotiations between Iran and the P5+1. Some heads of the Israeli security community preferred the diplomatic option and covert operations over a preventive strike. It is not clear what persuaded Prime Minister Netanyahu and Defense Minister Ehud Barak not to strike. Nevertheless an Israeli strike in face of objection from Washington would be unlikely.

The United States also provided Israel with financial support for the Arrow anti-ballistic missile system. The success of Iron Dome, and the hopefully similarly successful Arrow system, should give Iran pause for thought. However, a military confrontation with Iran would undoubtedly be several times more difficult than the conflict with Hamas.

As the negotiations between the P5+1 and Iran progressed, Jerusalem, under Netanyahu's leadership, was becoming worried that the emerging agreement would be bad for Israel. The main threat from Israel's point of view was that in exchange for restraining its nuclear ambitions, Iran was receiving legitimacy for becoming a threshold nuclear power. This result of ongoing negotiations between Iran and the P5+1 would formally allow the United States to state that it is not withdrawing from its commitment to prevent Tehran from acquiring a nuclear option, yet what may be satisfactory for the West is not necessarily adequate for Israel.

A de facto acceptance of a threshold nuclear Iran would imply different threats for the United States and the West than for Israel. A threshold nuclear Iran poses two threatening scenarios for Israel:

1. *A sudden breakout of Iran from threshold to operational nuclear status.* This could happen during an international crisis involving the United States in another region, or during an Israeli domestic or international crisis. Such an occurrence would represent only a remote existential threat for the United States, but would present Israel with an immediate existential threat.
2. *Proliferation of nuclear threshold states in the region.* Such a process could happen as a defensive response to a threshold Iran. A potential nuclear Iran, besides threatening the Jewish state, could result in other Middle Eastern states joining the nuclear arms race. The current candidates are Saudi Arabia, Algeria, Turkey, and Egypt. The US reassurance toward its regional allies that it would provide a nuclear umbrella would not satisfy their fears. Empirical research indicates that extended deterrence has failed in most cases (see the special *World Politics* (1990) issue dedicated to "Extended Deterrence").

A 2015 visit of President Vladimir Putin to Cairo resulted in the signing of a bilateral cooperation agreement on the construction of a nuclear energy plant. This was the first signpost on the road to proliferation. Given the mutual distrust between the major regional powers, one can assume that sooner or later the Middle East would turn into a system of fully nuclear-armed states. Such a system would be a nightmare for Israel. A declining US presence, accompanied by waning US influence, would further induce these developments. A more constrained United States in the world, and in the Middle East in particular, would open the road toward nuclear proliferation.

Taking into account the extreme hostility against the Jewish state, should Iran acquire nuclear weapons Jerusalem would have to bear in mind that, despite the low probability of an attack, a preferred target would be Tel Aviv. In light of the existential direct threat from Tehran, Jerusalem is unable to take risks, and hence cannot afford to wait until the West or Washington move to contain Shi'ite Iran, as well as the emerging Jihadist regimes in the Syria-Iraq region.

The above rationale of circumventing a nuclear balance of terror would apply to any Middle Eastern state aspiring to go nuclear. The United States would be the preferable power to stop proliferation in the Middle East. Should it give up on this task, Jerusalem would have to weigh its military options in order to prevent the emergence of nuclear states in the region.[2]

Conclusions

Following the 1967 and 1973 wars, a new balance of power emerged between the Jewish state and the Arab countries. A major contributor to the new equilibrium was the United States. Washington's active support of the conventional balance of power (by maintaining Israel's technological advantage), the demand of Israel for secure borders as outlined by UN Resolution 242, and tacit acceptance of Israel's strategic deterrence doctrine, have prevented the outbreak of a general Arab-Israeli inter-state war since 1973. This balance of power was not sufficient to eradicate violence, however, which instead has shifted to the sub-state level.

The main concern of this chapter has been to evaluate the implications of a changing US role in the Middle East on Israel's national security and on its strategic doctrine. Current US foreign policy indicates a reduction of US commitments, accompanied by constraints on unilateral involvement or on leadership of military campaigns. It is against this background that we could foresee a potential reduction in US commitment to Middle East security.

A reduced US presence in the Middle East would lead to regional instability and upset the balance of power between Israel and its neighbors. Accordingly, Jerusalem may have to reconsider its national security doctrine. Each pillar of Israel's national security strategy would be affected.

Despite the growing qualitative gap in favor of Israel, a reduced US involvement in preserving the conventional balance of power might send the wrong messages to its enemies. Given the current weakness of some Arab states and the disintegration of others, the main threat would originate from Muslim states on the periphery of the Middle East. But a revitalization of Arab states is still a possibility. The rise of new state actors, such as ISIS instead of Syria, or a takeover of territory by Hezbollah and Iranian forces bordering the Golan, are not beyond the imagination.

The revival of pre-1967 Israeli strategic features such as preventive and preemptive strikes, and disproportionate punishment in deterrence, would reflect growing regional instability, and indicate a return to recurring inter-state wars. In parallel, it is realistic to expect the continuation of sub-conventional warfare and its potential widening as a result of the state-disintegration process in the Middle East. A declining US presence would enhance this phenomenon. In order to minimize this threat, Israel would have to adopt a mixture of flexible and massive responses directed at the origin of the threat or its proxies on its borders.

A partial US exit would also increase Israel's threat perception, and hence its need for strategic depth. One possible response would be for Israel to unilaterally annex strategic areas, with the intention of ensuring strategic depth. A security border along the Jordan River and full annexation of the Golan Heights would improve Israel's capability to defend a potential invasion from the east, and especially the northeast.

Finally, without a committed United States to prevent a nuclear Iran, Israel may feel more compelled and less restrained than ever to strike, in order to prevent the nightmare of a potential Iranian "breakout," and/or the emergence of several threshold Middle Eastern nuclear states.

Given the above analysis it is recommended that the United States not abandon the Middle East. Its continued commitment is vital for maintaining relative stability in the region; a decision to turn away from the region would result in a drastically more unstable situation.

Notes

1 It is significant that following Netanyahu's address to the US Congress on March 3, 2015, Faisal J. Abbas (editor in chief of the Saudi al-Arabiya network) called on President Obama to pay attention to Netanyahu's warnings on Iran (Jewish Business News 2015).
2 For a comprehensive analysis of the US–Israeli interaction on the nuclear Iranian threat, see a report by Brigadier General (res.) Kuperwasser (2015). Yossi Kuperwasser was chief of the research division in the IDF Intelligence Corps, and subsequently director general of the Ministry of Strategic Affairs. See also the text of Netanyahu's March 3, 2015 address to Congress (*Washington Post* 2015).

Bibliography

Allon, Yigal. 1970. *The Making of Israel's Army*. London: Sphere Books.
Ball, George, 1977. "How to Save Israel in Spite of Herself." *Foreign Affairs* 55 (3): 453–471.
Ben-Yehuda, H., and Shmuel Sandler. 2002. *The Arab-Israeli Conflict Transformed: Fifty Years of Inter-state and Ethnic Crises*. New York: SUNY Press.
Cohen, Avner. 1998. *Israel and the Bomb*. New York: Columbia University Press.
Dayan, Uzi. 2010. "Defensible Borders to Secure Israel's Future." In Dan Riker, ed., *Israel's Security Needs for a Viable Peace*. Jerusalem: Jerusalem Center for Public Affairs, 22–32.
David, Steven. 1996. "The Continuing Importance of American Interests in the Middle East after the Cold War." *Israel Affairs* 2 (3–4): 94–106.
Dayan, Moshe. 1966. *The Sinai Campaign*. New York: Schocken Books.
Eiland, Giora. 2009. *Defensible Borders on the Golan Heights*. Jerusalem: Jerusalem Center for Public Affairs.
Gladstone, Rick. 2011. "Iran Admits Western Sanctions Are Inflicting Damage." *New York Times*, December 20.
Gold, Dore, 2010. "The US and 'Defensible Borders': How Washington Understood UN Security Council 242 and Israel's Security Needs." In Dan Riker, ed., *Israel's Security Needs for a Viable Peace*. Jerusalem: Jerusalem Center for Public Affairs, 34–51.
Haaretz. 2010. "Bush: Olmert Asked Me to Bomb Suspected Syria Nuclear Plant," November 5.
Hoffman, Bruce. 1992. "Current Research on Terrorism and Low-Intensity Conflict." *Studies in Conflict and Terrorism* 15 (1): 25–37.

Horowitz, Dan. 1984. "The Israeli Conception of National Security 1948–1972." In Benyamin Neuberger, ed., *Diplomacy and Confrontation*. Tel Aviv: Everyman's University, 104–148.

Inbar, Efraim, and Shmuel Sandler. 1993. "Israel's Deterrence Strategy Revisited." *Security Studies* 3 (2): 330–58.

Inbar, Efraim, and Shmuel Sandler. 1997. "The Risks of Palestinian Statehood." *Survival* 39 (2): 23–41.

Inbar, Efraim, and Eitan Shamir. 2015. "Mowing the Grass: Israel's Strategy for Protracted Intractable Conflict." *Journal of Strategic Studies* 37 (1), January: 65–90.

Jewish Business News. 2015. "Al-Arabiya Editor in Chief: President Obama, Listen to Netanyahu on Iran." *Jewish Press*, March 4. www.jewishpress.com/news/breaking-news/al-arabiya-editor-in-chief-president-obama-listen-to-netanyahu-on-iran/2015/03/04.

Kissinger, Henry. 1984. *Nuclear Weapons and Foreign Policy*. Boulder, CO: Westview Press.

Kissinger, Henry. 2004. *Crisis*. Jerusalem: Shalem Center. [Hebrew.]

Kober, Avi. 1995. *Military Decisions in the Arab-Israeli Wars 1948–1982*. Tel Aviv: Ma'archot. [Hebrew.]

Kuperwasser, Yossi. 2015. "The Struggle Over the Iranian Nuclear Program: A Status Report." BESA Center Perspectives Paper 289.

Oren, Michael B. 2002. *Six Days of War: June 1967 and the Making of the Modern Middle East*. New York: Oxford University Press

Osgood, Robert. 1957. *Limited War: The Challenge to American Strategy*. Chicago: University of Chicago Press.

Rabin, Yitzhak. 1991. "Israeli Strategic Thinking after Desert Storm." In *Thoughts on the Concepts of National Security* (1996). Ramat Gan: BESA Center for Strategic Studies, 1–9.

Reich, Bernard. 1995. *Securing the Covenant: United States–Israel Relations After the Cold War*. Westport, CT: Greenwood Press.

Sanger, David E. 2012. "Obama Order Sped Up Wave Of Cyberattacks Against Iran." *New York Times*, June 1.

Schelling, Thomas. 1972. *Arms and Influence*. New Haven: Yale University Press.

Toft, Monica Duffy, Daniel Philpott, and Timothy Samuel Shah. 2011. *God's Century: Resurgent Religion and Global Politics*. New York: W. W. Norton & Company.

Tucker, Robert. 1975. "Israel and United States – From Dependence to Nuclear Weapons?" *Commentary* 60 (5): 29–43.

Washington Post. 2015. "The Complete Transcript of Netanyahu's Address to Congress," March 3. www.washingtonpost.com/blogs/post-politics/wp/2015/03/03/full-text-netanyahus-address-to-congress/.

White House. 2002. "President Delivers State of the Union Address." Office of the Press Secretary, January 29.

World Politics. 1990. "Special Issue: Extended Deterrence." 42 (2).

Index

Page numbers in *italics* denote tables, those in **bold** denote figures.

9/11 attacks 15–16, 149, 183, 190, 215

Abbas, Mahmoud 191, 192, 258
Abe, Shinzo 118
Acheson, Dean 143
Adams, John 32
Afghanistan 21, 34, 36–7, 49–50
Afghanistan war 15, 66, 149, 170; US public opinion 21–2, 71, **71**
Ahmadinejad, Mahmoud 184, 204
air strikes 53, 56, 189; on nuclear facilities 209, 268, 272, 278
AKP (Justice and Development Party), Turkey 213, 218, 219, 220, 221, 222–4
Albright, Madeleine 28
Alien and Sedition Acts 32
Allawi, Ayad 186
alliances 27, 36, 45, 142, 145
anarchy, international 42
anti-Americanism 2, 3; Latin America 160, 162, 165, 166–7; Turkey 214, 215, 216, 221
Anti-Ballistic Missile Treaty 129
APEC *see* Asia-Pacific Economic Cooperation Forum (APEC)
Arab League 53, 191
Arab Spring 50–1, 129, 131, 188–90, 231, 242
Arab–Israeli conflict *see* Israeli–Palestinian conflict
Arak heavy-water reactor, Iran 206, 208
Argentina 163, 164, *166*, 168–9, 171
armed diplomacy 29, 33–5, 37, 39
armed forces 17
Armenian genocide 218
Arrow anti-ballistic missile system 279

ASEAN *see* Association of Southeast Asian Nations (ASEAN)
Asia, Obama's pivot to 45–7, 96, 110, 114, 118, 153
Asia-Pacific Economic Cooperation Forum (APEC) 45
al-Assad, Bashar 36, 54, 55, 56, 188–9, 217, 242
Association of Southeast Asian Nations (ASEAN) 45, 157
al-Attiyah, Khalid Bin Mohamed 240–1
Australia 45, 153
Azerbaijan 129, 130

Ba'ath Party, Iraq 21
Bachelet, Michelle 168
Bader, Mahmoud 236
Baghdadi, Abu Bakr 187
Bağış, Egemen 220
Baker, Andy 163
Baku-Tbilisi-Ceyhan pipeline 130
Ball, George 270
Ballistic Missile Defense (BMD) Program 129–30
"Ban the Aid" campaign, Egypt 236
Bandow, Doug 113
Bangladesh 144, 145
Barak, Ehud 263, 279
Barno, David 20
Barzani, Massoud 187
Baştürk, Levent 219
Bell, B.B. 115
Ben Ali, Zine El Abidine 188
Benghazi, Libya 53
Biden, Joe 53, 210–211n5, 210, 212, 216, 217, 228
bin Laden, Osama 72–3, 182, 183, 190

bipartisanship 79
black special operations 18, 23
BMD *see* Ballistic Missile Defense (BMD) Program
Boehner, John 76
Bolivarian Alliance *see* ALBA (Bolivarian Alliance for the Peoples of Our America)
Bolivia 164, 166, *166*, 168, 171
Brazil 166, *166*, 168, 170–1, 173
"Bright Star" military exercises 235
Brzezinski, Zbigniew 188
Bush, George H.W. 38, 154
Bush, George W. 1, 2, 3, 22, 35, 38; India 139, 149, 150; internationalism 28, 271; Iraq 186, 278; Israel 276; Latin American perceptions of 169–71

CAFTA *see* Central American Free Trade Area (CAFTA)
Calvo doctrine 161
Caribbean 161, 162, 170, 171, 174
Carter, Jimmy 65, 112, 146
Castro, Fidel 167, 168
Castro, Raúl 168, 171–2
CELAC (Economic Community of Latin American and Caribbean countries) 163, 164, 172
Central America 34, 161, 162, 163, 170, 174
Central American Free Trade Area (CAFTA) 170
CFC *see* Combined Forces Command (CFC)
Chávez, Hugo 160, 164, 167, 168, 171
chemical weapons 54–5, 189
Chicago Council on Global Affairs 64–6, **65**, *66*, **67**, 82
Chile 166, *166*, 168, 169, 170, 173
China 24, 37, 46–7, 91–105; domestic stability challenges 96–8; and India 145, 146, 147, 153, 157; international identity 98; and Iran 201; and Latin America 173; military expenditure 2; nuclear weapons 46, 146; public perceptions of US 91–2, 99–100; relationship with United States 93–6; South China Sea 46, 157; and South Korea 117–19, *118*; *see also* P5+1 group
CHP (Republican People's Party), Turkey 218, 219
Chung Mong-joon 113

civilian nuclear programs 199
Clinton, Bill 114, 147–9, 153
Clinton, Hillary 28, 51, 231, 232
cognitive-psychological attacks, Russia 133
Cold War 36, 124; India 144–7
collective security principle: NATO 128, 132–3; Nuclear Non-Proliferation Treaty 199
Colombia 163, 168, 170, 171
Combined Forces Command (CFC) 115
Combined Security Transition Command – Afghanistan 23
Commander's Emergency Response Program (CERP) funds 19
competitive strategies, Russia 127–8, 131–4, 135–6
Comprehensive Nuclear Test Ban Treaty (CTBT) 147
Congress Party, India 141, 154, 155
conservative internationalism 28–39, **29**
Consolidated Appropriations Act 235
conspiracy theories, Turkey 215, 221, 223, 225n4
conventional deterrence strategy, Israel 268, 269, 272–3, 275
credibility, United States 54–5, 58, 271
Crimea 48, 128, 132
CTBT *see* Comprehensive Nuclear Test Ban Treaty (CTBT)
Cuba 161, 162, 163, 164, 168, 170; Obama's policies 75, 84, 165, 167, 171–2

Danish cartoons crisis 183
Davutoğlu, Ahmet 213, 221, 240–1
defense budget: South Korea 115; United States 2, 45
democracy 29, **29**, 30, 32–3, 35–7, 52; Chinese opinion of 101; Iraq 186; Latin America 162; Russia 124, 125, 130; Turkey 33, 35, 37
Democratic Party 79–82, **80**, *81*, *82*, 146
democratization, Russia 124
diplomacy 27, 28, **29**, 66; armed 29, 33–5, 37, 39; with Iran 47–8, 200–8; Russia 133
disarmament, unilateral 24
disproportional punishment doctrine, Israel 272–3
Donilon, Tom 51, 53
DP (Democratic Party), Turkey 219

Eastern Europe 36, 66

286 Index

economic liberalization: India 147, 152; Russia 124
economic sanctions 28; on India 148; on Iran 47, 48, 75, 184, 185, 201, 203, 204, 208, 215–16, 270, 279; on Iraq 16; on Russia 49, 135
economy: China 2, 96, 117–19; European Union 2; Russia 124–5, 126; South Korea 115, 116, 117–19, *118*; United States 2, 96
Egypt 131, 133, 230–43; and Israel 51, 52, 230, 231, 232, 233–4, 235, 236, 238–41, 268, 269, 270, 271, 272, 273; and Israeli–Palestinian conflict 233–4, 238–41, 258; Mubarak 51, 188, 230–1; Muslim Brotherhood 51–2, 230, 231–4, 235, 236, 238, 239; nuclear proliferation 280; Obama's policies 51–2, 188, 231, 237; and Russia 236, 242–3; terrorism 238, 239, 240
Eisenhower, Dwight D. 144, 269
energy: India 153, 156; Russia 130
Erdoğan, Recep Tayyip 216, 217, 221–4
Ergenkon affair, Turkey 222
European Union 2, 36; and Iran 75, 184, 203, 209; and Russia 133–4, 136; and Turkey 219
extended deterrence 114, 131, 280

Fahmi, Nabil 237, 238, 242
FARC (Revolutionary Armed Forces of Colombia) 168
Fissile Material Cut-off Treaty (FMCT) 147
foreign direct investment, Latin America 160
France 134, 148, 249; *see also* P5 + 1 group
Free Trade Area of the Americas (FTAA) 164, 168, 170
freedom 29, 30, 31, 32–3, 34, 35–7, 38, 39n6; *see also* democracy
FTAA *see* Free Trade Area of the Americas (FTAA)
Fulbright, William 270

Gandhi, Indira 139, 140, 145–6
Gandhi, Mahatma 43, 141
Gates, Robert 50, 51, 53, 54
Gaza conflict (2012) 52, 233–4
Gaza conflict (2014) 192, 238–41, 258, 278
Gazprom 130
genocide 145, 218, 220

geostrategic borders, Israel 275
Germany 34, 36, 37, 134, 143; *see also* P5 + 1 group
Gezi Park protests, Turkey 222–3
global security, Latin American views on 172
global war on terror 129
Golan Heights 268, 275, 276
Gorbachev, Mikhail 34, 124
Guadalupe Hidalgo, Treaty of 38
Gülen, Fethullah 220, 224, 225n11, 226n12
Gülen movement 220, 223–4, 225n11, 226n12
Gulf war (1991) 16, 38, 214

Hamas 191, 192, 216, 233–4, 236–7, 238–41, 258, 274, 276, 278
Hezbollah 274, 275
High Council of the Egyptian Armed Forces 232
humanitarian interventions 42; Libya 53–4
Hussein, Saddam 16, 21

IAEA *see* International Atomic Energy Agency (IAEA)
imperialism, Islamic 182–3
India 139–57; armed forces 46; Cold War 144–7; early years of independence 142–4; energy 153, 156; and Iran 153; non-alignment policies 142, 145; nuclear weapons 146–50; and Obama 140, 151–2, 155–7; and Pakistan 142, 144, 145–6, 148–9, 153, 154; terrorism 149, 153, 154; World War II 141
Indian diaspora 154
Indo-Soviet Treaty of Friendship and Cooperation 144
INF *see* Intermediate-Range Nuclear Forces (INF) Treaty
information warfare, Russia 133
Intermediate-Range Nuclear Forces (INF) Treaty 34
International Atomic Energy Agency (IAEA) 153, 184, 185, 199, 206, 207, 209
international institutions 29, 31; *see also* United Nations
internationalism 28, 32; conservative 28–39, **29**; liberal 29, **29**, 39n2, 94–5; public opinion 64–6, **65**, *66*

investment, Chinese in United States 102
Iran 21, 24, 275; and India 153; Israeli public support for attack on 262–4, **262**, **263**; and Latin America 164, 167, 169; nuclear weapons program 47–8, 75–6, 184, 200–10, 258, 270, 278–80; Obama's policies 47–8, 279; and Russia 129, 201; sanctions on 47, 48, 75, 184, 185, 201, 203, 204–5, 208, 215, 270, 279; and Syria 55; threat of military force against 208–9; and Turkey 215–16
Iraq 36–7, 129; Gulf war (1991) 38; Israeli strike on nuclear facilities 278; Obama's policies 49, 66, 73, 75, 186–8; *see also* Islamic State
Iraq war 15–25, 149, 200; Latin American opinion of 170; Obama's policies 49, 66, 73; and Turkey 37, 213–15; US public opinion 21–2, 24, 72, **72**
Iron Dome anti-missile system 278, 279
ISIS (Islamic State in Iraq and Syria) *see* Islamic State
Islamic imperialism 182–3
Islamic State 55–7, 72, 73–4, 75, 131, 136, 182, 183, 187, 216–17, 258, 259, 274
isolationism 58–9, 131, 271; public opinion 64–6, **65**, *66*, **67**
Israel: democracy 35; and Egypt 51, 52, 230, 232, 233–4, 238–41, 268, 272, 273; and Iran's nuclear program 75–6, 270, 278–80; manhunting operations 18; nuclear weapons 268, 270, 278–80; Obama's policies 75, 76–7, 269, 270, 276, 279; public opinion of Obama's policies 248, 255–60, **256**, **257**, **259**; public perception of US 248, 251, **252**, **253**, **254**, **255**; public support for attack on Iran 262–4, **262**; terrorism 238; and Turkey 216, 219, 275, 277; US in Israeli strategy and politics 249; *see also* Israeli national security strategy; Israeli–Palestinian conflict
Israeli national security strategy 267–82, **269**; composite US–Israeli strategic relationship 269–71; conventional deterrence 268, 269, 272–3, 275; strategic depth 268, 269–70, 275–8; strategic deterrence 268, 270, 278–80; sub-state level conflict 273–5
Israeli–Palestinian conflict 190–2, 216, 273–4, 277; and Egypt 233–4, 238–41, 258; Obama's policies 75, 77, 190–2, 239, 277; Operation Pillar of Defense 52, 233–4; Operation Protective Edge 192, 238–41, 278; and Turkey 192, 216, 239–41; US public opinion of 75, 77, *81*

January 25 Revolution, Egypt 230, 231, 234
Japan: alliance with 36, 45, 153; and China 46, 105; democracy 33; reconstruction of 37, 143; and South Korea 37, 110, 114, 118; World War II 46, 141
Johnson, Lyndon B. 269, 270
Joint Plan of Action (JPOA) 47, 185, 200, 203–4, 207–8
Joint Strategic Vision for Asia-Pacific and the Indian Ocean Region 156
JPOA *see* Joint Plan of Action (JPOA)
June 30 Revolution, Egypt 236, 242

Kargil war 148
Kefaya movement, Egypt 234
Kennedy, John F. 145, 161
Kerry, John 54, 191, 192, 217, 239, 240, 241, 243n2, 258, 270
Khamenei, Ali, Ayatollah 184, 185, 204
Kılıçdaroğu, Kemal 219
Kim Dae-jung 112
Kim Jong-un 118
Kirchner, Christina Fernandez de 160, 171
Kirchner, Néstor 168, 171
Kirkpatrick, Jeane 30
Kissinger, Henry 93, 140, 270
Korean war 115, 143
Kurdish Peshmerga 217
Kurdistan Regional Government (KRG) 187
Kurds 187, 274; and Islamic State 55, 56, 217; and Israel 216; PKK (Kurdistan Workers' Party) 214–15, 219, 220; and Turkey 214–15, 216, 217, 218, 220, 221

Latin America 159–74; historical relations with United States 159–60, 161–3; and Iran 164, 167, 168, 169; public perceptions of Bush 169–71;

Index

Latin America *continued*
  public perceptions of Obama 171–2; public perceptions of US 160, 163–74, *166*; role in world 172–3
Lavrov, Sergei 242
"leadership from behind" concept 67, 189
liberal internationalism 29, **29**, 39n2, 94–5
Libya 23, 53–4, 129, 173, 189
Lotus Revolution, Egypt 230, 231, 234
Lula da Silva, Luiz Inácio 168, 170, 171

Mao Zedong 145
Marshall Plan 125, 143
Mashal, Khaled 238–9
Meir, Golda 273
Menem, Carlos 168
Mexico 38, *75*, 161; public perceptions of Bush 169–70; public perceptions of US 163, 166–7, *166*, 174; role in world 173
MHP (Nationalist Movement Party), Turkey 218
Middle East 35, 267–8; disengagement in 23–4, 271, 274; Islam 181–3; and Russia 129, 131; *see also* Egypt; Iran; Iraq; Israel; Israeli–Palestinian conflict; Syria; Turkey
military aid: to Egypt 235–6, 230–8, 242, 243; to India 144, 145; to Israel 249, 269
military containment, of China 95, 96
military expenditure: global 2; United States 2
missile defense systems: Israel 278, 279; South Korea 118
Modi, Narendra 140, 151–2, 154, 155–7
Morales, Evo 168, 171
Morsi, Mohammed 51–2, 231, 232–4, 235, 236–7
"mowing the grass" strategy, Israel 275
Mubarak, Hosni 51, 188, 230–1
Mullen, Mike 23
Mumbai terror attack, India 154
Muslim Brotherhood 51–2, 182, 189, 217, 231–4, 235, 236, 238, 239, 274

Nabucco pipeline 130
NAFTA *see* North American Free Trade Agreement (NAFTA)
nation building 30, 36, 37
National Forces Alliance, Libya 189
national security, Russia 127, 128, 129

national security strategy: United States 182; *see also* Israeli national security strategy
NATO 33–4, 36, 276; Afghanistan war 22, 23; Libya intervention 53; and Russia 49, 128–9, 132–3; Turkey 214, 221; US public opinion 66, **67**
Nehru, Jawaharlal 139–41, 142–4, 145
neoconservatives 30, 216
neoisolationism 24, 271
neoliberalism 162, 164
Netanyahu, Benjamin 76, 77, 191, 192, 238, 250, 254–5, 258, 263, 269, 270, 279
New Strategic Arms Reduction Treaty 129
Nixon, Richard 27, 145, 146, 270
NNWS *see* non-nuclear weapons states (NNWS)
non-alignment policies, India 142, 145
non-nuclear weapons states (NNWS) 147, 198, 199
non-state actors (NSAs), Middle East 275
North American Free Trade Agreement (NAFTA) 167
North Korea 46, 112–13, 115, 116, 118, 119, 198, 200
NPT *see* Nuclear Non-Proliferation Treaty (NPT)
NSAs *see* non-state actors (NSAs), Middle East
NSNW *see* non-strategic nuclear weapons (NSNW)
nuclear counter-proliferation policies 28, 198–210; military force 208–10
nuclear facilities, Israeli air strikes on 209, 268, 272, 278
Nuclear Non-Proliferation Act 146
Nuclear Non-Proliferation Treaty (NPT) 146, 198–9, 210n2; and India 146, 147; and Iran 200, 202, 206, 209; and Israel 270
nuclear weapons: China 46, 146; India 146–8, 150; Iran 28, 47–8, 75–6, 153–4, 184–5, 200, 209–10, 258, 270, 280; Israel 268, 270, 278–80; North Korea 46, 198; Pakistan 147, 154; proliferation in Middle East 267, 280; Russia 49, 129–30, 132; South Korea *113*

OAS *see* Organization of American States (OAS)

Obama, Barack 1, 2, 3, 20, 24, 41, 43–59, 63–4, 181–93; Afghanistan 22–3, 49–50, 66; Arab Spring 50–1, 188–90, 231; China 95–6; Cuba 75, 84, 171–2; Egypt 51–2, 188, 231, 237; foreign policy goals 66–7; India 140, 151–2, 155–7; Iran 47–8, 75–6, *75*, 184–5, 205, 279; Iraq 49, 66, 73, *75*, 186, 188; Islam 181–3; Islamic State 55–7, 72, 73–4, *75*, 182, 217, 256–9; Israel *75*, 76–7, 250, 269, 270, 276, 279; Israeli public opinion of policies 248, 255–60, **256**, **257**, **259**, **260**, **261**; Israeli–Palestinian conflict 77, 190–2, 256–8; Latin American perceptions of 171–2; leadership approval ratings **69**; Libya 53–4; nationalism 28; pivot to Asia policy 45–7, 96, 110, 114, 118; public opinion of foreign policy 63–4, 82; realist policies 44; South Korea 109, 110; Syria 36, 54–5, 188–9; terrorism 66, 72–4, **73**; Turkey 216, 217, 218, 219–20, 221–2, 223, 224; Ukraine 48–9, *75*

OIC *see* Organization of Islamic Cooperation (OIC)

Operation Pillar of Defense 233

Operation Protective Edge 238, 258, 278

Orange Revolution, Ukraine 130

Organization of American States (OAS) 171

Organization of Islamic Cooperation (OIC) 214

Osirak reactor, Iraq 268

Oslo Accords 38

P5+1 group 28, 75, 184, 198, 201–3, 204, 206, 210–211n5, 258, 279

Pakistan 21, 37, 46, 50; and India 142, 144, 145–6, 148–9, 153, 154; nuclear weapons 147, 154

Palestine Liberation Organization (PLO) 273–4

Palestinian Authority 191, 238, 241, 258

Palestinian–Israeli conflict *see* Israeli–Palestinian conflict

Pan-Americanism movement 161

Panetta, Leon 54, 116

Park Chung-hee 112

Park Geun-hye 109

Paul, Rand 24, 28

Peaceful Nuclear Explosion (PNE), India 146

Peres, Shimon 263

Petraeus, David 20, 23

pivot to Asia policy 45–7, 96, 110, 114, 118

PKK (Kurdistan Workers' Party) 214–15, 219, 220

Platt Amendment 162

PLO *see* Palestine Liberation Organization (PLO)

popular culture, Chinese opinion of US 101, 102–3

post-9/11 conflicts 15–25; *see also* Afghanistan war; Iraq war

preemptive strike doctrine, Israel 268, 273

psychological attacks, Russia 133

public opinion abroad 1; Chinese perceptions of US 92, 99, 104–5; Indian perceptions of US 152; Israeli opinion of Obama's policies 248, 255–60, **256**, **257**, **259**, **260**, **261**; Israeli perceptions of US 248, 251–5, **252**, **253**, **254**, **255**; Israeli support for attack on Iran 262–4, **262**, **263**; Latin American perceptions of US 160, 164, *166*; Russia 134; South Korea 109, 110, 111–12, 113, *113*, 115, 117–19, *118*; Turkish perceptions of US 214, 220

public opinion in United States: Afghanistan and Iraq wars **71**, **72**; isolationism versus internationalism 64–6, **65**, *66*, **67**; NATO 66, **67**; Obama's foreign policy 83–4; Obama's leadership 82–3; United States' standing in the world 77

Putin, Vladimir 48–9, 126, 135, 136, 242, 280

Qadaffi, Muammar 53, 189

al-Qaeda 15, 16, 21, 22, 66, 72, 80, 81, 190, 274

Quit India movement 141, 142

Qutb, Sayyid 15

Rao, P. V. Narasimha 147

Reagan, Ronald 30, 31, 32–4, 38, 39n6

"red line" policy 54, 56, 189

renationalization program, Russia 126, 130

Republican Party 79–82, **80**, *81*, *82*

"Reviving Sovereignty" campaign, Egypt 236

Rice, Condoleezza 16, 30

Index

Rice, Susan 190, 217
Rodó, José Enrique 162
Roh Moo-hyun 112, 116
Roosevelt, Franklin 27, 34, 139, 141, 142
Rouhani, Hassan 184, 185, 203, 204
Rubio, Marco 28
Russia 2, 24, 123–36; annexation of Crimea 48, 128, 132; competitive strategies 127–8, 131–4, 135–6; and Egypt 236, 242–3, 280; energy 130; and India 148; and Iran 129, 201; and NATO 49, 128–9, 132–3; perceptions of United States 123–31, 134–5, 136; public opinion 134–5; and Syria 54, 55, 129, 131, 189, 242, 243; terrorism 129; and Ukraine 37, 48–9, 128, 129, 131, 132; *see also* P5 + 1 group; Soviet Union

Sadat, Anwar 273, 277
sanctions 28; on India 148; on Iran 47, 48, 75, 184, 185, 201, 203, 204–5, 208, 215, 270, 279; on Iraq 16; on Russia 49, 128, 135
Sanders, Bernie 24
Santoro, David 113
Saudi Arabia 55, 234, 239, 241, 243, 280
Senkaku/Diaoyou islands 46
Sèvres, Treaty of 220, 225n7
Shultz, George 30
Sinai Peninsula 237, 238, 243
Singh, Jaswant 148
Singh, Manmohan 139, 150
al-Sisi, Abdel Fatah 52, 133, 232, 234, 236, 238, 240, 242, 243
Snowden, Edward 151
soft power 66, 93, 101, 133, 214
South China Sea 46, 157
South Korea 109–19; alliance with 36, 45; and China 117–19, *118*; command structure 115–16; democracy 33; and Japan 35, 37, 110, 111–13, 114, 118; nuclear policy 111; public opinion 109, 110, 111–12, 113, *113*, 115, 117–19, *118*; self-perception 111
Soviet Union 30, 34, 38, 144; *see also* Russia
Steinberg, James 95
strategic competition, Russia 123, 127, 129, 135–6
strategic depth strategy, Israel 268, 267, 269, 271, 275–8, 281
students, Chinese in United States 102

Stuxnet computer worm 279
Suez Canal 230, 243n1
Sulaymania incident, Turkey 215
Syria 23, 36, 54–5, 183, 188–9; chemical weapons 54–5, 189; and Israel 273; Israeli strike on nuclear facilities 273, 279; and Latin America 164; and Russia 54, 55, 129, 131, 189, 242, 243; and Turkey 55, 216–18; *see also* Islamic State

Taiwan 33, 46, 96
Talbott, Strobe 148
Taliban 16, 17, 21, 49–50, 149
Tamarud movement, Egypt 234, 236
tanks 235
Tantawi, Muhammad Hussein 231, 232
television shows, Chinese opinion of US 102
terrorism: 9/11 attacks 15–16, 149, 183, 215; Egypt 238, 239, 240, 243; global war on terror 129; Hamas 238; India 149, 153, 154; Israel 238; Obama's 66, 72–4, **73**, 182; Russia 129; *see also* Islamic State; al-Qaeda
threat perception: Israel 272; Russia 123, 128
tourism, Chinese in United States 102
trade embargos, Russia 133
Treaty of Guadalupe Hidalgo 38
Treaty of Sèvres 220, 225n7
Truman, Harry S. 33–4, 144
Turkey 213–25; democracy 33, 35, 37; domestic events and US 222–4; and Egypt 234; foreign policy discord with US 215–18; and Iran 215–16; and Iraq war 37, 213–15; and Israel 216, 219, 275, 277; and Israeli–Palestinian conflict 192, 216, 239–41, 258; and Kurds 214–15, 216, 217, 218, 220, 221; nuclear proliferation 280; Obama's policies 216, 217, 218, 219–20, 221–2, 223, 224; political attitudes towards US 218–20; public perceptions of US 214, 215, 216, 220–2; and Syria 55, 216–18

Ukraine 23; Crimea 48, 128, 132; democracy 35; Obama's policies 48–9, 75; Orange Revolution 130; and Russia 37, 48–9, 128, 129, 131, 132
United Arab Emirates 55, 243
United Kingdom 18, 134, 189; *see also* P5 + 1 group

United Nations 27, 75, 142, 170
United Nations Security Council 53, 148, 170, 191, 201, 203, 214, 241, 269–70, 274; *see also* P5+1 group
uranium enrichment 47, 76, 185, 199, 200, 203–4
urbanization, China 97

Vajpayee, Atal Bihari 147–9
Vargas Llosa, Mario 164–5
Vázquez, Tabaré 168

Wang Jisi 100, 104
weaponization, Iran 206
weapons of mass destruction (WMD): Iraq 200; Libya 53; *see also* nuclear weapons
Weinberger, Caspar 30
West Bank 191, 192, 238, 273, 276, 277, 278
World War II 49, 57, 141

Xi Jinping 97, 118

Yangju highway incident, South Korea 112
Yazidis 56
Yom Kippur war 249, 269, 273

zero-sum game 94, 128, 203

Taylor & Francis eBooks

Helping you to choose the right eBooks for your Library

Add Routledge titles to your library's digital collection today. Taylor and Francis ebooks contains over 50,000 titles in the Humanities, Social Sciences, Behavioural Sciences, Built Environment and Law.

Choose from a range of subject packages or create your own!

Benefits for you
- Free MARC records
- COUNTER-compliant usage statistics
- Flexible purchase and pricing options
- All titles DRM-free.

REQUEST YOUR FREE INSTITUTIONAL TRIAL TODAY

Free Trials Available
We offer free trials to qualifying academic, corporate and government customers.

Benefits for your user
- Off-site, anytime access via Athens or referring URL
- Print or copy pages or chapters
- Full content search
- Bookmark, highlight and annotate text
- Access to thousands of pages of quality research at the click of a button.

eCollections – Choose from over 30 subject eCollections, including:

Archaeology	Language Learning
Architecture	Law
Asian Studies	Literature
Business & Management	Media & Communication
Classical Studies	Middle East Studies
Construction	Music
Creative & Media Arts	Philosophy
Criminology & Criminal Justice	Planning
Economics	Politics
Education	Psychology & Mental Health
Energy	Religion
Engineering	Security
English Language & Linguistics	Social Work
Environment & Sustainability	Sociology
Geography	Sport
Health Studies	Theatre & Performance
History	Tourism, Hospitality & Events

For more information, pricing enquiries or to order a free trial, please contact your local sales team:
www.tandfebooks.com/page/sales

 The home of Routledge books

www.tandfebooks.com